· YANKEE ·
SAMURAI

AMERICAN MANAGERS SPEAK OUT ABOUT WHAT IT'S LIKE TO WORK FOR JAPANESE COMPANIES IN THE U.S.

DENNIS LAURIE

HarperBusiness
A Division of HarperCollins*Publishers*

HarperCollins books may be purchased for educational, business, or sales promotional use. For information, please write: Special Markets Department, HarperCollins Publishers, Inc., 10 East 53rd Street, New York, NY 10022.

FIRST EDITION

Designed by Ruth Kolbert

Library of Congress Cataloging-in-Publication Data

Laurie, Dennis.
    Yankee Samurai : American managers speak out about what it's like to work for Japanese companies in the U.S. / Dennis Laurie.—1st ed.
      p. cm.
    Includes bibliographical references and index.
    ISBN 0-88730-552-0
    1. Corporations, Japanese—United States—Management—Case studies.   2. Corporations, Japanese—United States—Employees—Interviews.   3. Corporate culture—Japan.   4. Corporate culture—United States.   I. Title.
    HD70.U5L34   1992
    331.25—dc20   91-58508

---

92 93 94 95 96   AC/HC   10 9 8 7 6 5 4 3 2 1

To the One who made this happen

*The Samurai thinks not of victory or defeat
but merely fights insanely to the death.*
—THE CODE OF BUSHIDO

CONTENTS

●

ACKNOWLEDGMENTS

●

> *Gratitude is one of the least articulate of the emotions, especially when it is deep.*
> —FELIX FRANKFURTER

I was a Ph.D. student of Peter Drucker's for several years at the Drucker Graduate Management Center at Claremont. His work, particularly as it deals with Japan, has been an inspiration, as has his personal encouragement for this book. I will always be indebted to him. Thanks also to the school's dean, Sid Harris; the faculty, including especially Richard Ellsworth, David Drew, and Paul Albrecht; as well as the wonderful administrative people for their encouragement.

I want to thank another dean, Dennis Aigner of the Graduate School of Management at University California Irvine, where I have taught global management. John Graham of UCI has great expertise in international marketing and communication and has been both helpful and a good friend.

Larry Arn does a fine job as President of the Claremont Institute. I thank him for his encouragement and support. My appreciation also goes to a leading China scholar at the Institute, Steve Mosher, who has been a considerable help to me.

It was Emerson who said that "An institution is the lengthened shadow of one man." In the case of Arco, that one man is its chairman and CEO, Lod Cook. I had the opportunity to work for him for many years, and owe him a great deal for what he taught me as well as for his friendship.

Kris Foster, Takeko Tanaka, and Miyuki Cunningham were very helpful in reviewing the text and sharing their knowledge of Japan and Japanese terminology.

I owe thanks to the many people who looked at early drafts of the book, including Mike Tharp of *U.S. News & World Report*, who has spent many years in Japan.

A special thanks goes to Virginia Smith, my editor at HarperBusiness. I was very fortunate to be able to work with her. Additional thanks to Ann Adelman.

All of the companies in the study were very cooperative. I am indebted to Messrs. Koji Kobayashi of NEC: Yukiyasu Togo, Jeff Smith, and Jim Olson of Toyota Motors U.S.A.; Fritz Kern, John Reilly, and Kozo Sakaino of American Isuzu; John Rehfeld and Hiroshi Fukino of Seiko Instruments; Cedrick Shimo, Kurt Antonius, and Shigeyoshi Yoshida of Honda North America; John Lawler and Takashi Kiuchi of Mitsubishi Electronics; Masayuki Kohama and Peter Kendall of Hitachi; Oki Komada of Mitsui Fudosan; Kazutoshi Hagiwara, Ron Cabibe, and Bill Burfiend of Nissan; Jiro Ishizaka of Union Bank; Rich Belliston of Tokai Bank; Larry Clarke of JAL; Tim Trujillo of Mitsubishi Consumer Electronics; Hideharu Takemoto and Kai Hoshi of Canon; Larry Runyon of TEC America; Gene Kunde and Yasuhiro Tsubota of Epson America; Rob Carlson and Akira Tsukada of Mitsubishi International; Naofumi Okamoto of Apricot Entertainment; Masahiro Shimizu and Koichi Yoshimine of Dai-Ichi Kangyo Bank; Yukio Suzuki, Yasuo Yamaguchi, and Gyo Shinasaki of Hochiki America; Hitoshi Arai of Personna; Juichi Tsuda of IBJ; Phil Wendel of Yamaha; and Norm Baker of Mitsubishi Motors.

Many doors were opened to me by people intimately involved in advancing U.S.-Japan relations. I owe special appreciation to: Saburo Yuzawa, Chief Executive Director, JETRO; Walter Beran of Ernst & Young; Steve Clemons, Executive Director of Japan America Society; and Gerald Yoshitomi, Director of JACCC.

My personal thanks also go to each of the some 250 Americans and

Japanese who gave me their time to be questioned and interviewed. I wish every one of them the best of fortune.

Closer to home, Ellie and Cyndi Laurie have always been supportive and Mildred Laurie very proud. Infinitely more than thanks goes to my sons, Michael Laurie, M.D., and Andrew Laurie, M.D.

INTRODUCTION

•

> *Japanese car companies shouldn't be
> defensive. Detroit's Big Three caused their
> own problems and are wallowing in
> hypocrisy because they import plenty of
> Japanese cars and parts on their own.*
> —RICHARD RECCHIA,
> President, Mitsubishi Motors U.S.A.

There was something almost metaphoric about a flu-stricken American president slumping to the floor and retching at the feet of the Japanese prime minister at an internationally televised state dinner. The January 1992 meeting between President Bush and Prime Minister Miyazawa in Tokyo marked a decisive turning point in U.S.-Japan relations. America's economy was struggling and the American people were sensing that the world political, military, and economic leadership which they had enjoyed since the close of World War II was slipping away. At the same time, Japan seemed poised to begin what could well be "The Japanese Century."

The pride of America's industrial might, the auto industry, is particularly troubled. The Japanese now control 32 percent of the U.S. market and Ford, General Motors, and Chrysler are hemorrhaging. Collectively, they lost a record $7 billion in 1991; 1992 doesn't look much better. Some two thirds of the $41 billion American 1991 trade deficit with Japan was in autos and auto parts. The fault, said the chairmen of the Big Three, who joined Bush in Tokyo, was that Japan didn't play fair. They issued an ultimatum to their Japanese counterparts at Toyota, Nissan, Honda, Mazda, Mitsubishi, Isuzu, and Daihatsu: Eliminate the trade deficit 20 percent a year over the next five years . . . or else.

Not all the American people agreed with this get-tough stance, particularly those among a special group of Americans whom I call "Yankee Samurai"—Americans working for Japanese companies in the United States. There are now about 400,000 of these Americans, and their numbers will likely rise to 1 million by the turn of the decade. One of them, Richard Recchia, president of Mitsubishi Motors U.S.A., who is quoted in the epigraph at the beginning of this chapter, was particularly outspoken. He pointed the finger of blame squarely at Detroit itself. Mr. Recchia and his fellow Yankee Samurai are playing a critically important role in bridging the vast cultural gap that exists between the United States and Japan. Certainly they know the Japanese well—or at least better than most Americans.

The story this book tells about the inner workings of U.S. subsidiaries of Japanese firms, and peripherally U.S.-Japan relations, will be seen largely through the eyes of Americans working for those subsidiaries. I interviewed and questioned some 250 of these Yankee Samurai. Their thoughts are directly relevant to the management of the Japanese firms in the United States, to the American competitors of those firms, and more broadly to the people of both America and Japan. Unlike other books that have described Japanese manufacturing operations in the United States, the focus here will be entirely on the white-collar office environment. Those interviewed and questioned ranged from mail clerks to chief operating officers, and were drawn from a range of automobile, electronics, transportation, banking, entertainment, and service firms. They are among Japan's finest:

Apricot Entertainment
Canon Trading U.S.A.
Dai-Ichi Kangyo Bank
Epson America
Fuji Research
Hitachi Sales Corporation
Hochiki
Honda
Honda International Trading

Industrial Bank of Japan
Isuzu
JAL
Mitsubishi Consumer Electronics
Mitsubishi Electric
Mitsubishi International Trading
Mitsubishi Motors
Mitsui Fudosan
Mitsui Manufacturers Bank
NEC
Nissan
Personna
Secomerica
Seiko
Sumitomo
TEC America
Tokai Bank
Toshiba Electronics
Toyota
Union Bank
Yamaha

The style of much of the book is patterned after the fascinating work done by Studs Terkel in exploring American working life, in which people are simply allowed to talk about their experiences. Here are a few "sound bites" from later chapters that will give you a sense of what is coming.

In early 1992, Lower House Speaker Yoshio Sakurauchi provoked a furor when he was quoted in U.S. newspapers as having asserted that American workers were lazy and illiterate when compared to their Japanese counterparts. What do some of the Yankee Samurai think of this issue? Here is a corporate auto-marketing manager with his observations:

I went through a Japanese trim plant last year. Under each of the work stations were photographs of poor work that had been done at the plant. The people there had great pride and didn't want something they did to show up on a photograph for all to see. If you tried to do that at a UAW plant in the United States, they would cut your balls off.

In Toyota City, where about 60 percent of the people are di-

rectly affiliated with the firm, the bars and lounges are closed at
eleven each night because they want people alert for work the next
day. Single women employees living in company-owned dormitories must abide by a ten o'clock curfew. Can you imagine trying
to do that in Flint, Michigan?

The metals coordinator for a major trading company added:

> They look at it [work] as life! Even on their days off, that is all
> they talk about. You are dealing with guys that work fourteen
> hours a day, every day, seven days a week, The natural result of all
> that work has got to pay dividends. You have a whole nation of
> people like that.

And how about the issue of American illiteracy raised by Mr.
Sakurauchi? Listen to the American employment manager for a major
Japanese auto firm:

> As I look at the young people coming into the work force, I'm
> convinced we are seeing a terrible decline in educational levels.
> The workers coming in are substandard. I see it daily.
>
> I have seen people with college degrees who cannot fill out an
> employment application. Perhaps 95 percent of them make mis-
> takes in spelling and half have trouble writing a simple sentence.
>
> People coming into the clerical ranks can't spell and can hardly
> speak English in many cases. Part of the problem is California. We
> have the charge of assimilating a lot of these different cultures.
>
> I remember in college reading about the Dark Ages where civ-
> ilization and learning almost disappeared in Europe. America is
> moving into its own Dark Ages. In Dante's *Divine Comedy*, he
> described Hell as some pit deep in the earth. I hope there is a
> special hell reserved for those who have allowed our education
> system to become what it has.

The issue of women and minorities working for Japanese firms in the
United States has received considerable media attention over the last
few years. It will be discussed in some depth later in the book. For now,
here is a preview, beginning with the thoughts of a black business
research clerk at a large Japanese bank:

> At my bank the Japanese don't like to hire minorities, especially
> blacks. There are no black men here, and only three other black
> women. The Japanese view blacks as Michael Jordan, Michael
> Jackson, Michael Tyson, or as thugs and undesirables.

Yet a Hispanic woman who works for one of the second-tier auto firms as an accounts receivables supervisor says:

> With my limited education, I'm very fortunate to have this job; it's the best I've ever had. The Japanese are always very polite and treat me with respect. Some of my friends say the Japanese are chauvinist, but they [the Japanese] remind me of all the Mexican men that I know and I don't have any problem with that [*laughs*].

Had you talked personally with the soft-spoken Vietnamese-American auditor working for a major Japanese bank, you probably would have come away as touched as I did:

> America is supposed to be a melting pot, but there is discrimination everywhere in the job market. It is deep-rooted and difficult, or impossible, to eradicate. But I am accepted by the Japanese. My family knows how hard I searched to find an appropriate place to work in this great land. Here at [bank name] I feel stable, secure, pride, and comfort.

Finally, here is the manager of production planning who said:

> Men or women, it doesn't matter. There is the tribal issue. You are never, ever, ever, going to be a member of the tribe. If they cut off your legs at the knees, reattach your feet, and change your eyes, you still ain't going to be a Japanese. In Japan it is the same way. You can look at the Koreans and Chinese and half-breeds, they are treated very poorly because they are not of the tribe. It is inbred and cannot be changed in this generation or the next.
>
> I would like to see the operation management of my firm be completely American and the advisers from Tokyo take a lower role. I see that coming about, but it is being fought tooth and nail.

Japanese CEO salaries are a fraction of their American counterparts. How do the Yankee Samurai feel about this issue? Here are the thoughts of the American chief operating officer of a high-tech Japanese electronics firm:

> . . . If I were a Chrysler worker and I saw Iacocca getting a $6 million bonus, I would say, "&*#$^@ 'em," and do everything I can to get mine. The high salary and unbelievably generous retirement package for G.M.'s Roger Smith [$1.2 million a year for life] has to be very demoralizing for the worker on the line.

Management style as practiced by the Japanese in their U.S. subsidiaries will be a fundamental topic of this book. One dimension of that style is the firm's absolute commitment to its mission and task at hand. Listen to the perception of a vice president of marketing for a major laptop computer company:

> The Japanese certainly are committed. Suppose a Fourth of July picnic was planned in the strawberry field just to the west of our Los Angeles plant. If the big one [earthquake] came along the day before and instead of the strawberry field there was the Pacific Ocean, then by God, on the Fourth of July, we would all go marching into the water.

And how well do the Americans, the Yankee Samurai, interrelate with their Japanese colleagues? Here is the experience of a young Mexican-American banker:

> The Americans and Japanese do not interact that much at work. It hardly exists at all. We never even go to lunch together. . . . When I got married, I invited the Japanese; that broke a lot of ice. The president of the bank came; that was amazing [shakes his head]. I never would have expected it. There were tables of Japanese there right in the middle of my Mexican family.

A good number of the Yankee Samurai thought they were changed by the experience of working for the Japanese. The auto firm's distribution manager was one of them:

> The biggest adjustment for me has been the Japanese tendency to never leave anything alone. It doesn't matter whether it's a written report or a piece of hardware; it is never finished and improvements can always be made. That drove me crazy when I first came here. I used to sit in on meetings and think to myself, "Come on, come on . . . let's get on with it, it's fine." But the Japanese always look for ways to make things better. I understand that now and think it is a wonderful trait; they call it *kaizen*.* Still, to be honest, you can go too far with it.

And what of another Japanese management style characteristic—the penchant for thinking long term? Here is a floor manager for a large trading company:

---

* For this and other Japanese terms that follow, see the Glossary on pp. 353–55.

The Japanese look at what will be making money not today, but in the future.

They like to tell a story about a three-man office. One man brings in $100,000 a year, another $5 million, and a third only $20,000. They ask who is the better employee. It is not necessarily the $5 million man, who might have inherited a cash cow. It may well be the $20,000 man, who is putting together a new grass-roots business that will be generating profit for fifty years.

Firms in Japan are known for their lifetime employment policy. What about the Japanese subsidiaries in the United States? Do the Yankee Samurai enjoy lifetime employment? Listen to the electronics firm's assistant general counsel: "My resposne to anyone who thinks there is lifetime employment here is 'bullpucky.' We have 'at will employment,' and make that very clear."

Later in the book you will be hearing from some two dozen Japanese chairmen, CEOs, and senior vice presidents I interviewed, asking them their views of the Americans they work with, of U.S.-Japan relations, and their personal experiences in the United States. You will hear, for example, the chairman of one of the world's largest automobile firms recalling that:

> My earliest recollection of the war as a child was the bombardment by B-29s. So many people died and we were of course destroyed. We have very bitter memories about that. But after the war it was a night-and-day difference. The American GIs were so tall, shiny, bright, enthusiastic, and friendly. I was very impressed. They were so generous, especially with children. We were always hungry while the war was going on, but during the occupation they gave us chocolate, chewing gum, and I remember Lucky Strikes—LSMFT, Lucky Strikes Means Fine Tobacco [*laughs*]. I thought it was so wonderful. So the Japanese have not forgotten the war, but the impression of the generous GIs and the Red Cross is very strong. I will never forget what they did.

The reminiscences of this Japanese executive go back nearly half a century. That is a long time. But today builds upon yesterday; this is particularly true for Japan. You will see a thread of history weaving through much of what follows. It is the only way that today's Japan, and U.S. relations with Japan, can be understood.

Before you turn the page, I'd like to share with you my primary motivation for writing this book. Throughout nearly my entire life,

America's political, military, and even economic policies have been largely driven by the existence of what was the Soviet Union. Its implosion has left a chaotic and dangerous Eastern Europe with an uncertain future; civil war and the renewing of ancient rivalries and hatreds are more likely than unlikely. And in Western Europe, while no one has yet officially recognized it, Germany's Fourth Reich began with the collapse of the Berlin Wall. Hitler's Third Reich didn't make it to a thousand years as he proclaimed it would. Hardly ten. This one will do much better. All of this means that there are both opportunities and threats to America in the new European order that is emerging. Because of that fact, and because our roots overwhelmingly trace from Europe, we will continue to look east across the Atlantic. That is as it should be.

Yet, for a whole generation of Americans just now coming of age, it is not the USSR or Western Europe but rather the Pacific Rim that will dominate their lives. They will look not east but west, across the Pacific Ocean, to the setting sun . . . to Japan. It is the bilateral relationship with that nation that will directly and indirectly influence the lives of the American people far more than any other. For almost half a century now, that relationship has been based upon close friendship in spite of two strikingly different cultures. My reason for writing this book ultimately comes down to the hope that it can contribute, even in some very small way, to maintaining that friendship, which will be sorely tested in the years ahead.

Dennis Laurie
Fullerton, California
February 1992

1

Achilles' Heel

> *The mighty Achilles, slayer of Hector, and*
> *hero of the Trojan War was himself*
> *destroyed by his one vulnerability.*
>
> —HOMER

THE HESSIANS

The crack of the final musket shot, in what had been a fierce ninety-minute battle, was instantly consumed by the fury of the blizzard that roared through the small village of Trenton, New Jersey. The last wisps of black smoke from the exchange of cannon fire drifted upward amid snow flurries, flurries so thick that it was difficult to discern enemy from friend.

Before the white-steepled Methodist church at Fourth and Queen Streets, behind the picket fences, near the neat homes and small shops of Second, Third, and King, and in the apple orchard beyond Assunpink Creek Bridge lay the dead, wounded, and dying Hessians. Only the night before they had drunkenly celebrated Christmas and gone peacefully to sleep, some of them perhaps dreaming of their German homeland and their families and friends a world away across the Atlantic. But the warm embrace of those dreams suddenly became the reality of piercing cold, the cacophony of shouts of warning, roar of cannon, staccato of musket fire, screams of the wounded, and the struggling from sleep to face an early morning surprise American onslaught. General Washington and three elements of his Continental Army had quietly crossed the Delaware during the night, moved down the Sullivan Road, and attacked the unprepared Hessians. It was a Hessian disaster. Over a thousand of their number had been taken prisoner, killed, or wounded, while the Americans suffered only a handful of casualties.

The Hessian leader, fifty-year-old Colonel Johann Gottlieb Rall, a heavy-drinking, grizzled veteran, fell to enemy fire early in the battle. He had arrived in this foreign land three months before, strong, healthy, and vigorous; now he lay with two gaping musket ball wounds in his side. Just before lapsing into coma and then death some thirty hours later, several of his officers heard him mutter, "Had I known, I would not have been here."

However, he *was* there, along with the rest of his Hessians, German mercenaries, who had been hired by the British to augment their own forces in the struggle against the rebellious Americans. But the Hessians did not fight as well as the British. Communication between the English-speaking British and the German-speaking Hessians was poor; Colonel Rall himself spoke no English. Further, it was difficult for the Hessians to adjust to the British style of fighting, and their officers had little hope of rising to leadership in the British Army. The Hessians did not share the British sense of mission, lacked the British commitment, and were generally left out of critical strategic decisions made by the British officers. Often they were transported by sea rather than marched through the countryside where some of them were likely to desert. In short, the Hessians added little to Britain's struggle to carve out an American empire.

The Americans' stunning success at Trenton on the day after Christmas 1776 was a significant turning point in the Revolutionary War. A bloody five years later, the British surrendered at Yorktown. There, as the Union Jack was lowered, British officers and men, government officials, and businessmen sullenly boarded ships bound for their home . . . the small island-nation of England. With them went English hopes of hegemony over America.

THE YANKEE SAMURAI

Today, in a Rod Serlinglike kaleidoscope *Twilight Zone* tale, the players upon the stage have changed, the uniforms are different, and neither the weapons nor the form of combat are the same; yet the basic story line is essentially unaltered. To the United States from Japan, another small island-nation, on the wings of JAL and All Nippon Airways, have come the men of the great Japanese trading, financial, construction, service, and manufacturing companies. They are charged with the responsibility of building a strong presence on American soil and by so doing advancing their firm's global strategy. And the growing number of Americans working for those Japanese firms might be considered modern-day Hessians, the hired mercenaries. There are about 400,000 of them now, and their ranks may well rise to over a million before the end of the decade. These Americans are the Yankee Samurai of this book.

The chapters that follow will explore whether indeed there are similarities between the Yankee Samurai of today and the German Hessians who fought in the freezing streets and fields of Trenton over two hundred years ago. Do communication problems exist between the Americans and Japanese? Do the Americans understand and accept the Japanese management style? Are there opportunities for Americans to rise to a leadership position in parent companies in Japan? Do these Americans—the Yankee Samurai—lack the commitment and work ethic of the Japanese; are they aware of the Japanese mission and allowed to take an integral part in key decision making? And finally, do the more aggressive among them "desert" for better opportunities with competitors?

The Japanese, of course, are not alone in pursuing global ambitions and in their efforts to assimilate foreigners into their companies. As the world has divided into three dominant trading blocs—the Pacific Rim, the European Community, and North America—American and European firms also seek empires beyond their own borders. Their goals and objectives are no different from those of the Japanese, and the problems that they face are much the same. But because the Japanese in many respects are further along in their global efforts than either the Americans or Europeans, and because their presence in the United States, and around the world, has grown so rapidly in the last decade, they and the Americans who work for their firms on American soil are highlighted here.

JAPAN'S GLOBALIZATION VIS-À-VIS AMERICA

A starting point to becoming a truly global company is to structure a strong export base from the home country. Arguably, the companies of no nation have been more successful at this than those of Japan.

Japanese-manufactured automobiles, home electronics, cameras, machine tools, computers, construction equipment, motorcycles, and more, all of the finest quality, have gained large and in some cases nearly total market share in the United States. Initially, beginning in the early 1950s, these products, made in Japan, were sold for the most part through trading companies and U.S.-based distributors.

That phase was an unqualified triumph as Japan's favorable merchandise trade balance with the United States steadily increased, from about $5 billion in 1980 to $57 billion in 1989. In 1991, it stood at about $41 billion. But with a labor shortage at home, still less than 5 percent of manufacturing carried out abroad, a strong Yen, a growing threat of tariff barriers and trade sanctions imposed by the U.S. Congress, and a need to gain proximity to markets, there has come an even greater challenge for the Japanese. Now they face the implementation of phases II, III, and IV: establishing manufacturing, then later white-collar administrative support, and later still service operations, all within the United States.

The Japanese foray into manufacturing in the United States began in earnest about a decade ago and has since accelerated. Today, all but two states (Montana and North Dakota) have such operations; there are nearly 1,500 in total, with a concentration along the West Coast, and in the Midwest and Southeast. They generally have an efficient factory layout, make effective use of robotics, take advantage of advanced inventory and quality-control methods, maintain tight-knit supplier relations, assure close coordination between design and manufacturing personnel, and employ a largely rural and suburban nonunion work force—even in the few union operations, relaxed work rules have been negotiated. The quality of Japanese products produced in these operations using American blue-collar labor is arguably higher than corresponding American products produced in American firms using American labor, but generally not quite as high as that produced in Japan using Japanese labor. With a few notable exceptions—such as early problems with Sanyo in Arkansas and Kyocera in San Diego—on balance this manufacturing phase II has been a significant success for the Japanese. The third phase—the development of U.S.-based white-collar operations in support of, or supplementary to, manufacturing that employs Americans in marketing, finance, R&D, human resources, advertising, planning, law, accounting, and public/government relations—has been seriously under way since about 1985.

Beyond this, in what might be called phase IV, Japanese service-oriented firms in general support of manufacturing, but sometimes operating independently, have been rapidly increasing in the United States over the last few years. In banking, real estate, construction, shipping, entertainment, insurance, travel, financial services, communications, executive search, media, and more, such firms are growing by the hundreds all across America.

These latter three phases of the globalization process have given rise to a brand-new phenomenon: Americans, or Yankee Samurai, working for Japanese firms in the United States. Like it or not, this means that the Japanese are now dependent, at least to some extent, upon their American "hired mercenaries." These blue-collar and especially white-collar American executives, managers, professionals, and administrative staff, and the Japanese ability to manage them, may determine the ultimate success or failure of Japanese companies in the United States. The British use of mercenaries contributed to their failure to maintain a foothold in America two hundred years ago. Will the Japanese now fail also, albeit in a much more benign quest, but for similar reasons?

Will the apparently invincible Japanese economic juggernaut stutter to a standstill, unable to overcome the daunting objective of assimilating contemporary "Hessians" into their corporations thereby failing to effectively operate their American subsidiaries and by extension failing in America? Could this be the Japanese Achilles heel?

For Japan, a Special Challenge

This assimilation of outsiders presents a special challenge for the Japanese. The reason lies in Japan's history and culture. Dating from the first written reference to Japan found in 2,300-year-old Chinese archives, that nation has been largely isolated from external forces. Having somehow successfully leaped the waters of the Sea of Japan, the Yellow Sea, and the East China Sea, influences from Korea, China, and the islands to the south are clearly identifiable in Japan's history and contemporary culture. Yet even when a foreign language, a philosophic or artistic principle, a religion, or a technology made its way to Japan, an inexplicable metamorphosis took place, rendering it uniquely Japanese. Nothing and no one enters Japan without being changed. Adding to the relative isolation was Japan's centuries-long policy of avoiding close trade and diplomatic ties with other countries. Nor has military conquest by another nation left a mark on Japan. The only foreign troops to tread the sacred Land of the Gods were the crewcut, C-ration and cigarette-toting American GIs after World War II. Even that largely amiable occupation, led by General Douglas MacArthur, lasted less than a decade.

Historically, Western influences have been relatively limited. Portuguese traders and missionaries first came to "the Japans" in 1537, bringing with them new technology and a Christian God. The British and Dutch followed in later years. The very real British navigational pilot, Will Adams (known as Angin-san in James Clavell's book and television saga *Shōgun*) was among them. But by 1640, the powerful Tokugawa Shogunate—ruling military-dominated government—became apprehensive of several hundred thousand Christian converts and the increasing encroachment of Western culture. Edicts were issued: all foreigners were driven from the land and every trace of Christianity eradicated, often with brutal executions. With the exception of the small artificial islet, Deshima, in Nagasaki Harbor, where a few ships annually flying the Dutch East India Trading Company flag were allowed to call, Japan was officially sealed off from the world; an invisible shield was drawn about the country. Free from the maelstrom of outside influences and peacefully united under Tokugawa, there followed relatively golden halcyon days, indeed centuries, during which the culture of Japan was forged, tempered, and honed.

The country largely remained that way until July 8, 1853, when American Commodore Matthew Calbraith Perry, seeking trade agreements, intrusively eased his four-ship squadron into Tokyo Bay. The two state-of-the-art black ironclad steamships and the two accompanying sailing ships with their combined 61 guns and complement of 967 armed officers and men boldly confronted a panic-stricken and technologically primitive people. The nation was forced to open herself to the brute strength of the "tall, big-nosed, red-haired and blue-eyed arrogant barbarian." Little more than a decade later, Japan grudgingly entered the Western world. Yet ever since it has tried ambivalently to do so with its approach of *wakon yosai*, or "Western technology and Japanese spirit." To this day the Japanese struggle to square the circle by holding dear their sense of "Japaneseness" while at the same time seeking to become "internationalized."

Japan's long history of chosen isolation has created a people that are the most homogeneous of any large nation in the world, with a unique and deeply imbued sense of culture, and an almost tribal-like identity with their nation-state. Might this strong parochialism then preclude Japan's enterprising corporations with global ambitions from ever welcoming and accepting *gaijin* (foreigners) within their ranks? Or, to the contrary, will the Japanese be able to learn, adjust, and bring the Yankee Samurai into their firms, thus rendering them true samurai and achieving the ultimate step in globalization?

Peter Drucker has written that "In the years ahead the successful multinational firms will be those that have learned to manage the host country employees and make full use of their abilities." How will the Japanese adapt their management style to the American workplace? Will they be able not only to manage their Yankee Samurai but to gain full community acceptance in the towns and cities of America where their firms operate, by adapting to the local standards of corporate social responsibility, ethics, and political lobbying? Or, rather than adapt, might not the Japanese approach to industry, politics, and society in general begin to influence the American ethos?

AMERICAN SUBSIDIARIES OF JAPANESE FIRMS

Much of the examination that follows is done through the eyes of the Yankee Samurai themselves. A total of some 250 of them working for 31 firms were interviewed and questioned for this book. These Americans, all of whom are white-collar employees ranging from mail clerks and secretaries to CEOs, will provide a window through which we can view their everyday work life in a Japanese firm operating in the United States. You will hear their words and share their thoughts, learn what attracted them to Japanese firms, why they are succeeding or failing, how their families feel about their employment with Japanese companies, their concerns, their ambitions, how they might differ from other Americans working for American firms, their perceptions of how women and minorities are treated in their companies, how they view the Japanese expatriates with whom they work, their opinions of U.S.-Japan relations, and their thoughts about Japanese management style.

You will also hear from several dozen very senior-level Japanese posted in the United States whose formidable task it is to manage in a culture so very different from their own. These leaders must balance the demands placed upon them from a distant and sometimes intransigent corporate headquarters in Japan with the realities of the American marketplace and their American work force. You will share their professional views about the Americans who work with and for them, as well as their personal thoughts on U.S.-Japan relations, and their experience of living in the United States.

Suggested from all of this are lessons for the Americans now working for Japanese firms and the ever-growing number of Americans who are considering doing so in the future. There are lessons as well for Japanese expatriates eager to discover how better to manage their American work force. American managers of American companies will learn how their Japanese competitors operate and draw valuable conclusions. Finally, and more broadly, there are lessons here for the people of America and Japan. These combined 375 million people form only 6 percent of the world's population yet generate 40 percent of the world's income; their destinies are inextricably linked and they are just beginning to learn about one another.

JAPANESE MANAGEMENT STYLE

By ten o'clock in the evening, cigarette smoke hangs heavy in the air of the restaurants and bars filled with Japanese *sararimen* (salarymen— elite of the white-collar work force). They are vigorously working at relaxing after a long day of intensive corporate warfare. After dinner, where attentive hostesses filled their plates with sushi, sashimi, yaki- soba, sukiyaki, tofu, and tempura, they adjourn to one of the several *karaoke* (singing) bars, where they burst into song, bellowing out their favorite (often bawdy or maudlin) tunes to the accompaniment of high- tech recorded music.

Decibel levels rise as discussion turns to the closing prices of the Nikkei Index, the government's proposal to include Special Defense Forces in U.N. peacekeeping operations, the growing labor shortage, and the sumo performance of the young Takahanada. These after-hours nightspots are havens of male bonding among the companymen of Nissan, Toyota, DKB, Hitachi, Honda, Sumitomo, and the other Jap- anese *kaisha* (corporations). Foreigners are looked on with a measure of suspicion.

This is not Osaka, Nagasaki, Hiroshima, Nagoya, Kyoto, or Tokyo itself. It is rather Little Tokyo, located some 7,000 miles from Japan, and only a few minutes from downtown Los Angeles, where Mitsui Fudosan has just completed a magnificent new fifty-two-story building, where Shuwa has purchased the twin fifty-one-story ARCO Towers, and where other Japanese interests combine to control 40 percent of the office space. With over 1,600 Japanese firms operating in Southern California, a large proportion of the roughly 40,000 Japanese expatriates in the United States are located here.

There is a story going around this Japanese enclave in the land of Disney, palm trees, Rodeo Drive, and sunshine about three international businessmen who have been caught up in a revolution inside a small Third World nation. The three—an Englishman, an American, and a Japanese—have been arrested and ordered put to death. They are, however, granted a final wish. The Englishman opts to sing "God Save the Queen" in his last moments on earth. The Japanese solemnly chooses to give a lecture on Japanese management style. And the American requests—in fact, demands—to be executed first so that he doesn't have to listen to another damn speech on Japanese management style.

After numerous rounds of sake and imported whiskey, upon hearing the story, the Japanese laugh good-naturedly with slightly nodding heads that seem to say, "That is probably the way it would be."

Japanese management style, particularly as it is practiced in the white-collar environment in the United States, is indeed a major focus of this book; several chapters will be devoted to it. But it is impossible to truly understand that management style without considering something far more basic . . . the national culture of Japan.

THE ROLE OF CULTURE

The management style of any nation's institutions, public or private, is significantly influenced by the surrounding society's culture, that is, by its beliefs, traditions, values, institutions, myths, language, history, and vision. This book is ultimately about culture and the clash of cultures.

If there are problems with the Yankee Samurai working for Japanese firms, they are generally not because of who the Americans are as individuals. Rather, it is that they have been nurtured in a culture that is at near-polar extremes from Japan's. It is difficult to conceive of two cultures more different from one another. That is fundamentally important because those cultures shade views of the workplace, govern the sense of time perspective, set the limits of self-interest, influence the work commitment, define the views held of women and minorities, circumscribe relations with co-workers, determine employee loyalty, fix the sense of business ethics, and the relation of the firm to the nation. The role of culture will emerge as an underlying theme in much of what follows.

As the curtain rises on the economic, political, and military World Super Bowl of the twenty-first century, each nation will bring to the international competition its arsenal of wealth and power: foreign reserves, natural resources, infrastructure, capital base, technology, international alliances, and military personnel and weaponry. But in the long run, these are of secondary importance, and in a larger sense they hardly matter at all. What matters ultimately is only the people themselves of each nation—their knowledge, skills, and more broadly, their culture.

The Japanese are forever analyzing who they are, what their culture is and is becoming, their sense of both uniqueness and superiority, and quite simply what it means to be Japanese. Americans seldom are so introspective. Yet every major issue that confronts America today is a reflection of its culture. An alien from somewhere in the solar system could learn much of American culture in 1992 by perusing any large-city daily newspaper. Our visitor would find a pastiche of issues: S&L crisis, litigation gridlock of 800,000 lawyers, collapse of whole segments of the education system, lagging productivity, decaying infrastructure, growing welfare-supported underclass, 2.5 million reported annual cases of child abuse, blighted inner cities, 350,000 "crack" or other drug babies born a year, a pandering entertainment industry, aggressive unions, CEOs taking home 100 times the salary of entry level workers, world's highest criminal incarceration rate, deluge of illegal aliens, 52 percent divorce rate, insurmountable federal deficit, greed driven Wall Street financial institutions, Third World infant mortality rate, AIDS epidemic, arrogant congress propped up by myriad special interest groups, environmental disregard, and deep-seated racial conflict. It is not a pretty picture. Yet it is a reflection of our culture.

The serene world of *Ozzie and Harriet, Leave It to Beaver,* and *Gunsmoke*—"There is only one way to deal with the killers and spoilers and that is with the U.S. Marshal and the smell of . . . gunsmoke"—of the 1950s certainly had its own set of concerns, but nothing as pernicious as these. The societal cancers identified here are new, metastasizing only in the last generation. This scourge has struck America not because of any act of God, nature, or preordained destiny, but because of who we are, and have become, as a people. We created them; they are culturally induced. There is no easy, short, or superficial fix to these intractable and systemic problems. Resolution, if it is to be attained, will only occur when we change who we are as a people—when we change our culture.

Econmic competition between the United States and Japan in the years ahead will not depend per se upon the victors of the clash of titans: General Motors and Toyota, General Electric and NEC, IBM and Fujitsu, Nomura and Merrill Lynch, or DKB and Citicorp. Nor in the long run will it depend upon the largely tactical skirmishes of who first comes to the marketplace with HDTV, the success of Toys 'Я' Us in cracking open the labyrinthine Japanese distribution system, whether the Japanese lower trade barriers for American rice, how many *biggu makku* the Japanese consume at Makudonarudo, whether T. Boone Pickens is given a seat on the board of a Toyota subsidiary, or whether Hollywood sells itself to Sony and Matsushita.

Victory will certainly not depend upon feckless congressmen, on the steps of Congress, childishly swinging sledgehammers into Toshiba VCRs while smiling stupidly into cameras set up for an infamous (1987) photo-op. Nor will it depend upon growing American-bashing rhetoric coming from extremist Japanese ultranationalists.

And victory is unlikely to depend upon the outcome of tiresome, protracted, and only marginally effective trade talks. U.S. Trade Negotiator, Carla Hills, has made some modest progress in "leveling the playing field," but in the long run her efforts hardly matter. Losers complain of playing fields not being level and whine about "unfairness." Winners silently go about their work. The American Chamber of Commerce in Japan—which consists of dozens of firms, including IBM, Coca-Cola, Schick, Disney, Exxon, Du Pont, Eastman Kodak, Motorola, Caterpillar, Caltex, Texas Instruments, Merck, Mobil, General Electric, and Amway—recently published a report arguing that there is great opportunity in Japan for any American company with a quality product or service that is prepared to invest in the long term. The trade talks and final signed agreements are fine as a means of maintaining open lines of communication and nudging the Japanese government to do that which it wanted to do anyway but could not because of domestic opposition (*gaiatsu*). But ultimately the forces of change are far too powerful to be altered in any significant way by pieces of paper. International agreements, be they trade, military, or political, have always been swept aside when it was convenient for one of the signatories to do so. The trash barrel of history is filled to overflowing with them.

In the final analysis, the competition is cultural. Victory, in this hopefully friendly but probably strained (possibly at times very strained) competition, will depend upon the nation whose culture is best fitted to the vicissitudes, demands, and constraints of the arena in the twenty-first century. It will involve a clash of beliefs, traditions, values, institutions, myths, language, history, and vision. Possibly only one culture will survive.

Concomitant with British power in the last century came the diffusing of that nation's language, common law, and culture throughout the British Empire and beyond. Along with American power in this century has come the near-worldwide attraction for American culture, and the

rendering of English, or at least American English (George Bernard
Shaw said that "The Americans and British are two people separated by
a common language"), as the near-universal language of science and
business. It is a historic verity that economically and militarily powerful
nations extend their culture well beyond their own borders. This was
true of Nebuchadnezzar's Babylon, Pharaoh's Egypt, Alexander's
Greece, Caesar's Rome, Montezuma's Aztec Empire, Suleiman's Ot-
tomans, and Bonaparte's France.

What, then, of Japan in the next century? If, as Ambassador Michael
Mansfield, and so many others, have said, "The next one will belong to
Japan," will Japanese culture and the Japanese language come to heavily
influence the nations of the Pacific Rim, including the United States?
If some 1,500 years ago, "All roads led to Rome," will it be true in the
year 2010 that "All roads lead to Tokyo"? If that is so, the Yankee
Samurai of this book may not be Hessians at all, but rather among the
first of the American disciples of the "Japanese Way." They are bridging
the two cultures, and it may be they who will bring the gospel of Japan
to their fellow Americans. Certainly, they are at the cusp of history.

American business practitioners and scholars jet to Japan seeking the
Holy Grail of Japan's success. They study manufacturing methods,
including *kanban* (Toyota's version of just-in-time inventory), in-house
unions, *kaizen* (continuous improvement philosophy), quality-control
circles, and robotics, and they observe Japanese management style as it
relates to managing people. These American visitors analyze the organization structure of the *keiretsu*, with their family of companies, and
explore the unique role of the major government ministries and their
highly cooperative relationship with Japanese industry.

They return to the United States intending to implement what they
have observed in Japan. They generally fail. Emerson would have understood why when he wrote, "The field cannot well be seen from
within the field." What these Americans have missed is the field—
Japan's culture. What works in Japan is unlikely to work in the United
States. The cultures are just too different. America and Americans
might be far better served if those who studied Japan focused instead
upon the essence of that nation's unprecedented achievements—its culture.

Over two centuries ago, Adam Smith, David Ricardo, and other
classical economists began their search for the true source of a nation's
wealth; the search continues. Recently, the Harvard scholar Robert
Reich, and the internationally known Kenichi Ohmae, have concluded
that "A nation's ultimate wealth is its human capital, the skills and

knowledge of its workers." That is getting close, but it can be argued that there is something even more fundamental than human capital in determining a nation's wealth.

That something more is the culture within which people labor. Even a nation rich in human capital, with a cadre of the most superbly trained men and women, will not be able to generate lasting national wealth if those people are overburdened by government regulation, forced to live in crime-ridden cities, lack a sense of nationalism and social responsibility, and are of such diverse ethnic, racial, and religious backgrounds that communication breaks down and it becomes impossible to share a national vision. Nor can they be truly productive if they have the morality of an Ivan Boesky or Michael Milken, work in an environment devoid of foreign and domestic competition, are repressively taxed to bear the burden of massive numbers of nonproducers and malcontents, and are without a higher spiritual or religious guidance. It is culture that is the true source of a nation's wealth.

Listening to the Yankee Samurai and the Japanese expatriates interviewed here helps make clear the fundamental role of national culture in influencing management style, and indeed in largely determining national well-being.

America's business, academic, media, entertainment, and political leaders should have a riveted concern in this. They are the caretakers with whom the nation has placed its most sacred treasure . . . its culture. It is their primary responsibility to preserve it. But beyond the leaders, perhaps even more important, each one of the 250 million of us in our personal and professional lives influences and is influenced by the national culture. That culture is America's destiny.

So, too, is Japan's culture, and Japanese readers of this book may well look to cultural changes that have occurred in the United States over the past generation. Might those changes vault the Pacific from east to west and invade their shores? If Japan will be better for those changes, then fine. If it will not, how should that country position itself to be a political, financial, economic, and military leader internationally, or even a major participant in world affairs, while still remaining protected from vitiating cultural influences from America and other lands? This is not the seventeenth century, and there are few Tokugawas in today's Liberal Democratic Party (LPD) prepared once again to draw a veil of isolation around the country; no doubt it would be impossible to do so in any case. Japan faces a cultural challenge no less intense than that of the United States.

2

Stars and Stripes and the Rising Sun

INTRODUCTION

Up on the forty-fifth floor of a Japanese bank's new office building was the firm's boardroom aerie. The view from full-length windows provided an ugly, smog-drenched panorama of the city of Los Angeles on a pizza-oven-hot June afternoon. Some 30 miles to the west beyond the brownish yellow gunk lay the Pacific Ocean. Looking down, far below, what appeared to be a vast parking lot filled with toy cars was in fact city streets at near gridlock resulting from construction work on an underground metro-rail. Behind the wheels of those cars were their frustrated drivers, many of them cursing in the various 130-odd languages spoken in this most polyglot of cities. Tiny traffic officers frantically waved their even tinier white-gloved hands, attempting to bring order to the madness.

In sharp contrast was the richly wood-paneled room interior, with its thick, dark gray carpeting. Delicate calligraphy and prints depicting feudal Japan adorned the walls. Near the doorway was an exquisite ebony cabinet, which displayed an ornate seventeenth-century samurai helmet and sword. Against the far wall hung an oil painting of one of the bank's Osaka born founders. He was an older, very distinguished-looking man, whose countenance seemed to say, "All here is strong, safe, and enduring."

A silent office lady had just placed expensive porcelain decanters of freshly brewed coffee and tea in the center of the table and then somehow vanished from the room. The barely perceptible hum of an air conditioner and purifier came from somewhere overhead.

Seated in high-backed black leather chairs around the brilliantly polished mahogany conference table were ten of the firm's Yankee Samurai. They had been put forward by the bank's management to be interviewed and questioned as part of the research that was to become this book. I was meeting with them to provide some background.

The atmosphere was professional but friendly. Several people voiced considerable interest in my project and pleasure at the opportunity to participate. However, while everyone else in the room laughed generously at an anecdote I told to lighten the mood, one woman just sat glaring at me through her designer glasses. She was in her late thirties, wearing a dark suit with a cream-colored blouse. She sat sullenly with her arms crossed.

Puzzled, but sensitive to the "politically correct" environment of Southern California, I said: "Excuse me, but I hope I have not done or said anything to offend you. If I have, I really apologize." She mumbled something about everything being fine and that there was no problem. She continued to glare.

After the meeting, I approached her in private and asked again if there was a problem. With apparently barely controlled fury, she blurted out, "You are referring to us as 'Yankee Samurai'! I am no 'Yankee Samurai.' I am an *American!*" She almost shouted the word.

That woman's anger, amid the sedate boardroom setting of a Japanese-owned bank in a Japanese-owned building in the city of Los Angeles, located at the very edge of an ocean beyond which some 5,000 miles to the west lay the great island-nation of Japan, all came together in my mind as a striking epiphany.

Was her chauvinism an aberration, or did she voice a feeling that is perhaps latent among many of the Yankee Samurai? How do the Yankee Samurai feel about relations between the United States and Japan? What are their views of the trade deficit and of Japanese investment in the United States? Do they think that Japanese products are superior to American products, and if so why? How do their perceptions differ from those of the American public at large?

Answers to these questions were obtained both by written survey and interviews. The results provide some insights into the thinking of the Yankee Samurai, who are in the uniquely ambivalent position of being Americans, yet at the same time dependent for their livelihood upon a Japanese-owned firm. This issue is of great importance to the Japanese firms, and indeed to U.S.-Japan relations, because these Americans could be an important free trade and lobbying constituency, or at the very least objective, neutral observers. If, on the other hand, the Yankee Samurai feel as the chauvinist "I am an *American!*" quoted above, then the Japanese assuredly do have a great challenge in winning American hearts and minds.

THE SURVEY

Thirteen statements relating in a general way to U.S.-Japan relations appeared on a survey completed by most of the Yankee Samurai in the study. They dealt with issues including: trade, investment, product quality, and comparative work ethic. Each response was scored on a scale of 1–5:

1 Definitely no
2 No
3 Neutral
4 Yes
5 Definitely yes

On the following page are the actual statements and the average scores of all the respondents:

U.S.-Japan Relations

Statement		Average Score
1.	Japan should make a very special effort to open its markets to American products.	4.4
2.	American firms should do a better job of trying to sell to Japan.	4.4
3.	The United States should impose a heavy tariff on goods imported from Japan.	2.2
4.	The United States should bar imports from Japan.	1.5
5.	The current presence of Japanese firms in the United States has helped to overcome trade frictions.	3.0
6.	Japanese products are generally superior to American products.	3.6
7.	Japan should contribute more to its own military defense.	3.7
8.	In the long run, a significant increase in Japanese investment in the United States could lead to an American public opinion backlash.	3.8
9.	Japanese investment in the United States should be restricted.	2.9
10.	Americans generally know very little about Japan.	4.2
11.	The relationship between Japan and the United States is far more important to the former than the latter.	3.1
12.	By the turn of the century Japan will have the strongest economy in the world.	3.6
13.	In general, the Japanese work harder than Americans.	3.7

The average scores translate into a story of their own.

While the Yankee Samurai do believe that Japan should make a special effort to open its markets to American products, they also believe that Americans must do a better job of selling in Japan.

There was general agreement that Japanese-imported goods should neither be barred in the United States nor have a heavy tariff imposed upon them.

The respondents were almost evenly split over the question of whether the presence of Japanese firms in the United States has helped to over-come trade frictions. But they were largely in agreement that Japanese product quality is superior to that of the United States.

The majority of the Yankee Samurai felt that Japan should bear a heavier burden for its own military defense.

A 75 percent majority believed that Japanese investment in the United States would ultimately lead to a public opinion backlash. Even so, they were evenly divided over the question of whether limitations should be put on Japanese investment.

There was near-unanimous opinion that Americans know very little about Japan.

While the Yankee Samurai were neutral in their judgment as to whether the relationship between the two countries was more important to Japan than America, they were largely in agreement that the Japanese work harder than Americans, and that by the turn of the century the Japanese economy will be the strongest in the world.

These Yankee Samurai views compare to a recent national public opinion poll indicating that a startling 80 percent of Americans want to limit foreign investment in the United States and 40 percent want to halt it all together. A majority of them at least want full disclosure. More Americans fear Japan's economic power than Russia's military power, 60 percent feel that the Japanese are unfair in their trading practices, and 68 percent blame the Japanese for America's economic problems. One *BusinessWeek* survey indicates that 70 percent of Americans favor quotas to assure access of American products to the Japanese markets, and 69 percent favor quotas that would limit Japanese products in the United States.

The Yankee Samurai survey responses, with only a few exceptions, appear to generally be far more sympathetic to the Japanese presence in the United States and to the Japanese position on trade than do those of the average American. Perhaps that is because they are closer to it all, more knowledgeable, and indeed have their own interests much at stake. The interview responses yielded similar conclusions, but were far less sterile than the summary statistics of the survey. "Where's the beef?"

the Wendy's commercial used to ask. The beef is in the interviews. Just listen to them.

The Interviews

The interview questions directed to the Yankee Samurai focused upon: (1) the causes of the trade deficit; (2) comparative product quality; (3) the impact of Japanese investment in the United States; and (4) likely relations between the two nations in the year 2000.

Trade Deficit

The interview responses were split over the issue of cause for the continuing U.S. trade deficit with Japan. Roughly 40 percent felt that unfair Japanese trading practices were responsible, while the others believed that it was America's short-term-planning horizon, government interference, poor product quality, and union indifference that were to blame.

The Fault Lies with Japan

Typical among the Yankee Samurai who believed that the cause of the trade deficit was Japanese unfairness was the response of the blunt-speaking manager of procurement and materials for a major electronics firm:

> A weakness of our cultural morals is that we try to be overly fair so everyone has equal footing. It is kind of like the code of the West. But the Japanese don't look at it that way. For them, business is war. If they can play on an uneven field and win, then so be it. American business leaders and the American government have to learn that is the way the game is played.

The bank's chief financial officer, who had been with his firm for several years, reflected upon an earlier experience while with an American bank in Japan:

> I used to work for Security Pacific's Tokyo branch; the Japanese government virtually managed the level of profits. However, when the Japanese come here, they operate like everyone else. This is really an unfair situation. [Things are changing. Over the last few years the Japanese government has been aggressively deregulating

the banking and securities industries for both domestic *and* foreign banks. There is nothing altruistic about this; the action is taken to catapult Tokyo into the position of leading world financial center, surpassing both New York and London. Our CFO quoted here would find a measurably different working environment today for a foreign bank in Japan.]

The electronics firm's credit manager raised the issue of culture as it relates to trade, which turned out to be a recurring theme of the Yankee Samurai:

> From the cultural standpoint I'm not sure the Japanese are willing to accept products from other lands as readily as we do. Japan is a very cohesive country in the sense of knowing who they are and looking to things to achieve as a nation much more than us. That makes it very difficult for American companies to gain market access.

The laptop computer firm's marketing vice president also raised the issue of culture:

> The Japanese culture has a philosophy of export or die and has perhaps practiced that too long. If a country continually has a trade surplus, it is because the nation has not allowed its consumers to enjoy a high enough standard of living.
>
> I continue to believe, for example, that there is a deeply in-grained Japanese cultural prejudice against buying foreign machine tools. At the same time, [Japanese] consumers seem to like American jeans. That is great, but we are not going to resolve the U.S.-Japan trade imbalance with jeans. [Who knows? . . . Used Levis made in the 1950s, with the real leather patch and inside copper rivets, are selling today for as much as $2,000 a pair in Tokyo; America's West has always fascinated the Japanese.]

Finally, there was the outspoken young metals-trading coordinator, who spoke Japanese fluently and knew the Japanese culture from having done missionary work for his church in Japan. His frustration and anger with the Japanese, mingled with great respect for them, spilled into these remarks on trade, the work ethic, and once again culture:

> The United States must increase its exports to Japan. But the Japanese are unreasonably unfair in their trade practices. They have a mind-set that it is themselves against the world; they are paranoid-protectionist.

They think they are different from other people and that rules that apply to other nations do not apply to them.

The plain simple reason for the Japanese "miracle," in my view, is the culture. The Americans put their family first and then maybe religion. It [their job] is something you do eight hours a day and not on weekends.

The Japanese do not look at the job that way. They look at it as life [*gestures with arms spread widely*]. Even on their days off, that is all they talk about. You are dealing with guys that work fourteen hours a day, every day, seven days a week. The natural result of all that work has got to pay dividends. It must eventually pay off for people having that kind of commitment, even if they are not competent. You have a whole nation of people like that.

The Fault Lies with America

For all of this finger pointing abroad to explain the cause of the U.S.-Japan trade deficit, the Yankee Samurai also placed blame squarely on the perceived faltering shoulders of their fellow country-men. The majority of them were harder on the United States than on Japan. One of the issues raised was the short planning horizon of the Americans as compared to the Japanese.

Some 60 miles to the west of Tokyo is the majestic 12,368-foot Mount Fuji, which dominates the countryside. Its near-perfect symmetry, pristine beauty, and often cloud-shrouded peak combine to give the mountain an almost sacrosanct bearing. The Japanese often refer to it as "*Fuji-san*" (san is generally affixed to a *person's* name as a sign of respect).

Whatever the turbulence of the moment, the mountain has stood, stands now, and will always stand. It provides a sense of continuity to the future as well as a link to the past. The 1992 salarymen of Sumitomo, for example, know that the 2092 men of their firm—men not yet born—will look up at the same mountain and ponder the mystery of the future just as they now do, and just as their predecessors did in 1892.

The sun, another symbol of Japan, like Mount Fuji, has about it an eternal nature. So, too, do the dozens of mountains, waterfalls, lakes, and forests, as well as countless centuries-old man-made shrines and gardens all so popular with Japanese tourists. Perhaps it is this that causes many contemporary Japanese to be so aware of the world they have come from and the one they will leave to those who will follow long after them.

They plan accordingly, often decades ahead. Their personal future is secondary. What matters is the long-term growth of the companies for which they labor; what matters is the ultimate glory of Japan; what matters is that there will always be a *Fuji-san*.

It is as though a never-ending Kabuki play is being performed. The Japanese workers and managers are the actors, and while they as individuals change from generation to generation, the basic roles are immutable: they are stewards with the sacred responsibility of assuring the preservation and advancement of their individual firm, and in the process the preservation and advancement of Japan. Like some *Star Trek* traveler, the Japanese ship-of-state continues its voyage into infinity; only the crew changes over time. This view is captured in the words of Yoshio Maruta, past president of Kao Corporation:

> A company is not an entity which you are in charge of for only a set period of time; it continues indefinitely. So even if the flowers do not bloom now, it pays to make the effort to see that they bloom in the next age. Our bodies will waste away, but the company is eternal.
>
> It is more important that you make the effort to carry the company on into the next age than to pay out healthy dividends while you are in control. You shouldn't worry about getting applause for your efforts today.

This kind of thinking translates into a planning horizon for Japanese companies that is far more distant than that for typical American firms. It is not unusual for some of them to think literally half a century ahead. The Yankee Samurai were aware of this and condemned the American companies for their relative myopia.

Listen to the Yankee Samurai floor manager for one of Japan's largest trading companies:

> The Japanese look at what will be making money not today, but in the future.
>
> They like to tell a story about a three-man office. One man brings in $100,000 a year, another $5 million, and a third only $20,000. They ask who is the best employee. It is not necessarily the $5 million man, who might have inherited a cash cow. It may well be the $20,000 man, who is putting together a new grass-roots business that will be generating profit for fifty years.
>
> I have some projects that have not made a cent in ten years, but we continue to try. I have traveled all over America attempting to sell Australian silica sand and nothing happened. The Japanese

say, "Don't worry, we will just keep it on a back burner." How is America ever going to compete with the Japanese when they have such a long-term perspective?

The senior credit officer of a major bank was another of several dozen respondents who commented on the American inability to take the long view:

> I have contended that American business is very shortsighted. They look for day-to-day earnings and believe the future will somehow magically take care of itself. They are concerned with quarterly earnings to keep the stockholders happy. Because of that we have lost our ability to reindustrialize.
>
> We have to take a long-term view as to what we are in business for, what our products are, and how we are going to do business.

Staying with that theme of short-term orientation of American firms was the marketing manager of a large electronics company. He related this anecdote:

> I had occasion recently to call upon most of the major American retail chains and met with the top people. I noticed that the executives had daily, and in some cases hourly reports brought to them, indicating their firm's stock price along with that of their competitors.
>
> When I happened to relate this to my [Japanese] boss here at my company, an absolutely puzzled look crossed his face. After a long pause he asked, "Why?" He didn't understand how stock prices, especially daily stock prices, were at all relevant to the firm's long-term objectives.
>
> I tired to explain to him American firms' penchant for executive stock option plans and the need for high stock prices to ward off raiders and to satisfy the demands of aggressive pension plan managers. He still didn't understand.

The electronics firm's national manager of human resources believed that short-run answers to America's problems would not suffice:

> We must recognize that we are now in a global economy. Legislation and monetary fixes are short-run answers at best. Although the Japanese do have to open their markets a little more, we have to stop making excuses for ourselves complaining about Japanese subsidies and unfair practices.

I grew up in the Midwest and we used to have a saying, "A farmer cleaning up horse dung from his barn knows damn well that the mess did not come from the outside." Well, America's mess didn't come from the outside. We did it to ourselves over the last twenty to thirty years.

We have to move toward the way the Japanese manage. They turn to those people who are closest to a particular problem for answers, listen to them, and then reward them.

Some of the Yankee Samurai, like the auto firm's accounts payable supervisor, thought that government was at the source of America's problems:

The role of government in the two countries is quite different. In Japan, the government tries to promote business and cooperate with industry because that supports the economy.

Here government is constantly in an adversarial "watch dog" role when it comes to business. You know a watch dog is used to guard against thieves, rapists, robbers, and I guess even child molesters. That is how our government views business. No wonder the Japanese have an advantage over us. We spend half our time fighting among ourselves.

Another auto firm's director of corporate administration thought that the failure of American business to meet customer demands, coupled with personal greed and incompetence, has contributed to the problem:

The Yen-dollar relationship should help the United States, but the American firms must be more willing to find out what the foreign countries really need and create that product for them. The Europeans, Asians, and Third World nations are finding out what the United States needs and delivering it.

We tend to go in and say, "This is what we have, why won't you buy it?" That is the philosophical difference that the United States has to get over.

About four years ago, when our Secretary of the Treasury, I think [Baker], engineered a dramatically weakened dollar, the domestic auto firms were in a great position to increase market share. [Company name] was very concerned, and we spent hundreds of hours devising counter strategies. But my old friends at G.M., Ford, and Chrysler didn't take the opportunity. Instead, they jacked up prices, making annual short-run profits surge, yielded to more blackmail from the unions, and all the executives paid themselves fat bonuses.

Now, a few years later, they are whining again about Japanese imports and want protection. Something is fundamentally wrong with the way Detroit, and for that matter much of America, does business.

Some Simple Solutions

Perhaps it was a lack of understanding of the complexity of the trade deficit and associated economic issues that caused some Yankee Samurai to suggest rather problematic solutions to, and explanations for, the trade deficit. Or maybe it is all simpler than we think.

The electronics firm's national account manager observed:

> The deficit could be resolved with a mutually agreed upon exchange of product between the two countries. We certainly have something such as food that they need; basically a barter system. [The only categories where the U.S. runs a significant trade surplus with Japan are food, beverages, cigarettes, and raw materials. Modest surpluses totaling only $5.2 billion exist for pharmaceuticals, aircraft, computers, and chemicals.]

I told him that the United States already exports more food to Japan than any other nation and has more land under cultivation to feed the Japanese than Japan itself has. I then asked what else America produces that the Japanese might want. After a long pause, he simply shrugged.

Then there was the thirty-four-year-old Louisiana-born project manager who felt that:

> Manufacturing is now a nonexisting thing in the United States. Back in the 1950s and 60s when we did have cars, textiles, and capital goods manufactured here, we did not face such an economic downfall. It cannot be blamed upon Japan, Taiwan, Singapore, or any other trading partner. Our government chose to disallow tax advantages to U.S. production companies. [Actually, manufacturing is still about 23 percent of GNP just as it was in the 1970s; employment in the sector has proportionately declined somewhat.]

Finally, the assistant to the general manager of a trading company had what she thought was a wonderful idea that will be greeted with deafening silence or perhaps a deep groan by the people at Exxon,

Texaco, Mobil, and Arco: "American firms, particularly oil companies, should pay higher taxes because they earn tremendous amounts of money. That can go to paying the trade deficit."

PRODUCT QUALITY

Until relatively recently, the American product quality-control expert W. Edward Deming was mocked or largely overlooked in his own land. Yet in Japan, he is revered and a recipient of one of the emperor's highest medals of merit. Brought to that country in 1947 by American occupation forces, Deming set to work teaching the Japanese about product quality. The attentive students learned their lessons well. "Made in Japan" changed from its prewar meaning of shoddy to an imprimatur of excellence. Today, the annual Deming Award for quality is perhaps the most prestigious that a Japanese firm can earn. (Belatedly, America introduced its Malcolm Baldrige National Quality Award a few years ago; Cadillac, Federal Express, Xerox, and IBM have been recent winners.)

Associated with the trade deficit, certainly a contributing cause, is the issue of comparative product quality. The interviewed Yankee Samurai were asked: "How in general would you characterize the differences in quality between American- and Japanese-produced goods?" The answers were consistent with the survey responses, which generally indicated Japanese superiority.

Here, for example, is the director of marketing for a large electronics company:

> Let me relate a story. Recently, Mazda's president addressed the U.S. Chamber of Commerce and was speaking about his firm's manufacturing activity in the Michigan area. He spoke of his dismay with U.S. vendors whose quality assurance levels were no better than 90 or 95 percent. But Mazda as a minimum required 99.5 percent. The vendors could not meet those standards.
>
> That explains the Japanese demands for quality versus what the Americans are used to getting.
>
> We have the same problem with our manufacturing activity in Oregon. Our goal is to obtain at least 50 percent assembly here, but we cannot achieve it. We have a team whose sole mission is to find U.S. vendors who can provide us with components for our fiber optics, cellular telephones, and multiplexors. But it is very difficult. We are still importing about 85 percent from Japan because the [local] vendors are few and far between who can meet the standards.
>
> I bought a General Motors car and expect a certain amount of

defects. There is nothing that you can do about that. It is a part of life that you have to argue with the service manager and fight for your rights under the warranty. We have simply come to accept that.

The Japanese don't accept that. They expect a product to work when they buy it.

Many of the Yankee Samurai, all white-collar people, were convinced that American labor unions were the fundamental cause for the poor state of product quality. Those unions are strikingly different from Japan's.

In the years immediately following World War II, violent leftist and Communist-dominated labor unions emerged on the Japanese scene. With full cooperation from the American proconsul, General Mac-Arthur, they were smashed by the government with support from right-wing Yakusa elements. (More about the Yakusa, which bears a distant resemblance to America's Mafia, in chapter 11.) What has evolved is a union movement poles apart from America's.

With the exception of employees of some government- or quasi-government-operated enterprises or federations of individual labor unions, unions in Japan are essentially in-house company unions. While the 764,000-member Confederation of Japan Automobile Workers is somewhat similar to the American United Auto Workers (UAW), there is little in the way of adversarial relations between worker and management. Days lost to strikes and absenteeism are a small fraction of what they are in the United States; strikes are often scheduled for the lunch hour so as not to interfere with production. Japanese union leaders often become part of their firm's management—in the mid-1980s, Mazda's CEO, earlier in his career, headed the company's union, and 16 percent of the director-level people in the largest five hundred Japanese companies are erstwhile union officials. The worker views vacations as a privilege and seldom takes all that is allotted; he accepts overtime or unscheduled shifts, flexible work rules, and job rotation without question, and will even docilely tolerate an occasional supervisor's disciplinary slap. American contingency-fee-paid lawyers salivate over the idea of such an occurrence in a Japanese plant in the United States—it hasn't happened.

The Yankee Samurai are generally aware of these labor union differences in the two countries. That has perhaps colored their perceptions of the American labor scene, which were largely disapproving, sometimes vehemently so.

Here, for example, is the electronic firm's manager of mobile service who embraced the view that America's problem is the unions:

> We can't afford good quality; too many concessions have been made to the unions. The unions have outlived their usefulness. My father worked for Bethlehem Steel for many years. He felt he actually earned thirteen weeks vacation a year! No wonder we can't compete with the Japanese.

The corporate marketing manager with a major auto company also felt that unions were part of the problem, although he believed there were other cultural factors at work:

> The product quality traces to differences in the cultures of the countries. It involves attention to detail.
>
> I went through a Japanese trim plant last year. Under each of the work stations were photographs of poor work that had been done from that plant. The people there had great pride and did not want something they did to show up on a photograph for all to see. If you tried to do that at a UAW plant in the United States, they would cut your balls off.
>
> Quality is a management commitment, a worker attitude, and is ingrained in the culture.
>
> In Toyota City, where about 60 percent of the people are directly affiliated with the firm, the bars and lounges are closed down at eleven each night because they want people alert for work the next day. Single women employees living in company-owned dormitories must abide by a ten o'clock curfew. Can you imagine trying to do that in Flint, Michigan? The culture of Flint and Toyota City are as different as the cultures of any two cities can be.
>
> There are really three kinds of products: those produced by American firms, by Japanese firms, and by Japanese firms in America. The Japanese-produced products are far superior to the American-produced. Those produced by Japanese firms in America fall somewhere between.

Samuel Gompers, the turn-of-the-century George Washington of America's union movement, no doubt paused in his negotiations with St. Peter on organizing the harp players to listen to the remarks of a tough-talking corporate marketing manager:

> The Japanese product quality is far and away superior to ours. The thing that killed American quality is the labor unions. We are

slaves to those unions; they have long since outlived their usefulness.

Japanese unions look to the welfare of the company, the American unions look to their own welfare at the expense of the company.

Who was the union leader? I think it was Lewis [John L. Lewis, president of the UMW, 1920–60] who had this one-word philosophy of "More." The unions will continue to demand more, even if that means destroying the firm as they did at Eastern [Airlines]! The Japanese don't operate that way. We are going to have to learn to cooperate. And we are going to have to learn that very quickly before it is too late.

The manager of accessory marketing repeated the point about there being three levels of product quality—Japan made, American made, and Japanese transplant made—and also commented on the Japanese workers' focus on quality:

I think I have had five Japanese cars. I have seen production facilities all over Japan and the attitude of the production worker. I have seen supervisors every morning sit down with the workers and talk about product quality. It is not a "them-against-us" thing. It is this team of management *and* worker.

They are all absolutely dedicated to quality. We can't touch them on that basis. We will never develop that in this country.

A percentage of this firm's manufacturing is here in Oregon. The difference between Oregon and Japan is product quality. It is reasonably close, but Oregon makes more mistakes; just careless mistakes. It is not technology, it is not component quality, it is human mistakes. The Japanese have a dedication.

I don't know how the United States can ever compete with Japan. The educated people in this country understand that we must compete, that we must deliver a product that is at least as good as the Japanese product. But the vast majority of Americans don't know and don't care.

I think that competition is really good for the Americans. It is really great. I want to have a choice for the product that I buy. I would like the Americans to live under the threat of knowing that if they do not get their act together, then the consumer will go elsewhere.

I drive an American company car now; which is the only reason I drive it. It is a year old and an absolute piece of junk. I wrote to

General Motors and they don't care. So I think that we need the
Japanese; otherwise next year we will pay $50,000 for a Buick that
is going to be junk. [The Buick people must have been listening.
With a far greater attention to customer demands and product
quality, Buick is experiencing something of a renaissance after
several years of decline: it was the only G.M. division to increase
sales in early 1991 and was also ranked first in 1990–91 among the
U.S. brands by J. D. Powers & Associates in absence of problems.
Still, the foreign imports—Lexus, Mercedes-Benz, and Infiniti—
did better.]

You may have had work done in your home or office. Every
time I contract with someone, the work is not completed on time
and it is not quality. Then there is an argument about what price
should be paid. It is not that way in Japan. If you buy something
in Japan and there happens to be a problem, they will apologize
like hell and fix it.

I get really disgusted with this country. I consider myself an
American, but I am mad and disappointed.

I perceived three levels of quality, the low, the middle, and the
high. The low being the American product manufactured by
Americans, the mid being product designed in Japan and manufactured by Japanese and Americans together here, and the high of
course being the product designed and manufactured in Japan.

It is not the technology. It is the worker; he has a tremendous
influence on quality.

Such a large percentage of American workers are only interested
in what time of day it is. They have no pride in their workman-
ship. To see it in Japan for the first time, it is incredible; you just
can't believe it.

The auto company vice president is a Japanese-American man in his
sixties, who spoke of the differences in quality expectations between
Japanese and American consumers:

We believed that the product quality of our cars produced in this
country was of the highest order. But when we began to export to
Japan, it was found that we did not meet the expectations of the
Japanese customers.

All of the cars have had to be reworked and our assembly plant
in Ohio upgraded. What is considered good here is still not good
enough in Japan. [Since the interview the company has apparently
resolved many, if not all, of its problems. A new American-

designed station wagon from its U.S. operation is being exported to Japan. The vehicle seems to be selling pretty well and soon will be marketed in Europe, assuming the Europeans accept the Japanese transplant-produced cars as *American.*. The combined exports from the U.S. of Toyota, Honda, Nissan, Mazda, and Subaru was 50,000 units in 1991; the figure will double well before the end of the decade.]

Things Are Getting Better

Several of the Yankee Samurai acknowledged that American product quality trailed the Japanese but believed that, thanks to the Japanese competition, progress was being made, and that the United States was catching up.

The electronics firm's manager of procurement and materials held that view:

> Japanese product quality is far superior, but we are beginning to improve. We are capable of that, but whether management will create the environment and government will cooperate will be determining factors. As far as our skills and technology are con-cerned, we can do it. We certainly have the resources.
>
> The American worker is starting to really take exception to hav-ing it thrown in his face that he is not as good as the Japanese worker. I see a definite trend, even in the hard-core unions of steel and autos, where the workers are saying, "Bullshit! I am as good as any guy over there." We could be as good and in certain areas better.

The quality-control manager from one of the smaller Japanese auto-mobile firms also thought the Americans were starting to improve:

> Most people know that Japanese automobile quality is excellent. I certainly believe that to be true. I know it is true. What is not so well known is that Detroit is getting better. They are beginning to adapt various Japanese management style techniques. They are running scared, which is good. But Detroit, especially Ford, is better than most of the public knows. That is fine with us at [company name], the competition will make us stronger.

Healthy competition was also the essence of remarks made by the senior finance vice president for a moderate-sized electronics company:

> The other day several of us went out to lunch at the Velvet Turtle [popular, up-scale, and much frequented by business peo-ple].

When we sat down, I happened to be telling my friends about a recent trip to Kyushu and the restaurants there. The service was impeccable: glasses and silverware were spotless, wine was poured without *any* spilling, plates were delicately placed, not dropped, on the table, glasses were always filled, and the food itself on the plate was picture-perfect. I mean, you almost wanted to just look at it instead of eating it.

Well, right about this time our usual waitress, Denise, comes over, and because of the conversation we had just been having, all of us kind of watched her perform. She did spill the wine when she poured. Not a lot, in fact, only a few small drops that generally people would never notice. But *we* did notice. We also noticed small portions of Caesar salad falling out of the mixing bowl as she prepared it. Again, not a lot but some.

Now pretty much the whole meal went like this. By American standards—in fact, by my standards before I went to work for the Japanese—it was a fine meal served by a pleasant and competent young woman. But my standards now are higher. I am demanding more.

This is what the Japanese have done for us. As Americans we will have to get better, and the Japanese have shown us what better is. I think we might just rise to the challenge. I am seeing some signs of it.

The Impact of Japanese Investment in the United States

As we will see in chapter 4, Japanese direct investment in the United States is large and growing. For the Japanese it is a way to overcome trade barriers, take advantage of a strong Yen, better understand the U.S. marketplace, and earn higher returns than are available in Japan.

With that investment, however, has come a growing unease among Americans. The survey results indicated that the Yankee Samurai were about evenly divided over the issues of limiting Japanese investment and whether current investment has overcome trade frictions; there was general agreement that the potential for American backlash is great. The interview responses seemed somewhat more favorably disposed to the Japanese perspective, but there were concerns about the growing Japanese real estate purchases in the United States, which totaled $71 billion as of December 31, 1990. A significant amount of that money found its way to Hawaii and California, a fact that you will see the Yankee Samurai picked up on.

Representative of those believing Japanese investment has a *positive* impact on the United States was the middle-aged executive vice president of a major bank:

> I don't see any problem at all with Japanese investment in the United States, although we do have to be careful about enforcing laws here.
>
> Here at the bank we have had $150 million of cash investment from the parent. We have not sent a dime of dividends back. In addition, we employ 750 people and have $2.3 billion in loans outstanding. All of that adds to the strength of the American economy.
>
> The man on the street is not sophisticated enough to understand the positive impact of Japanese investment. There have been a couple of billion dollars of Japanese investment in real estate in Los Angeles alone. Well, we didn't export anything over there, but it has exactly the same impact as if we had.

At the other extreme was the soft-spoken Japanese-American general affairs associate with a large trading company. His concern about Japanese investment was linked to childhood memories of internment during World War II by his own U.S. government. He and his family had suffered then simply because they were of Japanese heritage:

> With all the Japanese investment in the United States, it kind of scares me because I am a citizen here. I wonder what is going to happen? Does this mean that in five or six years the Japanese are going to own the country?
>
> Several years ago Sanyo bought a company in Arkansas and has recently had to shut the firm down. The situation became ugly, with laid-off employees throwing rocks and shouting epithets. Things like that are happening and [*voice drops, very concerned*] that is very scary.

JAPANESE-AMERICANS: A BRIEF ASIDE

The anxiety of this Japanese-American man leads to an important brief aside regarding Japanese-Americans and the presence of Japanese investment in the United States. While no exact figures are available, there appear to be a disproportionately large number of Japanese-Americans working for the transplanted Japanese firms; there were about twenty among our interviewees.

They have been markedly successful in their companies, even though a surprisingly large number of the youngest among them speak little or no Japanese. The language spoken among the older Japanese-Americans traces back to the Meiji era of the late nineteenth and early twentieth centuries, and is subtly different from modern Japanese spoken by contemporary Japanese nationals. Still, there is perhaps an innate cultural comfort level that exists between the Japanese and the Japanese-Americans, and the latter are helpful in explaining American viewpoints. There is also tension; the sources are two-fold.

The first generation of Japanese immigrants (Issei) arrived in America beginning around the turn of the century. They and their children and their children's children (Nisei and Sansei) have done very well in the United States: they have one of the highest per capita incomes of any racial or ethnic group, near-crime-free communities, high educational achievement, and a superb record of bravery among the Japanese-American units, including the 442nd Regimental Combat Team that fought against the Germans in World War II. Less well known and documented was the critical role played by the several thousand Japanese-Americans in the Pacific campaign, where they served as prisoner interrogators, interpreters, and codebreakers. Most found themselves caught up in battle and many lost their lives.

But even with all of that success since coming to the United States, the Japanese-Americans chose after all to *leave* their homeland to seek a fortune elsewhere. It is perhaps human nature for those who stayed to feel a measure of pique, particularly when there is such a strong sense of national identity and pride as exists in Japan. Why would anyone want to leave paradise, the veritable Land of the Gods? This idea may lurk, at least subconsciously, in the minds of the Japanese nationals and be a source of tension.

A second issue deals with hierarchy. The Japanese have a passion for order, for everything and everyone properly in place and ranked. That is the rub. For the most part, the Japanese executives are among the elite of Japan. They tend to have been born into families of relatively higher income and have endured the boot-camp rigors of one of the world's most competitive educational systems. That contrasts with the rural-poor roots of many of the Japanese-American Issei. (Not all came from such backgrounds. Some emigrated to avoid the newly installed Meiji-era national conscription, and still others because they lacked opportunities, being a second, third, or fourth son in a land where all inheritance still passed to the first son.) Delicately subtle stresses evolve between the Japanese and the Japanese-Americans as a result.

Today's 847,000 Japanese-Americans have established a fine record of achievement and citizenship, yet there is a certain anxiety amongst some of them. That anxiety may grow as the Japanese presence in the United States increases and as Americans lash out at easily identifiable targets. In 1986, a Chinese man was beaten to death in a Detroit bar by several men who thought he was Japanese and therefore somehow to blame for that city's continuing economic woes. And even though the Congress has voted to compensate Japanese-Americans who were interned during the war, a *Newsweek* poll showed that a full 34 percent of Americans believed that the internment was justified.

There is enormous drama here. The Japanese-American story is a story within a story. If it is indeed true that our Yankee Samurai are at the cusp of history, then it is also true that the Japanese-Americans are at the cusp of the cusp.

JAPANESE INVESTMENT IN THE UNITED STATES—CONTINUED

Throughout the 1930s, Japan, seeking to expand its empire in the Pacific, was challenged by American, British, French, and Dutch interests that were already there. In July 1940, the United States attempted to checkmate Japan's advances with an embargo on aviation fuel, scrap iron, and steel that would ultimately cripple Japan's economy. Even with the realization that America was vastly its economic superior, Japan felt itself compelled to continue its chosen path. On December 7, 1941, the Japanese struck at America's island outpost at Pearl Harbor as well as other Allied targets in the Pacific. Four years of bloody conflict followed in which both sides fought with courage and gallantry. By war's end Japan was economically and militarily all but destroyed, while America had emerged as the mightiest nation in the world. Less than half a century later, the same Japan, now fully recovered and an economic Goliath, has returned to the same island-outpost of an economically weakened and politically divided America—and bought it. There is some hyperbole here but not much. History is rich in irony, but there are few stories to match this one.

Most of the Yankee Samurai who were troubled by Japanese investment focused upon real estate, especially Hawaiian real estate. A 1990 poll by the *Honolulu Star-Bulletin* showed that nearly half of Hawaii's residents thought their state was on the verge of becoming a Japanese colony. Over 90 percent of all foreign investment in the state is Japanese. Japanese interests now control some 80 percent of the most expensive Waikiki beachfront property on Oahu, as well as investments in homes, offices, restaurants, hotels, and tracts of raw rural land; all of this totaled $17 billion in 1991, which is 23 percent of all Japanese real estate investment in the United States. Hawaii has become one of the favorite locales for honeymooning Japanese couples, single Japanese women with some extra vacation money to spend, retired Japanese executives, and Japanese real estate counterparts to the wheeler-dealer Donald Trump.

Typical of the concern about Hawaii are the auto firm product information manager's comments:

> What people are complaining about out here in Los Angeles, San Francisco, and Hawaii is that the Japanese are coming in and buying up the downtowns. That is very visible and doesn't add anything to employment. There is some negative public reaction to that.

The issue of Hawaii was also raised by a Japanese-American woman who serves as the marketing manager of a major electronics firm:

> I am a fourth-generation Hawaiian. The feeling there among the local people is that the Japanese are taking over the islands. We also see that in California. [Japanese real estate investment in California and Hawaii combined is $40 billion, or 57 percent of the total U.S. portfolio.] Unless there is a great deal of assimilation by the Japanese and a respect for the American people, animosity will grow.

The corporate import distribution manager has been with his automobile firm for almost twenty years and has rotated through a number of important positions, which augers a fine future. His views are typical of most of the Yankee Samurai, who felt some ambivalence over the question of Japanese investment:

> Japanese investment in the United States is a good idea, but it is a very sensitive area. Conflict over the next several years between the United States and Japan will center about the issue.
>
> Foreign capital does bring jobs, money, and expertise. The United States is still the number-one foreign investor. It was okay when we were bottling Coca-Cola everywhere and making Singer sewing machines.
>
> International business investment is a good idea; you cannot hide from the world economy. To turn the clock back would be catastrophic.
>
> But it is a highly emotional issue. There are very serious problems in Hawaii. You have to feel for the poor guy in Honolulu who is trying to buy a house and sees Japanese investors buying up

individual residences right and left for purely speculative reasons. I can understand why the mayor of Honolulu, or the governor of Hawaii, might want to take some action to somehow protect the homeowner from speculative investment.

But that has to be differentiated from [his firm's] spending $1 billion for a production plant in Georgetown, Kentucky, that will employ 3,500 people.

The manufacturing planning manager also has mixed feelings about the Japanese presence:

Japanese investment in the United States is providing jobs. But I would hate to see it reach the point where the Japanese controlled any segment of our society.

My father fought in the war against Japan. He is concerned about our being manipulated by another society. Looking back at history, through either military or economic means, one country has taken over another.

I have family in Hawaii who are very much aware of the Japanese infiltration of business and real estate. There are more Japanese on the roads than Americans and conditions are very crowded.

In California it is still somewhat under the surface; it is going to be interesting.

A large number of those who held ambivalent feelings about Japanese investment in the United States did so because their paychecks came from Japanese-owned companies. A personnel manager said: "I feel some concern, as do many Americans, about the level of Japanese investment in the United States. At the same time, as an employee of a Japanese-managed company, I benefit from certain opportunities. I have mixed feelings."

The same feelings surfaced from an accounts receivables supervisor who has been with her electronics firm for six years: "Because I am working for a Japanese company, I think that Japanese investment in the United States is a good idea. If I wasn't, I am sure that I would have second thoughts. If I was working for an American firm, chances are that we would be taken over . . . there could be a backlash."

There is of course an entirely different perspective on Japanese investment that none of the Yankee Samurai noted. Almost every one of the fifty states in the United States has offices in Japan with responsibility to aggressively seek Japanese investment for their home constituency. And it is American sellers of real estate who are bombarding the

Japanese with investment opportunities. Tokyo newspapers daily carry full-page ads featuring American houses, office buildings, and shopping centers for sale. No American has had a samurai sword brandished overhead forcing him or her to sell. Even so, the Japanese government has begun to recognize the sensitivity of the issue and has admonished investors to eschew high-profile hotels, office buildings, and "trophy" properties like the Rockefeller Center and the Coral Gables Golf Course.

Indeed, with the current bust in Japan's real estate market, the Japanese have recently slowed their investments abroad and have even been doing a little selling. That has brought a whole new set of problems, with Americans concerned about falling property values. "My God," came the cry of the 1980s, "the Japanese are *buying* the United States!" "My God," comes the cry of the early 1990s, "the Japanese are *selling* the United States!"

U.S.-JAPANESE RELATIONS IN THE YEAR 2000

Finally, the Yankee Samurai were asked to foresee the economic and political relationship between the United States and Japan in the year 2000. Survey responses were about evenly split over the question as to which nation needed the other more. Eighty-five percent believed that the Japanese economy would be as strong or stronger than that of the United States by the turn of the century. That compares to a recent *Newsweek* poll indicating that 58 percent of Americans believe Japan *already* is stronger. About 75 percent of our Yankee Samurai thought that the Japanese should provide more for their own defense. These relative shifts in economic and military position must influence future U.S.-Japanese relations, yet there was no consensus among the Yankee Samurai as to the direction that influence would take.

Among those who believed that relations between the two countries would become more strained over time was the young engineering supervisor who spent some time in Japan before going to work for his company:

> I see relations between the two nations becoming progressively worse. Everything I hear coming out of Japan is Japanese nationalism. This generation [of Japanese] now believes it is the favored race in the world. That is going to intensify. If it does not lead to militarism, it certainly will lead to an increasing economic ferocity.

How Americans might respond to a more powerful Japan was discussed by the dealer/liaison manager for a major automobile firm:

Japan is already on the way to superpower status and will surpass the United States by the turn of the century. When the average American becomes aware of that, there is going to be a panic. Some articles have been written about that but the issue has not yet been brought home.

The general manager of one of Japan's smaller but growing automobile firms saw little in the future but conflict between the two countries:

The [Richard] Gephardts of this world forget that for every sin they can find on the Japanese side, the Japanese can find an equal number on our side. I just don't think we are going to work this thing out any time soon. We have a long, long row to hoe. There is going to be a whole lot of friction between the two countries in this decade.

The advertising coordinator from a major electronics company, a recent UCLA graduate, said:

Our advertising emphasizes how [company name] is playing such a large part in America by employing thousands of Americans and reinvesting profits into the economy.

We think that is an important message because there is a real negative feeling out there about foreign firms coming in and invading the American economy. There are still strong feelings about World War II and there are stereotyped prejudices about the Japanese and other foreigners.

I think that our advertising helps some, but still I believe that the years ahead will be strained.

There were a few, however, like the electronics company's accounting manager, who were quite optimistic:

Relations between the two countries should be as good, or better, by the turn of the century. Eventually the Japanese are going to have to open up their society.

I think the American economy will come back, although the Japanese will remain a very strong presence.

Most of the Yankee Samurai felt that the relationship would somehow symbiotically muddle through. The corporate marketing manager of Japan's largest auto firm held that conviction:

I see the relationship between the United States and Japan continuing along without either great warmth or hatred for several more years.

As Americanization [of the Japanese-owned firms in the U.S.] continues, the relationship will get stronger. The United States needs Japan; Japan is funding much of the U.S. debt. On the other hand, the Japanese need the U.S. market. The two countries should become stronger allies.

The deputy division manager, an alumnus of the American Graduate School of International Management at Thunderbird, had a somewhat similar view:

The United States and Japan have to work something out. If [relations between] these two countries fall apart, the whole world will have serious problems. The United States depends upon Japan, second-largest after Canada, for exports, as well as being a major source of important imported products.

I suspect that the United States will remain quite strong politically on the world scene in the year 2000, and economically probably will be stronger than today.

Gradually I think we will see a strengthening of the Japanese military. That raises both positive and negative concerns throughout the world.

Summary

Earlier in this chapter, we saw polls indicating the growing anti-Japanese sentiment held by the American public. That sentiment has been greatly influenced by various opinion leaders who have taken what is, or has been interpreted to be, a very hard line against Japan and Japanese practices. These anti-Japanese paladins are found in the media, Congress, academia, and corporate boardrooms.

Washington has found Japan to be a vulnerable target. House Majority Leader Richard Gephardt of Missouri has been outspoken in his claim of unfair Japanese trading practices—it was a major theme in his 1988 run for the presidency. Today, in early 1992, there are both Democrats and Republicans seeking their party's presidential nomination making veiled and not-so-veiled threats to Japan. Beyond that, Japan's trading and investment practices are a major issue in congressional campaigns across America this year. With about two thirds of the U.S. trade deficit with Japan comprised of automobiles and parts, almost the entire Michigan congressional delegation, led by Senator Riegle, is pushing draconian legislation that would all but eliminate imports.

Among businessmen, the corporate raider T. Boone Pickens has bitterly expressed his feelings about Japanese business practices. He was denied a seat on the board of directors of Koito, a Japanese auto parts manufacturer, even though he held a substantial financial interest. The Koito people raised concerns about Pickens's business ethics. They observed that his oil company, MESA Petroleum, was slipping into bankruptcy in the summer of 1983 when he discovered the leveraged buyout, junk bonds, green mail, and the whole armamentarium of the paper entrepreneur that led to his fortune. This is anathema to the Japanese.

Arguably Japan's most vocal business nemesis is Chrysler's Lee Iacocca. He has asserted that the Japanese transplants have an unfair advantage: "They start with a young work force, no health care, and no pensions, which saves them $600 a car. So should I go to Iowa to build a plant and screen workers to make sure they are young and they haven't been on drugs? Do that kind of screening in Detroit, and you won't have anybody working for you." Iacocca has been lobbying Washington to force production from Japanese auto plants in the United States to be counted as part of the "voluntary" export quotas that are already in place. Almost without exception, the Yankee Samurai working for Japanese auto firms bristle at the very mention of the name "Iacocca."

A rough survey of books written by American authors over the last several years dealing with Japan shows that the majority of them are critical—some of them extremely so. For example, James Fallows would like to see an across-the-board 25 percent decrease in Japanese imports; Karl van Wolferan denies the legitimacy of the entire Japanese social system; Pat Choate claims that secrecy, deceit, camouflage, and betrayal are an integral part of Japanese politics and business; and Chalmers Johnson has argued for a far more balanced field in international trade.

While each of these detractors may indeed raise at least some valid issues, our Yankee Samurai generally do not share their extreme views and are far more favorable to Japan and the Japanese presence in the United States than is the American public at large.

Recall the woman introduced at the onset of this chapter who asserted she was no Yankee Samurai? Perhaps not, but she was for my purposes here a stalking-horse. Her barely concealed anti-Japanese feelings, which came through both in that quote and in later private discussions, turned out to be something of an anomaly among the Yankee Samurai. The majority of them were far more balanced. In fact, many of them were extremely critical of labor, management, and government in their own country. Still, there were not many among them who have fully accepted and endorsed the positions of the Japanese government, people, and business interests. Their views tend to be somewhere in between, which is perhaps to be expected.

The Yankee Samurai are generally neither totally Yankee nor totally Samurai. They are a brand-new world phenomenon, a unique blend of Occident and Orient, still learning how to bridge two cultures. Their future role could be of great importance, both in terms of moderating relations between the two countries and in serving as the conduit through which Japanese business and societal culture passes into the United States.

Seldom in history has a body of people lived at a specific time of significant historical change and been clearly *aware* of such change. Even less seldom have there been people able actually to *influence* the direction of change. Our Yankee Samurai may turn out to be just such people. Japanese literature and philosophy is replete with the concept of *karma*, or fate and destiny. It may be the karma of these American men and women to nudge history into a direction it might not otherwise have gone.

The McCarthy hearings, the Berlin airlift, the Hungarian uprising, the Korean War, Khrushchev's U.N. table-pounding, the Cuban missile crisis, Vietnam, SALT I and II . . . these images of the Cold War era have dominated the attention of this generation of Americans and been indelibly stamped on their minds. But for the Americans just now coming to maturity, the hammer and sickle will become a distant memory, replaced by a blazing red shield on a field of pristine white. It is Japan that will become the focus of American attention in the ensuing decades.

With the collapse of the USSR, the international political–economic–military deck has been reshuffled. The "evil empire" that Ronald Reagan condemned is no more. Yet, no sooner had the last shovelfuls of dirt been tossed on the Communist coffin than new apocalyptic scenarios began to be spun, with Japan as the adversary:

(1) The linchpin of U.S.-Japan relations since the late 1940s has been America's fundamental geopolitical need for Japan as a Far Eastern bastion against communism.

(2) With that need now lessened or eliminated, there will come a reduced American tolerance for what is perceived as "unfair" Japanese trade practices.

(3) That in turn will be met by a growing Japanese impatience with

America's unwillingness to put its own house in order and its continuing scapegoating of Japan as the source of all the problems.

(4) Both Japan and the United States then begin to compete for markets as well as allies in the Far East.

(5) The United States, with its powerful Navy, then threatens to interdict Japanese oil shipments from the Gulf and raw material supplies from Australia, Indonesia, and Malaysia.

(6) Japan, with the third-largest military budget in the world, steps up spending to counter the American threat.

(7) The two nations then find themselves on a collision course that looks chillingly like the mid- to late 1930s. This is déjà vu, but with a whole new arsenal of weapons and infinitely more at stake.

Until very recently, no one had even begun to think in these incendiary terms. You can expect more of it. There is a fundamental historical sea-change at work. Japan has fully emerged as a great nation. The relations between the United States and Japan are beginning a brand-new chapter; the junior partner has grown to full adulthood. Most Americans are as yet oblivious to all of this. But the Yankee Samurai are one step ahead and could be instrumental in helping to assure that America and Japan remain close allies and friends, albeit, no doubt, aggressive economic competitors. Even the economic competition will likely be mitigated by growing joint research and business ventures, as well as the increasing success of American firms in Japan. There are many reasons to believe that by the turn of the century—cemented by close interdependent business, scientific, and personal contacts between the two peoples—the relationship will be even more positive than today. Each of us as Americans and Japanese will play a role in building those ties. The Yankee Samurai will have a special role: they bridge the two countries.

In the final chapter, "Lessons," some practical suggestions will be made as to just how the Yankee Samurai and their companies might go about positively and objectively voicing their views in the public arena, and thereby play a role in altering U.S.-Japan relations for the better.

You have now been introduced to the Yankee Samurai and have gained some understanding of their views on the global issue of U.S.-Japan relations. Yet, as these words are being read, it is unlikely that this larger issue is paramount in the minds of the Yankee Samurai themselves. Their thoughts no doubt remain fixed on the far more prosaic matter of daily working relationships with the Japanese.

3

American and Japanese Manager Relations

*Unity is always better than disunity, but
an enforced unity is a sham and
dangerous affair; full of explosive
possibilities. Unity must be of the mind
and heart, a sense of belonging together
and of facing together those who attack it.*

—NEHRU

INTRODUCTION

There are an estimated 40,000 Japanese expatriates in the United States and a corresponding 400,000 Yankee Samurai, roughly 300,000 of whom are blue-collar workers. The overall ratio of one Japanese for every ten Americans belies differences from firm to firm. Among the companies from which data were drawn for this book, the figure ranged from 3 percent Japanese expatriates for some of the electronics companies to 20 percent for several of the banking and trading firms.

Generally, the Americans were present in greater numbers if the operation was more market-oriented, or if there was a requirement for an American public interface—in, for example, legal, community, or government affairs. With the high cost of posting Japanese in the United States, low or semi-skilled administration work was also reserved largely for the American staff.

But whether the Japanese are present in large numbers or small, we ask what is the relationship between them and the Americans they work with. Is there a unity between them that is merely enforced by the circumstances, or is it indeed ideally, as Nehru would have said, "of the mind and heart"?

INDIVIDUALITY

Standing at the end of a Mitsubishi television assembly line in Irvine, California, one watches as the identical units complete their final test. Within hours, they will be shipped across the United States; a buyer in Salem, Oregon, will have a large-screen color TV set indistinguishable from that of another buyer in Tampa, Florida.

To many outsiders, Japanese managers, like the television sets, often appear to be identical clones coming off an assembly line somewhere in Tokyo. From a distance they all seem to look, talk, and behave the same. But the Yankee Samurai who have worked closely with the Japanese have learned otherwise. For these Americans, their working environment often greatly depends upon the individual Japanese managers with whom they interface. The personality and management style of individual Japanese is as important as Japanese management style per se; perhaps it is more important.

The twenty-year-veteran sales manager of one of Japan's leading airlines commented:

> The Japanese do have certain national characteristics just as do Germans, or French. But having said that, there are just as many individuals in Japan as in any other country. I have worked for some really excellent and outstanding men, and also [*pauses and shakes head*] a few real bastards.

The Japanese would probably smile a little between themselves listening to the words of a bank lending officer, a UCLA graduate who has been with her firm for less than a year and who seemed incredulous as she said, "I have seen a range of personalities among the Japanese; they are human just like we are!"

As assistant to the general manager of a large trading company, one world-traveled European-born woman has been able directly to observe Japanese-American manager relations:

> While there still are no Americans in top management, in general the relationship between the Americans and Japanese is im-

proving. There have been some rough times when some employees felt that it was "us against them."

Some of that comes down to simply differences in individual personalities. Sometimes there have been terrible clashes, and sometimes people get along wonderfully.

Each Japanese department manager has a somewhat different style, just as Americans do. Some departments relate to their people very differently than others. Some are very formal, with almost no interaction; for others there is much more camaraderie and sense of working together.

A senior bank credit officer also noted great differences between individual Japanese:

You relate to some people and some you do not. People are people. I find that personalities among the Japanese are wide and varied.

Even with the Japanese culture that enforces certain behavior, there is a bunch of loose cannons running around. Some of them are fine and others you cannot stand. One of the nice things is that you know they will be returning to Japan sooner or later. [Smiles] [The Japanese typically rotate managers every three to five years.]

A corporate employment manager for a major automobile company said:

You get the idea that the Japanese are these benevolent people and can't be harsh and demanding. That is not true. Don't let anyone tell you that they are all these benevolent smiling people. They are individuals just like we are.

Some can be harsher taskmasters than you could run into in a U.S. company. When they say, "Bow," they are accustomed to people doing that. When we get one like that here, we ostracize him. I have seen it happen.

You need not be a Freudian or Jungian acolyte to read into the last quote a measure of repressed (perhaps not so repressed) anger. Quite coincidentally I discovered that the man no longer works for the same company. He recently left for some vague reasons which seemed to come down to lack of a good fit. What personality characteristics give rise to a good fit? What mix of personal traits should an American have, or develop, to succeed and indeed flourish in a Japanese firm? We will talk about this in the final chapter entitled "Lessons." Between now and then, as this story unfolds you are likely to begin drawing some conclusions of your own.

Finally, let's listen to a thoughtful senior project engineer, reflecting upon the management of his electronics firm:

> The leadership style here is very much a function of who sits in that office [*points to president's office next to where the interview is being held*]. The last man was polite and gracious but also very quiet and did not communicate much. The new man has really changed the environment here. He has adopted a Western name, speaks English very well, and even played in a softball game we had a few weeks ago. He has set a very different tone and we [Americans] are responding much better.

COMMUNICATION

A recent *Fortune* survey reported that some 90 percent of large American company CEOs believed that the morale of their employees was quite high. Yet the majority of the employees themselves thought the reverse. Never in recent memory has it been lower. In the words of the warden in the film *Cool Hand Luke,* "What we have here is a failure to communicate." Whether it is because of differing perceptions, lack of trust and openness, failure to read nonverbal symbols, poor listening skills, technical jargon, diversity of the labor force, noise in the channels, or the sheer size of the larger companies, good communication in corporate America today is a greater challenge than ever before. It is all the more of a challenge in the Japanese transplant operations.

Only relatively few of the Yankee Samurai speak Japanese. That places the burden of communication largely upon the English-speaking ability of the Japanese. Even though Japanese junior and high school students pursue years of English, the instruction often emphasizes writing rather than speaking or conversation. The result is that while some Japanese are perfectly fluent, many are not, particularly in the banking and trading firms, where English-speaking skills do not seem as well developed as they are among expatriates in the electronics and auto companies.

The issue goes well beyond mere verbal communication. Japanese conversations tend to be punctuated by protracted silences during which body language and facial expressions serve to communicate. Americans tend to feel uncomfortable with this emptiness of sound and often rush in to fill the silences with conversation, whether relevant or not. There is a Japanese saying that translates roughly as "He who speaks first is a dumb ass." Well, Calvin Coolidge, Clint Eastwood, and the taciturn New Englanders don't fall into that category; most of the rest of us do.

Not only is interpreting silences a problem. The Japanese language is filled with subtlety and nuance; there are literally sixteen ways for the Japanese to say no. Frequently the Americans understand none of them. Some words or phrases are more properly used by women than men. Even a smile or the sucking in of breath has special meaning that is difficult for an American to comprehend. Americans and Japanese also have a different perspective on eye contact: appropriate for the former and often inappropriate for the latter.

Other factors add to the difficulties. Americans making a presentation have a hard time adjusting to Japanese coming and going during a meeting. They also do not quite know what to make of after-lunch or late afternoon meetings at which a Japanese is observed "listening with his eyes closed." (I remember the first time that happened to me about six years ago. I was making an after-lunch speech to a group of about a dozen Japanese. I had barely launched into the topic when one of them, the U.S. president of a large Japanese auto firm, began to "listen with his eyes closed." Somehow I maintained my composure and stumbled through the remarks.)

Something as simple as a joke can lead to problems. Americans invariably begin presentations with a humorous or light remark. That is often taken askance by a Japanese audience as not being serious. It is far better to start with an apology perhaps for being late, even though the speaker was on time, or the poor quality of the remarks to follow, even though they will be masterful. It doesn't matter. This is a nice touch, showing respect for the audience and the time its members are taking to listen to the speaker. The opening apology is nevertheless disconcerting for the American. And a speaker showing verbal virtuosity and a measure of dramatic flair also raises doubts in the minds of the Japanese. On the other hand, a speech that is simply read, no matter how drearily, shows that the speaker is "prepared."

In meetings between Americans and Japanese not well known to each other, Americans tend to direct their attention and conversation to the most English-literate among the Japanese. That could be a mistake. English "specialists" are often the least senior among a group of Japanese businessmen.

All of these things add a carnival-mirror distortion to the already static and noise-filled corporate world of the Japanese transplant. With only a few exceptions the Yankee Samurai voiced their concern about the problems of communication.

One of the few exceptions was the manager of public relations for a very successful automobile company: "The Japanese managers are about 3 percent of the people here. There is a great deal of communication and dialogue. The two groups commingle at lunch and you kind of forget that they are Japanese."

Far more typical was the response of an executive secretary:

> Communication between the American and Japanese managers is not that good, and is a big problem.
>
> It is hard for the Americans to know whether the Japanese are saying yes or no. The Japanese can be nodding their head yes, but meaning no.

Voicing his frustration, the bank assistant cashier said:

> I have the patience of a saint; I really do. But communication between the Americans and Japanese is difficult.
>
> It's surprising that the Japanese send people here whose English is not very good.

Many of the companies have introduced Japanese-language courses taught in house. Several dozen of the Americans either are, or have been, enrolled in such courses, but they tend to drop out after a short period.

The manager of materials and procurement, with more than a hint of American arrogance regarding his language, said:

> I started a program for my staff a few years ago to learn some words and phrases [of Japanese], but it was a total flop. The general attitude of the Americans is that if you are going to do business in the United States, English is the worldwide business language.
>
> Most of the Japanese assigned here have a better understanding of English than I will ever have of Japanese.

An Australian-born management technical adviser commented with a smile:

> One of the ideas that I have come up with is that no Japanese is spoken in my presence; I consider that an offense. When it happens, I launch into French. I once started a sales seminar in front of eight hundred people in French. I was trying to get the Japanese to understand how we feel. The point got across [laughs].

The manager of special projects for one of the world's largest electronics firms admitted: "I don't speak Japanese but do understand about 30 percent of what they say. They [Japanese] don't like that; it scares the hell out of them." The computer company's import administrator commented: "My supervisor is Japanese. I have always had a Japanese supervisor. Sometimes there are communication problems and it is hard to understand. You have to listen very carefully to what they are trying to say." The U.C. Berkeley MBA who was director of marketing in the mobile radio division of an electronics firm thought that "Communication skills [of the Japanese] range from excellent to poor."

One assistant to the president of a large auto firm is fluent in Japanese. He had some thoughts about Americans learning the language:

> I speak Japanese and am very comfortable with it. But people who come to me and say they would like to learn Japanese should have a very good reason. If the reason is that they want to better communicate with the Japanese, I would recommend that the time would be better spent studying about the Japanese culture and how the Japanese think and approach problems.
>
> Our corporate language here is English. Our Japan staff meets once a month and they speak in English. But you will hear the Japanese use their language amongst themselves. They try very hard not to do that in front of Americans. But after a full day of that they are pretty worn out. So when they go out in the evening and have a chance to be together, it is not a rebuff to the Americans but only a chance to unwind.

Finally, the executive vice president of a major bank commented:

> Today, the head of our national corporate division dealing with the American companies is a Japanese who can hardly speak English. A *Fortune* 1000 treasurer will not want to take the time to deal with him. That is terrible.
>
> I think that the more appropriate structure would be one where the best American man can be found and given a strong Japanese as his deputy.

Yukiyasu Togo: Door to Door in Canada — A Brief Aside

Most Americans having just read the last quote are probably mentally nodding their heads in agreement. How inefficient, how inappropriate, how stupid to send a man who speaks broken English to call upon busy senior American corporate treasurers! But you might think again after listening to a story told to me by Mr. Yukiyasu Togo, the articulate and charismatic president and CEO of the $16 billion Toyota Motor Sales U.S.A.

In an earlier assignment in the mid-seventies, Mr. Togo was appointed president of Toyota Canada, where the Toyota name was not well known. His task was to help change that. Yet his English-speaking skills were still somewhat rudimentary, and his personal knowledge of Canada and the Canadians was meager at best.

He perused all the available information: predecessor experiences, sales, competitors, and demographic data. He listened to co-worker and management theories and speculation about the best way to proceed. All of this he carefully studied and then set aside. He began to sell his cars . . . door to door. Well over 2,000 Canadians answered his polite knock and found a middle-aged Japanese man standing before them, smiling nervously. As he launched into his sales presentation, most of the Canadians were polite, some were rude, many were absolutely baffled, and a few—a very few—actually bought an automobile.

Mr. Togo ventured alone and unarmed into the Canadian world, forcing himself to sharpen his speaking skills and heighten his sensitivity to the needs of a people so different from his own. The few cars sold were of secondary importance. The knowledge learned of the Canadian people was invaluable. How did they think and feel, what were their hopes, ambitions, and fears, what pleased them, what angered them, who were these Canadians? No written report could tell him that. Mr. Togo sought to see, touch, and feel the market himself. His direct experience made the impalpable palpable. When he stepped down after seven years, sales had reached 6 percent of the market and a solid base had been formed upon which a still stronger Toyota presence in Canada was ultimately built.

Magnificent! This is the stuff of legend and myth upon which great companies and indeed great nations and empires are built. This is the kind of story that used to be told with great pride about Americans who, beginning with nothing but their own courage and vision, overcame mountainous obstacles and countless naysayers. Each of you has your own pantheon of business heroes who have done just that. It might include: Alexander Graham Bell, Andrew Carnegie, Thomas Watson, Henry Ford, Henry Luce, Ray Kroc, Pierre Du Pont, Thomas Edison, Bill Gates, H. Ross Perot, Steve Jobs, William Boeing, Walt Disney, John D. Rockefeller, and more; add Yukiyasu Togo to that list.

You might also now rethink the wisdom of the Japanese banking executive discussed earlier (p. 50) with his halting English calling upon American companies. Twenty years from now he might be the CEO of the world's largest bank and his early stumbling efforts in the United States told to younger executives as a kind of rite of passage, as an exemplar of grit, courage, and indomitable spirit.

The next time you hear an American querulously mumble about how unfair the Japanese are and how unbalanced the playing field is, you might ask why there are not more, or indeed any, American salespeople, let alone company presidents, in Japan going door to door selling their products and services. Why is there only a handful of Americans now enrolled in Japanese-language, or for that matter any foreign-language, classes at our universities? Why do Japanese businessmen operate in well over one hundred nations around the world and manage, however haltingly or proficiently, to speak the local language?

The Japanese Work Ethic—and Long Hours

Mr. Ishii stood under the pulsing shower in the bathroom of his hotel room. It was late on a warm July afternoon in 1990, and once again he was away from home in a foreign land. Over the last ten months as a manager in the machinery division of Mitsui & Company, he had traveled to Moscow eight times and had spent 150 days on a variety of overseas business trips. At home his weekends were fully occupied escorting foreign guests around Japan.

The peripatetic Mr. Ishii seemed always to be struggling with jet lag, found himself exercising less, smoking more, and entertaining business clients far into the night. He could not remember when he last took a vacation, and he missed his family. The exhaustion he felt was almost physically painful. Sleep, a long sleep, beckoned him. But the warm shower was refreshing and reminded him of hot baths he used to take as a child. As his mind turned to those pleasant days, driving out thoughts of a contract he was trying to close with the intractable Russian apparatchiks, a sudden dizziness came over him. He reached for support, but his hand would not obey him; it would not move. The vision in his right eye blurred and then blackened as though a shade had been drawn over it by some unseen force. He tried to call for help but could utter no sound. Moments later he lost consciousness and crumpled to the floor; the shower water, like the rest of the universe, continued to pulse.

Mr. Ishii was dead of a stroke at the age of forty-seven. No one will ever know what flashed across his mind during those last moments:

terror, relief, family, childhood, the Russian contract? Or perhaps his last thoughts were of his warrior heritage and the Code of Bushido: "The Samurai thinks not of victory or defeat but merely fights insanely to the death." Mr. Ishii died for Mitsui just as his distant ancestors died for their *Daimyo*, or provincial lord. But unlike those ancestors, Mr. Ishii was not destined to go quietly to his grave.

Two weeks after his death, the bereaved widow broke all precedent and took an action whose repercussions are still being felt in Japan; she did the unthinkable and applied for workmen's compensation, claiming her husband had "died from an accumulation of fatigue caused by murderous overseas trips." Newspapers quickly picked up the story and the bureaucrats at the Ministry of Labor found themselves inundated by insistent calls from hundreds of generally self-effacing widows whose corporate husbands had died of heart attacks or strokes; they were inquiring whether they too might qualify for government benefits. Shock waves reverberated throughout the world of the Japanese salarymen, who typically put in minimum eleven-hour days and work weekends as well. A new word entered the Japanese lexicon: *karoshi*—"death from fatigue."

Studies of international work ethics indicate that few people, with the possible exception of the Koreans, work more hours than the Japanese. The Japanese factory worker puts in the equivalent of *six weeks a year* more on the job than his American counterpart. Overall, the Japanese average some 15 percent more hours than Americans (Koreans average 25 percent more). A typical Japanese salaryman leaves home at 5:00 or 6:00 A.M. and does not return until ten or eleven in the evening. Saturday is often a workday. It is not unusual for a Japanese manager to see his children actually awake only on Sundays.

Unlike most Americans, the Japanese are reluctant to take earned vacation. Part of the reason is the group orientation culture of the Japanese workplace. It is difficult to leave for a carefree holiday knowing that your colleagues will have to labor harder to take up the slack. If you are a salaryman, your wife does not make things easier for you, either. Listen to the typical story of Mr. Takashi.

Mr. Takashi had not taken a full week's vacation in the sixteen years he had been with his shipping company. One Friday afternoon, Mr. Fukui, his superior, concerned about Mr. Takashi's health, strongly encouraged him to take the next Monday and Tuesday off. Very reluctantly he agreed.

The following Tuesday afternoon Mr. Fukui needed to check some information with Mr. Takashi and called his home. His wife answered and was puzzled by the phone call. As far as she knew, her husband had awakened early Monday and Tuesday and gone to work as usual. When Mr. Fukui mentioned this to Mr. Takashi upon his return Wednesday morning, the guilt-stricken man admitted what he had done. Being too ashamed to tell his wife of the time off because she would think him lazy and irresponsible, he spent his two-day "vacation" miserably walking the streets of Tokyo. This is very difficult, almost impossible, for most Americans to understand.

The Japanese bring their work ethic with them to the United States. A cultural collision with the Americans often results.

Many of the Yankee Samurai made mention of the strong Japanese work ethic and very long hours. Surprisingly, only a few had great respect for it; many, perhaps feeling a little contrite, resented it.

One man, however, who did hold the Japanese work ethic in high regard was an automobile firm's manager of distribution, who said:

> The Japanese work very long hours. You almost cannot work long enough to be the last one out of the building. I have left here at ten or eleven o'clock at night and still seen Japanese on the job. It's not terribly uncommon for them to stay here all night if there is an important project to work on.
>
> It all goes back to the idea that they just cannot fail. It is a mission that just has to be done, and they have to give it their best. I certainly admire that; it is a marvelous trait.

But typical of the somewhat defensive and resentful Yankee Samurai was the auto firm's corporate marketing manager, who said:

> I get here at six in the morning, but I don't stay late. Most of the Japanese stay until eight or nine at night. Many of the American managers stay with them.
>
> I made up my mind to be with my kids and leave about five. [Voice hardens] I can walk out with my head high after having put in an eleven-hour day.

The director of human resources for a large and successful consumer electronics firm had similar problems with work hours:

> The Japanese think nothing of working fifty or sixty hours a week. That creates a certain subtle pressure for the American manager to put in extra time and have the same level of dedication and commitment. That is perceived as a question mark along the American managers.

One thing I would like to change is the Japanese understanding of the American culture. Americans believe that the most effective way to do a job is to get it done in the least amount of time, not the most.

The Japanese seem to respect the amount of time that you put in and equate that with commitment, capability, and performance. The Americans look at it inversely. The most capable managers are those that can get a job done in the *least* amount of time. That is an issue that needs further discussion and possibly some change.

The bank vice president also questioned just why it seemed to take the Japanese so long to finish their work: "The Japanese are very detailed and methodical. They stay very late to complete reports. But even though Americans do not stay that late, I feel that we can do the same kind of report in half or three quarters the time."

The young trading coordinator—one of two graduates of the respected School of International Management at Thunderbird in the survey—indicated his view of late working hours.

My boss has been in America for two years and has never yet had a meal with his family. Even on the weekends he finds some business-related thing that he goes and does.

I told him right off the bat, "Don't ever plan for me to do anything on a Sunday; that is just out of the question."

I will work on a Saturday if it is something of an urgent nature.

I don't have any problem with overtime, unless it is just staying around because you don't want to go home. I won't play that game and have told them so. I am my own self.

This thing about how late people work being a measure of how good the worker is makes no sense. I think everyone should leave by five-thirty. The poor secretarial staff sometimes stays here all night long working on things that could wait.

It is bad for morale when at five o'clock all of the Americans stand up and leave while the Japanese, and Japanese-Americans, stay. It creates hard feelings both ways. The Japanese think the Americans are lazy and the Americans think the Japanese are making them look bad.

We have said earlier that culture is a theme that weaves itself throughout this book; here we are looking directly at a clash of cultures. Americans and Japanese start from a different cultural base.

Confucian ethics pervade contemporary Japanese society as they have for some 1,300 years. Fundamental to those ethics is an individual's demonstration of loyalty to that society. Loyalty is demonstrated by self-sacrifice. In the case of a Japanese salaryman, the society to which he belongs is his firm. He shows his loyalty to that firm by sacrificing his personal life. This is a virtue . . . in Japanese eyes!

Listen to a manager of research who commented, "I have seen the Japanese boast among themselves about who has put in the most hours and not been home the longest. It is a macho kind of thing." Couple that sense of loyalty with a culturally determined, Buddhist-based work ethic that goes well beyond just putting in long hours to include attention to detail (Japanese garbage truck drivers can be seen early every morning polishing their vehicles), a belief that no task is ever completed and that there is always room for improvement (*kaizen*), a philosophy that spiritual and social life is to be found within the workplace, and a national sense of fear and vulnerability, and you begin to understand a little better the Japanese work ethic.

Yet the Americans must ultimately be influenced by the Japanese example and begin to ask themselves, "Is it really Miller time?" and should we "Thank God it's Friday"? And the Japanese watching the Americans enjoy a more rounded life may begin to question their own culture. The battle between two cultures is being played out within Japanese-owned operations in the United States. There is push and pull, tug and shove, frustration, anger, and occasionally enlightenment. Out of this witches' brew will come something that no one can yet foresee.

THE COORDINATORS

The Japanese transplants have not yet determined the organization structures that can most effectively bring together Americans and Japanese. The structures differ from firm to firm. Some literally have parallel operations: one American and one Japanese. One auto firm has a Japanese counterpart for every American of rank. Others mix the Japanese throughout the organization in key positions. Still others have variations on this.

In nearly every organization structure, however, the Japanese do have the dual responsibility for day-to-day operations as well as reporting back to Japan. One of the reasons the Japanese put in such late hours until nine or ten at night is to communicate with Japan, where early morning business is just getting under way.

While the Japanese generally form a small percentage of the subsidiary's work force, they tend to hold all, or most, of the senior positions. Those Americans who do hold high management rank frequently find themselves bound Siamese twinlike with Japanese "coordinators," sometimes referred to less euphemistically as "shadows" or "spies." The Yankee Samurai are typically more than a little uncomfortable with this.

A major automobile firm's sales vice president described his coordinator:

> There is a Japanese coordinator who I work with. He does not report to me, and I do not report to him. His office is next door and we talk all the time. His primary responsibility is to serve as a bridge between this operation and Japan. He has a rather awesome task.

The corporate marketing manager from the same firm, who had an office right down the hall, commented:

> I would say that the relations between the Americans and Japanese managers can be best characterized as cautious.
>
> Americans have a confusion, or concern, about what their Japanese counterpart is supposed to do, and what his responsibilities are. Many Americans are not clear about just what their coordinator's real mission is supposed to be.
>
> My coordinator is probably the most Americanized in the company. That is fortunate because marketing has a lot of showmanship about it that is not easy for a foreigner to understand.

The director of corporate auditing for a major automobile firm observed:

> The upper-level Japanese include the president and the vice presidents of finance, planning, and operations. They are generally here three to five years.
>
> Below them there is a level known either as deputy vice president or assistant to a vice president. The more senior Japanese get the deputy title.
>
> These men report to an American vice president and are the communicators with Japan as well as the coordinators with the Americans. Sometimes we affectionately call them the "factory spies." They stay here until late at night and call Japan to convey information back and forth.
>
> Some of those people are very political and know where their

roots are. They will do everything possible to make it convenient for themselves when they return to Japan; they respond to the wishes of their Japanese supervisor. But other people have been good at finding the middle ground and working with both the American and Japanese side. In the long run I think those people will go further.

The "Lessons" chapter will explore some useful suggestions for organization structures that make effective use of both the American and Japanese skill-set. It will also have some thoughts about policy relating to the rotating of Japanese.

Rotating Japanese

You are an American businessman or woman who has been painstakingly nurturing the "Fujisori" account for well over a year and are just on the verge of closing your first sale with the firm. Mr. Iinuma, your primary contact, has received all of your price, quantity, and delivery schedule information. Beyond that, a good personal relationship has developed between the two of you. Several evenings have been spent together at local restaurants where you smilingly gagged down sushi. You even made your company's box at Dodger Stadium available to Mr. Iinuma and his family. You personally like the man.

You call his office to arrange for what you expect to be the culminating meeting. "*Konnichi wa* (Good afternoon . . .)," you say to the secretary who answers the phone. "May I please speak to Mr. Iinuma?"

"Oh, I am so sorry," (favorite and in many ways so civilized Japanese phrase, which nevertheless seems to annoy some Americans), she replies in that gracious and polite voice so typical of Japanese secretaries. "Mr. Iinuma has been reassigned to Japan and has been replaced by Mr. Hamada. Perhaps you would like to speak to him?"

Welcome to the world of Japanese companies and their penchant for job rotation. Like Sisyphus ever destined to push a giant boulder to the top of a mountain, only to have it roll back down just before the summit, you must begin anew with Mr. Hamada.

As difficult as it is for those trying to do business with a Japanese firm or government agency because of the way the personnel rotate so frequently, it is often more difficult for Americans working in Japanese firms. Expatriate rotations generally occur every three to five years, but shorter stays of six months to a year are also common. Many of the

Yankee Samurai noted this and were concerned that the relatively short stay kept the Japanese and Americans from ever really understanding one another.

The thoughts of a young Wharton MBA (the only Wharton graduate in the survey—in general the Japanese have not yet begun to recruit aggressively from the top American universities), who is manager of strategic planning at a very large electronics firm, were most incisive:

> I understand the reasons for the Japanese rotating their people. It ultimately greatly improves the decision process because people have an opportunity to look at problems from many different vantage points. It also avoids the not-invented-here syndrome. No doubt it is also more self-fulfilling for the Japanese to expand their experiences. In fact, I really wish American employees here had the same opportunity [*slowly shakes head*].
>
> But there is a significant downside to the Japanese rotation for us [the Americans]. The Japanese typically are rotated every three to five years. That is hardly time for the Americans and Japanese to adjust to one another. When progress finally seems to be made, a new man comes in. We lose continuity.
>
> There is another problem. The Japanese know they are here only for a short time and that their future career depends so much on their relations with the home office. They tend, either consciously or subconsciously, to make decisions that may or may not be in the best interests of our operation [here in America]. For example, they might accept a boatload full of obsolete product knowing that it cannot easily be sold but that it will help a friend back in Tokyo.
>
> For our long-term success here, I would really like to see some of the key Japanese people stay for longer periods rather than simply having their tickets punched. Some of them, however, are afraid to stay too long. They may be looked at with a measure of suspicion for having become too Americanized if they are here for extended periods.
>
> There is also a personal issue if they have children. Education here is terrible and the youngsters are simply unprepared when they return to Japan. Many of them [the Japanese] leave their older children at home in Japan so they don't fall behind. I don't think I could do that.
>
> I guess I really don't have any answers. But it will all somehow work out. I sense that the Japanese are dedicated to making this

operation a success. They, or hopefully we, will continue to improve.

A Chinese-American young woman, a trading analyst for a major trading company, commented bluntly:

> What you have here is a group of Japanese managers that stay for five years and leave. All the seminars that are put on trying to explain the American psyche really go in one ear and out the other. The Japanese come directly from Japan, stay a couple of years, and then leave. It is difficult to believe that an Americanization process is really going to happen.

The product information manager working for a leading automobile firm observed that:

> For many of the Japanese, the American assignment is like a flicker of brightness while they are here. They have power and income. They have large homes in Palos Verdes [high-income Southern California residential area overlooking the ocean].
>
> Their wives can become like American women. Some of the women do not want to go back to Japan.
>
> So, when they are over here, it may be one of the happiest times of their lives. When they go back, they might find their return not well received.

From the viewpoint of the chief financial officer at a large bank, the problem is severe:

> The Japanese rotate every three to five years. Of the thirty-five Japanese officers [here] there are about twenty who interface with Japan. If they left tomorrow, we would not miss a beat. But the others are in key functional areas.
>
> The problem is that their eye is across the pond; that is where their careers lie, and they don't want to get in trouble here. Credit is a risk-taking business and you cannot have someone who is afraid to take a risk. They are too damn afraid to make a mistake. That hurts the bank.
>
> They cannot be totally objective because of their culture and tradition as well as their recognition that their career resides in Japan and not here. They cannot properly address risk-oriented matters under those circumstances.
>
> Then there is also the problem of losing all the experience and knowledge when they return to Japan.

By way of preview to chapter 8, where rotation of the Yankee Samurai will be discussed in more detail . . . there isn't much of it. It is the Japanese expatriates for the most part who are doing the rotating.

OVERALL RELATIONS

With only a few very angry exceptions, the viewpoint among the Yankee Samurai was that overall relations with the Japanese were cordial, respectful, and friendly, but with little or no true socialization. The bank's assistant cashier quoted earlier felt that:

> The Americans and Japanese do not interact that much at work. It hardly exists at all. We never even go to lunch together.
>
> But we have been invited to the homes of the Japanese for an evening. When I got married, I invited the Japanese; that broke a lot of ice. The president of the bank came; that was amazing [*shakes his head*]. I never would have expected it. There were two tables of Japanese there right in the middle of my Mexican family.
>
> In general, the Japanese are very cordial and very nice. But we really do not work together.

The executive vice president and CFO of still another bank commented:

> The Americans realize that we do not have the same position that the Japanese have. In Japan, the bank is one of the most premier in the country. They interview about 1,500 of the top college graduates and only hire 150 of them. That creates a certain elitism.
>
> There is still, and always will be, a certain degree of mistrust. That attitude is understood by all the Americans. Even though we work very closely with them, indeed become friends, there is still a difference.
>
> There is most definitely a feeling on the part of the Japanese officers that they can do a better job than the Americans.

The manager of special projects with one of Japan's largest electronics firms noted:

> There are very few Japanese in the company. But those that are here hold all of the top slots or sit next to senior Americans.
>
> We could use a lot of help with the relationship between the American and Japanese managers. They send managers here without teaching them anything about how Americans think.

> There is a short honeymoon period during which the Japanese
> will let the Americans manage while they sit back and learn; but
> when they feel confident, they take over.

For the bank's head auditor, there had been a time, when his bank
first opened, that relations between the Americans and Japanese were
very close:

> With earlier Japanese managers there were a lot of times when
> we went out after work and had a drink with them and commin-
> gled with them. We discussed various policy matters after hours.
> But with the current managers, they stick with themselves. We
> deal with them only at work. They are very friendly and answer
> your questions, but there is not so much social relations.
> I really miss the way it used to be.

The electronic firm's manager of procurement and materials had this
to say:

> In general the relations between the Americans and Japanese
> managers here are excellent. There is a great deal of mutual re-
> spect between the two groups. Although I still sense that the Jap-
> anese view themselves to be a cut above the Americans. You can
> detect that, but it is very low-keyed; it is not flaunted and thrown
> in our faces.

In another electronics firm, the Americans felt more shut out and the
Japanese were thought to be more distant. Here is the director of materials control for that firm:

> The American managers have to choose their words carefully
> and be patient with communication. The Japanese managers tend
> to be very focused on the goal and seldom take the initiative to
> include Americans in decision making or sit down and explain the
> overall situation. So, neither side seems willing to take the time to
> communicate.
> The Japanese have all the top management jobs, so they are
> responsible for the key promotions.
> We sometimes scratch our heads at some of the Japanese ideas
> or policies, but that is what we have to operate under.
> Men or women, it doesn't matter. There is the tribal issue. You
> are never, ever, ever, going to be a member of the tribe. If they cut
> off your legs at the knees, reattach your feet, and change your eyes,
> you still ain't going to be a Japanese. In Japan it is the same way.

You can look at the Koreans and Chinese and half-breeds, they are treated very poorly because they are not of the tribe. It is inbred and cannot be changed in this or the next generation.

I would like to see the operation management of my firm be completely American and the advisers from Tokyo take a lower role. I see that coming about, but it is being fought tooth and nail.

The Iranian-born young woman who has traveled widely brings a somewhat broader perspective to working for a Japanese firm. She is a customer sales assistant for a rather tradition-bound trading company:

The kinds of problems that you see here are not unusual. American firms would have problems working in Japan, and an Italian company would have difficulties in Libya. It doesn't matter, when there are cultural differences there are managerial problems. It is universal.

The Japanese are not really flexible. But they realize they must learn to be because they are in a country where the culture is so different. I hope that they try hard to achieve that or there will remain great conflict between the Japanese system and the American employees. I don't know where it will lead.

The Japanese will be more successful if they try for more flexibility, especially when it comes to women and human relations in general. I hope they take into account what really works here.

Both the Americans and Japanese are trying to get along with one another and accepting the other's principles.

Having been born in Iran, I have a greater understanding of the Japanese than most Americans. My country has almost the same perception of mutual respect among people as exists in Japan. With Americans, there is a big difference. The Americans have a very different view of respect [for one another] and are very open in their relations.

Perhaps the assistant to the vice president of a highly successful electronics firm summed it up best when he said:

We are finding that there is very little interface between American and Japanese managers beyond what is required, very little at all.

We are looking for ways to get the Japanese more involved so that they will understand what, and why, we do things. At the same time, we are sending more people to Japan to try and understand why they make the decisions they do. Hopefully then we can either accept the decision without fighting it, or find ways to help them understand our position.

Overall the relationship is a love-hate, or required, relationship.

CONCLUSION

What is the working relationship between the Americans and Japanese inside U.S. subsidiaries of Japanese firms? From the perspective of the Yankee Samurai, the relationship between the two often depends to a great extent upon personality traits and management styles of the individual Japanese. Communication, both verbal and nonverbal, is a problem. The long working hours of the Japanese are a point of friction, making the Americans feel either grudgingly obligated to go along or guilty if they do not. Many believe the long work hours are a waste of time. Japanese "coordinators" play a critical but somewhat shadowy role that tends to make the Yankee Samurai uncomfortable. The three- to five-year rotation policy between Japan and the United States among Japanese managers creates discontinuity in their relations with Americans. Overall, the association can be described as cordial, respectful, and friendly, but not approaching anything that might be called true camaraderie or a "unity . . . of the mind and heart." There has been only marginal melding of the Japanese and Yankee Samurai.

In light of the relatively short time that most of the Japanese firms have been operating in the United States, you would probably evaluate the American-Japanese working relationship as not bad at all; indeed, pretty good. Even so, in almost every firm one senses a strong desire to make things better. Everyone is still learning.

4

The Foreshadows

The present state of things is a
consequence of the past.
—SAMUEL JOHNSON

INTRODUCTION

It can be argued that everything and everyone we see about us has a certain continuity with, and is a consequence of, the past. "Every great drama," said Emerson, "has its foreshadow." Few things in our real world have simply "appeared" before our eyes like a shooting star on a clear winter night.

So, too, with the some 400,000 Yankee Samurai who are now in our midst. Over the last half century, an extraordinary series of events as well as powerful international economic and political forces have fallen into place like a giant picture puzzle from which has stepped the Yankee Samurai. To fully understand the Yankee Samurai—their position in the companies for which they work and their still larger role in U.S.-Japan relations—and to speculate upon what the future might hold for them, requires some knowledge of that past.

For a good starting point, let's fast-rewind to September 2, 1945,

aboard the U.S.S. *Missouri* anchored in Tokyo Bay. Allied and Japanese
representatives had just finished signing the document ending World
War II as General Douglas MacArthur stepped forward and declared,
"Let us pray that peace now be restored to the world and that God will
preserve it always. These proceedings are now closed." With superb timing, just a few moments later over a thousand carrier planes and B-29s
roared across the dark sky, flaunting U.S. airpower and corresponding
Japanese impotence. The proceedings were indeed closed. The guns of
World War II were silenced and the killing had ended.

Japan, at that moment, was powerless, crippled, and a pariah among
nations. Every major city was virtually razed, with factories and housing
all but destroyed. Tokyo itself, victim of dozens of American incendiary-
bomb raids, was little more than a massive slum, with cobbled-together
pieces of metal, wood, stone, and cardboard serving as rude hovels.
Hiroshima and Nagasaki were moonscapes where 170,000 people had
been radiated and incinerated by a technology never before or since
unleashed upon another nation. Japan was occupied for the first time in
history by a foreign power, and confronted with a freezing winter and
starvation. Japan was decimated, as few losers of a major war have ever
been, while the United States stood alone as the world's leading economic and military power.

Yet within one generation, the "Rising Sun" rose again. It rose from
the rubble, the horror, and despair to achieve the economic miracle that
is Japan 1992: higher per capita GNP than the United States (Japan's
total GNP is projected to pass that of the U.S. by the turn of the century,
even with half the population), world's leading creditor nation, second-
largest exporting nation, world dominance in automobiles, consumer
electronics, semiconductors, industrial equipment, and dozens of other
industries, home to eight of the world's ten largest banks, rapid ascen-
dancy to dominance or at least equality in nearly all high-tech fields, a
land value for the greater Tokyo area alone equal to that of all the
United States, and the world's most generous foreign aid donor.

In fact, the unprecedented recovery from so near death to the glory
that is Japan today was no "miracle" at all; it was the result of several
very real world factors.

The Culture

Arguably the most important factor in Japan's rebirth has been the
Japanese people themselves. Only two weeks before the events of the
U.S.S. *Missouri*, on August 15, 1945, the 70 million people of Japan

heard a radio broadcast that changed their lives irrevocably. The voice they listened to had never before been publicly heard in the land. In fact, it had been considered lèse majesté for the common people even to look at the man who now spoke. Through the background crackle of static came the "Voice of the Crane," the emperor Hirohito:

> Let the entire nation continue as one family from generation to generation, ever firm in its faith of the imperishableness of its divine land. Unite your total strength to the construction of the future. Cultivate the ways of rectitude; foster nobility of spirit; and work with resolution so that ye may enhance the innate glory of the Imperial State and keep pace with the progress of the world. . . .
>
> The hardships and sufferings to which we will be subjected will be great. But it is the dictate of time and fate that we have resolved to endure the unendurable and suffer the unsufferable.

Centuries from now, historians will take special note of the twentieth century postwar generation of Japanese men and women who listened carefully to that speech and then, samurailike, did as they were told: endured "the unendurable" and suffered "the unsufferable." Their legacy is the economic behemoth which is modern-day Japan. The key to their unprecedented accomplishment is captured in some of the emperor's words and their underlying meanings: sense of family, nationalism, mission, rectitude, future orientation, work ethic, and stoic dedication. These are the very essence of Japan's culture. Two thousand and more years of that culture flowed through the veins of the men, women, and children of Japan on that August day nearly half a century ago. In retrospect, they were in fact invincible; culture is destiny.

But Japan's recovery and rise to prominence was aided by a number of other factors, some planned and some merely fortuitous.

THE OCCUPATION

The MacArthur-led occupation of Japan was both progressive and benign. American shipments of clothing, food, and drugs helped to allay some of the most immediate basic problems. War-crime trials were limited to just a few of the more notorious Japanese leaders, including War Minister Hideki Tojo; Iwane Matsui, the commander charged with responsibility for the 1937 "Rape of Nanking"; and former Prime Minister Koki Hirota. No reparation payments were ever made.

The Supreme Command of Allied Powers (SCAP), which pretty much came down to General MacArthur along with his small staff, ordered the breakup of the *zaibatsu* (which within only a few years reformed as the modern-day *keiretsu*—more on these industrial giants later in this chapter), launched a land redistribution program, and helped draft a constitution calling for universal suffrage, anti-trust enforcement, collective labor bargaining, freedom of speech, and the controversial Article IX that would "forever" limit the use of military force to a defensive posture.*

If the emperor ever had political power (a much-debated question), after the war he was officially deprived of it and transformed by a SCAP pen stroke into a purely symbolic figurehead for the country. The judicial system was made more independent and a newly formed Supreme Court was established. The Japanese Diet, or Parliament, with its two houses, was given absolute power, with the prime minister, who appoints the cabinet ministers, elected by the lower house. The Liberal Democratic Party has dominated politics since the mid-1950s with relatively weak challenges from the Social Democratic and Communist parties. This overall political system, fully endorsed by SCAP, has yielded one of the world's most stable postwar governments and a cooperative partner with Japan's business interests.

America's banking and industrial experts—including Edward Deming, the quality-control guru mentioned earlier—were sent to Japan to share their expertise. Seventy-eight percent of all foreign investment in prewar Japan came from the United States. Dozens of American companies that had done business in Japan before the war returned.

Disregarding Lincoln's admonition of "malice toward none and charity to all" following America's Civil War, northern carpetbaggers, like swarms of locusts, crossed the Mason-Dixon line and imposed their will, at the point of a gun barrel, on the crippled South. Their objective was to strip what remained of the Confederacy of its wealth, pride, its very culture. Even now, after a century and more has passed, the bitter dregs linger still in the hearts and souls of some southerners.

There were no carpetbaggers in SCAP. It was SCAP's intent to make Japan a viable, democratically governed, and economically stable state; a kind of Little America on the other side of the Pacific. When the

---

* Irony of ironies: in direct contradiction to that same Article IX, the American government put great pressure on the Japanese to send troops to aid the allies during the 1991 Gulf crisis; 78% of Japan's population agreed with its government's refusal to do so.

military occupation ended in 1952, Japan was well on its way to achieving that—and more.

Korean Conflict

"We stopped too God damned soon and have given those sons of bitches half of Europe. Let me have a few divisions and in ten days I'll have us at war with those Mongoloid Bolshevik bastards and kick their ass all the way back to Russia where they belong." As the war with the Nazis wound down in Europe in 1945, it was evident to General George Patton that Stalin posed just as serious a threat to world peace as Hitler had. He was right, but the American higher command, including Dwight Eisenhower, who had his eye on the presidency, would not listen. Patton was censured for his outspokenness; he died only a few months later. Shortly thereafter, the Iron Curtain descended on Eastern Europe; the Cold War had begun. The Japanese, seeing what was coming, were euphoric.

Because the United States needed an anti-Communist bastion in the Far East, the outbreak of the Korean conflict in 1950 served to reinforce close ties between the United States and Japan. Japan's leftist-oriented labor unions were smashed with the tacit approval of the MacArthur occupation forces, and the U.S. military provided a defensive umbrella over the Japanese islands and sealane approaches.

Of even more value to the Japanese, the war also created a de facto "Marshall Plan" for their economy, as American war-related orders poured into fledgling factories for a variety of light manufacturing products, as jobs relating to servicing American military bases became available, and as American servicemen stationed in the country spent freely while on leave.

Even today, there are twelve Americans bases in Japan that continue to modestly stimulate the economy, although the Japanese are now assuming about one third of the costs. Far more important, the American military presence has provided a security shield for Japan, allowing the Japanese to focus upon economic development without overextending themselves militarily.

Japan has not needed too much encouragement from America to be wary of Russia. Even before the 1905 Russo-Japanese War, in which the Japanese brilliantly defeated a Russian armada in the Tsushima Straits, there was antipathy between the two countries. That was exacerbated by

the Bolsheviks' rise to power in 1917. Japan's leaders were deeply apprehensive of the Communist threat only a few hundred miles northwest
across the Sea of Japan. Relations became even further strained in the
closing days, almost hours, of World War II when the USSR declared war
on an all-but-decimated Japan and grabbed the northernmost Kurile Islands. In mid-1991, Mikhail Gorbachev began tentative negotiations
with Tokyo to see if the Japanese government might be interested in *buying* the islands back. Who needs fiction when you have history?

In sum, the Cold War since the mid-forties has provided common
ground in bringing America and Japan together, and indeed keeping
them together. It has been the cornerstone of U.S.-Japan relations and
a blessing for the Japanese. It was critical for their success.

TECHNOLOGY LICENSING FEES

In retrospect, the United States pursued a myopic policy of providing
Japan advanced technology with "2 for 99 cents"-priced licensing fees.
From 1950 onward, those fees amounted to only 1/180th of all U.S.
R&D expenditures. Yet much of what the Japanese learned from that
technology has been translated into products that help to account for
Japan's continued trade surplus with the United States.

To this day the Japanese are still licensing U.S.-developed technology
and buying into American R&D firms. Many American companies apparently lack the capital, will, and commitment to bring the technology
to market. As some of our Yankee Samurai pointed out earlier, American
firms have much too short a time perspective; quarterly profits matter.

The Japanese have made good use of American technology as they
position themselves for the twenty-first century with their fusion reac-
tors, supercomputers, X-ray lithography, biogenetics, low-temperature
conductors, advanced semiconductors, fiber optics, ceramics, computer
manufacturing, cyrogenics, and more. In many of these key areas, the
Japanese are at least on a par with America, and in several others they
have already progressed well beyond.

It is a myth spread by complacent and "whistling in the graveyard"
Americans that the Japanese are only capable of copying and lack creative ability. Bill Gates, Microsoft's chairman, has said: "There is this
notion that the Japanese are not creative; that for instance they cannot
write software, and it is not true." In fact, Japanese high school students
invariably finish first in international science and mathematics exams
that feature problem solving, while America's young scholars finish

fifteenth or sixteenth, barely ahead of Third World nations. Japan graduates twice the number of engineers and scientists as the United States,
issues more patents, and takes advantage of the natural penchant to work
in teams through which so many technical breakthroughs are now
made. America's "Desert Storm" victory was due in no small part to the
exceptional performance of its weaponry, a significant part of which
used advanced Japanese technology. The self-effacing Japanese do not
make an issue of this—the hawk never shows its talons. They are perfectly willing to go along with the American-held foolishness of their
own superiority while day by day twenty-first-century "science cities"
such as Tsukuba, 35 miles northeast of Tokyo, are sprouting up throughout Japan. The government, in cooperation with business and academe,
has carefully planned and launched nineteen such science cities, each
the equivalent of America's Silicon Valley. Japan by the turn of the
century will be one huge high-tech archipelago. It will have become the
Mecca of technology, and the entire world will worship there.

No doubt the Japanese would have reached their current prominent
level of hi-tech accomplishment without U.S. shortsightedness; still,
the American jump start certainly helped. It was Aeschylus who wrote,
"So in the Libyan fable it is told that once an eagle, stricken by a dart,
said when he saw the fashion of the shaft, 'By our own feathers and not
by others' hands are we now smitten'." The United States has been
smitten by its own technological feathers.

JAPAN INC. — THE ROLE OF GOVERNMENT

"It's difficult to know where government ends and the private sector
begins," said Commerce Secretary Robert Mosbacher in a mid 1991
speech. It has been widely argued by American observers that Japanese
government industrial policy has been a critical factor in the nation's
economic achievements. That policy included infant industry protection, tacit permission of cartelization, low interest rates, industry and
personal tax incentives, as well as the business "guidance" of the Ministry of International Trade and Industry (MITI) and the financing
policies of the Ministry of Finance (MOF).

While the central planning role of the Japanese government may
have been overstated, there is little doubt that there is, and has been, a
strong element of collaboration and cooperation between business and
government. Two years ago, the Ministry of Transportation finalized a
report calling for a third air carrier to compete in the Far East with

Singapore and Korean Airlines. The other two Japanese carriers, All Nippon Airways and Japan Airlines, had too high a cost structure. As has often been the scenario in the past, the report became a springboard to policy. The airline is now flying profitably. This kind of thing has occurred thousands of times all across Japan's industrial landscape.

One reason for the apparent success of the Japanese industrial policy are the skills and abilities of ministry officials who determine and influence that policy. These men (and I do mean men; more about this later) are the elite of Japan, having survived the rigors of a brutally competitive education system. At the apex of that system is the law department of Tokyo, or Todai, University. Its top graduates go on to take positions at the MOF or MITI. Graduates from other departments and from other top universities serve in other various powerful ministries.

Following successful government careers, key bureaucrats take their post-retirement "descent from heaven" (*amakudari*) by joining the executive ranks of a major corporation (Mazda's past chairman, as well as a current member of Toyota's board of directors, for example, were both ranking MITI officials); heading a quasi-government corporation; or entering the Japanese Diet, one third of whose members are past bureaucrats. This further contributes to the blurring of lines separating government and industry and to the strengthening of cooperation. Old school ties enhance relations among the nation's leaders; the same graduating class that sends some of its people into government sends others into industry, science, media, politics, and academe. Class members remain in touch with one another. These ultimately are the men who lead Japan.

Collaboration is further reenforced by near-constant discussion and consensus building among the hundreds of councils, panels, and advisory groups, comprised of representatives of various constituencies, who come together to hammer out policy. There is for instance the powerful Keidenren which represents some 100 industries and over 800 corporations; the Keizai Doyukai, with well over 1,000 individual top executive members; the Nikkeiren which brings together the management leadership of some 30,000 firms to deal with labor-management issues; and the 6 million-member Japan Chamber of Commerce. Long-term membership in these organizations forms a "social memory" that contributes to an almost clanlike body politic of 125 million people.

This is not to say there are not disputes—sometimes bitter ones—between various government agencies, industrial sectors, or factions within the ruling Liberal Democratic Party, or that there are not environmental or civil rights issues raised by various dissident groups. Nor is it to say that there are not fierce competitive battles between companies to seize domestic market share—in fact, the Darwinian struggles are so intense that winners find their well-honed and tested products and services easily exportable to a far less demanding international market. But to an extent beyond the comprehension of most Americans, the Japanese resolve their societal differences in a largely nonadversarial manner. Much of the legislation voted upon in the Japanese Diet is drafted by the ministries, and a good deal of it passes unanimously or nearly so. The last time the American Congress passed anything of substance unanimously—unless you want to count congressional pay raises—was the declaration of war against Japan in 1941.

All of this combines to form an image of the totality of Japan's people, land, and capital resources as a kind of mega-company traded on some universal stock exchange: "Japan Inc." Prussia was once referred to as an army with a state. Japan can be called an economy with a state. That image is neither pure reality nor pure myth; but it is more the former than the latter and has greatly contributed to Japan's success. It is a direct reflection of that nation's group-oriented culture.

KEIRETSU

Some have credited Japan's economic achievements to the industrial organization structure, dominated by the *keiretsu*. This will be discussed in some detail in chapter 6, "Japanese Management Style," and once again in the final chapter, "Lessons."

Briefly here, however, we should note that the *keiretsu* are families of companies that can be thought of as a wagon wheel with a hub and spokes. The hub is generally a bank, and the spokes a variety of service and manufacturing companies. Interlocking directorates, cross shareholdings, monthly presidents' meetings, and business dealings between firms, including loans from the hub bank, characterize these *keiretsu*. The firms from different *keiretsu* tend to compete vigorously with one another.

The wagon wheel design is simple, beautiful in its symmetry, and superbly functional. Those wheels carried America's heroic nineteenth-century pioneer men and women across the West to a new land and prosperity. The same structure in a different context has helped to carry the Japanese to new lands and prosperity in the late twentieth century.

Japan's national flag today is of course the blazing red disk on a clean white background. But pause for a moment and recall the Japanese flag as it appeared from 1933 to 1945. It was a red circle with red rays extending from it all on a white background. Now put an imaginary circle around the rays, and the circle becomes the rim of what might be called a wagon wheel. Metaphysically, this no doubt has absolutely no meaning at all—but it is still fascinating. It is no less fascinating that the Japanese Navy readopted its wartime flag in 1952.

THE U.S. MARKET

No major power is more dependent upon raw material imports than Japan, as the following table shows:

• KEY RESOURCE FOREIGN DEPENDENCY •

RESOURCE	JAPAN	UNITED STATES
	%	%
Energy sources	87	42
Iron ore	99	30
Copper	96	34
Aluminum	100	64
Lumber	69	4
Wool	100	23
Cotton	100	− 84
Wheat	93	− 147

Japan must import to survive, but foreign reserves to purchase those imports can only come by exporting—a task that Japan has done with splendid success. A relatively open American market was fundamental to that success; Japan probably could not have achieved its present state without it.

In 1975, the Japanese merchandise trade surplus with the United States stood at $2 billion. By 1980, the figure had reached $10 billion, and from 1982 to 1987, the increase continued: $16, $17, $21, $37, $41, and $55 billion. By 1988, even with the weak dollar, the figure still stood at over $50 billion; three years later, it was $43 billion. The United States today accounts for 27 percent of all Japanese exports, although that percentage has been declining over the last decade as Japan has expanded its markets into Europe and Asia.

The 250 million omnivorous American consumers have been, and are, a vital market for Japan's products. The net of almost $500 billion has flowed from America to Japan over the last decade and a half. That has been a megadose stimulant for the Japanese economy. No one should underestimate the difficulties the Japanese have had to face in competing in this American market: foreign language(s), bafflingly diverse cultures, vast distribution networks, combative trade unions, mystifying legal labyrinths, complex federal, state, and local political systems, powerful opposing special interests, in-place competitors, and more. Yet America's belief in the principles of capitalism and free enterprise has allowed the Japanese to compete with restrictions generally no less onerous than those imposed on American firms. That opportunity, which the Japanese seized, has been a critical factor in Japan's economic success.

A Revised Strategy

One begins to sense at this point just how closely Japan's postwar world has been linked to America: from the MacArthur occupation, to a joint anti-Communist political-military alliance, to technology licensing, to open markets, and more. The relationship was one of *oyabun-kobun*, or "father-child role," with the United States of course being the nearly omniscient and omnipotent father, highly respected by the Japanese son. Or so it was until roughly 1980, when the son began to flex his newfound strength.

By the late 1980s, the dollar had weakened by some 50 percent from a few years earlier. The Japanese held a vast sum of those dollars, and there was a clamor for protectionist legislation from within the halls of the U.S. Congress, which in 1988 passed a bill aimed at any foreign nation guilty of "unfair" trading practices. Strip away the facade, and the bill's tacit target was Japan. Many Americans were worried, and some special interests feared the continuing flood of imports from Japan. The Japanese realized that and began revising their export-driven strategy. The new strategy included both portfolio and direct investment in the United States.

Portfolio Investment

The Commerce Department reports that in 1987 Japanese portfolio investment in the United States totaled some $10 billion of corporate bonds, $13 billion of corporate stock, and $70 billion of government

securities. By early 1989, the Japanese Central Bank held $90 billion of
U.S. Treasury bonds. In mid-1990 in a typical U.S. Treasury bond
sale, the Japanese bought 25 percent, or $2.5 billion, of notes. Today,
Daiwa, Nikko, Nomura, and Yamaichi purchase upward of 20 percent
of all U.S. federal securities offerings.

Eight of the ten largest commercial banks in the world are Japanese,
and they hold 9 percent of all commercial loans in the United States.
Japan is already the largest creditor nation in the world, and by 1995 the
people of this planet, a large portion of them Americans, will owe $1
trillion to that California-sized island-nation. That works out at about
$8,000 for every Japanese man, woman, and child.

Japan's rationale for the portfolio investment strategy is evident: higher
interest rates in the United States, a home for its huge number of
dollars, and a means of smoothing out exchange rate fluctuations. Perhaps not so evident is the ultimate power and influence that investment
buys. Even the hint of the Japanese failing to participate in a U.S.
Treasury bond offering, or worse yet, a dumping of their massive holdings, would panic U.S. financial markets. That provides the Japanese
with a negotiating sledgehammer in dealing with the United States in
other matters of politics and trade. Further, the Federal Reserve Board
has lost at least some of its independence. A move by Board Chairman
Alan Greenspan to lower interest rates for the purpose of stimulating the
economy may drive foreign (Japanese) capital away. Power—the ability
to guide its own destiny—is slipping away from America.

DIRECT INVESTMENT

There are three convenient categories of Japanese direct investment
in the United States to be considered: real estate, commercial joint
ventures, and so-called "green field" operations. The Department of
Commerce reported that in 1987 those three categories totaled about
$30 billion and the following year approached nearly $50 billion. By
1991, the figure was over $100 billion.

Real Estate.

The Shuwa Corporation epitomizes the aggressiveness of the Japanese in the real estate market. In 1987, the company purchased $1.8
billion worth of buildings in the United States, and another $2 billion
the following year.

In 1988, other firms spent an additional $4 billion, the leaders being Dai-Ichi Mutual Life, Sumitomo Life, Mitsui Fudosan, and Mitsui Life. Several joint ventures have also been struck between, for example, Nomura and Cushman & Wakefield, and Kumagi Gumi and William Zeckendorf. More recently, however, as the Japanese have gained knowledge and confidence, they have been going it alone.

Japan has been under a great deal of U.S. Commerce Department pressure to increase imports of American beef and citrus products. The Japanese have begun to comply, but only in their own inimitable way: Sumitomo has just invested $54 million in a Florida citrus operation and Otaka has purchased a 31,000-acre Colorado cattle ranch. Large tracts of California's verdantly lush San Joaquin Valley are beginning to fall into Japanese hands. Oranges grown in Japanese-owned groves and cattle raised on Japanese-owned land in America will soon be exported to Japan.

A recent study by the Kenneth Leventhal Company showed that the Japanese invested $13 billion in real estate in the United States in 1990. Since 1985, that brought the total in 1991 to over $76 billion.

The largest investors have been construction and development companies, followed by individual "Donald Trumps"—even Japan has a few of those. About 40 percent of investment has been in office construction and another 30 percent in hotels and resorts.

Recall our Yankee Samurai concerns over Japanese investment in California and Hawaii real estate. They were onto something. The Japanese have spent $24 billion and $16 billion respectively in these two western outpost states, which amounts to 34 percent and 23 percent of the Japanese portfolio. The Hawaiian investment includes 80–90 percent of Honolulu's beachfront hotels and nearly half of the condominiums along Waikiki Beach.

The Japanese love America's Sunbelt. California, Arizona, Hawaii, Florida, and Texas account for 65 percent of their total real estate investment. The two Northeast states that have attracted the Japanese are New York ($16 billion) and Illinois ($11 billion).

Investment in Guam, a U.S. territory since 1950, totals over $1 billion. Golf is a major attraction. It is cheaper for the golf-addicted Japanese to make a three-hour plane flight to Guam for an eighteen-hole round than to play on many of the courses in Japan. And if the growing number of Japanese senior citizens (12 percent over sixty-five in 1991; 18 percent in 2005; and 24 percent in 2020) do not mind the occasional earthquake and typhoon, and more than a few snakes,

Guam's 75 to 85 degree year-round weather, beautiful coral reefs, white
beaches, and scenic mountain interior may also serve as a potentially
desirable haven for retirement communities; a kind of Miami Beach of
Japan. Plans are on the drawing board.

Japanese investors now own over one third of downtown Los Angeles
office space, and in New York have purchased the Exxon, ABC, and
Citicorp buildings, as well as Rockefeller Center. Even the Aladdin and
Dunes hotels in Las Vegas and the Bel-Aire Hotel in Beverly Hills are
now in Japanese hands.

Part of the Japanese interest in the United States stems from the lack
of opportunity at home. Although Japan is roughly the size of California, only about 20 percent of the land is habitable, the remainder being
generally too mountainous. So land prices throughout the 1980s increased from 10 percent to as much as 50 percent a year. Even though
prices fell in 1990–91, they still remain high by American standards.
Prices remain highest in Tokyo. In the Marunouchi banking district,
there has been essentially no building sold for twenty years; and in the
prime shopping areas of the Ginza, property values exceed $500,000 per
square yard. A piece of land the size of this page will cost you roughly
$22,000. Land represents three fourths of the cost of a new project in
Japan, compared to one fourth in the United States. At current exchange rates, Japan's total land value of about $14 trillion is twice that
of the United States, even though the latter is twenty-five times larger
and rich in natural resources. The Imperial Palace and its surrounding
grounds in the very midst of Tokyo have a land value greater than that
of the entire state of California.

Another attraction the United States has for Japanese real estate investors are the greater tax advantages; furthermore (helped by a weakened dollar), the return on investment is more than twice that in
Japan—or at least has been until a weakening in the United States real
estate market the last few years.

All of this has made Japan the largest foreign real estate investor in the
United States, recently surpassing Great Britain. But the Japanese are
interested in more than being America's landlord.

Commercial Joint Ventures.

There is an ever-growing number of commercial joint ventures between U.S. and Japanese firms. The alliances touch almost every sector of the U.S. economy. Perhaps the most well known is the

NUMMI project of General Motors and Toyota, with their automobile-manufacturing facility in Fremont, California. Not so well known is G.M.'s smaller-scale partnerships with a dozen other Japanese firms, including Isuzu and Suzuki. Ford with Nissan, Mazda with Yamaha, and Chrysler with Mitsubishi have their own Japanese partners.

Beyond the automobile industry, joint ventures are found all across U.S. industry. Nippon and Inland Steel have now put into place a $525 million co-venture called I/N Tek; ProQuip, a manufacturer of integrated circuit-test equipment, is linked to Shinko Shoji; Young & Rubicam has teamed up with Dentsu in advertising and Goldman & Sachs with Sumitomo Bank. Plant Genetics has joined with Kirin Brewery, Nippon Oil with Texaco and Chevron, Honeywell with NEC, AT&T with Mitsubishi, Kawasaki with ARMCO, LSI Logic with Sharp, Kodak with Canon, Komatsu with Dresser, Boeing with Mitsubishi, Hitachi with Texas Instruments, Texas Instruments with Kobe Steel, Alcoa with Fujikura, Alumax with Mitsui and Nippon Steel, Motorola with Toshiba, Intel with NMBS and Matsushita, Sony with AMD, and Sanyo with Micron Technology; there are thousands more of these American and Japanese linkages.

So extensive and far-reaching are these joint ventures that they are likely to lead to the third major issue in U.S. and Japan economic relations. The first is the ongoing Japanese trade surplus; the second is today's Japanese investment binge in the United States (with dollars earned from the trade surplus); the third is the extraordinary degree of linkage between American and Japanese companies. Perhaps a "U.S.-Japan Inc." is on the horizon.

These joint ventures provide the Japanese with a window into U.S. technology, an opportunity to better learn the marketplace, and a springboard for export to Europe—putatively being an "American" company, and hence not encountering EC restrictions that would be imposed on exports from Japan. Exchange rate fluctuations are moderated, and (of great importance) cries for American protectionist legislation are muted. Further, these ventures create American jobs (although some argue that they are the wrong kind of jobs, largely in assembly and marketing, while the Japanese keep for themselves jobs in plant design, product engineering, finance, and strategic planning—a debatable point); reduce the current account balance, at least temporarily, until income starts to flow back to Japan (not highly debatable); and help to build an American political constituency for the Japanese.

Green Field Operations.

The term "green field" refers to the start-up of a brand-new operation. Such a literally green field of several hundred once agricultural acres is found in the Torrance-Gardena area of California. There, Honda is building its Versailleslike U.S. headquarters. The firm is now America's fourth-largest automobile company and has begun to export to Japan. Toyota is only a car length or two behind Honda. Both have their turn indicators on poised to pass Chrysler and will likely do so within the year.

Nissan has a new truck plant in Tennessee and Toyota has a $1.1 billion manufacturing facility in Kentucky, as well as a forklift operation in Indiana. Mazda is in Michigan, Honda in Ohio, Sony and Kyocera are in California, Komatsu in Tennessee, Sanyo in Arkansas, and Matsushita is in Illinois. A new $370 million Sony plant in Pittsburgh will manufacture 1 million television sets a year.

All across the United States, governors and local officials make pilgrimages to Tokyo to sing the virtues of Forrest City, Arkansas; Flat Rock, Michigan; Smyrna, Tennessee; Anna, Ohio; and Lafayette, Indiana, as the perfect locations to build a new plant. Forty states have permanent offices in Japan manned by American officials, who seek Japanese investment leading to employment for their constituents at home. The Japanese are responding—and making friends in the process.

In a 1991 survey by the quasi-governmental Japan External Trade Organization (JETRO), 1,435 manufacturing plants in the United States were found to be either owned by the Japanese or to show significant Japanese investment. This was a 40 percent increase from a previous count made in 1989. Employment in these plants increased from 200,000 to 300,000.

The Japanese have now, either separately or in partnerships, erected ten automobile plants in the United States with a capacity of 2.5 million cars. That is the equivalent of a brand-new company twice the size of Chrysler.

Only the people of North Dakota and Montana find themselves so far without a Japanese presence. The locations of choice include California, which has the most plants, Oregon, Washington, the industrial Midwest, and the Southeast. At least half of the factories export products from the United States, and 75 percent of them use U.S.-supplied materials for at least half their manufacturing needs.

Almost a decade ago, it was recognized that the Japanese would need

to take countermeasures to alleviate the problems that their trade surpluses were creating. Those countermeasures included portfolio and
direct investment. Japan is now the third-largest direct foreign investor
in the United States, after the United Kingdom and the Netherlands.
With the inclusion of portfolio investment, it is the largest foreign
investor.

THE WHEEL COMES FULL CIRCLE

Some of the hundreds of billions of dollars that Americans sent to
Japan for Canon copiers, Nissan trucks, Sony VCRs, Epson Computers, Mitsubishi television sets, Toyota Celicas, Nikon cameras, and a
cornucopia of other products, are now coming back. Those dollars are
buying U.S. investment portfolios, real estate, joint ventures, and
start-up operations. Solomon Brothers reports that at the close of 1991
the Japanese held $115 billion of U.S. government and corporate se-
curities in addition to direct investments and bank liabilities totaling
$140 billion. The process has only just begun. The Japanese still hold
vaults filled with neatly stacked greenbacks, and in spite of a weakened
dollar, the accretion of trade surplus with the United States continues,
thus adding to those vaults.

Japan's intention is made clear by Saburo Okita, adviser to the Japanese government's Economic Planning Agency, when he asserts that
"Overseas direct investment will continue to increase." A recent survey
of the largest Japanese firms indicated that one third of them expected
to expand operations in the United States. The Economic Planning
Agency in its "Future 2000" report indicated that Japan will inevitably
shift from being a major trading power to a major power in direct
investment. American observers come to the same conclusion. They see
the Japanese becoming true multinationals, aided by the rising Yen.
Direct investment is predicted to reach $200 billion in the United States
by 1995, with commerce and finance investment added to manufacturing. The Japanese-owned sector is growing 400 percent faster than
the rest of the U.S. economy.

The Japanese are learning the merger and acquisition games of Wall
Street. In 1987, Reichold Chemical became victim to a Dainippon Ink
hostile takeover; 1988 saw over $10 billion of acquisitions, including
Union Bank by the Bank of Tokyo, Firestone by Bridgestone, MCA by
Matsushita, and Gould by Nippon Oil. In 1989, Sony added Columbia
Pictures to its vertically integrated entertainment holdings. Japanese

firms are loaded with cash to buy more—much more. Of the twenty-six international companies having $1 billion or more in net cash, nineteen are Japanese. Toyota leads the list with $14 billion. And all of that cash says nothing of potentially greater borrowing capacity.

The Japanese presence is not a short-run aberration. They have the patience, the will, the resources, and the vision. A Japanese proverb says: "A journey of a thousand miles begins with a first step." The Japanese have already taken that first step—toward building a powerful U.S. presence.

Americans working for Japanese interests, the Yankee Samurai, will be an integral part of that presence. Out of Japan's humiliating and total defeat in World War II, the benign MacArthur-led occupation, the Korean War, technology licensing fees, the role of government, *keir-etsu*, trade surpluses, and recent investment in the United States, has come, finally, the Yankee Samurai. Perhaps a few among them are the sons and daughters of American military personnel who were aboard the U.S.S. *Missouri* on September 2, 1945. We have come full circle.

5

Yankee Samurai: Personal Insights

"Who are you?" said the caterpillar to Alice.

ALICE IN WONDERLAND

INTRODUCTION

Understanding the events leading up to the coming of the Yankee Samurai; the Yankee Samurai views on U.S.-Japan relations and Japanese management style; and the role that the Yankee Samurai are playing in Japanese transplants in bridging the cultures between the United States and Japan are several objectives of this book. So, too, is simply getting to know these American men and women. Who are they?

What are their vital stats: years with the firm, gender and racial mix, job descriptions, education, and age? What attracted them to a Japanese firm? Are they fluent in Japanese? Have they worked before in a Japanese company, and what influence did earlier experience have on their decision? Are they somehow different from other Americans? How do their family and friends feel about their employment with a Japanese company? What is their overall view of working for a Japanese firm? And finally, how have they personally been changed as a result of their working experience?

VITAL STATISTICS?

No one perhaps will ever know who the first Yankee Samurai was, but some of Japan's trading companies trace their local roots to the turn of the century; the idea of Americans working for Japanese firms on U.S. soil is not new. Still, they numbered only in the hundreds or very few thousands until the early 1980s when, as the last chapter indicated, the Yen rain of Japanese investment began to fall upon America. One of the earliest referenced estimates of 70,000 Americans working for Japanese firms in 1985 was made by Harvard's Japan watcher, James Abegglen. The numbers have grown ever since. The following figures are drawn from several sources:

• ESTIMATED NUMBER OF YANKEE SAMURAI •

YEAR	NUMBER
1985	70,000
1986	105,000
1987	175,000
1988	230,000
1989	250,000
1990	300,000
1991	400,000
2000 (proj.)	1,000,000

These figures include only American blue- and white-collar workers directly employed by Japanese firms in the United States. Excluded are outside consultants, legal counsel, advertising agents, lobbyists, or other vendors who are supplying products or services to the Japanese companies. Also excluded are the ever-growing number of Americans whose American-owned company is in a joint venture with a Japanese company—Yankee Samurai cousins, so to speak. Then there are those Americans who have borrowed from Japanese banks for their homes or businesses . . . they are not counted. Finally, not included are those people working for American firms providing products and services sold directly to Japan—Japan is America's second-largest export market, and per capita the Japanese import more American products than Americans import Japanese products.

Including all of these additional Americans the figure would rise easily to 6 million. Multiplying that by the conventional factor of 4 to take account of multiplier effects (e.g., the economic well-being of Andy's Barber Shop, located just outside a Toyota plant, is dependent upon the salary of the Toyota workers) yields 24 million Americans, roughly one tenth of America's population, involved directly or indirectly in Japanese commercial dealings. And of course this says nothing of the 90+ percent of us who have purchased Japanese-made products, or the underclass of some 30 million receiving government welfare money that has been previously borrowed from Japan through Treasury bill offerings.

With only a little hyperbole, it can be said that there is no American untouched by Japan. The reverse statement is also largely true. The ties that bind these two nations—which together account for only 6 percent of the world's population but 40 percent of its wealth—are becoming more tightly bound every day.

Our focus here, however, is only on those Americans, the Yankee Samurai, working directly for Japanese-owned firms in the United States. To put the current estimate of 400,000 in perspective, America's labor force now numbers about 110 million. The Yankee Samurai then are only 0.4 percent of the total. The manufacturing percentage, however, is higher, at about 1 percent. The numbers are still relatively small, but the Yankee Samurai are found in some of the most critical industries of autos, electronics, and finance; 20 percent of all new manufacturing jobs in the United States are with Japanese-owned firms. Even more important, what the Yankee Samurai are learning, and the examples they are setting, may well transform the American workplace.

How representative of the nation's 400,000 Yankee Samurai are those who have been questioned and interviewed for this book? As we saw earlier, one very significant difference is that all our people were white-collar workers. The Japanese companies are now building the marketing, finance, and distribution infrastructure to support their manufacturing operations. In the years ahead, hiring in this white-collar sector can be expected to increase more rapidly than in the blue.

A second difference is geographic. Many of the Japanese manufacturing facilities, by design, have been located in small rural towns in the Midwest, Southeast, and Northwest. Yet for communication and logistic purposes, as well as the ability to recruit, white-collar operations must of necessity be located in or near larger cities.

The Yankee Samurai you have been meeting here are all Southern

California men and women, who are probably typical of their white-collar counterparts working for Japanese companies in New York, Boston, Chicago, Atlanta, Seattle, or San Francisco.

YEARS WITH CURRENT COMPANY

The Japanese firms are relatively new to the United States; there are a few exceptions: Toyota, JAL, and Sumitomo, for example, have had American operations for over a quarter century. The 5.1 year average tenure of the Yankee Samurai among those interviewed is a reflection of this. Only a handful of them have been with their firms for over twenty years.

From the standpoint of organizational behavior and management style, these newly fashioned companies are special, if for no other reason than that they are new. Young and rapidly growing companies are usually marked by a strong family orientation among the core employees, rapid promotions, and a struggling to find appropriate operational, organization, and human resource management styles. The corporate culture has not yet evolved. Japanese management merely adds a further complicating layer.

THE ROLE OF WOMEN

Early on this study I called the New York office of one of the world's largest electronics companies, seeking to speak with the Japanese president. Before getting through to him, I chatted with his American secretary, who told me: "Your contacts are very good and I am sure that they will give you people to talk with. But they will only be safe people and certainly will not include any women."

Well, "they" did give us women to talk with, 38 percent of the total, which is just a little less than the roughly 45 percent national average in the American work force. Women were represented all the way to the manager and director rank in the firms involved here. The issue of women in Japanese companies will be considered later, in chapter 8 . . . it is a hot topic.

Just how "safe" the people were to whom I spoke you will have to judge as the book goes on. But I think you will be struck by just how outspoken the Yankee Samurai are, especially the women. The Japanese seemed to be not at all bothered by this and were far more willing to open their doors to me than American firms might have been.

Racial Mix

Based upon Southern California's overall racial mix, there was a disproportionately large number of Caucasian (78 percent) and especially Asian-Americans (13 percent) among the Yankee Samurai interviewed.

More than half of the Asian-Americans I spoke with were Japanese-American. They seemed to enjoy a somewhat special position in their firms, interfacing more with the Japanese nationals and holding a significant number of management positions. This was true even though not all of them could speak Japanese.

Other Asians were a mix of Chinese—Hong Kong or Taiwan-born—Thai, Vietnamese, Filipino, and Korean. The Asian population in California has exploded over the last decade and now comprises some 8 percent of the population. The majority of the new immigrants are carving out economic lives for themselves as small entrepreneurs working within their own, often thriving, communities. They have tended, for the most part, to shun the corporate world, but those who have ventured into it often have found far greater receptivity among the Japanese firms than among American companies, where they form only about 1 percent of the *Fortune* 1000 managers. There is perhaps a sense of cultural affinity and comfort in the Japanese firm.

Here, for example, is a poignant story that might be titled "Only in America." A well-educated, middle-aged Vietnamese man escaped the hell of Vietnam with his family and fled to the United States, but was unable to obtain any responsible position with an American firm. He never got past snickering employee-relations people who saw nothing but a small, self-effacing man still struggling with his English. With boundless forbearance and fortitude he continued his search for almost five years, all the while working in a restaurant to keep his family intact. That was yesterday. Today, he is an auditor for one of the major Japanese banks, where he was welcomed. I remember the deep emotion in his voice as he said, "My family knows how hard I searched to find an appropriate place to work in this great land. Here at [bank name] I feel stable, secure, pride, and comfort."

Look for many more Asian-Americans to become Yankee Samurai, even if that brings charges of discrimination by other Americans; it already has.

The blacks and Hispanics among the Yankee Samurai with whom we spoke made up only about 10 percent of the total; they form about 30 percent of the local geographic region. The 10 percent figure, however, is probably typical of the white-collar professional corporate environment in American firms located in the same area. The disappointingly small percentage is largely a reflection of limited educational opportunities. The high school dropout rate in Southern California among disadvantaged minorities is some 40 percent, and approaches 50 percent in many of the inner-city schools. Even graduates are often woefully ill-qualified to compete in the labor force.

The Japanese companies are growing ever more solicitous not only of their black and Hispanic employees but of the corresponding communities from which they come. There is reason for concern; in February 1992, Benjamin Hooks, NAACP president, called for a black boycott of Toyota, Nissan, and Honda because there were too few black dealerships. More on this in later chapters.

JOB DESCRIPTIONS

The Yankee Samurai placed themselves in one of four job categories: senior management, technical or professional, middle management, and other.

Senior management included chief operating officers, chief financial officers, vice, executive, and senior vice presidents, and directors. They accounted for 11 percent of the total. Over the last several years, nearly all the newspapers stories dealing with Americans working for Japanese firms have focused upon senior executives. Their views are not always shared by others lower in the organization.

General legal counsel, engineering specialists, business systems analyst, and auditor were typical of titles in the technical or professional category. They made up 10 percent of the respondents.

There was a full spectrum of middle management positions, ranging from contests and incentives manager to strategic marketing manager. They accounted for the largest percentage of the sample at 47 percent.

The category "other" made up the remaining 32 percent, and included such positions as: executive secretary, human resources administrator, accounting clerk, marketing coordinator, and customer services representative.

There were no blue-collar employees. That is important to keep in mind; it will later come up as an issue.

EDUCATION

About 10 percent of the Yankee Samurai had only a high school education, while 25 percent had done post-college graduate work. The average years of education was 15.5, just short of a four-year college degree; that is considerably higher than the national average of 12.9, and reasonably typical of the large American company professional white-collar work force. Still, we stumbled onto an interesting phenomenon. Even among the more senior-level managers, few had graduated from big-name business schools. Many came from state universities, and some holding fairly substantial positions graduated from third-tier universities, diploma mills, even two-year junior colleges; a few managers only had high school educations, albeit with experience in the military. Even the most senior of the Yankee Samurai tend not to hold the cachet of graduation from major universities. There are some very good reasons for this, which will be explored in chapter 8.

AGE

The Japanese penchant for hiring younger people in their factories was not particularly evident among our white-collar people. Specific data were not tracked, but anecdotally the work force appeared to be little different from that of an American company in terms of "graying." In fact, many of the banks had a disproportionate number of older men who had been caught in the mid-eighties downsizing of such American institutions as Security Pacific, Wells Fargo, and Bank of America.

JAPANESE-SPEAKING SKILLS

Certainly an anomaly, when compared to an American firm, was the fact that about 8 percent of the Yankee Samurai spoke reasonably good Japanese. Many of them were accounted for by Japanese-Americans, but there were several exceptions. Two young men with a trading firm learned the language while doing missionary work in Japan. A few others, including one young woman who had modeled in Tokyo, picked up their skills while working or studying in Japan; only a handful learned Japanese in U.S. universities. Many of the companies have introduced Japanese-language courses taught in house. Several dozen of the Americans either are or have been enrolled in such courses, but tend to drop out after a short period.

An American's facility in the Japanese language is by no means a prerequisite for his or her promotion and success. Yet we saw earlier how severe the communication problem is between the Yankee Samurai and the Japanese expatriates; it cannot be doubted that the ability to speak Japanese would be a great asset for an American.

PREVIOUS JAPANESE EMPLOYMENT

Since less than 1 percent of the U.S. labor force works for a Japanese-owned firm, a surprisingly large 15 percent of our Yankee Samurai were found to have previously worked for a Japanese company. The explanation probably lies in the relatively dense concentration of Japanese companies in the area—five of California's ten largest banks are Japanese, and there are over 1,500 Japanese-owned firms in the greater Los Angeles area alone. The observed job-hopping generally occurred within either the electronics or automobile industries. The evidence indicates that most people who left their initial Japanese employer did so of their own accord.

INFLUENCE OF PRIOR KNOWLEDGE

Americans are generally rather casual in their choices of the firms for which they choose to work. While alternatives between companies might be carefully weighed and pondered, these are not taken to be "bet your life" choices. That is nothing more than a practical reflection of the American workplace. If one opportunity fails to be realized, then another will be sought and is generally available. No country in the industrialized world has a more nomadic labor force. The average American white-collar worker has 4.3 employers after the age of twenty-one—compared to less than half of that for the Japanese salarymen.

Thus, some of the Yankee Samurai showed an almost cavalier attitude in choosing their firm. There were a few who initially were not even aware that the firm was Japanese. There were others, however, who made their choice only after a great deal of research and who knew exactly what they were doing. Some of their responses follow.

A vice president and senior counsel for an electronics firm said: "The fact the firm was Japanese was not significant in my coming here. I was influenced by the rapport with those I interviewed with, salary package, and financial performance of the firm." The recently hired woman personnel manager commented, "The fact that the firm was Japanese was not even known to me when I interviewed for the job. It was not at all significant."

The director of materials control has been with his electronics firm for over ten years, having joined it just out of junior college. The company is now Japan's largest in its field. Nevertheless he observed, "it is a little embarrassing to admit, but when I first interviewed here, I did not even know who [company name] was." The middle-aged director of materials controls for a very large electronics firm commented, "To be honest, I had never heard of the firm before [*grins and shrugs*]."

PRODUCT AND INDUSTRY INFLUENCE

Of particular interest were the several dozen people who were influenced not by the fact that the firm was Japanese, but by the product or industry. The remarks of an automobile firm's manager of public relations were somewhat typical: "I had respect for the very little that I knew about the company, but it was not an important factor. Had the company been called 'Smith' but made cars of the same quality, I would have been just as influenced." And the electronics company's manager of mobile service who learned his engineering as a technician in the Air Force indicated, "It was the industry, not the fact the firm was Japanese, that attracted me here. I walked in here blind." A similar point was made by the laser printer project manager: "The firm's manufacturing reputation, not that it was Japanese, drew me here."

POSITIVE INFLUENCE

Roughly 40 percent of the Yankee Samurai, however, were quite aware of the Japanese ownership of the firm, which *did* significantly influence their choice in a very positive way.

A recently graduate Cal State Long Beach MBA said, "After studying Japan's 'economic miracle,' quality circles, and consensus decision making, I decided in college that I wanted to work for a Japanese firm."

The credit manager of a mid-sized electronics firm commented:

> The fact that the firm was Japanese had a tremendous impact on my decision to come here.
>
> Japanese companies in general have a strong reputation for being more of a family unit, working as a team, and with less of a "cover your ass" philosophy. I thought the environment would be very positive, with an aggressive attitude and good track record.

The electronics firm's procurement manager was an organized and disciplined man, who knew exactly what he was doing in joining his firm:

> I came here by design having set out to work for a Japanese company.
>
> I had always been loyal to my employer and had pride in workmanship. Long before people became aware of the Japanese presence in the United States, I started reading articles about the Japanese management style and manufacturing methods. I said to myself that the Japanese do business the same way that I would.

The director of employee relations for a large-screen television manufacturer commented:

> Having been through a leveraged buy-out situation with an American company and seen the terrible disruption on people's lives, there was a high degree of attractiveness about working for a Japanese firm. I liked the stability, and the reasonable assurance that the job and company would be there tomorrow.

Finally, a vice president of electronic banking operations observed that:

> I viewed working for a Japanese-owned firm as a plus for several reasons.
>
> Much has been written recently about the strength of Japanese strategic planning, product quality, and the value placed on the individual worker.
>
> They are more focused on long-term rather than short-term results, which American companies are notorious for. To me, this translated into a sense of career stability and security.
>
> I felt that the firm would view the employee as a valuable asset and not just a disposable, or expendable, commodity.

Negative Influence

An estimated 10 percent of the Yankee Samurai did have prior knowledge of Japanese firms and their management style; they joined their respective firms *in spite of* that knowledge.

The director of channel development for a major electronics firm, a young woman, said: "I was aware of the opinion that Japanese firms do not provide a positive environment for women but was assured that was not the case here. I also chose to deal with consensus decision making as a challenge, not a hindrance."

The electronics firm's marketing vice president also overcame some initial qualms: "The fact that the firm was Japanese was actually negative in my choosing to come here. I had an image of the Japanese ripping off American technology and competing with us with our own products. But the product was exciting and the facility's location very convenient."

The manager of system implementation, a very outspoken woman, observed:

> I worried about working for a Japanese company. There was a lot of talk on the news that the Japanese were taking over everything and buying Hawaii. There are so many Orientals now on the West Coast and they have all of the money. It makes you think twice about continuing to feed these people. I still think about this.

Another concern was raised by the contests and incentives manager for a world-class automobile company: "I was cautious about the role that U.S. employees might play in corporate management."

Do the Yankee Samurai Differ?

You have been listening to the Yankee Samurai now for some ninety pages and the thought may have crossed your mind, "Are these men and women somehow different from other Americans working for similar American firms?" The Yankee Samurai themselves were almost evenly split over the issue, with about half seeing no difference whatsoever and half seeing significant differences.

The auto firm's public relations manager voiced a typically repeated view: "If Americans working for Japanese firms are different, I am really not aware of it. I really don't think they are." A bank executive vice president had a somewhat more extreme reaction: "The people here have come from Security Pacific and other American banks and so are not different from other Americans. There is no noticeable affinity for the Japanese; in fact, there is a slight degree of antipathy. There are no Japanophiles."

The electronics firm's vice president of consumer product marketing said flatly, "I can think of absolutely no difference between Americans here and those working for American firms. We recruited our people from those firms." The sixty-four-year-old electronics firm's consultant didn't see any difference, either: "The Americans who are here could walk across the street and work for a competitor; they are no different. In fact, most of the people have come from the competition."

On the other hand, about half of the Yankee Samurai saw notable differences between themselves and their counterparts working for American firms. They felt specifically that there were differences in individual personality, work ethics, appreciation of Japanese culture, and a desire to make a career with the firm.

A Japanese-American assistant manager spoke for many when she said:

> The Americans that stay with the company have certain characteristics that I have noticed. They are not as typically aggressive as other Americans and tend to be more soft-spoken. They frequently are looking to experience some degree of the Japanese culture that they have known elsewhere.
>
> The ones who have left either have had communication problems, or felt frustration at the speed at which management responded to their ideas.

The manager of inventory control is in his tenth year with a major electronics firm and recently returned from a six-month training program in Japan. It was an opportunity not afforded many Americans:

> I would say that every American has to go through a learning curve in coming to work for a Japanese firm. For some it takes six months, for others two or three years, and some never learn it. Those people leave the company.
>
> The Japanese have their own way of doing things. Americans come in and immediately want to do things their way; it is not going to happen.

The bank corporate account officer thought that skill in dealing with ambiguity made the Americans at his firm different from other Americans:

> The Americans here are different. They seem to adjust better to ambiguous situations. There is no real defined job description. An individual's responsibilities depend upon the initiative that he takes. Those needing structure and direction become frustrated; we have a high turnover. Americans who succeed here do so without an awful lot of signposts to give them direction.

The airline sales manager who has been with his company for almost twenty-five years commented on the typical American's lack of patience:

The American airline employees would not work very long for a Japanese company. The demands upon them are too great and the benefits that you get come with tenure rather than at the start. The new Japanese employee understands this, but the American does not. He will not wait to work his way through the necessary steps. Those who stay, for whatever reasons, are differently motivated than other Americans.

The trading company credit manager said:

For the Americans who remain with the firm, there is a need for adjustment. They must have more patience regarding their future promotions and responsibilities.

Some people feel uncomfortable because everything is not spelled out and many things are left ambiguous. There is a need to develop a base of knowledge on your own.

Success in the firm requires flexibility. You simply cannot stubbornly hold onto viewpoints no matter how strong you might feel about them.

The assistant to the general manager of a major trading company has worked for several international companies and is world-traveled. She thought that Americans at her firm were indeed different from Americans in general:

The Americans working here are very definitely different from Americans working at an American firm. At the secretarial, clerical, or support staff levels, the people are pretty much the same as you would find elsewhere. But at the manager trainee level, the people tend to be better educated and more conservative. They are conservative in their ideals, political views, appearance, and behavior. Those are the kind of people that [company name] likes.

It has been interesting because I have seen a lot of people come and go. Those who do leave lack certain qualities, including an understanding of human nature and a willingness to work with people and not against them. They lack the ability to meet someone halfway. The people who have left tend to be those who have no experience with other cultures.

Several people made a point of the Americans being different in terms of accepting limited career opportunities at a Japanese firm. Some asserted that the Japanese accept mediocrity among the Yankee Samurai.

An auto firm marketing vice president thought that was at least partly true:

People do not come to a Japanese firm without realizing that they are never going to get to the top. They can enjoy a good career, but cannot aspire to become president.

I am always reading about some whining "hot shot" American executive who has sued the Japanese firm he works for because of limited career opportunities. But to me they are not being honest with themselves. What are their chances of becoming president of an American firm? Some of those I have seen here could not rise to even mid-levels in an American company.

A bank senior vice president noted that "Americans who are real achievers tend to get frustrated in the Japanese environment and leave. There are many who stay who are probably overcompensated and could not get a job elsewhere." And the manager of major projects commented that "The Japanese often settle for mediocrity among their American employees. A lot of the Americans in Japanese firms would have a difficult time working for an American company."

But the auto firm's manager of environmental control chafed when the question of mediocrity among the Yankee Samurai was raised:

Sometimes I hear people say that American employees of Japanese firms are only mediocre. I resent that; it makes me damn mad. Maybe I don't have a $60,000 MBA and maybe I don't wear $500 suits and spend all my time politicking, kissing ass, and letting everyone know how great I am. We had a lot of people like that at [American car company, his last job] but there are very few here; it is not the Japanese way. If not being like that is mediocre, then I guess I am mediocre and proud of it.

EXPLAINING THE CONTRASTING VIEWS

Are the Yankee Samurai different from other Americans or not? You have heard two starkly contrasting views. In fact, both are correct, and they reflect a reality that was articulated by the young deputy division manager who, after college, spent several years in Japan doing missionary work:

There are a certain group of employees who are interested in a long-term commitment and the Japanese culture; they enjoy working in this environment.

I see another group who are here just for the position; for them it just so happens they are working for a Japanese firm. Those people are no different than any other American.

I think that in the long run those who have an understanding of and compatibility with Japanese culture can do very well with this firm or most any other Japanese company.

So many Americans refuse to recognize that they work for a *Japanese* company. They are either oblivious or cavalier; they have no respect [*shakes head*]. [Update on this young man: he has recently been promoted and transferred to another facility. Everyone I have spoken to in the company thinks very highly of him and foresees an even brighter future.]

REACTION OF FAMILY AND FRIENDS

If an American worked for Shell, British Petroleum, Daimler-Benz, Unilever, Nestlé, BASF, Electrolux, Barlow Rand, AlCan, Fiat, Michelin, or Thomson, his or her family or friends would think little about it; yet these are all foreign firms. But what if the firm is Japanese? This was probed with the following results.

• FAMILY/FRIENDS' VIEW OF JAPANESE EMPLOYER •

SCORE		%
1	Very unfavorable	5
2	Unfavorable	12
3	Neutral	49
4	Favorable	21
5	Very favorable	13

The scores average 3.3—just above Neutral, and leaning toward Favorable. Only 17 percent held an Unfavorable or Very unfavorable opinion. Memories of World War II, male chauvinism, limited career opportunities, Japanese market dominance, and even a little racism were at the root of the concerns that family and friends have regarding Yankee Samurai employment. The following is a range of typical responses from Unfavorable, to Neutral, to Favorable.

The human resources administrator, a woman in her thirties, has some differences of opinion with her family and friends: "My father is still bitter because of World War II and the Mitsubishi bombers, and refers to the 'sneaky Japanese.' And many of my women friends question Japanese male chauvinism."

The manager of mobile telephone service had a father-in-law who has made things uncomfortable for him:

> To this day my father-in-law has a problem with my working for a Japanese firm. He was a Nebraska farm boy who served in the "Great War." The man is very concerned about the Japanese influence and thinks that they are taking jobs from American workers. Holidays when we are together are always a little awkward.

The accounts receivable supervisor for an electronics firm said, "I am the first member of my family to work for a non-American firm. My family is very union-oriented. They don't say anything to me, but I know what their silence means."

The laser printer project manager was also having some in-law problems:

> Typically, my family and friends have no problem with my working for a Japanese firm, but there have been some difficulties with my wife's side of the family. They are fourth-generation southerners. Many of them fought in World War II and the Korean War. Initially they thought I was working for those "commies" or those "Japs." I am not sure that they even knew the difference.
>
> But now with the Louisiana economy so depressed, any job is good, and it is okay, or at least they do not make as much of an issue of it.

The auto firm's corporate marketing manager remarked, "Some of my neighbors and 'friends' back in Detroit were pretty cool to me when they learned that I was leaving and coming here."

And the advertising supervisor commented about her family:

> My family lives and works at Cape Canaveral. The atmosphere there, among my family, is very pro-American. They would not work for a foreign firm nor buy foreign products. Since they see my growth and opportunity, my employment here has become a topic that we just don't talk about.

The electronics firm's marketing vice president smiled when he said, "I have heard the term 'selling out' many times from my classmates at Rice and Stanford. My parents back in Alabama also have a little problem. But no one can deny the success that we have had here and the great opportunity that this has become."

The young trading coordinator found relations strained with both family and friends:

My family and friends are all leery of my working here. They do not understand my business interest.

My wife's family is very conservative and they distrust the Japanese. They worry about everything that I do. I am currently selling to Iraq, which bothers them a good deal. [This interview took place about six months before "Desert Storm" and the products sold were not military.]

The twenty-five-year-old Chinese-American who is an account rep with a major trading company said:

When my parents first heard that I was coming here, they questioned my choice because I am a female. They live in Hawaii and there is a very large Japanese influence there. My parents know how sexist the Japanese can be. My friends felt the same way, but I thought I would give it a try. [The young woman recently resigned, complaining of male chauvinism.]

On the other hand, roughly half of the family and friends of our Yankee Samurai were either without any opinion or had mixed feelings. The young business systems analyst was typical, noting that "There have been no real comments made, one way or another, about my employment here." Or, here is the electronics firm's credit manager, "I don't think that my family and friends think twice about my working for a Japanese firm."

The assistant secretary to the general manager of a major trading company is British-born and says she has had, "mixed reactions from my family and friends about working here. Some say that it is terrific but others are pretty negative. They say you should be working for an American company. They don't like the idea that the Japanese are here to stay."

The assistant manager of inventory planning is a black young man who said: "My family thinks that the experience I am getting is very good. But my friends don't buy a lot of Japanese products; they don't like the idea of money going out of the United States. Some of them work for G.M. and others think they [Japanese] are racist."

The electronics firm's director of employee relations was a man in his mid-fifties who was getting positive feedback about his employment from everyone but his septuagenarian mother: "The view of my family friends about working here is anywhere from neutral to positive. My mother is an exception; she was aghast. She still thinks the Japanese are our enemies and can't understand how I can be working for them [*laughs*]."

Finally, just about one third of the family and friends were very supportive of the Yankee Samurai choice of employment. Here, for example, is what a black business research clerk said: "My family thinks that I have died and gone to heaven."

The electronics firm's manufacturing schedule manager commented:

> In my family, working in this kind of field is pretty unusual. My brothers are in construction and my dad was in the military. They were limited in their views of Japan and the Japanese firms. Over the years they have seen that I have had the most stable employment of anyone in the family, and they realize that I made the right choice.

The auto firm's sales vice president, a hearty, outgoing man, responded: "My California friends were very positive about my coming here and have indicated how fortunate they thought I was. For my friends at Chrysler, the response to my coming here was mostly envy. Several wondered if I could find a place for them."

A black woman in her late thirties serves her electronics firm as travel department coordinator. She was enthusiastic: "My husband loves the fact that I work here; my kids think that it is great because they get some products at discount." The young electronics firm's purchasing clerk just graduated from high school. She said: "Many of my friends are very envious of the benefits and working conditions that we have here." The middle-aged secretary to a Japanese executive noted, "My family and friends are proud of my working here. They have a lot of respect for the Japanese."

In conclusion, let's hear the reaction of an electronics firm's manager of product development who is a recent European immigrant to the United States: "My family and friends are very proud of my working here. [Company name] is one of the largest companies in the world. I think that over time the Japanese-owned companies will be the most prestigious to work for."

Overall View of Japanese Company

The Yankee Samurai were asked to summarize their overall experience with their firm, using both quantitative measures (shown below) and appropriate comments.

• YANKEE SAMURAI OVERALL VIEW •

SCORE		%
1	Very unfavorable	1
2	Unfavorable	7
3	Neutral	18
4	Favorable	55
5	Very favorable	19

The scores average 3.8 indicating a Favorable overall view. Seventy-four percent were either Favorable or Very favorable. A recent *Fortune* survey of American firms showed a comparable figure of only 55 percent. This works out to a pretty strong endorsement for Japanese firm employment. Don't lose sight of this as you continue through the book. You have heard, and will hear in the pages that follow, the Yankee Samurai grumble and voice their unhappiness about this or that, yet they are very positive about their overall work experience. The following were some typical responses ranging from Unfavorable through Neutral to Favorable.

A middle-aged auto firm manager with a UCLA MBA said, "I don't work as hard as I used to when I believed that professional and career advancement were possible. Now I just do my job; nothing more."

The field support supervisor with a large electronics firm voiced her frustration:

> The Japanese believe in pushing product but not spending money to do so. The pay is minimum and people use the firm as a training ground before moving on. Minimum wages do not attract experience.
>
> We cannot communicate! The Japanese translate our language into something completely different from what was relayed.
>
> I will still try to persuade them to see my point of view on issues, even though I know that I am wasting my breath. My patience has just about run out.

The manager of marketing administration was a University of Southern California MBA who was looking for opportunities elsewhere:

> The Japanese expect hard work and loyalty from the Americans, yet career paths and personal development do not exist for us. I feel myself driven to work harder to fulfill an unnecessary whim. But the work is not rewarded. I am simply biding my time before I move on.

An executive secretary who had been with her firm for over twenty years said:

> Over the years I have never had to worry about my work or went home frustrated. I always felt secure and enjoyed my job. About six years ago I began to get some anxiety.
>
> When you get older, you become concerned about your future. You hear comments that the Japanese are attracted to the younger girls. You start to ask whether dedication and loyalty means anything. Were all the things that you were taught meaningful? Are they looking at that or at the pretty young girl outside their office for status?

A vice president and senior counsel for a major bank thought that "Working for a Japanese-owned company is no different, better or worse, than working for an American-owned company." Another banker, an assistant vice president, had mixed feelings: "The farsightedness and commitment to employees is good. However, the cross-cultural difficulties, language problems, and lack of quick response have not been positive. It has not improved with time. Perhaps the biggest problem is lack of communication."

The vast majority, however, viewed their experience very favorably. For example, the electronics company's young parts department manager explained:

> I have had the opportunity to be creative and make things happen. I have been promoted several times and gained more experience than I thought possible at my age.
>
> I feel more committed and motivated than ever before and am more fulfilled.

A young Hispanic banker also sounded as if he had found a home:

> I could easily go to another bank and get a higher-paying job. But that will defeat my purpose. I have been given a lot of additional responsibility, really enjoy my job, and am in this for the long haul. [Not too long after this interview, the young man received a promotion to vice president.]

The bank chief financial officer reflected upon the past fifteen years he has spent with his firm:

> I have put in the cream of my working career here. The experience has been very fulfilling. But I am not likely to have any higher titles because I am not Japanese.

I like the firm because we don't play a lot of politics around here. I also don't have to put up with being told to do things that are illegal; that is important to me.

There are pros and cons to staying here. I don't necessarily see myself as retiring from [bank name], but on the other hand I might.

The senior consultant in his late sixties was enthusiastic about his electronics firm: "This is a great company to work for . . . positively great. I went from a small salary to six figures; there is a tremendous bonus plan. I am very, very happy."

A Japanese-American who rose to a top senior position with his auto firm was approaching retirement when he summed up his over two decades: "I have had an absolute ball." (Now in retirement he seems to be having an even bigger ball, remaining intensely loyal to his company and attending a variety of company picnics, reunions, and dinners.)

The manager of special projects for a large electronics firm commented: "Once someone learns how to get something done in a Japanese company, you can be very happy here. You are not pigeon-holed and are exposed to a myriad of problems. Your opinion is of value to them." And the mid-thirties deputy division manager of a major trading company at one point in the interview simply blurted out: "It is so exciting to be with this firm and in this industry. I love it!"

How I Have Changed

Finally, the Yankee Samurai were asked how their Japanese firm working experience has changed them. Roughly half did not feel that they have changed at all. They were basically the same people you heard from earlier who thought that the Yankee Samurai were no different from Americans working for American firms; that tells you something. But for the others, the changes have been striking.

The auto firm's public relations manager noted his earlier experience with General Motors:

I have lost some ego and belief in self-importance but probably quintupled my sense of job satisfaction. I have twenty times the responsibility I had at G.M.

There are a lot of long hours. We have an extremely lean management. Sometimes that is frustrating because there is overwhelming work to get done. But I have learned to actually "enjoy" the challenge. There is a certain fulfillment in coming home very tired; it is almost like how you feel after a good workout at a gym. I would never go back [to G.M.].

The black assistant manager of inventory planning was very enthusiastic as he said,

> This has been a tremendous learning and growth experience for me. I knew very little about business when I came here. It has been a kind of university. The rapid change in the environment has been almost overwhelming. I have watched the firm grow from a small distributorship to the corporation we are today.
>
> At times going through the changes was very difficult for me. But from it I have learned self-discipline and an ability and confidence to operate in different environments.

The auto firm's new product research manager was a man in his mid-forties. He is working on an MBA, but his workplace seems to have changed him more than the educational experience at UCLA:

> Almost since kindergarten all the way through college I have been told what to do . . . what assignments were to be and when they were to be completed. My experience in industry was the same way with its MBO [Management by Objectives]. I knew exactly what was expected of me.
>
> When I walked in here, it was very different; it was Future Shock. My boss [Japanese] gave me only the vaguest of directions. I was supposed to figure it out myself. I would go home and tell my wife that I didn't know what I was doing or even what I was supposed to be doing. I wanted to be told what to do; what my goals were.
>
> It has now been about six years since my coming here, and in the process of holding several jobs I'm starting to understand. The Japanese do not see the world as some neat and structured theoretical model. It is filled with uncertainty, ambiguity, and change. Your thinking has to match that reality. You cannot look at a problem narrowly, but rather you must consider it in all its possibilities. You have to do what needs to be done, whatever that may be, and without being told.
>
> How have I changed since coming to [company name]? I now see the world as a lot more complicated than I thought it was and am learning to deal with that.

The electronics firm's chief operating officer, one of the highest-ranking Americans in any Japanese firm, commented about how he had changed:

> As an American I used to say, "Let's go to lunch or dinner and fix this problem," and 95 percent of our time would be spent dealing with that problem. For the Japanese, they go to dinner just to get to know one another better. I am beginning to understand how important that is and am trying to practice it.

The auto firm corporate marketing manager has also experienced great changes since joining his firm:

> I have learned an awful lot over the last four years. The Japanese are looking for opinions from many different sources. That has forced me to learn other parts of the organization and get out of the niche mentality that I had been in at G.M.
>
> In my business approach I am much more analytical than I was at G.M. We are always producing papers here about why we want to do things. The papers are done mostly with graphs and pictures. That is a new way of thinking for me and can be very effective.
>
> I am now a little more tolerant of people, and have learned that one person cannot change a firm.
>
> I have never worked so hard. This has been the toughest but most satisfying four years of my life.

The auto firm's engineering specialist has an engineering undergraduate degree and an MBA, both from Midwest schools. He said that

> the main personal change for me has been to look more at the long-term impact of decisions. At [American firm], we would find problem solutions without really thinking about follow-on implications; I never questioned that. Yet when I first came here I remember being in meetings where people were seriously talking about, and planning, products and designs into the next century [*amazed*]! I now at least *try* to think several steps and years ahead.

The bank's research clerk is a young black woman who has recently graduated from Los Angeles City College. I am still puzzled by her statement. It might be very meaningful, and I wish I could have probed further: "I change every morning when I walk in the door. I feel wonderful. At least on the outside I have become Japanese; the best there is."

Here is another minority young woman, a Hispanic human resources administrator. She is a recent graduate of Cal State, Los Angeles:

I have learned a lot about patience and group dynamics. In a way that has not been too difficult for me; we [Mexican-Americans] are raised to be respectful of others and accept not always getting what we want. I have also learned to work much harder. I honestly feel that any future job will seem easy compared to the demanding pace here.

The bank's accounts payable clerk has been with her firm for five years and says: "I now feel more responsible and proud of my work and that of the department. Before coming here the emphasis was just on finishing the task as quickly as possible, with no attention to detail and no follow-up."

Stay with that theme of "finishing the task" for a moment and listen to the auto firm's distribution manager, who has been with his firm for twelve years and held several different positions. He will be introducing you to *kaizen*—the process of continual improvement—a concept that will appear many more times in the pages that follow:

> The biggest adjustment for me has been the Japanese tendency to never leave anything alone. It doesn't matter whether it's a written report or a piece of hardware; it is never finished and improvements can always be made. That drove me crazy when I first came here. I used to sit in on meetings and think to myself, "Come on, come on . . . let's get on with it, it's fine." But the Japanese always look for ways to make things better. I understand that now and think it is a wonderful trait; they call it *kaizen*. Still, to be honest, you can go too far with it.

The senior credit officer, a man in his early forties, has found that he has changed considerably over his six years with his Japanese bank:

> I was a psychology major in college, but not much of what I learned was helpful when I came here. I have been spending a lot of time studying the Japanese and their culture. As a result I have become much more flexible and patient . . . that is a definite virtue in working here.

The senior vice president of real estate at a large bank also felt the working experience had changed him: "One requires more dedication, patience, and teamwork here. I have learned to suppress some of my ego."

And finally, an auto firm's human resources manager and ex-Navy airman said:

I have refined my management style since coming here. I am now more of an orchestra leader providing the opportunity for each of my people to perform their own area of expertise.

I also am more frequently assessing whether a particular goal is my personal goal, or whether it is one that is in the best interests of the company. I generally do away with 99 percent of those goals that are personal only. I work harder at discussing new ideas with management, and I have had to move more slowly. My timing and the way I approach problems has changed.

SUMMARY

The great anthropologist Margaret Mead, early in the century, introduced Americans to the relatively unknown people and cultures of the Pacific Islands. To many Americans, the Yankee Samurai are as unknown today as those islanders were then. But we are starting to learn some things.

There are an unexpectedly large number of Asian-Americans and especially Japanese-Americans among them. Roughly 8 percent of the Yankee Samurai interviewed and questioned had some Japanese-speaking ability and 15 percent had previously worked for a Japanese company. About half sought employment with their firm without considering, or even being aware, that it was Japanese. On the other hand, almost 40 percent specifically sought out employment with a Japanese firm, based upon what they had read about Japanese management style, believing that it would be a good personal fit for them.

Some 85 percent of family and friends had a neutral to positive view of the Yankee Samurai working for a Japanese firm—many of the friends were envious. At the same time there were some quite strong negative feelings among family and friends who were from the older generation of Americans who had experienced World War II, as well as others concerned about limited career opportunities, growing Japanese presence in the United States, and male chauvinism.

There was a sharp division, almost fifty-fifty, over whether the Yankee Samurai were somehow different from other Americans. Half thought that there were no differences at all. The other half believed that the Yankee Samurai were more appreciative of the Japanese culture, team-oriented, able to deal with ambiguity, flexible, and patient. A few thought that the Yankee Samurai were more mediocre than Americans at American firms. There is anecdotal evidence that those in the second group, who think they are different, are doing substantially better with their firms.

There was again a split, roughly fifty-fifty, over the question of how the working experience had changed the Yankee Samurai. Half didn't see much change. On the other hand, the other half thought they had changed a great deal. The latter had learned to suppress their own ego, had developed skill at working with numbers and thinking quantitatively, and had become more flexible, patient, team-oriented, and sensitive to the human and social dimension of the workplace. They thought further into the future, had adjusted to the continuous improvement, or *kaizen*, policy, better understood and appreciated Japanese culture, adjusted to ambiguous work situations, and enjoyed, or at least accepted, the rigor and satisfaction of long work days. Those who saw a change in themselves were by and large the same ones who believed that they were different from other Americans working for American companies.

Finally, the Yankee Samurai spoke in overwhelmingly favorable terms about their work experience. Almost 80 percent viewed it as Favorable or Very favorable. In spite of some of their gripes, complaints, and carping, the Yankee Samurai are pleased . . . more than pleased with their firms. Even with all of the difficulties we have heard and will be discussing later, the Japanese transplants pass that critical test: *Americans truly like to work there*. They are at least as positive in their feelings as Americans working for American companies.

We turn now to a key theme of this book: Japanese management style. To what extent have the Japanese brought their style with them to the United States, and how have our Yankee Samurai adjusted to it?

6

Japanese Management Style: The *Keiretsu*

> *Style has no fixed laws; it is changed by the usage of people, never the same for any length of time.*
>
> —SENECA

INTRODUCTION

Contrary to Seneca's view about style constantly changing, many of the characteristics of the Japanese management style trace back a thousand years and more. Four of its more important defining characteristics are consensus decision making, the "Whole Man," mission, and destiny. These form the titles and topics of ensuing chapters. They deal respectively with how the firm makes decisions; how it values its employees; the crucial role of its mission; and its approach to dealing with the future.

It is important to underscore that the management style described here should not be construed as practiced uniformly throughout Japan. There are differences from industry to industry, within industries, and between larger and smaller firms.

For example, you will shortly see that top management's encouragement of a sense of harmony, consensus decision making, and family orientation is a general characteristic of the management style. Yet Honda's charismatic founder, Soichiro Honda, was just as demanding and autocratic as Henry Ford. Following Mr. Honda's retirement in 1972, the company began to assume a more typical Japanese team-oriented management style. Today, Honda, ever the maverick, is challenging the system once again by moving toward a more top-down management approach.

Seiji Tsutsumi, chairman of Seibu Saison Group, and Isao Nakauchi, founder and CEO of Daiei, the supermarket and department store chain, are two of a dozen and more contemporary Japanese senior executives whose outspoken and imperious ways seem not to fit the Japanese stereotype.

Even the vaunted Japanese lifetime employment (to be discussed later) in fact holds for only about 30 percent of the work force. Excluded are essentially all women, part-time workers, those employed by smaller firms, and employees of the millions of family-owned firms in what some would mistakenly call the inefficient distribution network.

Beyond this, management style is influenced by the natural interplay of personalities and office politics familiar to Americans. Intrigue, petty jealousies, fall guys, tyrants, power seekers, and sycophants in Japanese companies are factors just as they are in American companies. As you heard one of our Yankee Samurai say earlier about the Japanese, "They are human just like we are!" Another Yankee Samurai, one of the few who has been rotated to Japan, commented: "In Japan, if all the employees in our firm would take just half the time they spend in internal entertainment and political maneuvering and spend it with customers, we would be so dominant that no one would ever touch us."

Having made this point, it should not be overstated. While the Japanese certainly have a range of emotions and behavior patterns similar to Americans, group orientation with its enormous peer pressure, as well as an individual sense of *giri* (duty) to family, company, and nation, are powerful suppressing forces that help to keep human foibles in check. Still, you should be aware that "office politics" exists. The management style described in later pages will make little mention of it, but it is there like background elevator music.

Having said all this, consensus decision making, lifetime employment, and other dimensions of the Japanese management style do tend generally to be practiced among the salarymen of the large *keiretsu* firms. It is their management style that is the focus of what follows. But, what are these *keiretsu*?

KEIRETSU

While Japan's history reaches back 3,000 and more years, it was not until the early seventeenth century that the land was united. The man who achieved this was the great Ieyasu Tokugawa—Lord Toranaga for fans of James Clavell's *Shōgun*. For nearly 250 years thereafter, the Tokugawa Shogunate ruled by wisdom and strength. One of its earliest acts after coming to power was to draw a cloak of isolation around the country, virtually expelling all foreigners and keeping contacts with the outside world to an absolute minimum. During that period of "The Great Peace," a culturally homogeneous, peaceful, and largely agrarian society was built.

That idyllic world was torn asunder in 1853, when Admiral Perry sailed his heavily armed warships into Tokyo Bay demanding that Japan open up to Western commerce. Japan, with its rudimentary military technology, was defenseless against the American dictate, and there followed more than a decade of bitter internal debate and civil war over how to respond. Should Japan suicidally fight to fend off the intruder in a futile but honorable effort to hold on to the past, or should the nation enter the contemporary world? What ultimately emerged by 1868, under the banner of "Powerful Army and Wealthy Country," was the beginning of the Meiji era: Japan would compete with the West.

As an initial step, the government sold off various inefficiently run state-operated enterprises (privatized in today's jargon) and provided business charters and capital to a small number of well-connected families with names like Sumitomo, Mitsui, and Mitsubishi. Each proceeded to build up a powerful combine of companies or groups of businesses in shipping, mining, manufacturing, and banking. The families were known as the *zaibatsu* (financial clique) and were Japan's first great capitalist-industrialists.

Within one generation, the *zaibatsu* system helped to cleave the nation from its agrarian feudal past and propel it into the twentieth century; history has seldom seen such dramatic change in so short a time. With Japan's shocking victory in 1905 over the supposedly powerful Russia in the Russo-Japanese War, the United States and Europe suddenly realized that a new industrial power had emerged in the East. In just one generation the country had become a player on the world scene.

The *zaibatsu* continued to flourish, but because—beginning in the late 1920s—they aligned themselves with the military and forged the weapons of war, the post-World War II occupation forces expropriated their holdings in 1946. An era ended—but a new one quickly began.

By the early fifties the *zaibatsu* had largely reappeared, metamorphosed as the *keiretsu*. Gone were the individual family members, but the groups of companies remained. They have since flourished. Today, the firms of the six largest groups number only 10 percent of all those traded on the Tokyo Stock Exchange but account for 78 percent of the value of all shares and 17 percent of the nation's GNP. The figure rises to one quarter when the other smaller *keiretsu* are included; roughly the same percentage holds for assets and profits. *Keiretsu* companies form less than 0.1 percent of the total in Japan, yet they dwarf the rest; Mitsubishi's 190 member companies alone account for $300 billion in sales. The *keiretsu* are the driving force of Japan's contemporary economy. Half of Japan's largest firms are members.

Additional groups have formed over the postwar years, including Hitachi, Toshiba, IHI, Nissan, Toyota, and Matsushita. Some of these, such as Toyota, can be characterized as a "supply *keiretsu*." Toyota has some 175 primary suppliers and 4,000 secondary ones. Americans might recognize this as "vertical integration," with Toyota often maintaining some equity holdings among its primary suppliers, as well as providing them with technical assistance in the form of both hardware and personnel training. The primary suppliers in turn have secondary suppliers with whom they work. It was out of this structure that Toyota developed its *kanban*, or "just-in-time" inventory system, which works only if there is precision timing and the closest of cooperation and trust with suppliers. As much as 50 percent of the business done by the supply *keiretsu* is within the group.

During trying economic times it tends to be the suppliers lower in the hierarchy who are squeezed. If there are layoffs and cutbacks, that is where they occur.

The twenty to fifty core members within each so-called "bank-centered group" maintain interdependent strategies, share R&D efforts, form interlocking directorates, interchange executives, and make use of a common bank—hence the name. An average 25 percent of a firm's shares are held by group members; that figure rises to 90 percent for banks. These holdings are seldom if ever traded. Indeed, with various "stable shareholding agreements" with large institutions, some 60 to 80 percent of the shares are never traded at all. Close relations among the group companies are further cemented by a policy that often brings retired managers from the major firms into positions, at a reduced salary, in the smaller vendor firms. In addition, banks frequently place their own people into key positions at a firm to which they have lent heavily if that firm has fallen on hard times.

The group members try to do as much business as possible with one another: a computer manufacturer will buy semiconductor chips from another firm in the *keiretsu*, and an automobile firm will purchase steel from a sister family company. The *keiretsu* stress long-term relationships, some with roots that go back to the last century. One of the reasons that American companies have had such difficulties breaking into Japan's market is that *keiretsu* members tend to give preferential treatment to one another both as customers and suppliers.

This industrial structure may appear noncompetitive; the reverse is true. A significant factor explaining Japan's lax enforcement of anti-trust laws, forced upon the Japanese by MacArthur, is that competition is fierce—considerably more so than in America. That competition takes the form of *keiretsu* versus *keiretsu*: in electronics, Toshiba of the Mitsui Group battles Fujitsu of the DKB Group, Mitsubishi Electric of the Mitsubishi Group, Sharp of the Sanwa Group, and so on. It is because the competition is so savage that the government can allow its anti-trust laws to languish.

There is enormous financial power in each of these *keiretsu*. Consider the DKB Group. By tradition, members meet monthly at the *sankin-kai*, or president's council. Seated about the table are the presidents of Dai-Ichi Kangyo, the world's largest bank; Asahi Chemical, the world's largest textile company; Fujitsu, the world's second-largest computer company; along with the heads of Kawasaki Steel, Isuzu, Sheseido, and a dozen others. Like DKB, each *keiretsu* pursues (and for the most part succeeds in) a *wan setto shugi*, or "one-set principle," with a company in each industry.

An issue that will soon be making headlines in the American press deals with the *keiretsu* operating on U.S. shores. Half of the Japanese manufacturing firms in California are associated with the *keiretsu*, as is 68 percent of all investment in U.S. high-tech companies. Whose anti-trust laws will hold, Japan's or ours? Watch for this to become a flash point of contention. There is already an incipient stirring at the General Accounting Office, U.S. Federal Trade Commission, and the Justice Department.

The *keiretsu*, then, can be thought of as giant economic entities with the characteristics of vertical integration, conglomeration, and holding company. Although there is no American equivalent to the groups as a whole, the individual firms are roughly comparable to the larger firms in the United States included in the *Fortune* 1000.

THE ALPHA GROUP IN THE YEAR 2002

It is true that today there is no American equivalent to the *keiretsu;* but that may well change. The world is looking very closely at the success of the Japanese industrial model. In fact, the Koreans and Taiwanese have families of companies structured much like the *keiretsu.* Should the United States learned from the Japanese and follow suit? Charles Ferguson of MIT, Lester Thurow of Sloan, and a growing number of other scholars, business leaders, and government people think so.

It is the year 2002, and the brutally intense international business competition in both the Pacific Rim and Europe has forced a myriad of near-revolutionary political and economic changes in America. The nineteenth-century Sherman Anti-Trust and the twentieth-century Glass-Steagall acts (1933) have been voided. Horizontal and vertical integration and conglomeration are no longer proscribed, and banks are allowed—in fact, encouraged—to hold an equity interest in corporations to which they loan funds. With that have come several industrial behemoths. One of them is the Alpha Group.

The Alpha Group

Boeing
Liz Claiborne
Coors
Corning
Lyondell Petrochemical
DEC
General Electric
RJR Nabisco
International Paper
Tenneco
Gillette
Alcoa
Ford
Bell South
Union Pacific
Asarco
Johnson & Johnson

Time-Warner
Arco
Goodyear Tire
Xerox
Colgate-Palmolive
Burlington Holdings
Lorillard
Mattel
MCI
Harley-Davidson
EDS
Bank America
Merrill Lynch
Aetna Life
Wal-Mart
UAL

These firms employ about 2 million people, or 1.5 percent of the 2002 work force, and have combined assets of $733 billion. There are cross stockholdings among them and some 20 percent of all business is done intragroup. Bank of America and Aetna Life are a primary source of capital for group members. The monthly president's meeting brings together the CEOs to plan interdependent strategies. Hundreds of smaller companies are linked to the group and nonmembers are tacitly shut out.

There are half a dozen other similarly sized groups and dozens of smaller ones. They all compete vigorously with one another and with the Japanese *keiretsu*.

This system is guided and refereed by the departments of Commerce, Banking, Energy, Transportation, Technology, and International Trade; the latter two were formed in 1996 following that year's presidential campaign. The departments are staffed by the top 1 percent of college graduates, each of whom is driven by the goal of American economic leadership. Much of the legislation passed by Congress originates from these departments, which work closely and cooperatively with business.

That is the American *keiretsu* of the future. Don't dismiss it too quickly. There are signs even now that such groups, or something very similar to them, may be on the horizon. (More of this in the final chapter.)

Japanese Management Style

The Japanese management style considered in the next several chapters, with the caveats noted earlier, is that largely practiced among the salarymen working for the core members of the *keiretsu* in Japan. Be clear on this. We are talking about salary*men*; more on this as the book proceeds. They comprise only about 30 percent of the Japanese labor force but are the white-collar elite. Except for the fact that they are all male, they are roughly comparable to the educated mid-management and up American employees of the *Fortune* 1000. Indeed, they are roughly comparable to most of the Yankee Samurai of this book.

What are the major characteristics of the management style of the *keiretsu* salarymen, and to what extent are they practiced among the Yankee Samurai? Have the Japanese transported their management style to their U.S. subsidiaries? Let's begin with consensus decision making.

7

Consensus Decision Making

> *Deliberate as long as you please, but when you decide it is once and for all.*
> —PUBLILIUS SYRUS
>
> *Swift decisions are not sure.*
> —SOPHOCLES

CONSENSUS DECISION MAKING . . . IN JAPAN

Caesar sat quietly alone atop a hill overlooking the river Rubicon. It had been a scorching day. Sweat still poured from beneath his tunic even as the setting sun reflected from the towers of the prize in the distance . . . Rome. On his shoulders alone weighed a historic decision. Below, his army restlessly waited. Each man knew that once the river was crossed to advance against Pompey, there would be no turning back and a battle to the death must follow.

But finally, as if abandoning calculation and casting himself upon the future, Caesar rose and shouted, "Let the die be cast," and he hastened to cross the Rubicon. His men followed.

How do Japanese organizations deal with the decision process in confronting their modern-day Rubicons? Are there Toyota, Nissan, Hitachi, and Fujitsu Caesars sitting behind desks in their top-floor corporate offices, pondering their personal responsibility to render fateful

decisions for their business empires? The evidence indicates that there
are not.

Unlike Caesar's imperious and autocratic approach, Japanese decision
making adheres to the very different *ringi* process, characterized by the
bottom-up origination of ideas, full participation of those even indirectly
affected by the decision, the harmony-seeking and vision-setting role of
senior management, decision boldness, never-ending rounds of both formal and informal meetings, final consensus agreement, and efficiency in
implementing decisions. The consensus process helps to assure that all
issues, no matter how minute, are raised, and that solutions are contributed by those closest to the problem. There are additional benefits ac-
cruing to the organization, including the strengthening of group relations
as problems are worked through together, and a corresponding improvement of the individual participant's knowledge base.

IDEA INITIATION

New proposals warranting decisions are generally initiated bottom up,
not top down. Ideas can emerge from any level of the organization,
although most come from middle management. Proposals range across
the totality of a firm's operation—from simple administrative issues to
critical matters of capital allocation and strategic planning. The superior
Japanese educational system, which yields 100 percent literacy and the
world's best-educated work force, assures a high level of competency
even for lower-level personnel; their opinions have merit. Initiative and
sound recommendations at these lower levels also occur because the
hierarchical seniority system (discussed in the next chapter) keeps gifted
people for a longer period in junior positions.

CONSENSUS ORIENTATION

Agreement on a proposal, whatever the issue might be, is consensus
agreement. It is based upon collective opinion or general accord. Informal meetings and discussions, known as "taking care of the roots"
(*nemawashi*), are held among all of those either directly or indirectly
involved. Matsushita's president says that "Idea interchange occurs between individuals regardless of rank and organization." The process
crosses both vertical and horizontal organization lines.

Arriving at consensus takes time. What would be perhaps a fifteen-
minute meeting in an American firm can turn into an all-day marathon
among the Japanese. There is a prevalence of such meetings.

Once a concept has taken substantive form, a written document summarizing the proposal is circulated. Each responsible individual appends a seal, rather than his signature, to the document—facing up for approval, down for disapproval, and sideways to indicate a need for more discussion.

It is only after all have been heard and differences resolved that a decision is rendered; it is a group decision. Each individual has accepted the judgment, albeit, for some, reluctantly.

THE ROLE OF SENIOR MANAGEMENT

With a decision process that is bottom up, consensus- and group-oriented, what is the role of senior management?

A Japanese firm's president does not run a fief or one-man show. There can be no CEO or chairman decision without organization acceptance. The Japanese senior manager blends into the organization. With only a few exceptions—Akio Morita of Sony comes to mind—there are not many highly visible and headline-seeking Iacoccas, Trumps, Lorensos, Geneens, Jobs, or Perots.

The senior manager is responsible for screening the proposals that come to him, delegating problems, communicating the mission, and building an atmosphere where creative and cooperative ideas can be generated, reviewed, and then acted upon. The senior man has to demonstrate magnanimity, compassion, vision, and wisdom; he leads by example, not authority.

Officers of publicly owned firms are often personally obligated for any outstanding corporate loans in case of default. Company presidents typically resign out of a sense of honor for any major company scandal, accident, or business failure. This was the case in the summer 1990 Nomura Securities scandal, when large and favored investors were surreptitiously reimbursed for their losses on the stock market; Nomura's CEO resigned. Top management has a sense of responsibility to the firm at the expense of self-interest. In trying economic times, salary reductions or resignations at the top are taken before there are any layoffs.

IMPLEMENTATION

While an autocratic, top-down decision can be rendered quickly, how efficient the overall process will be is another matter.

There is more to the decision process than just making the decision. Generating ideas, gathering information, analyzing, discussing, rendering a decision, and implementing it must all be considered. Viewing the process in this way, the *ringi* approach may take longer, but appears to be highly effective.

Further, there generally is no need for a quick decision. Most business crises are in fact "crises in slow motion" that have taken months, perhaps years, to reach a point of rupture. It should be rare for an astute and vigilant management to be caught unawares without at least some contingency plan. A good early warning system with continual data gathering and a thoughtfully crafted responding strategy is far more appropriate than the quick, knee-jerk response: quarterly earnings are down, let's cut the headcount by 5 percent.

Making a strategic decision is easy and can be done with the snap of the fingers; American CEOs do it all the time. But if the decision is based upon limited or inaccurate information and cannot be implemented, it is at best meaningless. One is reminded of the nonexistent armies that Hitler was moving around maps in his underground Berlin bunker during the closing days of World War II. He was making decisions and issuing orders that disappeared into the empty bombed-out streets above him. The decisions and orders were divorced from reality. So, too, with many modern-day top-down corporate decisions. Thorough analysis, feasibility of implementation, and the secondary and even tertiary effects which that implementation will bring must all be thought through. There is no shortcut.

DECISION BOLDNESS

There was an enormous risk for Japan associated with the December 1941 attack on Pearl Harbor and other targets in the Pacific. But risk characterizes many Japanese decisions. Brilliant individuals, who might otherwise be smothered by the hierarchy of the seniority system, can present bold ideas. They do so with the full knowledge that the group will carefully analyze their proposal, and that if the idea fails, senior management will take full responsibility.

Consensus in Japanese companies by no means necessarily translates into temperate decisions. To the contrary . . . Honda, the motorcycle manufacturer, entered the auto industry against already entrenched competition and considerable opposition from MITI, which was concerned about overcapacity. Toyota launched the Lexus to compete head-on with established American and European luxury car makers. Sony designed and sold the Walkman against all expert advice, and Canon, Minolta, and Ricoh, all camera makers, moved against the ostensibly invincible American copier maker, Xerox, and in six years took half the giant's market share. There are thousands of other examples. The Japanese have a saying: "To capture the baby tiger, you have to enter the mother tiger's lair." There is boldness here.

HISTORICAL ROOTS

Like so much of Japanese management style, the decision process traces back at least 1,500 years, to the Confucian principle of sacrificing oneself for the group. That is reflected in the constitution introduced by the emperor Taishi in the year 604. One of the articles, which could be a verbatim passage from a contemporary training manual for young Matsushita recruits, reads:

> Each person should calmly discuss matters and arrive at a decision that is reasonable from the viewpoint of the community as a whole. In the interest of harmony, each should accept the decision even if he may disagree.

Then, moving forward in time about a thousand years, came the teachings of the samurai-priest Jocho Yamamoto (1659–1719):

> Whenever there is to be a consultation, first talk to each person involved and then assemble the people whose opinion you need to hear, and make your decision. Otherwise, there will inevitably be people who resent your decision. Also, when there is an important conference, you should secretly ask the advice of people who are not directly involved. Since they have no personal interest at stake, often they understand the proper solution.

These traditions have carried forward. Consciously or subconsciously they have become part of the decision process of today's salarymen.

SUMMARY

Ringi, the Japanese decision-making process, emphasizes the group rather than the individual; the latter is willing to compromise to avoid disharmony. The system has the advantage of generating vast amounts of information, thus helping to assure that important factors have not been overlooked. A great deal of time is spent in informal discussion, *nemawashi*, as well as formally scheduled meetings. Bold and often risky ideas tend to be initiated from lower and middle levels within the organization and are freely and widely discussed. When consensus is reached, implementation is rapid as participants generally feel committed because of their earlier counsel. Senior management's role is largely to delegate problems, communicate the larger vision that sets the boundaries within which decisions are made, reinforce the corporate culture of creativity and harmony, and be ready to take full responsibility in case of failure. There are additional benefits of information sharing, team building, and decision effectiveness.

The great Caesar would not have made it at Mitsubishi Electric.

CONSENSUS DECISION MAKING . . . FOR THE YANKEE SAMURAI

Perhaps the authoritarian Caesar would not be successful at a Japanese firm in Japan, but what about a Japanese subsidiary in the United States? Does an American, a Yankee Samurai, see consensus decision making practiced? Have the Japanese brought this critical part of their management style to the United States and made the Americans an integral part of it?

We can learn some of the answers from both the quantitative survey and the interview responses.

Survey Results

The Yankee Samurai completed a survey dealing with a series of issues related to consensus decision making: degree of individual participation, role of top management, speed of decision implementation, low- and mid-management initiation of ideas, idea boldness, and time spent gathering and sharing information.

Each statement was scored on a scale of 1 to 5:

5   Definitely true
4   Somewhat true
3   Cannot say one way or another
2   Somewhat not true
1   Definitely not true

The C response, in the table below, relates to the current Japanese employer, and the P to a past American employer with which the respondent was familiar. Another J column has been added to reflect a theoretical value that might be expected from Japanese respondents employed by a large *keiretsu* firm in Japan. (Note that some of this kind of research has been done by the outstanding scholar, Naoto Sasaki, of Sophia University in Japan.) The C and P numbers that appear are average responses, and the asterisk * indicates a statistical significant difference between them at the 5 percent level. To you nonstatisticians, don't worry about it, it just means that the differences between the C and P responses are . . . well, significant, greater than what would be expected by chance.

The response to statement 1, then, is to be interpreted as follows: Ideas requiring major decisions at Japanese companies in the United States are initiated at low and middle levels to a statistically greater extent than in corresponding American firms (3.1 is greater than 2.6, and there is an *), but not to the same extent as in Japanese firms in Japan (3.1 is less than 4).

Consensus Decision Making

Question		C	P	J
1.	Ideas requiring major decisions often are initiated at mid-management and lower levels in the organization.	3.1*	2.6	4
2.	Senior executives take the leadership in problem solving.	3.4*	3.7	2
3.	A great deal of time is spent in meetings.	3.9*	2.9	5
4.	On those occasions when a project has failed, managers at each level take responsibility, with the most responsibility taken by top management.	3.1*	2.7	4
5.	Consensus is heavily emphasized in the decisions and actions of each unit.	3.4*	2.7	5
6.	Final decisions tend to have broad consensus support among all of those directly or indirectly affected.	3.4*	2.9	5
7.	Informal discussions regarding an issue often cut across functional organization as well as rank.	3.5*	3.1	5
8.	Management at all levels frequently delegate problems for solution.	3.6*	3.2	4
9.	People are encouraged to make their views known.	3.2	3.0	5

10.	Ideas requiring decisions range from the very conservative, low risk to the very bold, high risk.	3.4 3.3 4
11.	Implementation following a decision tends to be smooth and rapid.	3.1 3.2 4
12.	Top management spends a lot of time ensuring that the working environment encourages creative thinking and harmony among employees.	2.6 2.6 5

The statistical significance of many of the statements that compared the Japanese firms to American firms signals that there is a greater presence of consensus decision making, extensive discussion and communication, ideas originating low in the organization, broad consensus agreement, and senior management delegation and taking of responsibility for failure in the Japanese subsidiaries than in corresponding American-owned firms. That is, the C and P values differ from one another (*), and the C value is closer to the theoretical J value.

At the same time, comparing even the statistically significant C responses with the theoretical J values indicates that while the Japanese transplants have "come a long way" from American firms, there remains a gap when compared to what might be expected in Japan.

Several key statements failed to show any statistical significance, and even more than that, their average scores were low. For example, the response to statement 9 dealing with people being encouraged to make their views known had only an average 3.2 score for the Japanese firms— little different from the neutral 3.0. A similar conclusion holds for decision boldness, smoothness of implementation, and the role of top management, statements 10, 11, and 12, respectively.

The survey evidence overall, then, is somewhat mixed, but with pretty clear directional indications that aspects of consensus decision making do appear to be present in the Japanese subsidiaries to a greater extent than in corresponding American firms, albeit to a considerably less extent than in the same firms in Japan.

INTERVIEW RESPONSES

The interview responses were able to probe more deeply, and several specific trends were uncovered: the role of trust; clear cases where there was, or paradoxically was not, consensus decision making; the heavy influence of the style of the top Japanese manager; and finally a concept that might be called "consultative" decision making.

Trust

In one of the Japanese companies I have been dealing with, essentially the only consensus decision making going on is among the Japanese. The Americans are largely shut out . . . and resentful.

While probing for an explanation, I stumbled across a situation that had occurred in the company some eight or nine months earlier.

A new marketing vice president—we'll call him Bill McDonald—had been hired. He came to the firm with impeccable credentials: big-name school MBA, articulate, fine previous record, good-looking, and a set of excellent references. McDonald appeared to be the answer to the firm's serious marketing problems.

He was sent to Japan for an intensive three-month indoctrination and training program. There he learned the company's entire product line, pricing structure, upcoming product offerings, and five-year plan. So much confidence did the firm have in Bill McDonald that it shared this critical information with him. Armed with his new knowledge, immediately upon his return to the United States McDonald submitted his resignation and the next week went to work for a rival company.

The Japanese executives of the firm were dismayed and their natural instinct to trust no one but themselves was reinforced; they turned inward. It is not by accident that the Japanese word *gaijin* for "outsider" or "foreigner" has a pretty negative connotation, sometimes translating as "barbarian." Still, as an American, you cannot ask for a better friend than a Japanese friend, nor for a better working relationship than one with a Japanese firm. But that friendship and that working relationship come only with time. With time comes trust.

Bill McDonald set back that trust at the firm which hired him for many months, if not years. As the story got around within the Japanese business community—an informal but highly effective communication network—all Yankee Samurai, both current and future, were hurt at least marginally. The Japanese stereotype of Americans as self-interested gunslingers for hire was reenforced.

Emerson once wrote, "Trust men and they will be true to you." There may be some wisdom there, but Emerson never met Bill McDonald. For real wisdom, listen to the Yankee Samurai.

Here is the deputy division manager for one of Japan's largest trading companies. He has had over ten years, two of them in Japan, with his firm, and has slowly built up his reputation. He used the word "trust" three times in the space of a minute in the following remarks.

> Participation in consensus making depends a great deal upon who you are and your perceived role in the company. I am personally quite involved. It is important that I have worked in Japan and speak the language. I am perceived differently from most Americans.
>
> My experience [with the firm] in Japan was primarily aimed at developing human relations. The friends I met now make it very easy for me to do business. When I send a telex to Japan, they know they can trust me; they worked with me for two years.
>
> Building trust has been the key to my career. It is all a question of proving yourself. When I first came here, I performed duties that were really beneath my abilities, but I did them well and earned their trust . . . and was accepted.

The same basic point was made by the airline sales manager who has almost a quarter of a century with his firm: "I have worked my way into a position where I can make certain decisions. They are not all necessarily earth-shattering, but they are accepted because of trust that has built up over the years."

The *reverse* side of the trust coin was indicated by the marketing coordinator for a leading PC producer. She is in her early thirties, outspoken, and has an effusive personality. Her previous job had been in the Bahamas, in the tourist business. She has been with the firm for only two years:

> I used to be involved in procuring product from Japan and in that aspect we worked with the Japanese management. Half the time they didn't believe us. They would sit there and say "Uh-huh, uh-huh," and then just go out and order what they wanted to order. So I don't know if there is still this "we don't trust them and they don't trust us" kind of stuff. I think there is.

Finally, the trading company credit manager who has been with his firm for nearly a decade:

> Participative decision making varies, and that is frustrating to some. Much of it depends upon how you are viewed by the Japanese; how much they trust you and how flexible you are. Your reliability and reputation are important. If an individual is unwilling to maintain an open mind, he will not be consulted.

CONSENSUS DECISION MAKING: PRESENT OR ABSENT?

Roughly 40 percent of the Yankee Samurai saw little or no consensus decision making except that practiced by the Japanese among themselves.

The assistant manager of administrative planning is a young woman who is a third-generation Japanese-American. When asked the extent to which consensus decision making exists in her firm, she responded:

> The decision process begins at very low levels of management. An individual who has an idea will talk to his supervisor, and other associates, to see how they feel. This is an informal process, or *nemawashi*. That serves as a sounding board to test for any objections.
>
> The informal process continues before an idea is officially presented in the final stages. Usually by that time things have all been worked out.

At this point I interrupted her and said, "Let me be clear. You are saying that what you have described holds for everyone in the firm." She looked at me with some astonishment and replied, "Oh, no. This holds only for the Japanese executives. The Americans tend to neglect the approach and do not share their ideas with others, especially with other departments. The *nemawashi* process does exist, but mostly among the Japanese managers."

The personnel manager for a major electronics firm said:

> Japanese managers have a tendency to have meetings after hours that exclude the American managers. They make decisions and then later communicate those decisions to the Americans. It makes the Americans feel that they do not have a whole lot of say-so. It gets very frustrating for them. That is pointed out to the Japanese, but you still see it occurring.
>
> Maybe the reason is cultural and the Japanese just feel more comfortable dealing with their own peers. I don't know what the reason is, but it does cause a great deal of dissatisfaction among the Americans.
>
> We have a managers' meeting once a week where the Americans can contribute. But there is a feeling that decisions have already been made no matter what we say.

The UCLA MBA in his late twenties who is project manager for a new printer commented:

On the Japanese side it is very true that there is consensus decision making. As far as Americans getting involved in decisions dealing with America, all the people impacted by a decision are definitely not included in the process . . . definitely not.

Among the Americans here, decisions are made at a high level without consulting those below. That is much different than the way the Japanese do it.

This bank executive vice president has been with his firm for fifteen years, and a note of frustration was evident as he said:

The Japanese use consensus decision making. Every Monday morning, the Japanese senior officers have a meeting here in this boardroom. They go over everything. From an actual management of the bank perspective, that is one of the most important meetings, but there are no Americans included.

On Tuesday there is a meeting that includes the Americans, where ostensibly decisions are made. But from a practical standpoint [*voice hardens*] the decisions have *already* been made.

One could get very frustrated here if you let your ego get involved.

The thirty-five-year-old ex-high school football player is emerging as a star with his electronics firm. He was chosen for a rotation back to Japan, which is a clear recognition of how well thought of he is by the Japanese. His view on consensus decision making:

There is quite a bit of consensus decision making . . . but most of it is being done by the Japanese. There is a pretty tight community of the Japanese management here. Americans are only included from an operations point of view, dealing with how things should be done. Among the Americans there is not much consensus decision making.

The Japanese have a lot of meetings, almost to the point of going too far. But the result is that no rock is left unturned, even though some of them might have been turned thirty times [*laughs*].

The same message is heard again from the special assistant to the vice president at still another electronics firm:

When it comes to consensus decision making, unfortunately we are more of an American than Japanese company. There is only one person who makes all of the key decisions and that is our [American] general manager.

There are two sides of the house here. The Japanese staff make all of their decisions by consensus. If the Americans try to find out who made a decision, you cannot get an answer; it is the group.

On the American side, one person makes the decisions. He gets input from his vice presidents, sometimes myself, and a few others. But when it comes time to make a decision, he makes his own judgments.

The English-born and -educated assistant and secretary to the general manager at a large trading company said:

The very basis of Japanese management style is decision making from the bottom up. Issues here are talked about at length before moving up to the next-higher level, where the process is repeated all the way to the general manager. It then goes to New York and then finally Tokyo.

The Americans are not involved in this process. They may express their opinions, but the reason that none are involved is that none are at high levels.

The Chinese-American Claremont economics graduate is an account rep for a large trading company:

People talk about the *ringi-sho* system, where the decision process begins from the bottom and then moves up and around. In Japan, they have a piece of paper with a circle on it. As the paper is circulated, everybody named on the paper has to sign it.

Here there are two factions that they are trying to break down. There is the management, which is Japanese for the large part, and there is the clerical staff that is mostly American. At this firm there is consensus decision making among the *managerial* staff. There are about four out of thirty Americans included in that group.

One of my pet gripes is that whenever there is a strategy meeting, all of the Japanese disappear to attend. The Americans later find out just what happened.

The trading company general affairs associate responded succinctly to a question about consensus decision making: "The decision process is basically top down and controlled by the Japanese in New York and Tokyo."

Finally, here is the manager of a mobile cellular phone service company:

The consensus decision is always made on the Japanese side. Only sometimes is our input taken. That can be frustrating when we really believe that we have a viable solution to a problem. I have learned to feed things to the Japanese so that it becomes their idea. You cannot push or shove and must have all of your facts. If you are going to work here, you have to learn that.

Just as little or no consensus decision making was evident in a large percentage of the companies, it *was* evident within other companies. While there were some industry differences, there were also differences from firm to firm within an industry. Differences were also discerned within a company, depending upon the management style of individual Japanese managers.

Here, then, are the Yankee Samurai who felt themselves to be part of a decision-making process. The electronics firm's credit manager, a man in his mid-thirties, was one of them:

A recent memo was distributed by our new Japanese president emphasizing the importance of imagination and the individual's contribution to the organization.

At my level, every decision that affects our department is made with group input. We contemplate some action, discuss it, and then make a move.

No decision of mine has ever been questioned, and I have been included in the loop on major decisions.

At the very top level, direction is, at times, given via request. There was a recent situation where our president sent out a memo requesting support for a particular project that he indicated was very important to him. It is the way that it is put that can be so important.

I have never once been asked to do anything. But if you like someone and have respect for them, it is just like your mom or dad.

Some academic studies tend to beat to death the obvious: communication increases when people are placed in close proximity to one another. Conversely, it diminishes almost geometrically as the distance between them increases. In high-rise office buildings, direct communication between people separated by more than two floors falls to near zero. This may be obvious, but in a typical American firm, top management tends to be locked up behind security guards, electronic doors, and viragolike secretaries. Even moving down the organization, middle managers and supervisors have private offices. In fact, having such an office is a symbol of rank—especially if it is in a corner or boasts a window.

The structure in a Japanese office, in Japan, is generally quite different. Remember the schoolroom of a generation ago? There is the teacher in the front with her desk facing the students. The students' desks are deployed in neat ranks of four or five rows. That characterizes the Japanese office structure, with the manager (teacher) facing his staff (students). The physical office structure often takes the exact form that the firm's organization chart takes on paper. One very telling example of this open office structure is seen at the tenth-floor Honda headquarters in Tokyo. There the thirty top executives do business in an open tennis court-sized area. The result is significantly improved communication and increased consensus decision making. Everyone is right there, with no partitions or closed doors.

This office structure also serves effectively in Japan as a highly effective implicit control system. If an employee is on the phone with a personal call, on a break, or—horror of horrors—out sick or on vacation, it is evident to all. A subtle peer pressure enforces behavior. Americans, with the heritage of vast, seemingly endless plains and wilderness that span three time zones, generally find such a group orientation terribly oppressive.

Only the firm mentioned below and several of the trading companies approached the open Japanese office style; but even they made severe modifications, yielding to the American penchant for privacy. Listen to the auto firm's corporate import distribution manager:

> We do practice consensus decision making here at corporate headquarters. It is really just good solid communication.
>
> One of the important things that contributes to that is the office layout. The higher-level people, such as myself, have traditional closed offices. The lower-level managers, however, are in much more open areas.
>
> If we really operated as the Japanese do, we would all be in a big bullpen; my desk would be at the end of a row. It is a great way to communicate; there are no secrets in a Japanese company. Unfortunately, we have had to make a few adjustments here because of the American cultural preference for a measure of privacy.

Here is another auto man, a corporate marketing manager in his mid-forties, who experienced much more consensus decision making than during his years at General Motors:

> I spend an awful lot of my time in meetings with lower-level people generating a consensus of what we want to do. It never

happened that way at G.M. There, the guy at the top would decide what should be done and then just tell everyone.

Here there is a conscientious effort to get the ideas started in the organization at the bottom and ultimately end with the guy at the top. I would be less than candid to say that always happens. We do have a very strong American at the top and the Japanese president has been out of Japan for a long time. He has adopted many American management approaches; so there are some top-down decisions. But, I would say that the majority are bottom-up decisions.

The director of human resources for a computer company was a young woman in her mid-thirties:

You don't see a lot of single individual decision making here. If it is going to impact the organization in a significant way, there will be many people involved.

Now there might very well be a leader in each of the groups to whom the others will defer, but it is generally a consensus.

Many issues are first raised at lower ranks of the organization. Employees can bring up any issue with our top manager with no fear of repercussions.

Another woman, the import supervisor of a personal computer and electronics company, felt that even though her group was small, consensus decision making was evident: "They [the Japanese] always want our ideas. There are about four of us. They want us to work together, and are always willing to listen to suggestions for improving our work. It is an informal kind of thing. They don't just say, do it this way."

Here is the senior credit manager of a Los Angeles bank, with two teenage children. Their pictures were proudly displayed on his desk—something seldom seen on Japanese desks. He has had to be flexible:

I have to adjust my thoughts to accept group decision making. Sometimes it adds great pressure and time to resolve a problem. Something that I can handle in thirty seconds might end up taking two hours, requiring a number of discussions . . . that is a frustration you have to live with.

The middle-aged computer operations manager says his firm does practice consensus decision making, but it has not been well received by the Americans: "Americans find consensus decision making, with its intense emphasis on communication, a bit laborious and frustrating."

That raises an interesting point. Not all Yankee Samurai *like* consensus decision making. There were any number of examples of this. Here is a lending analyst with a major bank: "To try to give people more authority is difficult; a lot of them don't want it. We encourage consensus decision making, but many people just want to do their job, go home, and not think."

This last quote is grist for the long controversial academic battle over the issue of the empowerment of people in an organization. Douglas McGregor, at MIT, as far back as the 1930s was writing about his Theory X and Theory Y. The underlying premise comes down to how employees are viewed. Are they indolent, lacking in ambition, self-centered, resistant to change, readily duped, reluctant to take responsibility, and not terribly bright? If so, then it is top management's responsibility to organize accordingly: agree among themselves on the firm's vision, set strategy, and make critical decisions, while at the same time cajoling, deceiving, punishing, and controlling the work force to "get things done through people." If this is what you believe, then you are a Theory X, Machiavellian-type manager.

On the other hand, if you believe as Napoleon did that "Every private carries a marshal's baton in his knapsack," and that people have great creative ability, innate potential, and a desire to contribute, then you are a Theory Y manager. You manage by assuring that individuals are given appropriate independence, responsibility, and authority, and that they obtain personal and almost spiritual fulfillment in the workplace. You seek to satisfy the "Whole Man"—the topic of the next chapter. Theory Y people believe in consensus decision making; Theory X people do not. The Japanese, in Japan, are the archetypical Theory Y managers. But what of the United States? Is the Y or the X approach better suited to the American workplace? All of this is now being played out inside the Japanese firms here in America.

You were introduced earlier (see pp. 56–58) to the Japanese "coordinator," whose role it is to bridge the American and Japanese management. The auto firm's director of corporate administration described the coordinator's role in decision making this way:

> There is a lot of give and take between the middle and vice-presidential levels. And there is a fair amount of consensus in inner-departmental work. However, senior management does tend to pass things top down to the vice-presidential level.
>
> While that is going on, we do have a Japanese management structure here also. There is a Japanese president and some Japa-

nese vice presidents. There are also Japanese on the staff of the American vice presidents. They have their own inter-reporting structure brought from Japan.

If an American-run department wants consensus from the Japanese side, then the American vice president's Japanese assistant takes on the consensus decision-making task among the Japanese vice presidents.

The manager of public relations for another very successful automobile company that is often viewed as something of a maverick in the industry comments:

When a decision has to be made that has a financial and personnel impact, it is just a natural thing to get a number of people involved. People realize that there are different schools of thought. A lot of decision making is based just on casual conversations and information gathering. Slowly, almost out of the woodwork, there is developed a sense of direction, where everyone seems to feel that is the right thing to do.

When you finally get down to the decision, there is no surprise, it just seems right and natural.

If we want to implement a program, we ourselves talk about it, and get a kind of consensus. Then I will run it by my boss and maybe his boss.

Sales goals don't just come out of the blue sky. The president doesn't just say how many units we will sell, nor does an order come from Japan. That just doesn't happen. The goal evolves out of long discussions here in America, where our sales people are talking to our marketing people, and they are talking to our marketing research people. Then we have to discuss that with Japan to make certain they can meet the demands for the product. Ultimately the goal is very much agreed upon by everybody.

The young black assistant manager of inventory planning of a large electronics firm saw a growing increase in consensus decision making:

There are more and more people included in the decision making. In the past it seemed to be more top down. What was decided in Japan was what would happen here, regardless of what our [American] marketing people felt. We were selling the product that Japan wanted to produce, not necessarily what the market called for.

It is good that we are looking more to the ramifications of everyone involved. We are going in that direction.

The Man at the Top

In an earlier chapter, we saw how important the individual personality and style of the senior Japanese was in determining the organization's overall style. A manifestation of this is found in consensus decision making.

The vice president of marketing for a major computer products company had participated in the development of one of the firm's most successful laptop computer products:

> One of the things that I have learned here is the importance of consensus decision making. At Stanford, we had a class in organizational theory with Bill Ouchi; he tried to show us how consensus decisions are of better quality.
>
> I had graduated from Admiral Rickover's Navy and what Ouchi was teaching just did not stick. [Hyman Rickover was the father of America's nuclear-powered submarine fleet, who ruled with a tyrannical iron fist.] But over the years I have been seeing that not only are group decisions better, but implementation is far better. It is great when it is used.
>
> But we don't have it [consensus decision making] here; it is a real anomaly. Our Japanese top manager is very autocratic but is also very highly respected. That is just not consistent with what we hear about Japanese management. He is very much a superstar and makes decisions that do not have consensus; some of those decisions are pretty lousy. He is a real anomaly. [Update: our marketing V.P. has recently resigned, partly because of a feeling that he had an inadequate voice in decision making.]

The assistant legal counsel for a large electronics firm has a certain astuteness about management not often found among his brethren of the Bar. He also noted the importance of the man at the top:

> There has just recently been a change of management, with the president of the last six years returning to Japan, and a new gentleman replacing him.
>
> Under the previous president, I was not aware of any consensus building. It was strictly a matter of decisions coming from above, and that was that. There was not much discussion. Individual subsidiaries were run the same way.
>
> Since our new president came, we get a totally different impression. Committees are beginning to run the company and there is

an active seeking of views from different management levels and consensus is being built.

The national human resources manager for another electronics company said:

> Under the past [Japanese] management, individual involvement by the Americans in decision making has been very limited. The Americans didn't make the big decisions; for example, going from reps to our own sales force was determined in Japan.
>
> We have had serious communication problems. The Japanese are much more comfortable being among themselves, as are the Americans. There is consensus decision making among the Japanese managers for those issues that relate to them.
>
> When the Americans make decisions, they do not go through the process, and that is to our detriment. Now, there are negative aspects of consensus management, but the whole idea of giving ownership to an individual is very effective. That is just logic. You involve people that are going to be affected by the decision, so they will have ownership.
>
> The new Japanese president, who will be in place within the next month, unlike his predecessor, has told us that he intends to integrate the Americans into the consensus process. That will completely change the way we operate. We'll see.

Finally, the product information manager for a large auto company has observed a significant change just in moving from one department to another within the same firm:

> In my last assignment in the parts department there was a good deal of consensus decision making. It was like a team. That was the way the [Japanese] manager wanted it.
>
> The management here in product development, however, is totally different. The Japanese come to us and simply tell us what is the concept of the car. We have no hand in the styling, engine, or suspension. So, it is a case of their consensus put on us.

Consultative Decision Making

A variation of consensus decision making might be called "consultative" decision making, wherein information is gathered and shared throughout the organization but the final decision is solely in the hands of the senior people. There is a good deal of this in the Japanese subsidiaries. In fact, many of the Yankee Samurai interpreted this as being consensus decision making.

Here, for example, is the chief operating officer, a rising star among American managers of Japanese-owned firms. He talked about something of a compromise from consensus decision making, which he called "collaborative" decision making (my consultative decision making):

> Collaborative decision making is another case of adapting. So many Americans here when asked, did you talk to the field service guys or the MIS guys, say, "Oh, I didn't have time." They want to make a decision in the Lone Ranger mode and plunge ahead.
>
> In consensus decision making, you have to get 100 percent agreement from 100 percent of the constituency. Generally, Americans have discussions with 10 percent of the constituency. I say [that] in collaborative decision making you force yourself to go to 100 percent of the constituency, force yourself to talk to everybody and hear their point of view. But you don't have to have agreement. That is very powerful. It sounds easy and trivial, but the American guys around here don't do it.
>
> Americans are very heterogeneous. They may not want to talk to the field service guy because they don't like him or because they anticipate an answer different from their own. Americans tend to be culturally independent and want to charge off and do things by themselves.
>
> My [Japanese] boss is a very astute guy. He observes that Americans cover the whole spectrum with education, wealth, race, and lots of other things. The Japanese tend to be much more in the middle. They are very homogenous in everything. So here I am trying to gain a constituency from people that are all over the map. Obtaining a Japanese constituency is easier.
>
> For the most part, they [the Japanese] are going to be working together for thirty years. They understand each other very well and know how each other thinks. They spend a lot of time together. In task-oriented business they are together from eight in the morning until seven at night, and then they are together for another three hours at dinner just socializing, where business issues are discussed subtly. This is critically important for consensus decision making to work.

For another example of consultative decision making, here is the personnel manager of a medium-sized auto firm, who commented:

There is considerable input to a decision that goes all the way down to the clerical level. Depending upon the decision, employees at all levels are usually asked for their thoughts. Not all the managers use that information, but there is an opportunity to be heard.

The graduate of international management at Thunderbird, now with a large trading company, said:

I have studied Japanese management in school and have an understanding of how it is supposed to be. But here there has not been consensus management, although lip service has always been paid to it.

When a decision is going to be made affecting the entire division, there will be meetings where expressions are heard. So they do listen to us, but you know going into it that the decision has already been made.

The commercial bank senior vice president had this to say:

The Japanese have a belief, that is culturally and linguistically driven, that the only way they can be successful is to have a large contingency of expatriates in the organization. That core group becomes the dominant management presence. Among that group, consensus decision making takes place.

The American contribution to the consensus decision-making process is either accepted or rejected, depending upon what the core management wants to do. So, the Americans are listened to, but they may or may not have a voice in the final decision.

The distribution manager for one of the smaller automobile firms described his firm's decision making this way: "There is probably more consensus decision making here than in any company I have worked for [which happened to include another Japanese auto firm]. Even if we are not part of the decision, we are given an opportunity to provide input."

Summary

Dealing with over thirty firms here from several industries (automobile, electronics, banking, entertainment, trading, and service) makes generalizing a little difficult. Even companies in the same industry may differ considerably in their approach to consensus decision making, and for that matter there may be differences between departments within a company. Still, some clear patterns do emerge.

Overall, significantly more consensus decision making goes on in the Japanese transplants, among the Americans, than in corresponding American firms. The extent to which it is practiced is still small by Japanese standards, but relatively large by American ones.

There is a good deal of "consultative decision making," in which people are listened to even though they may not be part of the final actual decision making.

Trust is a key determinant as to whether an American is allowed to participate in the decision process; only time and performance builds that trust.

The extent of consensus decision making depends greatly upon the style of the top Japanese manager, whether he heads a group, a department, or a company.

There were evident differences in the degree to which consensus decision making was practiced from industry to industry, and for that matter among firms within an industry.

Consensus decision making, then, has traversed the Pacific, east to west, only moderately well. There are some very important cultural factors, both American and Japanese, that explain this. For the Americans, a heterogeneous population, a sense of individualism, a mobile labor force, gender clash, the need for a measure of privacy, and impatience, all preclude consensus decision making. On the other hand, Japan's culture influences the extent to which Japanese expatriates are willing to trust and communicate with *gaijin*, that is, the Yankee Samurai. Still, by selective recruiting of Americans—difficult with ever alert government Equal Employment Opportunity Commission (EEOC) watchdogs—intensive training, improved communication, team building, and the imposition of a strong corporate culture, the Japanese model can be approached in the United States. Indeed, what might emerge could be even better; a few gadflies here and there may not be a bad idea.

The electronics firm's manager of procurement and materials suggested something along those lines:

> Here, there really isn't any consensus making as it is traditionally thought about. When there are Japanese and Americans in a room, the Japanese try to push the consensus making, but there

are so many rabble-rousing Americans that they never quite get there. Things become derailed and the consensus never really happens.

What you end up with, if there is an American in authority, is his saying, "All right this is what we are going to do." But there is still a lot more discussion. Ideas are surfaced which might not otherwise have been, we learn something about another man's viewpoint, and there is not so much a feeling that things have been jammed down your throat.

We have become at least willing to listen to other views in a civilized manner. The result is not an autocratic decision, but neither is it consensus decision making; it is a hybrid, and certainly an improvement over what I have experienced throughout most of my career.

Well, East met West and something of a hybrid was born, at least for consensus decision making. Turn now to perhaps the most critical of the dimensions of Japanese management style, the "Whole Man."

8

The "Whole Man"

> *Man himself is the crowning glory of creation.*
> —GLADSTONE
>
> *So long as we live among men, let us cherish humanity.*
> —SENECA

INTRODUCTION

Several years ago the tag line for one of America's top ten companies at the end of a TV commerical ran: "People are our most important asset." What was so facilely proclaimed, and later quietly curtailed when management announced employee layoffs, is a reality for most Japanese companies.

Japanese management style, practiced in Japan, seems to truly reflect the belief of Gladstone, and Seneca, that the employee is the crowning glory of creation and should be cherished. The belief is translated into a corporate culture that makes employees the keystone of the firm. That requires much more than just providing them with a paycheck, no matter how generous. It means meeting the full spectrum of human needs which combine to nurture the "Whole Man": security, friendship, sense of belonging, self-worth, even self-actualization. It means that personal, social, and spiritual fulfillment are found *inside* the workplace. The company becomes a complete society in itself.

A business or profession in Japan has been called *michi* (the way). This refers not to whatever technical tools one might bring to a task (i.e., the way the job is done) but rather to the process of self-discovery. The job provides the vehicle, *the way*, whereby the employee reaches his or her full potential as a human being. Work is not separate from life; it *is* life. How does a Japanese firm provide such an almost religious experience?

Lifetime employment is one aspect of this. It is often viewed as the linchpin of Japanese management style; a good case will be made for this later in the chapter. But parts of the Scandinavian, Indian, French, and British industrial sectors, as well as the dead and dying Communist bloc nations, also have had jobs guaranteed for life. Here in the United States, the Post Office, many government agencies, and our higher-education institutions with their academic tenure, provide in essence lifetime employment. For decades, until late 1991, General Motors had such a practice for its senior executives and managers, and IBM's job-for-life policy had been the rule since its earliest days. Indeed, that was largely the case for most of the *Fortune* 500 until the LBOs, mergers, acquisitions, and resulting "downsizing" of the 1980s. Before Ronald Reagan stared down PATCO in 1980—a watershed year for the American labor movement—most unionized industries provided lifetime employment for union workers, especially those with seniority. The U.S. Congress, until this election year, has been structured so that it was virtually impossible to unseat an incumbent. Yet it is difficult to find many models of high efficiency, or effectiveness, among any of the above. Even America's great pride, IBM, has been badly wounded over the last five years, having lost almost ten points in world market share, from 30 percent down to 21 percent. There must be something more to the Japanese theory of the Whole Man than simply lifetime employment.

That something more is a complete body of policies, practices, and traditions that combine and complement one another to form a corporate culture, at the very center of which stands the "salaryman" (*sarariman*). Among the most critical of these are intense hiring practices, continuous training and job rotation, nonspecialized career paths, powerful human resources departments, seniority-driven promotions, good salaries and comprehensive benefits, secondary role for women and minorities, and a group/family orientation. Each of these, in addition to a policy of lifetime employment, is practiced in Japan.

HIRING . . . IN JAPAN

"We want only a few good men," say the U.S. Marines, along with Nissan, Canon, Toyota, Nippon Steel, Mitsui, Toshiba, Honda, Hitachi, Kyocera, Industrial Bank of Japan . . . The Japanese hiring system, with its painstaking evaluation of job candidates, reflects that view. If in fact the employee is the centerpiece of the Japanese firm, it is expected that the firm will initially choose him with great care. It does.

In what has become an annual tradition, with all the accompanying excitement of America's NFL draft for those involved, Japanese college graduates are recruited by the top corporations for what will almost certainly turn out to be a lifetime relationship between man and company. Even though Japan's divorce rate is very low by American standards, a salaryman is probably still more likely to leave his wife than his employer! Because of this minimum thirty-five-year commitment, the companies assiduously evaluate their potential recruits. The hiring practices are intense.

Male college students apply to their firm of choice during summer vacation of their final year. Formal testing, interviews, and evaluations begin in November, and continue until the following spring, when final decisions are made.

A survey taken by the Japan Recruitment Center in 1990 indicated that senior executives expect new employees to have been thoroughly tested and interviewed, with special emphasis placed upon character and personality; ability and knowledge are only fractionally as important. Personal appearance, unlike the case for many American firms, is of little significance. A potential candidate's school records, moral background, race—pure Japanese, with no trace of Korean, Ainu, *burakumin* ("untouchable"), Okinawan, or other "taints"—and health are rigorously examined, sometimes with the help of hired detectives. Former elementary and high school teachers as well as families and neighbors might be interviewed to probe aberrations in prior teenage and subteen behavior. The company also wants to ensure that candidates are not associated with some of the "New Thought" religions that have recently emerged in Japan, whose teachings might be anathema to company loyalty and a compelling work ethic.

Candidate testing does not focus upon any particular technical skills of the candidate. Rather, it is primarily designed to determine the applicant's character, loyalty, and potential for growth. Technical skills are expected to be learned largely on the job. This even holds true in the sciences and engineering, although the candidates are expected to know the fundamentals. The companies prefer having "blank slates" come to them, so long as those "slates" have a personality and character congruent with the firm.

The more prestigious the university from which the candidate has graduated, the stronger are his credentials and the more likely he will match with a major firm. Tokyo University stands atop the hierarchy, although Kyoto (another state institution) is also very highly regarded. The private universities of Keio, Hitosubashi, Waseda, and Sophia all have fine reputations. There are about a dozen others. The very best of Japan's young men are found in these institutions. The less prestigious companies recruit from the second tier of universities. Individual professors, as well as alumni with close ties to a particular company, may play a matchmaking role.

Those who successfully traverse the minefield of obstacles and are ultimately hired enter as a cadre—the "new rice crop"—numbering only a few for some of the smaller firms and several hundred for the larger. The class of '92, say, will train together and be promoted as a group into their forties. The bonding that will be built between them will be deep and strong, as will the all-but-unbreakable link between themselves and the company.

While the primary concern here has been, and will be, with the white-collar salarymen, a similarly intense hiring effort is made at the factory level, where recruits tend to be high school or vocational school graduates—27 percent of Japan's work force have college degrees, and 94 percent are high school graduates. Here again, there are close relationships between teachers or counselors and individual firms. Once again, character and the willingness to learn and to work well with others are crucial. With the exception of additional physical dexterity tests, the hiring procedures for the blue-collar worker differ little from those for the white-collar salaryman. (By way of contrast, at this writing an acerbic debate rages in Congress over the issue of whether employers in America have the right to request a high school diploma and transcript from applicants for entry-level jobs.)

In sum, then, the leading companies hire cadres of young men annually directly out of the best universities, after intensive examinations and interviews that focus less upon technical skills than upon character and personality. The latter are critical in determining if the candidate will be compatible with the firm. The companies are looking for latent ability and "the right stuff." The lives of the young recruits, including their family roots, ethnicity, and religion, are carefully evaluated. Those finally chosen become salarymen—the elite of Japan.

HIRING ... FOR THE YANKEE SAMURAI

Now compare this with hiring procedures for the Yankee Samurai as seen through their own eyes. Both quantitative survey and interview responses will be considered. The format of the table below is the same as that introduced in the last chapter. Recall the scale:

> 5 Definitely true
> 4 Somewhat true
> 3 Neutral
> 2 Somewhat not true
> 1 Definitely not true

The C and P figures are averages based upon current Japanese employment and past American employment, respectively. The J is a theoretical value you might expect to hold in Japan. The asterisk * indicates significance between C and P at the 5 percent level.

Hiring

Statement	C	P	J
1 The hiring procedures are very intense and thorough.	3.1	3.2	5
2. I was hired more for my general knowledge than any particular skill or area of expertise.	3.3*	3.0	5
3. The recruitment of personnel is based upon long-range personnel planning rather than immediate needs.	2.6	2.7	5
4. People are seldom hired from the outside and placed in senior positions.	2.5	2.8	5

There is little to indicate here that the hiring process is anything like that for the Japanese salaryman. In fact, with the exception of statement 2, the Yankee Samurai experiences with their previous *American* firms tended to be more like the Japanese system (P numbers were closer than the C numbers to the theoretical J values).

The response to statement 1 indicates that the hiring procedures were not terribly intense (3.1 compared to 5), and to statement 3 that unlike hiring practices in Japan, which take into account long-term personnel needs, the Americans are brought aboard to fill immediate requirements. The response to statement 4 makes clear that Japanese firms in the United States do *not* hire their Yankee Samurai in groups of young people upon their college graduation, as is the case in Japan. Rather, the Yankee Samurai are hired as individuals, as needed, and are oftentimes brought in at senior levels.

TOP UNIVERSITY GRADUATE HIRING

Nor is there a pattern of hiring the Yankee Samurai from the top business schools; there were only three such graduates among our sample of almost 250. This is probably not an accident. Privately, many Japanese managers will tell you that graduates of these prestigious institutions too often bring with them unwanted baggage, including their attitude, educational training, and salary demands. Consider each of these separately.

To the Japanese, too many of the newly minted MBAs see themselves as masters of the universe, ready to step into the CEO's position a week after joining the firm. Nor are they "blank slates." In fact, they tend to be impatient to apply the academic tools they have learned. The Japanese may feel that graduates from second-tier schools have smaller egos, are more malleable, better team players, and can adjust more readily to Japanese management style. In the long run, these people can be far more productive than the "golden ones," who may be alienated from the firm and so create "disharmony."

Beyond personality is the academic training itself. Much of what students have been taught, including an emphasis upon financial return, is viewed by the Japanese as being irrelevant at best and counterproductive at worst—finance departments are notoriously weak in Japanese firms and comparatively strong in American ones. America's business schools themselves over the last few years have begun to recognize a need for significant curricula adjustments. Among the proposed changes: an increased emphasis upon global business, foreign languages, manufacturing technology, information management, ethics, and interpersonal skills. Changes are beginning . . . glacially.

Finally, starting salaries can be 50 to 100 percent higher for top B-school graduates, which is a cost the Japanese feel they need not pay; Japanese tight-fistedness has been a samurai trait for centuries.

The Japanese in general are disdainful of America's business schools. Akio Morita, Sony's outspoken chairman, has gone so far as to claim (perhaps tongue-in-cheek) that his country's competitive advantage is that "Japan, unlike America, has no B-schools."

Having said all of this, how does one explain the roughly 18,000 Japanese enrolled in U.S. universities, many of them in MBA programs? They now account for some 5 percent of the students in the better business schools. Three fourths of these Japanese students are sponsored by their companies; roughly seven hundred came to the United States in 1990 alone. There is no paradox here. They do not come to learn and emulate American business practices; indeed, they find most of the curricula incomprehensible and of little value. They are here solely for the reason of learning about America. The MBA is a convenient vehicle to achieve that. It is often called "Mastering Being in America," which means honing language skills and obtaining an in-depth understanding of the American people and their culture.

INTERVIEW RESPONSES

Interview responses have the benefit of picking up nuances (e.g., the Japanese firms in the U.S. leave hiring practices and decisions largely to their American staff) and dynamic shifts not obtainable from a survey. That was evident here.

Like the quantitative survey results, the majority of interviewees indicated that the hiring practices for the Yankee Samurai were little different from those practiced in American firms and quite unlike those in Japan. A smaller number, perhaps 30 percent, did however see some Japanese influence on hiring practices and, more important, felt it was growing.

Here first are the majority viewpoints. The electronics firm's marketing vice president said: "Our hiring procedures are no different than for an American company. We certainly hire people for a particular skill-set who also have the capability to grow."

A few years ago, an American bank was taken over by the Japanese. The Americans who had been with the firm before the acquisition are in a unique position to compare the current management style under the Japanese with that previously practiced. A lending officer for the bank, a woman in her mid-thirties, said that "The intensity of the hiring process depends upon the level of the position. It is no different than it was before our merger with the Japanese."

The existence of an American-style hiring process was also evident to the sales vice president of a major auto firm. Comparing his previous twenty-two years with Chrysler, he thought that "the approach to hiring seems to be basically the American way." The manager of procurement and materials saw no Japanese involvement in the hiring process: "The hiring process is totally American. There is no difference from an American firm. There are no criteria laid down by the Japanese that I am aware of."

Unlike hiring in Japan, positions in the Japanese subsidiaries were generally filled by Americans to meet specific needs. Making that point was the electronics firm's advertising and public relations coordinator who said that "the Japanese are pretty body-count-oriented, and people are brought aboard to fill only specific, needed positions."

The auto firm's manager of purchasing observed that the hiring process was in American hands:

> The hiring process is totally American. There is no difference from an American firm. The hiring is done strictly through the human resources department, which has an American manager. I am not aware of any criteria laid down by the Japanese. We hire and fire just like an American company.

Not everyone held these views. Perhaps 30 percent of the Yankee Samurai felt that the Japanese influence was present to some extent and that it was growing: hiring practices were becoming more intense, greater consideration was being given to personality and character, and some people were being hired for general abilities.

Here, for example, is the Sansei (third-generation Japanese-American) assistant manager of administrative planning for a major bank:

> Tests are administered to determine the individual's skill levels, after which they go through a series of interviews. We are not so much concerned with a person's skill, per se, but how that person will fit into the organization in the long run. We look at the person's stability and how they would measure up in different situations.

Another Yankee Samurai who saw a positive Japanese influence was the trading coordinator who had spent several years in Japan doing missionary work for his church:

> I have been involved in about forty employee interviews; about 85 percent of the criteria looks at individual character rather than specific talents. I am starting to think like my Japanese manager that we should look for people who will fit into the organization.

The director of employee relations has been with his electronics firm for a little over a year; during that time, he has seen aspects of the Japanese management style in the hiring process:

As you move up the job level, the individual's team and group orientation is looked at very carefully.

The psychological fit becomes very critical at the management level. The environment here is one that suggests a high need for collaboration and cooperation. Candidates who are strong individualists without those traits just don't fit. Often that is a dominating factor, regardless of technical skill or education background.

Agreeing that hiring style was moving toward becoming more Japanese was another firm's national manager of human resources, who said: "We are on the track to improve the hiring process. Prior to my coming here there were very few reference checks and the interviewing process was somewhat perfunctory; that is changing."

Here is the import supervisor, a woman in her late forties with only a high school degree, who has also seen significant changes since she first joined the company: "The hiring process is different now. I may not have the qualifications if I now applied. Seven years ago, I just had a brief interview with one lady and one gentleman. That was it. Hiring goes through a lot more steps today."

The auto firm's corporate employment manager noted that there is a long-term trend toward the Japanese approach:

> We hire both for specific positions such as a computer programmer and to fill general management needs. We have a manager trainee program where people are brought in and go through different stages of parts, sales, and service development. This is relatively new and we are not yet at the point where we can supply all of our management needs internally. We have not had the time because of our growth. But I expect that will change.

Finally, the auto firm's public relations manager contrasted blue-collar hiring practices to white-collar. His comments are very significant, and we will return to them later because they indicate that the Japanese may view the blue-collar worker differently than the white; the former might be more highly valued:

> The intensity of the hiring process varies tremendously. The manufacturing operations do an extensive background check, an orientation, and series of interviews. Before an hourly worker is hired in our manufacturing facility, he goes through at least three interviews for an hourly position. We are trying to understand the candidate's work ethic and team orientation. There are also physical dexterity tests given. Unintentionally, we have developed

something of a youth orientation because our experience has been that the assembly-line pace can be pretty rugged and is difficult for older people.

Once hired, there is an orientation, and the family is asked to come in for part of that. That gives them an understanding of what the firm is all about. They understand what [company name] is doing globally. They start to get a sense that they are part of a global team.

Here at the sales, distribution, and administration arm [all white-collar], that orientation is not as deep and hiring practices generally are not as intense.

SUMMARY

In summary several things are clear. The Japanese do not hire Yankee Samurai in young male cadres of university graduates. While college-trained Yankee Samurai are present in the white-collar ranks in numbers roughly corresponding to American firms, it is unusual to find prestigious B-school MBAs among them. Hiring does not tend to be for general abilities; people are usually brought aboard to fill specific niches, oftentimes at senior levels. The hiring process itself, in terms of intensity of testing, interviewing, and background checks, cannot begin to compare with that in Japan; it is roughly similar to that found in American firms.

Still, there are signs things are beginning to change. Many of the Japanese firms have set up their American operations relatively recently and have not had the luxury of hiring for anything but to fill specific niches. Nor did they have the time or expertise to carry out intensive background checks of candidates. There is some evidence that the firms established longer in the United States have begun to pursue a more Japanese-oriented intensive hiring style. But even so, quite significant differences between practices in America and Japan remain.

There was one another important finding: it may be that the Japanese practice their hiring polices much more vigorously for their blue-collar Yankee Samurai than for their white.

TRAINING AND JOB ROTATION ... IN JAPAN

Japanese new recruits, as a unit, are put through exhaustive one- to three-year training problems, during which they obtain a broad overview of the company, bond together with each other, and have the firm's mission and corporate culture first branded upon them and then

over time inculcated into them. Physical endurance and spiritual training are frequently part of the overall program. The former is often
carried out at the government's Self-Defense Forces facilities and the
latter at various Zen temples.

Matsushita and Toyota are typical of many firms. New recruits complete an intensive two-year training program that includes office, sales,
manufacturing, and engineering courses; they thoroughly learn the
background, history, and culture of the company.

By Western standards, the three year-training program at Nomura,
the world's largest securities firm, is brutal. At live-in cement-block
training centers, and later austere Spartan dormitories, the new recruits
cook their own food, make their own beds, and share baths, showers,
and toilets. Their training includes a full understanding of the business:
sales, trading, analysis, stocks, bonds, and front and back office operations. Lectures can often last until two or three in the morning; frequent
examinations are set to test that assigned material is mastered. Just as
young medical interns review patient case histories with the attending
physician, the young Nomura men analyze and review, with their su-
periors, daily financial issues reported in the *Nihon Keizai Shimbun*
(Japan's *Wall Street Journal*). Poor performance wins a tongue-lashing
diatribe no less severe than that received by an inept American Marine
recruit from his Lou Gossett, Jr., drill instructor. Great emphasis is
placed upon sales experience both on the telephone and in person.
Large numbers of the calls are "cold." Failure is unacceptable.

After the passage of three years, every vestige of the young, fledgling
raw recruit who came to Normura has been burned away. He has been
reborn into a thinking and acting Nomura man, with the ability—
through intense concentration—to absorb and analyze massive amounts
of information. He can drink far into the night and after just a few hours'
sleep arise refreshed for an assault on a new, frenetic eighteen-hour day.
He has emerged with an arrogant and unerring belief that he is part of
a master culture.

In-House Training

This initial training is followed by de facto lifelong training . . . largely
in the form of job rotation. At Matsushita, 5 percent of all personnel
rotate every year. Sony moves its employees roughly every two years. At
Kao, each employee has at least three positions over a ten-year period.

There is little or no dependence on the universities for employee
training. Graduate studies at universities in Japan are rare. They are

designed primarily for those intending to pursue a career in academia. That is especially true in management, where there is no real equivalent to Harvard's Business School, although there are now four different universities fashioning business programs that are beginning to attract students; several American universities are discussing MBA joint ventures with a Japanese university counterpart. While some employees are sent to graduate schools abroad, most learn while on the job. That learning includes both technical training programs and pervasive character and social development. There is a focus on education at the work site, with emphasis on group learning.

Nonspecialized Career Paths

Widespread training and job rotation translates into nonspecialized career paths. Job rotation may take an employee from auditing to marketing, to engineering, and then perhaps personnel.

At Nomura Securities, generalists are revered; conversely specialization is denigrated. The nature of the training and job rotation assures creation of these generalists. There is a Japanese candy *kintaro-ame*, in which the filling is in the design of a face. It does not matter how one cuts into the candy; the same face will appear. That is the intent of the Nomura training program. No matter who an outsider might approach at Nomura, he will encounter the same face—a man knowledgeable about the company's business and imbued with the company's culture.

Job specifications, descriptions, and contents are not very clearly defined, and individuals do not tend to identify with a particular field of expertise. The employee simply refers to himself as a Nissan, Seiko, or Sumitomo man, not as an accountant, lawyer, engineer, or lab technician. What Peter Drucker calls the "Double-Headed Monster," referring to an employee's dual loyalty to his profession on the one hand and to his employer on the other, does not exist.

These nonspecialized career paths and vaguely defined job descriptions are consistent with the belief that the job should be made to fit the individual, not the reverse.

The Importance of Tradition

Somerset Maugham wrote years ago that "The great truths are too important to be new." So it is with the Japanese approach to work and training.

As far back as the 1920s, Mitsubishi Shipyards and Mitsui Mining had established their own trade schools. Training went well beyond the technical area to include courses in leadership, company culture, and individual character building. Literary, sports, flower arrangement, and other classes were formed so that the enterprise became something of a school. This is a pattern found today throughout most of Japan's major companies. But the principles of lifelong training and a broad generalized perspective go back even further in time. In the late seventeenth century, the samurai-priest Jocho Yamamoto wrote that

> A Samurai must know his shortcomings well and spend his life in training without ever feeling he has done enough.
> A man who earns a reputation for being skilled at a technical art is idiotic. He must develop proficiency in many areas to fulfill his total human role.

Another samurai-priest, Miyamoto Musashi, about a century before Yamamoto wrote: "Be knowledgeable in a variety of occupations and cultivate a wide range of interests in the arts. Continue to learn and perceive the truth in all matters."

Westerners look at Japan today and see one of the world's most advanced nations, in many ways the very avatar of the coming twenty-first century. What we do not see is just beneath the patina of modernity: a nation rich with samurai principles put in place thousands of years ago. It is not coincidental that both Yamamoto and Musashi were samurai-priests, experts not only in the multifaceted ways and weapons of war but in the arts, social behavior, and matters of the spirit as well. The lifelong training, job rotation, and the search to fulfill the entire human potential about which they wrote is still manifest today at Toyota, Canon, Honda, Mitsubishi.

To understand today's salaryman of the *keiretsu*, his company and indeed his nation, is to understand the history of Japan. In that salaryman's veins flows the same blood as Yamamoto's and Musashi's. The contemporary samurai-priest-businessman shares a social memory that encompasses some 3,000 years of Japanese culture. Culture matters; it is a nation's destiny.

As we continue to examine the Yankee Samurai, we will see how the smooth-functioning Japanese management style, practiced in Japan and based upon Japan's culture, begins to be buffeted when encountering the turbulence of a far different culture here in America.

Mr. Nagata

Cross-functional training—beginning with the most humble jobs—is pervasive in the *kaisha*, or Japanese corporation. It helps break down provinicialism by integrating people into all aspects of corporate life, thus giving them an appreciation for problems in other organizations. This is of fundamental importance in achieving consensus decision making. The rotation is a lifelong phenomenon, with lengths of stay seldom lasting more than three years. It is consistent with Japanese culture, which has traditionally disparaged the specialist. In the process of this training, whole legions of salarymen develop the skills and knowledge to step into positions of top leadership.

Perhaps a better summary of this fact of Japanese management style would be to examine the career pattern of someone we'll call Mr. Nagata.

Mr. Eiichi Nagata is a slim, handsome man who has worked for one of Japan's leading steel companies since graduating in 1968 from a top university at age twenty two, with a major in engineering. The chronology that you see below is the rule rather than the exception:

AGE	DUTIES
22	Orientation: senior executive presentations, plant tours, office and factory experience, physical endurance weeks, Zen spiritual training, company history and culture, sales and aggressiveness training. All of this done as a group member while living in austere company-provided dormitories.
23	Local plant—trainee (often performing most mundane of tasks, including routine maintenance and janitorial work).
24–25	Local plant—foreman.
26–28	Local plant—quality control section chief.
29	Local plant—open-hearth section chief.
30	Stanford Business School.
31–32	Chicago, Illinois-based U.S. sales office.
33–34	Tokyo office—studied possibilities of technological cooperation with foreign companies.
35–36	Tokyo office—technical development section chief.

37–38   Major 750-man plant—director.

39–40   Major 750-man plant—manager, technology department.

41–42   Tokyo office—member of human resources committee.

43–45   Tokyo office—manager, R&D department.

Nagata-san (roughly equivalent to "Mr. Nagata" but with an added element of respect) is now poised for what could well be the most productive of his years: he is a prime candidate to head a joint venture with an American firm. As a direct result of the job rotations, he has built a whole network of friends and obtained a broad overview of the firm's operations; he harbors no narrow-minded beliefs about the company's operations. The friends and companywide perspective are critical in building consensus around major decisions the firm will be making and in which he will be involved.

The steel company has no need for outside hiring because there are hundreds like him, equally well trained and capable of stepping into a variety of positions should that be required. He has worked and studied abroad, but not to the degree that he has lost his Japaneseness and become "suspect" by the Tokyo office. He has become a storehouse of social memory for the firm; younger men seek him out for counsel.

And finally, while he has a wife and two lovely daughters (on several occasions he has had to relocate without them—*tanshin funin*), his company has become his life. The grueling eighteen-hour days, six- and more day work weeks, the challenges he confronted and overcame in each of his assignments, the camaraderie among the men he has worked with, the security of knowing his firm will always support him, and a sense of enormous accomplishment all have combined to fulfill the deepest of human needs in the man.

How about our Yankee Samurai? Are they trained and rotated as Mr. Nagata was?

TRAINING AND JOB ROTATION . . . FOR THE YANKEE SAMURAI

Begin with a quantitative perspective. You should now be familiar with the table format introduced in the last chapter. (If not you might want to refer back to it.)

Training and Job Rotation

STATEMENT		C	P	J
1.	Planned job rotation is emphasized as a device for developing employee capabilities.	2.6	2.8	5
2.	The training here seems to be almost continuous.	2.9	2.9	5
3.	There is quite frequent job rotation.	2.7	2.7	5

Nothing in the responses above indicates that training and job rotation for the Yankee Samurai were even remotely similar to the experiences of Mr. Nagata. In fact, the situation appears to be essentially the same as in corresponding American firms (C and P numbers are similar), which typically assign all but a handful of the "anointed ones" into niches where they will work out most of their career.

Interviews told largely the same story, but there were some indications that modest changes were afoot.

THE RULE

Only a handful of the Yankee Samurai saw training and job rotation in their firms. There was, for example, the trading company's young training coordinator who said:

> They stress that you know what is going on in other departments. There is quite a bit of job rotation. One man in the oil department was transferred to electronics following the crash in oil prices a few years ago. The same holds for the tubular department, which depends upon steel. The people were just thrown into new departments.

The corporate marketing manager of a powerful auto company also saw some job rotation in his organization: "There is quite a bit of rotation from department to department. Every one of the twenty-two managers who has been with me over the last four years have been rotated off of their jobs. There is a great deal of movement."

THE EXCEPTION

Those views were very much in the minority. Fully 90 percent of the Yankee Samurai did not see much training and rotation in their firms. The following are some typical responses.

The electronics firm's vice president of marketing commented:

> There is a night-and-day difference between the Americans and
> Japanese. Japanese job rotation is legendary. It happens here every
> three years like clockwork. On the American side, there is no
> prospect for me to take a job in another division.

The Japanese-American marketing services manager of a large electronics firm noted, "What I have read about Japanese management style
and what I see here are really two different things. Training you just
learn on the job; I don't see any rotation of positions here."

The electronics firm's personnel manager, a woman in her mid-
thirties, observed:

> We are a little lax in ongoing training and job rotation, although
> we are trying to develop something now. We don't really have
> anything official.
>
> The Japanese on the other hand are here for three to five years
> and then rotate back to Japan.

The electronics firm's legal counsel noted that:

> The lack of training is almost a point of criticism. I have seen
> some job rotation among the managers, but it is not very extensive,
> and there is no plan whatsoever to rotate anybody from division to
> division to groom people for an overall view.

The Louisiana-born project manager has been with his electronics
firm for seven years. His view:

> We lack programs to achieve effective training and job rotation.
> Our personnel group that should be putting these programs in
> place is not doing so. I would like to see some vast improvement
> in that area. They have been talking about it for a while but there
> has been too much shake and not enough bake.
>
> There has to be some management training program if we are to
> get good people in higher positions.

The manager of mobile cellular phone service said that "On the
American side, we are job-specific. On the Japanese side, there is a great
deal of rotation and job training. It is a very broadening experience . . .
for them [*grimaces*]."

The auto firm's manager of environmental control was an engineering graduate of one of the local state universities:

Have you heard of the "In and Out" hamburger chain? The Japanese rotate in and out of here roughly every three to five years, although some are here for shorter six-month or one-year stays. But while the Japanese are in and out, we [Americans] are just *in*. I really don't know why that is. I'd like to have the same opportunity.

The importance of trust was raised by the electronics firm's manager of special projects. He has a strong interest in Japanese culture, and is both knowledgeable and articulate about Japanese management style:

What really scares me is the Japanese advancements in software. The firm trains its young kids. It is not like in an American company that goes outside to hire their experts; that is not done in Japan. Training starts immediately out of college within the firm; some are sent to American or European business schools.

In Japan, people are moved from fiber optics to cable to transmission to give them a broad view of the company. By the time management tests are taken [in a man's forties], an individual has a good background knowledge about how the company thinks.

On the other hand, there is very little job rotation here [among the Americans] that I am aware of. You have to be with the company many years and gain their trust before they would rotate you. They have to feel that you are going to stay with the firm.

Sometimes, but rarely, an [American] individual is sent to Japan for a year, and then brought back and reassigned. That only happens if the Japanese have the utmost belief in the man's loyalty to the firm.

The executive vice president and CFO of one of the world's largest banks is a thoughtful man, who has been with his firm for thirteen years. He says:

This bank is run like an American bank from a job rotation standpoint. Americans are all specialists. We are not suited, with our background and temperament, for the kind of job rotation that the Japanese have. They rotate in and out of the positions every three years, even if they are not really qualified.

Finally, the young laser printer project manager summed it up simply when he said: "There is a continual job rotation among the Japanese; job rotation among the Americans is zero."

In the last section you were introduced to the auto firm's public relations manager who thought hiring was more intense in the blue-collar environment than the white. He also drew a distinction when it came to job rotation:

> In the manufacturing facility [in the United States], there is a significant amount of rotation. If you are on a line installing radios, that does not mean that you will be installing them for the next twenty-six years. You will be doing related wiring harnesses or speaker subassembly and so forth. Training is related to how complex the job is. We send a lot of our "associates" to Japan when there is a model change. There they work at the lead plant. They will spend anywhere from four to eight weeks there, working with their Japanese counterparts.
>
> "Here [at white-collar corporate headquarters] there is not a lot of job rotation. In Japan there is a great deal more, where someone may be in manufacturing for a while and then go to a sales operation, and then a service operation. We have a fair amount here, but there is no set plan.

PROGRAMS STARTING TO BE INTRODUCED

The last chapter indicated that some changes were under way to render consensus decision making a little closer to the Japanese style.

In a similar way here we have seen some intensifying of the hiring process, and several dozen of the Yankee Samurai believed that new training and job rotation programs were starting to be put in place. Some of their responses follow.

The product information manager is in his mid-thirties and has been with his firm almost since graduation from college:

> We have been trying to become a little more like the Japanese in job rotating and developing broader-based employees.
>
> In the last fifteen months they have been conscientiously trying to move some people around that they feel are talented, or have potential, and give them a little more general experience.

The forty-three-year-old corporate distributions manager also saw some changes occurring:

> There is a desire to rotate people, but we often fall short. Our president [Japanese] is now looking at that; he really does not want to see people put in a niche and kept there. There is a desire to

create generalists with broad-based skills and some programs are being put into place.

The Japanese-American support engineer for peripherals noted some recent changes: "I think they are kind of starting into job rotation because they have had people come from the field into corporate. It strikes me as something very new."

SUMMARY

Job training and rotation practiced among the Yankee Samurai is nothing like that found in Japan, although there are some indications of change.

From interview responses, there appear to be three basic reasons why the Japanese have not pursued more training and job rotation among the Yankee Samurai; all three are culturally related.

First, the firms can always buy the needed talent. America's labor market is just that . . . a raucous Mideast bazaar dealing in the human commodity. Employees sell their services freely to employers and look elsewhere when better opportunities arise. Conversely, a firm needing a specific skill merely goes into the market and buys it; just as readily as that skill, and the man or woman within whom it is housed, is dismissed when no longer needed. An entire temporary and full-time employment, executive search, and outplacement industry has developed to service this market. So, there is no need for the Japanese firms in the United States to train their Yankee Samurai. The marketplace can ostensibly provide any particular talent that is required.

Second, many Americans feel a natural discomfort taking assignments outside of their expertise. Differences in culture are at work here. While Japanese philosophers of centuries ago spoke with contempt of the specialist, the Western world was embracing him. Americans have become children of Adam Smith's eighteenth-century concept of "division of labor," with its accompanying carving out of niches of specialization. This we believe to the source of efficiency. It is manifest throughout our society: in industry, the sciences, academia, the arts, and athletics. Even in those circumstances where an American is prepared to take on an assignment in a different field, he or she is likely to balk at the idea of a company ordered physical move to another part of the country, let alone a perceived exile outside the country. This is of course exacerbated by the now-prevalent two-income earning family . . . what about the spouse?

Finally, there is the issue of loyalty. It is senseless for a firm to expend resources to train a man or woman only to have the person resign at some point in the future, taking their obtained skills with them. The Japanese are very aware of the American nomadic penchant for seeking opportunities with other firms and act accordingly.

Even so, the fact that we have not seen a training and job rotation program for the Americans consistent with Japanese management style does not mean that the Japanese have not tried. Recall from an earlier chapter our Bill McDonald, who took advantage of his firm's trust to learn just enough about the product line, after a thorough three-month training program in Japan, to leap to a competitor. Too often, the Japanese encounter people like Bill McDonald. Listen to the Nomura experience.

Nomura's Experience

In 1982 Nomura Securities, looking to globalize its operations, decided to hire American nationals. Twenty-eight young men embarked upon a three-year training problem patterned after that of their Japanese peers. They were carefully selected, bright, athletic, and handsome business school graduates from the best universities.

Rebellion broke out the first day when the recruits arrived in Japan and found their rooms to be tiny Spartan cubicles, located in a barracks-style building that required an elevator to the basement for a shower or communal bath.

Within a week the facility, so meticulous when having previously lodged Japanese young men, looked like the fraternity house of *National Lampoon's Animal House*: furniture that had survived decades of Nomura men was damaged and broken, soiled clothes were strewn about the rooms, dirty cups and dishes were idly cast down, and pictures of nubile women hung from the walls. The recruits effusively cannon-balled into the communal bath without the mandatory pre-scrubbing, thereby leaving the water dirty for those who followed. They ridiculed the Japanese practice of bowing and were seen exaggeratedly doing so to one another and then laughing uproariously. The halls echoed with their banter; Jim Belushi would have felt right at home.

During lectures, the young men quickly began to challenge the instructors and provide their own opinions about how the firm should be run, even though many had not even bothered to study required homework material. Several felt they should immediately step into the management structure. When, late in the afternoon, the Japanese instructor, by way of silent example, cleaned up the classroom, there was no response except stifled laughter.

At a morning tour of Sapporo Brewery, the recruits freely sampled the sake offered to them. On the bus ride to their scheduled afternoon visit to Tokyo Electron, they downed the brewery's gifts of bottles of wine. Several of them were reeling drunk upon arrival. During a look at the firm's high-tech multi-million-dollar "ultra-clean room," against the strictest of policies, they removed their sanitizing masks and slippers and happily tossed them about, thinking it all hysterically funny. The Nomura people were terribly embarrassed and apologized endlessly to Tokyo Electron.

Things did not improve in the ensuing months. If anything, they became worse. Years later, one of the recruits, John Feree, reflected back on it all: "None of us had really ever heard of Nomura. We just wanted to travel, see Japan, drink, and chase women."

The denouement of the story: by 1985 the Nomura program collapsed as one by one the American recruits resigned; none completed it. Almost to a man, having touted themselves as "Japan experts," they walked into big six-figure jobs with Western firms.

There is a more recent update. Last year, IBM-Japan sought to introduce a program similar to Nomura's but with one crucial difference. The company instructed Recruit U.S.A., the Japanese search firm in the United States, to find about two dozen Americans—all of Asian descent, and all males under the age of twenty-five—to be sent to Tokyo for a two-year training program. It seemed logical to the Japanese that these young men, with their Asian cultural background, unlike the Nomura recruits, would nicely fit into their program. Perhaps, but the EEOC fined Recruit U.S.A. $100,000 for sexual, racial, and age bias in its search policies.

Human Resources Departments ... in Japan

There is a simple acid test for the premise that the Japanese firms value their employees so highly that they are the very centerpiece of the firm. That test is the power and influence of the human resources department. Its ostensible singular responsibility is to marshal the firm's most important resource . . . its human resource. If in fact it does wield great power, then the premise is correct; if it does not, then all of the talk of valuing the employee is empty rhetoric.

Be assured that it is not rhetoric. Those departments have great influence and prestige, and the most senior—and capable—of people are frequently assigned there. At Nomura, for example, the department has near-absolute power; usually every three years in an employee's career, it hands down promotion, demotion, and relocation decisions.

The status of the human resources manager is very high in the Japanese hierarchy. He is responsible for all aspects of the employee's career: hiring, training, relocation, promotions, as well as compensation and the resolution of superior/subordinate disputes. It is logical that he would be so highly regarded, given that he is the caretaker of the company's most valuable resource.

HUMAN RESOURCES DEPARTMENTS . . . FOR THE YANKEE SAMURAI

What has just been described deals with circumstances in Japan. Now apply that same acid test across the Pacific. How strong is the human resources department in the Japanese subsidiaries in the United States? Recall that the asterisk * indicates significance at the 5 percent level and that 1 = Definitely not true and 5 = Definitely true.

Human Resources Department

STATEMENT	C	P	J
1. A position in the personnel or employee relations department is sought after because of the prestige of that organization.	2.0*	2.3	4

In the entire survey, no statement scored lower than this. The C score translates to "Somewhat not true"—a full point less than the neutral score of 3.0

The department was even viewed as being significantly less prestigious than corresponding American firms (2.0 compared to 2.3), which is akin to being rated lower than the Cleveland Indians. Throughout most of American industry, human resources departments play little role in hiring, promotions, or firing decisions, except for low-level positions. Major responsibility is held largely by line managers—the reverse of the situation in Japan.

In American corporations, with the exception of highly trained compensation and benefits experts, and information systems people responsible for developing and maintaining employee information databases, much of human resource activity is largely bureaucratic. Minorities and women are disproportionately present in these organizations, especially in the areas of so-called "equal employment." Many American firms satisfy much of their de facto quotas of underrepresented groups by hiring into this area. An anomaly in terms of power and prestige in the human resource organization is its head, who is almost always a white male carrying the title of vice president. His primary responsibility is keeping members of top management—especially the CEO—happy with their cornucopia of salary and benefits. More recently he has also often had to play a lead role in finessing corporate downsizing. It pays well to be caretaker of these sensitive corporate concerns. In 1990 William Wayland, Textron's vice president of human resources, made $616,750, while his counterpart at GE, Bruce Carswell, made $672,000.

Seldom, if ever, is the American firm's human resource department viewed as powerful, influential, or sought after as an area of employment because of its great prestige. With the exception of the top job, surveys show that the department itself is generally considered a necessary evil at best.

Yet the Yankee Samurai see their human resources department as even less prestigious than that of a corresponding American firm. Listen to them.

The bank's sixty-year-old CFO described an event that occurred recently in his firm:

> One area where the Japanese managers do not interfere is in the American personnel policy: they tend to defer to the Americans. The Japanese have a high discomfort level in dealing with personnel issues. I think that is because in Japan they don't get involved in those things. It is done for them by the personnel department.
>
> That department is very powerful. Let me give you an example. [Name] is one of our most senior Japanese officers. Before this assignment he was the top man in Bangkok, and had held many other important posts around the world. Yet he virtually answered his phone one day and was ordered to pack his bags and report for a new assignment in Los Angeles in two weeks. He was told that by some second- or third-rank personnel officer! That would never happen in an American bank.

Here is the second-tier auto firm corporate marketing manager:

> I think it is pretty telling that our human resources department is not responsible for the Japanese expatriates. They are handled

completely by Tokyo. [The policy of Tokyo handling personnel matters for the expatriates is typical.] Our department [*mimes two thumbs down*] is only responsible for the Americans, and doesn't really do the best job.

Of all the Yankee Samurai who were interviewed, only three believed that their companies had strong and effective human resources organizations; each of them *headed* their respective firm's human resources departments. The views of two of the three follow.

He is the director of employee relations for a major electronics company, an articulate and thoughtful man with earlier experience at an American aerospace company:

In relation to the American firms, my department has a strong position. It is not the center, or most important part, but it does have more status, power, and influence than any American company I have been with.

My title is director, yet my peers at American companies are called managers. I am involved in all major decisions here. By and large we do maintain a higher status than comparable U.S. companies.

The personnel manager for another large electronics firm, a young woman quoted earlier, also felt that her department was very important:

I have been in human resources for five years now. I see the department as being the core of the division. We are depended upon quite heavily by both the Americans and Japanese.

In Japan, the human resources department handles all the hiring, training, and counseling; the Japanese managers are not used to doing these things. We have to edge them away from that and make clear to them that they are responsible for their employees.

In Japan, the human resources department is all-encompassing. It is probably the largest department and is extremely highly regarded. When they make a decision, that is it; there is no arguing over it. They recruit employees from the university system; management does not interview candidates. If an employee is not happy with his review, he does not go to his manager, he goes to the human resources people.

So, when the Japanese come here, they are not used to personnel matters. They do not understand all of the laws, the need to treat women differently, or promotion philosophy. That is why the function of human resources is so important.

Far more typical was the response of the manager of special projects working for the *same* electronics company as the personnel relations department head just quoted. His view:

> In a Japanese company [in Japan], the most powerful people are in personnel; they set the future of an employee. They take great pains to put the right person in the right spot. Here our personnel department is just like an American company that handles insurance, equal rights, and those kinds of things. In this country, the human resources department has no power at all.

And the manager of procurement and materials working for the same company as the director of employee relations quoted earlier (who believed his department to be highly regarded) thought that "Our human resource department is just like that in an American company. It is no better or worse, which is not saying much."

Many of the Yankee Samurai believed that not only was the human resources department of their firm no different from an American firm but it was in fact weaker. Consider the remarks of the inventory planning manager of a relatively small electronics company: "The human relations group in this office is just about nonexistent. The assistant to the general manager has the main responsibility. She is a very nice woman, but I don't think that she is explaining, or even knows, what the issues are."

The advertising and public relations coordinator commented that "A lot of big American companies have a pretty strong personnel department with many programs. I don't see that here." And the trading company credit manager agreed that his human resources group had even less influence than in an American firm: "The human resources group does not have the power and authority that it would have in an American company. A lot of it depends upon the managers."

The manager of system implementation was disillusioned with her firm's human resource department, saying: "The previous human resources director was recently let go. The department had a pretty bad reputation. There wasn't a whole lot of communication or training. They used to shut their doors every day at lunch, which was the time when many employees wanted to see them [*shrugs*]!"

An accounts receivables supervisor grimaced when asked about her firm's human resources department:

> The view about the human resources department seems to be getting a little better lately. Although there are questions about

why all of a sudden the area is being taken over by all women managers. And why only in that area? It is getting better. It used to be a joke.

They should not be involved in some of the final decisions that they are involved in. They are unorganized and slow to act on things. HR makes a policy to fit a situation and then changes it a few months later. That has happened, I don't know how many times. That is why I have become so cynical. Not just myself but other people.

The Japanese-American assistant manager of administrative planning for a large bank has been given some personnel relations responsibility, but she commented:

We don't actually even have a human resources department. The final decision-making determination is made by the Japanese managers. The Japanese cannot understand how women can hold management positions in a human resources department since in Japan that department is considered so powerful.

Finally, the politically perceptive special assistant to the vice president of a major electronics firm chose his words nimbly in saying, "The human resources department is supposed to be the clearinghouse for all social interfaces, training, hiring, firing, benefits, and salary reviews. I could not really be a judge of their performance at this time."

In sum, if it is true that a powerful human resources department translates into an all-encompassing view of the importance of the employee, then the conclusion is that the Japanese do not value their Yankee Samurai all that much. The human resource department, responsible only for the Yankee Samurai—the Japanese expatriates come under the aegis of Japanese human resource staff in Japan—may even be weaker than that in American companies.

The strength of these departments is a kind of litmus test of how the firms truly value their employees. While that strength is minimal now, watch for it to grow. This is one of several important topics in the last chapter of the book.

SENIORITY . . . IN JAPAN

Another element of the "Whole Man" approach to the Japanese management style, in Japan, is that of seniority. Promotions come slowly, over long periods of time, and are primarily driven by seniority.

People are not brought in from the outside, and there are no "stars" who are leapfrogged over several levels of management. Like so much of Japan's contemporary management style, this is not new. There is evidence of it as early as 1830 in the thriving textile industry, where the following structured career path existed:

AGE	RANK
12–18	Boy worker (*kodomo*)
19–21	Assistant worker (*koeki*)
22–30	Young fellow (*wakamono*)
31–38	Assistant manager (*fukushihai*)
39–50	Manager (*shihai*)
51 +	Retired worker (*inkyo*)

Increases in both job responsibilities and salary came with each advancement in rank, which was in turn a function of age. Little has changed today: it is still essentially a rule that rank must be equated to age.

The 51 + -aged "Retired worker" warrants a special note. To be fifty-one years old in 1830 was already pushing the odds of life expectancy. But if the man was still physically strong and mentally alert—a Japanese George Burns of the early nineteenth century—there were two options. If he was truly outstanding and capable, he might continue with the firm in some respected advisory or consulting capacity. If he was less capable, he might be posted to an affiliated smaller post at reduced pay.

His nearly exact counterpart is seen today. Normal retirement is at age fifty-five—although that is edging upward since Japan's life expectancy leads the world and the nation continues to "gray" at a rate even faster than America. But even with two to four years severance pay and a vaultful of saved money, the fifty-five-year-old retired salaryman generally continues to work . . . half of the men over sixty-five are still doing so. If he is a man of great achievement, he remains with his firm in a very senior position and may continue to be promoted well into his sixties and even seventies. Otherwise he may be transferred, at reduced pay, to one of the second-tier companies within the *keiretsu* family. The retiree who opts to continue to work then is able to maintain a source of income and the *keiretsu* family benefits from his years of experience.

Another characteristic of this seniority-based system is the slow pace of promotions.

SLOW PROMOTIONS: THE BEAUTY CONTEST

The Japanese approach to promotion is a beauty contest . . . with a twist. The twist is the time factor. The contest is a protracted one, and winners are not announced for as much as a quarter of a century. Promotions are slow, based primarily upon seniority until candidates reach the higher management levels in their mid- to late forties; at that time, merit does become an important factor and the "winners" begin to be named. Until then, everyone is kept in the race. Each candidate continues to run hard with his vision of achieving senior manager levels. There is harmony and camaraderie among the group members as they share the travails of the challenge—rather similar to that of young beauty pageant contenders. There is a limited sense of one against another. This is in stark contrast to the typical American corporate environment, in which "superstars" or "fast-trackers" are identified quite early, often in their mid- to late twenties, leaving the vast majority of the work force—perhaps a little sullenly or even jealously—to work out their years with the firm. The Japanese system maintains a group harmony (*wa*) as well as individual motivation.

It also contributes to the well-known long-term planning perspective and makes for far better decisions. There is no inclination for an individual, whether consciously or subconsciously, to champion a project with enormous short-run benefits but heavy long-term costs. Too often in an American company, a project or an action may yield very positive immediate results. The project leader is heralded and promoted. Only several years later is it discovered that the action has had terrible repercussions. By this time our hero or heroine has moved ever upward, always a step or two ahead of his or her wake. In the Japanese firm it does not pay for an individual to seek short-run Ponzi game strategies because he will still be there when the bills come due.

MENTORS

Throughout much of Japanese society, men have or strive to have a senior mentor to help them cope with life's social, economic, and emotional vicissitudes. The senior might be an older relative, corporate superior, or leader in a political clique.

This is seen inside the corporation, where it is a direct result of the seniority-based system. Such a relationship is referred to as the *oyabun-kobun*, literally, "father-child role." The *oyabun* guides the younger man through his career by providing him with counsel and interceding for him among senior management. The responsibility of the senior, or "godfather," goes beyond the workplace to include personal matters of health, finance, and marriage. In return, the junior, or *kobun*, gives his unswerving loyalty.

No section chief refuses to teach his subsection chief out of fear that he might ultimately lose his job to him, since promotions are based solely upon seniority. Conversely, the junior does not attempt to upstage his senior out of a Confucian respect and honor for age and elders; the senior in return has to acquire virtues worthy of respect.

No senior needs to feel threatened by any *Wunderkind* who reports to him. Indeed, he is pleased to have the outstanding younger man in his organization because the performance of the unit is improved.

SUMMARY

The Japanese seniority system drives the promotion process and makes possible an effective mentor system, with a healthy symbiotic working relationship between juniors and seniors. The juniors are patient, knowing that they have much to learn and that their turn will ultimately come. Merit-oriented promotions do not really begin until a candidate's mid-forties; until then, promotions are slow and based upon seniority. The "class of '92" will be promoted as a group until perhaps the year 2114 or so. No superstars are identified early in the race, and motivation and harmony within the entire organization remain high.

Japan's seniority system is based upon hundreds of years of Buddhist and Confucian tradition of respect for elders. It has survived the test of time. Like so much of Japanese management style, it is a reflection of national culture.

SENIORITY . . . FOR THE YANKEE SAMURAI

We have seen that the Japanese approach to hiring, training, job rotation, and the human resources department is measurably different in Japan compared to that practiced among the Yankee Samurai. How about the issue of seniority?

Seniority

Statement	C	P	J
1. Promotions are relatively slow in coming.	3.3	3.2	5
2. Manager's performance is evaluated over five to ten years.	2.6	2.5	5
3. Seniority is more important than merit in determining promotions.	2.6	2.7	5
4. People are seldom hired from outside and placed in senior positions.	2.5	2.8	5
5. Many people here seem to have mentors to help them.	3.2	3.1	4

The earlier pattern remains intact. There is a lack of statistical significance between the C and P values, and a large gap between those figures and the theoretical J values. The Yankee Samurai overall do not see a seniority system like that practiced in Japan; what they do experience is little different from the situation in American firms.

The average figures, though, hide the fact that about one third of the firms did practice the seniority system but were balanced by the others that did not. This will become more clear in the interviews.

The interview responses also helped to identify what appears to be a process in transition. About one third of the firms use seniority as the primary factor in promotion. Americans often resist, preferring merit to be the decisive factor, and demanding formal annual performance reviews; several firms have recently installed them.

Another one third of the firms tend to be merit-oriented, with the remainder using a mix of both seniority and merit. It is toward that mix that the process now seems to be moving.

SENIORITY: THE DECISIVE FACTOR

In an interview on a rainy Saturday morning in a virtually empty office building, the chain-smoking division accounting manager spoke of the promotion system at his electronics company: "It's a sore point with me that people that have been here for some time are paid more regardless of whether they are contributing more. That is probably typically Japanese."

The young trading coordinator also talked of the fact that she did not like her firm's seniority-based promotion system:

> There is no question but that promotions are based upon seniority. That's one of the frustrating things for me. It doesn't matter how well I perform. If someone down the hall was hired two days before I was, even though he wasn't doing anything, he would still be promoted before me.

The assistant and secretary to the general manager of a powerful trading company confirmed that the Japanese prefer the seniority emphasis:

> Promotions are generally based upon seniority. That is because the Japanese feel most comfortable with that approach.
>
> It is extremely rare for a younger person to be promoted over an older person.

The Japanese-American assistant manager of administrative planning indicated that his firm uses a seniority-driven system, but that it leads to increased employee turnover:

> Seniority is a major factor in promotions. It is difficult to promote someone strictly on merit. The normal tendency is to consider other employees who have been with the firm for a similar length of time and compare their abilities.
>
> This has frequently resulted in our losing some good people because the process takes so long and they do not have the patience to wait.

The Canadian-born director of human resources with a small electronics firm is a relatively young man, who only recently graduated from one of the local state universities. He noted the innate difficulty the Japanese have in identifying outstanding performers:

> The Japanese have a philosophy that everyone in their department is outstanding. They cannot distinguish. They do not want to identify someone as being better than another. They say it's impossible, so they rely on the seniority system for promotions.

MERIT: THE DECISIVE FACTOR

Many of the Japanese firms, about one third, have apparently succumbed to the more typical American approach of a merit orientation. That is not surprising given the unhappiness voiced by many of the Yankee Samurai above who endure the seniority system.

The giant auto firm's product information manager says, "From what I have seen, seniority has very little to do with promotions. Last year, one individual in our group received a raise of 2 percent while another got 8 percent. That never would have happened in Japan."

The vice president and head auditor of a major bank in his late thirties with eight years of seniority says:

> Among the Japanese staff, promotions are almost always based upon seniority; it's like a labor union. Individuals take positions, even if they are not qualified, because it is their turn.
>
> With the Americans, any promotions are based much more upon merit.

The same point is made by a senior vice president from a different bank:

> Promotions are based far more on merit than seniority. That is different than it is for the Japanese staff.
>
> Our bank is totally American from that standpoint. I want the best person for the job in a particular position; he will not necessarily be the one who has been here the longest.

TRANSITION

The policy of seniority rather than merit as a criterion for promotion appears to be in transition toward a mix of both factors. About a third of the Yankee Samurai responses were in that category.

The credit manager for a major trading company observed that "promotions are supposed to be based upon merit rather than seniority. But it is difficult for the Japanese to get away entirely from the principle of seniority. That is being grappled with and will take time, although things are changing."

Another example of transition was voiced by the office services supervisor, who has been with his firm for about eleven years: "Promotions now tend to be a mix of both seniority and merit, but leaning a little more toward merit. That is a shift from when I first came here."

Finally, a sign of changing times was indicated by the general affairs associate of a major trading company. He is a Japanese-American who has been with his company for over twenty years. He sees a weakening seniority system and he doesn't like it: "Promotions have been based largely on seniority, but lately the new college graduates coming into the firm are being evaluated much more on merit [*shakes his head disgustedly*]."

Mentoring

Mentors are a commonplace feature of management style in Japan, and directly related to the seniority system. But with only a few exceptions, they were unknown among the Yankee Samurai. The mentoring relationships that do develop from time to time are little different from what commonly occurs in U.S. firms. Some representative responses follow.

The mobile radio division director of marketing did observe mentoring—among the Japanese: "There is a mentoring program among the Japanese, but I have not seen it with Americans." Describing a situation similar to that in a typical American company, the customer services representative of a successful electronics firm commented: "There are a few people who I deal with that are high-ups who give me some insight; that's about it. This is very informal and depends upon who you know."

The national manager of human resources noted, "You are damn lucky if you find a mentor. There are a few people who have them, and have succeeded because of that. But it is an exception; there is no planned program to do that." And the electronics firm's office services supervisor reflected: "If there is a formal mentor program, then I wonder where mine is [*smiles*]."

The bank vice president and head auditor suggested that the Japanese practice of job rotation was one reason why there was little mentoring: "There is no formal mentor program, but sometimes people do just hit if off together and a good relationship develops. But it is hard to build these relationships because the Japanese continue to rotate in and out of the country."

The director of human resources has been with her electronics firm for three years. While two other Yankee Samurai did speak of a special monitoring program for a group of manager trainees, she was the only one who indicated that a broader two-way effort was being made:

> We are reviewing the possibility of an American mentor system for the Japanese who have just come to the United States. And we will be assigning a Japanese mentor to work with Americans enrolled in a—just-introduced—Japanese-language program.

SUMMARY

For the Yankee Samurai the Japanese approach to promotions, seniority, and mentors was not broadly evident. The Americans usually saw all of these things practiced "across the aisle" among the Japanese. Here, again, cultures were in conflict.

The roughly one third of the respondents who did speak of seniority as the driving factor in their firms often indicated an unhappiness with it. Newly hired younger employees were especially impatient with the process. Most wanted a highly structured annual merit review to serve as the basis for determining salaries and promotions. They complained that without such a process, when they did ask their Japanese seniors about their performance, they invariably were told, "Fine, Thompson-san, fine." The Yankee Samurai were as uncomfortable with this ambiguity as they were about the slow pace of promotion. Many firms were experiencing a higher turnover as a result.

The inability of the Yankee Samurai to "read" their Japanese managers regarding their own performance is also culturally based. In Japan, amongst the Japanese, feelings and impressions are communicated subtly and naturally, often without a spoken word. If you have lived with someone for a long time, as the Japanese salarymen do with one another, you understand this. You "sense" when your wife, or husband, or child has a problem. You finish one another's sentences and communicate without words. The Yankee Samurai and Japanese expatriates do not have that ability with one another—the cultural chasm is too great. The result is that the Japanese are forever complaining that the Americans do not know what to do and have to be told everything.

The Confucian and Buddhist respect for age is not prevalent in the youth-oriented culture of the United States. Yet this is a critical cultural base upon which the seniority system is built. Young American MBAs often lack a sense of loyalty to their seniors, and for that matter to their firms, and do not have the patience to wait. The American Management Association surveys indicate the substantial fear that many managers have of their young subordinates. Without a seniority system, that fear is often justified.

An effective mentor system is also difficult to sustain because of existing gender and cultural gaps between the Japanese and Yankee Samurai. Nor does the continued rotation of the Japanese help.

For largely cultural reasons, then, the seniority system appears not to work well in the United States. The Japanese transplants have come to recognize this and are moving toward a mix of seniority and merit in their promotion and compensation.

SALARY AND BENEFITS ... IN JAPAN

Fundamental to satisfying the needs of the Whole Man is providing him with security—economic security. What are the characteristics of Japanese company salary and benefits policies designed to do that?

The era of low salaries in Japan that began in the post-World War II period ended well over a decade ago. Today, white-collar workers gross incomes are actually somewhat higher in Japan than America. However, with Japan's high taxes—along with Sweden and Australia, the most progressive in the world—and high cost of living, especially for food and housing, the overall edge shifts slightly to the American worker. The age and wage profiles in the two countries are similar, rising gradually for workers in their early twenties and peaking in the mid-fifties. There is then a marked similarity in salary between workers in America and Japan, at least until you reach the executive suites.

TOP EXECUTIVE SALARIES

A conspicuous difference in the compensation practices between the two countries is found at the senior management level. In Japan, salary differentials between entry-level personnel and the topmost levels of management are no more than a factor of 5 to 15; they are 50 to 100 and beyond in America.

Japanese executives go without stock options, complex deferred-income packages, and the rich array of golden parachutes found in American firms. Even allowing for generous entertainment expense accounts, company cars, and subsidized housing in Japan, their American counterparts make substantially more. Top American CEO salaries in 1990 averaged $1.4 million, and in 1991 they approached $2 million. That was almost ninety times the entry-level salary for factory workers. Stephen Ross of Time-Warner topped the American CEO "Get what you can" derby, with $78.2 million in 1990. That was more than the *combined* salaries of the CEOs of Toyota, Nissan, Honda, Mitsubishi Heavy Industries, Sharp, Sanyo Electric, NEC, Fujitsu, Panasonic, JAL, Canon, Hitachi, Toshiba, Isuzu, Yamaha,

Nippon Steel, DKB, Hochiki, and dozens more! Is Mr. Ross worth more than the CEOs of the one hundred largest Japanese companies combined? With all due respect to him and the majority of other *Fortune* 500 CEOs who have a cozy relationship with their "independent" board of directors that determine their salaries . . . does this make any sense at all? What is more, over the 1980s CEO salaries rose three times faster than those of ordinary workers, and studies have consistently shown little or no correlation between company performance and CEO salary. The implications of this for worker morale and a company's sense of family will be considered in the final chapter.

BONUS

A unique characteristic of the Japanese firms' compensation system is that as much as one third of the total comes in the form of semi-annual or annual bonuses, which are generally a function of profitability.

This is ideal for the firm. It provides a hedge against an economic downturn, and can be viewed as a kind of corporate dividend to employees that may or may not be paid, depending upon the firm's performance. A second benefit is that it keeps funds in the corporate till, where they can be earning interest, for a longer period of time. From the company standpoint, it can be viewed as deferred income.

Employees tend to be pleased with the system, viewing the bonus as naively as Americans perceive their IRS refund check . . . something for nothing. The scene is played out in homes all across America in March, April, and May every year: a husband opens his mailbox and pulls free from the piles of junk mail a thin, official-looking envelope. Guessing its contents, he rips it open and rushes inside to share the news with his wife. "Honey, look what just came in the mail, a check from the government for $1,173.24. This is great! Tell the kids our summer trip to Disneyland is on." Never mind that the check is a meager return for the perhaps $24,000 of payroll deductions that invisibly flowed to Washington the previous year. This is how the Japanese view their bonus.

There is a decided national benefit to the Japanese bonus system as well. Japanese family budgets tend to be geared to the weekly paychecks. Bonus money generally finds its way into savings. This factor contributes to Japan's estimated 17 percent personal savings rate, compared to 4 percent in the United States.

BENEFITS

Family and group orientation are basic to Japanese management style. One manifestation of this are the almost paternalistic benefits provided to the employee. In addition to the medical, dental, and life insurance coverage familiar to Americans, a myriad of other benefits are available—including housing subsidies, commuting allowances, and access to vacation facilities; a few firms have even begun to build retirement communities.

With housing prices rapidly climbing out of reach in the Tokyo environs, Toshiba is constructing 2,700 apartments and 1,800 houses for its newly hired employees. Most firms provide subsidized housing for single employees and low-interest home loans for older married men. One company, in labor-short Japan, entices potential new young employees by advertising: "We will have you in your own home by the time you are thirty-five." Mitsubishi Electric is taking another tack by providing its top managers with bullet train passes that cost up to $1,000 a month. The trains, which travel at 170 mph, can swiftly reach new housing in regions north and southwest of Tokyo some 125 miles or even further away.

Pensions are provided at the conventional retirement age (fifty-five) in the form of lump-sum payments of two to four years annual salary. As we have seen, post-retirement opportunities are also frequently available, to work in a reduced capacity either with the parent firm or with one of the *keiretsu* subsidiary firms.

SUMMARY

The Japanese firms' compensation policies are characterized by very generous benefits, along with good salaries of which bonuses are a large part. With the exception of the executive ranks, the age and wage profiles look very similar to those in America, peaking in the early to mid-fifties. Executive salaries are small in comparison to those received by American CEOs. Perquisites including lush entertainment accounts, close the Grand Canyonlike gap a little, but only a little.

SALARY AND BENEFITS . . . FOR THE YANKEE SAMURAI

Now how about our Yankee Samurai? We begin as always with some numbers.

Salary and Benefits

Statement	C	P	J
1. A significant percentage of annual compensation comes in the form of a bonus.	2.8*	2.4	5
2. The firm has a salary and benefit package that is far above average.	2.8	2.8	3

This is pretty telling. The Japanese firms do tend to provide bonuses to a greater extent than corresponding American firms—note the * in statement 1, indicating statistical significance. At the same time, the 2.8 figure is less than the neutral 3.0. It will become evident in the interview responses that not all firms pay the bonus, and those that do make relatively small payments by Japanese standards.

The response to the second statement clearly indicates that the way the Yankee Samurai are compensated differs little from corresponding American firms, or for that matter corresponding firms in Japan.

These average figures, however, camouflage wide variations in company-to-company policy, as the interview responses below make clear.

POOR SALARIES AND BENEFITS

There was little consistency among companies in terms of salary and benefits policies. Roughly a quarter of them, as perceived by their Yankee Samurai, had poor salaries and poor benefits. The electronics firm's laser printer manager commented: "I would have to say that wages and benefits are below the average by quite a bit. There is an overall disgruntlement and a lot of turnover as a result." Another electronics firm's vice president of marketing noted: "We are behind our competition in the computer industry in terms of compensation. Our policy has been to provide average compensation and above-average opportunity, working conditions, and security [except that the firm recently had layoffs]."

The mid-sized auto firm's marketing vice president noted that

> Initially we thought wages were very generous. But the Japanese, perhaps out of naivete, overdid it in bonuses. We had very little overhead and got off to a pretty good start. Money, in the form of bonuses, was just poured on us.

Then, toward the mid-eighties, things got tough. Costs went up and profit margins went down. We went from almost corporate indulgence to a near curtailment. That is where we still are, and there is much disenchantment.

A Japanese-American loan officer at one of the major Japanese banks commented:

The pay and benefits here is on the low end. People who have friends working for other banks get feedback indicating that we may be the lowest paid. This is a large factor in explaining employee turnover.

They also tend to bring in people at too low a level. College graduates are brought in as first-level clerks [common in Japan]. So both pay and job level are too low, and people leave. Management is concerned about the turnover but seems unable to do anything about it.

GOOD BENEFITS AND POOR-TO-AVERAGE SALARIES

Roughly half of the Yankee Samurai agreed with the Chinese-American trading coordinator that benefits were very good, but that salaries were little more than average at best: "As with any Japanese firm, the benefits are excellent; the Japanese are hailed for their benefits. The pay, however, is less than desired. "I don't think that any of us are compensated very well." A somewhat similar situation was described by the electronics firm's human resources manager: "Our benefits package is Cadillac but not complete because we don't have a 401K plan. The wages are about industry average."

This emerges as a rather common theme. Here it is again from an accounting supervisor at a large electronics company: "The firm has a very good benefits package, and the wages, which have not been very good, are slightly better than they were two or three years ago."

The automobile firm's marketing manager made a similar point: "The wages and benefits are competitive, but not exceptional. I cannot attract people here on the basis that we pay a lot." The trading coordinator for one of the major trading companies added:

Some benefits are pretty good, but the wages are low. I have gone round and round with them on that. I do business that brings in hundreds of thousands of dollars in commissions, but they refuse to pay a percentage. It doesn't matter how successful I am because I am salaried.

GOOD BENEFITS AND AVERAGE-TO-BETTER SALARIES

Perhaps 25 percent of the Yankee Samurai were very pleased with their firm's salary and benefits policy. The airline sales manager was one of them who felt that:

> The wages and benefits package is very good indeed. We are not the best but are near the top. The Japanese are not leaders in this, but neither are they followers. They like to look at the industry as a whole and then take a position between the middle and the top.

The point is made again by the electronics firm's director of marketing: "The salaries and benefits are above average for the industry."

Believing his firm to be at the high end of wages and benefits was the vice president of an auto company's trading operation. "The firm's wages and benefits package is among the best." Agreeing with him was the young assistant cashier with one of Japan's largest banks: "The wages and benefits are excellent. I would never be making as much as I am here if I were still at a major American bank. I certainly would not have learned as much or had as much responsibility."

The electronics firm's human resources director was also pleased:

> I think that our wages and benefits would put us in the top 10 percent of the local community. We have a strong, all-encompassing, benefits package that is virtually all paid for by the company. Our wages tend to be among the top 25 percent with the hourly people and about the 50 percent level for the management people.

BONUS

Annual bonuses in Japan can run to 30 percent of total compensation. The Yankee Samurai did not see bonuses of that magnitude; more than half saw no bonus at all, but those that did were pleased. The electronics firm's manager of cellular radios was one of them: "The bonus is a great thing. It amounts to about 5 percent of the total salary. Everybody likes the idea." The trading company's deputy division manager commented, "I wish we had the Japanese-style bonus, but we don't. Around Thanksgiving, the nonexempt employees get a nominal gift, although they cannot always be counted upon. The maximum amount ever involved is one month's salary."

The Chinese-American trading company account representative noted: "I have heard that the Japanese staff received bonuses in their bank accounts. But that is only hearsay. Nothing was distributed to us [Americans]. I wish it was, because it would be a great thing."

An auto firm's human resources manager indicated that his firm was adopting a new bonus system:

> We are moving toward a true bonus system, where you are rewarded for your performance. In the past it was simply a deferred compensation program based upon the company's performance. The amount, depending upon your level, ranges anywhere from 5 to 40 percent of your base income.

Changes in an electronic firm's bonus plan were described by the company's human resources manager:

> In the past, we had the Christmas gift program, which was very Japanese. Everyone in the company received it, based on years of service; there were no performance criteria at all. We also had a mid-year gift, similarly based on seniority. But in the recent employee survey there were major complaints about this approach. There was no recognition of outstanding performance.
>
> We are introducing a revised program in which payment is based upon teamwork criteria. That is, how effective a team player is the individual?

The assistant manager of administrative planning is a Japanese-American who noted that "there is an end-of-year bonus program that is largely based upon merit. It averages about 10 percent of annual income."

An auto firm's vice president commented:

> The managers get a bonus that is a function of their grade. It is not like Japan, where you receive three or four months of your annual salary as a bonus, although it is getting close to it. The nonmanagers get a certain fixed bonus amount at Christmas time.

SUMMARY

Depending upon the firm, the Yankee Samurai experience a range of salary and benefits packages. With only a few exceptions, however, the Japanese companies did provide better-than-average benefits. Although it is difficult to quantify, overall the Japanese firms' benefits in the United States place them in the top 50 percent industrywide and they paid a salary that puts them somewhere in the 25th to 75th percentile.

No Japanese firm provides its Yankee Samurai with a bonus system like that in Japan, where the bonus accounts for as much as 25 percent of total salary. Some of the firms do have modestly paying systems, which are well received by the Yankee Samurai. A small number of companies are moving toward introducing the Japanese-style system.

Overall, then, the Yankee Samurai are by no means shortchanged in terms of having their basic economic needs met. Indeed, although it did not emerge in the interviews, even for the most senior-level Americans, while their salaries are generally lower than for their counterparts in American companies, they often are making considerably more than the Japanese managers they report to.

LIFETIME EMPLOYMENT . . . IN JAPAN

In the early and mid-1980s, Japan's textile, steel, petrochemical, and shipbuilding industries were floundering. Japanese firms were being driven from the international marketplace by low-cost competitors in South Korea, Brazil, and China. The financial losses were enormous. Today, all of those industries are thriving.

The turnaround was achieved in archetypical Japanese fashion. Under the guidance of the Ministry of International Trade and Industry (MITI), industry was "rationalized": overcapacity was eliminated and market share allocated. Some of the companies diversified into related industries. Financial needs were met with the help of cooperating bankers and shareholders. Most importantly, workers were *not* for the most part laid off, but rather were retrained and reassigned.

Unlike an American firm, where employees are generally viewed as little more than commodities that are set aside when no longer needed, the Japanese companies with their tacit lifetime employment contract do everything possible to nurture this precious asset. So much of Japanese management style follows as a direct result of this.

The value placed upon the employee translates into the great authority and influence of the human resources department. There is less resistance to change and technology because workers are assured that their jobs are not at stake. Training and job rotation become economically feasible. The seniority system works because younger people know that ultimately their turn will come. Cooperative company unions become possible since one of the most basic concerns for workers is job stability. A harmonious work environment is more likely since individual objections have to be resolved; there is nowhere else to go. Lifetime employment creates a stable work force, with a continuity of organization memory. That memory in turn facilitates the planning, control, and decision process. Finally, there is adequate time to develop a sense of family, and to inculcate the firm's mission and credo among its members.

LIFETIME EMPLOYMENT . . . FOR THE YANKEE SAMURAI

The centerpiece of the "Whole Man" philosophy is lifetime employment. Without it, much of the entire structure collapses. This raises the fundamental question: Do our Yankee Samurai enjoy lifetime employment?

Lifetime Employment

Statement	C	P	J
1. People stay alert to job opportunities outside the company.	3.5	3.6	1
2. We have not had layoffs and employment is generally understood to be for life.	2.7*	2.1	5

Just these few numbers tell a story by themselves. There are two sides to lifetime employment. One is that the firm offers it to the employee; the other is that the employee accepts it, making the commitment to stay with the firm for life. The response to statement 1 makes clear that the Yankee Samurai are not terribly interested in lifetime employment. They are reading the Sunday want-ads and taking calls from head-hunting firms; they have their eye out for other opportunities virtually to the same extent as if they were working for an American firm (3.5 and 3.6 are statistically indistinguishable). Most of the current crop of America's corporate employees recognize that for years, in spite of management rhetoric, their firms have treated them like little more than commodities. Now they have come to treat their firms the same way; they feel no long-term commitment. This holds for many of the Yankee Samurai, too.

The second response indicates that employment is far more stable with the Japanese firms than at corresponding American firms (the asterisk indicates statistical significance), but it is by no means for life. The 2.7 score is not even at the neutral 3.0 level, and the Yankee Samurai have experienced the trauma of layoffs in their firms.

The corresponding interview results told largely the same story: there is essentially no firm in which lifetime employment is offered to employees *and* the employees agree to commit themselves for life. The responses were, however, split roughly 60:40. The 60 percent felt that there unquestionably was no lifetime employment, while the 40 percent believed that some aspects at least were in place. Many people commented that when their firms first began to operate in the United States, lifetime employment was the rule, but the policy has been changed over time.

No, But . . .

Many of the Yankee Samurai were employed by firms where there was no lifetime employment per se, but still they found that the Japanese worked very hard at keeping people. Others observed that implicit pressures were introduced to encourage people to leave

The vice president and corporate secretary of a very successful automobile firm said:

> Is there lifetime employment here? I doubt it. People assume that they are here for a lifetime and that the firm does not fire except in extreme cases. However, people might be transferred to another area and eventually get the message and leave.

The Hawaiian-born Japanese-American associate trader is a young man in his mid-twenties. He described the situation at his bank this way:

> From what I heard the Japanese really don't like to terminate anyone, but they can make your life miserable until you quit.
> We have a high turnover rate; part of the problem is the wages, which are low, although the benefits are excellent. We also lose a lot of clerk-level people; I guess there is more work and responsibility than they can handle.

The customer services assistant for a large trading company has been with his firm for less than a year:

> I have heard that there is lifetime employment here. There are advantages and disadvantages. Security is an obvious advantage. On the other hand, people may not be challenged enough to work hard. I see this and I also see people become frustrated and leave.

The deputy division manager who had spent time in Japan commented:

I have never had anyone say to me that you have a job for life. I would not want to be tied down like that.

There is a general feeling that if you do not do anything really wrong, you are not likely to be fired. Looking around the office, that is generally true. People do get fired but very rarely. To a certain extent I would like to see a little more critical review of employees.

Ouchi's [Bill Ouchi, author of *Theory* Z] entire premise is based upon lifetime employment, but that does not exist in the United States. We are a product of instant gratification; I don't think we know what it is to sacrifice, and so people leave unless their immediate demands are met.

The auto firm's manager of distribution said:

When I joined the firm in 1970, lifetime employment was the ironclad rule, but I think that is changing.

I see people moving from one Japanese firm to another. That was absolutely unacceptable twenty years ago.

We have had to let people go, but as a corporate philosophy we really don't like to do it; it is a last resort.

The corporate marketing manager for another auto firm thought that his company also showed a strong reluctance to let people go:

No one tells you that you have a job for life. Still, when I first came here, I found some dead wood that had been laying around for a long time.

There was one individual who, in my opinion, was worthless. He had been with the firm for fifteen years. I wanted to find a way to get him out of the company. But the Japanese wanted to work with him. We did reduce his responsibilities. He is still here today and doing okay. I learned a lot from that experience and now agree with the policy of finding a place where people can contribute . . . so long as you don't have too many like that.

The Japanese do seem to make an effort to keep people. The anecdote above confirmed this. So, too, does the comment from the ex-high school football star who is now director of material controls for a major electronics firm:

I have had the pleasure, or displeasure, of firing a few people for nonperformance since I have been here. But I have never worked for a company that is more willing to give people a chance to get themselves out of trouble. People are given the extra mile.

In Japan, if someone is not performing, they are moved off to what is called a "window" job, where the individual just reads the newspapers all day. Or he might be sent to a subsidiary.

Finally, several people believed that the Japanese would like to have lifetime employment among the Americans and try to keep them aboard, but often fail to do so; Americans too often leave for greener pastures. For example, the young Hispanic cashier noted that "Lifetime employment does not exist here, although the Japanese management encourages it. They would like the Americans to stay for a long time. I know that if I left, it would be very difficult to tell them."

The automobile firm's national manager of human resources made a similar point:

In Japan, there is the idea that an individual comes to the company and stays there for his entire career; that doesn't hold in the United States.

The Japanese here know that the American staff moves around from company to company in pursuit of career goals. It's not always easy for them to accept that, but they are trying at least to understand it.

There is not a lifetime employment situation here, but we do try to create an environment that will encourage the Americans to stay.

NONE

Most of the other Yankee Samurai saw no lifetime employment policy at all. In fact, in order to guard against lawsuits from people who might be terminated, but who had been under the impression that they were hired for life, many firms have made their nonlifetime employment policy very clear. The large auto firm's corporate employment manager indicated that this was true at his company:

There is no lifetime employment here. We make an effort to tell people that. Everything has been taken out of our literature that would lead someone to believe otherwise.

There is a disclaimer on our application forms and in our offer letters making that clear. In bold type the language says, "**Employment with the firm can be terminated by either you or the company**."

When I first started here, there was an implication of lifetime employment. But for the last seven years that has not been the case. We are sensitive to this issue.

The assistant general counsel's remarks were a little earthy but incisive: "My response to anyone who thinks there is lifetime employment here is 'bullpucky.' We have 'at will employment,' and make that very clear." The same legal point was repeated by the electronics firm's project manager: "Everyone coming aboard here signs an 'at will' statement indicating that lifetime employment is not expected. The firm can lay people off if that becomes necessary and the employee certainly is free to leave if he chooses."

The trading company's credit management also made mention of the law in commenting that:

there is lifetime employment among the rotating [Japanese] employees. But for the Americans, the situation is different. They [the company] are very careful about that now because there has been some legal action. At one time lifetime employment was implied, but not today.

The young Japanese-American loan officer commented cynically:

There is no lifetime employment here. Nothing is said, but I get the feeling that they would like to bring you in with little experience to be trained for your job. Then after three to five years it seems as though you are expected to leave. I don't know why that is. Perhaps it is keeping down costs. Or maybe it is a control factor; if you get too high, you will know more and be harder to control.

The manager of computer data network resources is a quiet, soft-spoken man in his late thirties. He says that there has been tremendous turnover the last few years. "No one thinks lifetime employment exists here."

The electronics firm's director of marketing is a U.C. Berkeley MBA whose experience showed that:

While there is lifetime employment for the parent in Japan, there is not lifetime employment for the American subsidiary—at least for the Americans. It is very different here. We are hired to do a job, and if that cannot be done, people leave with no tears shed on either side, even if that means layoffs. [Federal courts have ruled that the Japanese are in their right to lay off Americans while keeping expatriates on the payroll of American subsidiaries. The same principle holds for American firms operating in Japan.]

SUMMARY

Perhaps the most fundamental characteristic of Japanese management style is the emphasis placed upon the "Whole Man." Fundamental to that in turn, is lifetime employment. Everything else flows from it: intensive hiring of youthful cadres, on-the-job training, the seniority system, mentors, implicit controls, imbuing of company culture and a sense of family, consensus decision making, company unions, employee willingness to accept new technology, employee loyalty, a more harmonious workplace, and a long-term planning perspective. Not only does each of these follow from lifetime employment, but each facet is related in some way to every other. They combine to form the entire management style. Remove lifetime employment and much of the rest simply collapses.

Earlier on, when we applied the acid test of how much value the Japanese firm places in their Yankee Samurai by how strong the human resources department was, the Japanese firms failed. Those departments were surprisingly weak. Lifetime employment is another test. Do the firms so value the American employee that he or she will never be let go? That is after all the case for the salaryman in Japan, as well as for the expatriates in the United States. The answer to the question is somewhat mixed.

In general, the Yankee Samurai do not have a job for life. But this is not necessarily the choice of the Japanese. Indeed, many firms sought to keep their Americans, who for one reason or another decided to leave. Even in those cases where there have been layoffs or firings, there is often a strong reluctance on the part of the firms to do so. The Japanese firms in the United States are much more sensitive to this than corresponding American companies. An American can find more employment stability with a Japanese firm than with a U.S. firm, even though it may not necessarily mean a job for life.

WOMEN AND MINORITIES ... IN JAPAN

WOMEN

In spite of warnings in an earlier chapter, some readers may have become a little nettled by now at the constant use of male-designated terms, such as "salaryman" or "salesman," in describing the Japanese workplace. If so, I did not mean to offend, but that is the reality. The Japanese workplace is *otoko no shakai*, "a man's world." While women compromise some 40 percent of the labor force, they occupy almost none of the influential positions. The women are a part, but not really a part, of the major corporation. They generally enter the job market immediately after completing their education and work only until they marry, or at the latest have their first child. Older married women who return to work after their children have grown fill largely unskilled and nonmanagerial positions.

Women at Nomura, the world's largest security investment firm, are somewhat typical. The personnel department recruits only the most attractive, single, and demure "office ladies" or "Nomura girls." Young women directly out of high school or two-year colleges are hired as sales assistants and are much preferred to four-year college graduates, who are viewed as poor investments. The OLs (sobriquet for "office lady") are trained in smiling, bowing, walking (with the back straight and small steps), answering phones (always on the first ring and smile while you talk), and making tea. After being fitted for slightly coquettish blue and white uniforms, they spend their years greeting visitors, working elevators, fixing tea and coffee, and doing light secretarial work until they marry. A little over 40 percent of the "Nomura girls" will marry a "Nomura man," with initial introductions made by the firm's own marriage brokerage service. Such services are common in many of the larger firms.

Marriage and family are of the highest priority for most Japanese young women. Indeed, if they are not married by age twenty-six, they become "Christmas cake." What do you do with Christmas cake on December 26? You toss it out; it is old, stale, and beyond use.

Under some international pressure, in 1986 Japan did pass an equal employment law, but it has largely gathered dust; there is no penalty for lawbreakers. Women themselves are not flocking to the equal employment banner. For the most part they do not see much in a man's life to envy, and they believe that home and the family responsibilities of raising children, handling all finances, and caring for elderly parents and in-laws are both important and fulfilling. No woman apologizes for being "just a housewife." The home is her private domain and run like a thinly disguised matriarchy. The salaryman is often little more than a nocturnal border, who turns over his entire paycheck and receives a weekly allowance in return from his purse-string-holding wife. The raising of the children—the pride of Japan—is left largely to her.

The quite separate roles of men and women will be looked at in more depth later, but it should be clear even from the brief comments here that a Japanese salaryman, nurtured in Japan and arriving in America for the first time, undergoes severe Future Schock in encountering a confident and well-educated woman MBA.

MINORITIES

The question of minorities in Japanese management style is basically a nonissue. Less than 1 percent of the population is of Korean ancestry; even though most of these people have been in Japan for generations, they have not been assimilated into the larger culture and are still required to hold a Korean passport and undergo fingerprinting.

Another minority group numbering perhaps 1 million are the so-called "unclean people," or *burakumin*, who are the descendants of butchers, leatherworkers, and gravediggers. They are somewhat akin to India's "untouchables" and remain largely an outcast community. It is all but impossible to marry outside of the group, even though individual *burakumin* have absolutely no discernible physical differences from other Japanese. Painstakingly accurate genealogical records are kept to avoid intermarriage.

There is also prejudice against those of Ainu lineage. Some anthropologists believe that these people, with their strong Caucasian features (including heavy beards), may have been the first to occupy Japan. They are found largely in the northernmost parts of the country, in the Kurile Islands and the northern part of Hokkaido. The Japanese view the Ainu much as Americans view Native Indians. While Americans pursued their "manifest destiny" as nineteenth-century conquistadors, moving west and subjugating Native Indians in the process, the Japanese, centuries ago, moved north against the Ainu with the same objective and the same result. The fate of the Ainu is, at best, to live on the outermost fringes of a larger society that has leaped technologically infinitely beyond their reach. They are no part of Japan Inc.

In addition to the Korean-Japanese, *burakumin*, and Ainu, there are a mix of Okinawans, Taiwanese, Filipino, Chinese, and other nationals who combine to total at most a few hundred thousand. The Japanese have even been very resistant to accepting Vietnamese "boat people," and the few thousand who have come to Japan have been kept largely quarantined from the rest of society. The entire "minority" population of Japan forms well under 3 percent of the total. These minorities play little or no part in the corporate world of the *keiretsu*.

WOMEN AND MINORITIES . . . FOR THE YANKEE SAMURAI

I have had the good fortune of knowing one of Hollywood's most prolific actors, Eddie Albert. I recall him describing to me an almost sure-hit movie plot . . . "the fish out of water." It has dozens of variations: a tough black Chicago cop is assigned to the elegant Beverly Hills Police Department (*Beverly Hills Cop*—Eddie Murphy); a young and beautiful millionairess finds herself traveling cross-country without any money (*It Happened One Night*—Claudette Colbert and Clark Gable); a Kansas farm girl awakes from a deep sleep in a magic land filled with midgets, witches, and talking lions (*Wizard of Oz*—Judy Garland) . . . easily one third of today's films show some variation of this theme: take someone from one background and drop them with no preparation into an entirely different one. It almost always makes for a good story.

Over time, each of us builds a set of automatic responses to new situations that we encounter. Some of these are natural and instinctive, but most are culture-based. We know how to deal with most situations because they have been seen before. We become "nervous" when encountering new situations . . . when we become fish out of water. We don't know how to act or what to say, and generally resort to doing what worked before in a totally different setting. The result can often be a disaster.

This is what the Japanese face in America in their relations with Yankee Samurai women and minorities. Perhaps there is no greater cultural trauma experienced by the Japanese men when they first step onto the tarmac of an American airport than this. The Japanese become fish out of water. If they fall back to natural responses appropriate in Japan, where minorities are essentially ignored and where women play no role in the man's world of business, disaster ensues.

Let's start with some numbers.

Women and Minorities

Statement	C	P	J
1. Minorities and women have considerable opportunities within the firm.	2.7*	3.3	1

There are several conclusions to be drawn here. The asterisk * indicates the statistically significant difference of the Yankee Samurai perception that opportunities for minorities and women are less in Japanese compared to American firms. At the same time, even the 3.3 figure for the American experience is only just above neutral, indicating that American firms also are certainly not thought of as havens of fairness and justice. And finally, the 2.7 figure is pretty far removed from the theoretical J value of 1. So Yankee Samurai women and minorities have vastly more opportunities than their counterparts in Japan, but apparently not as much as their peers at American companies.

To probe a little further, here are the figures for responses to the same statement presented by gender and race.

• VIEW OF MINORITY OPPORTUNITY •

RESPONDING GROUP	C	P
Male Caucasian	2.8	3.3
Female Caucasian	2.6	3.3
Male Black	1.5	2.5
Female Black	2.6	2.6
Male Asian	3.0	2.9
Female Asian	1.8	3.9
Male Hispanic	2.5	3.0
Female Hispanic	3.5	3.3
All females	2.6	3.4
All minorities	2.5	3.2
Overall	2.7	3.3

Female Asians and black males perceived there to be the least opportunity, while Hispanic women and Asian men viewed their opportunities to be better than at corresponding American firms. White and black females held the same views regarding their Japanese employer; and black females believed they were treated no differently than at corresponding American firms. Male Caucasians thought that opportunities for women and minorities were better than the women and minorities themselves thought them to be. Some explanations for all of this emerge from the interviews.

The interview responses split roughly into 20 percent who felt that women and minorities are doing quite well, 30 percent who believed that the performance of women and minorities was somewhat mixed, and 50 percent who thought that women and minorities are not doing well at all. The following are representative responses.

WOMEN AND MINORITIES: DOING QUITE WELL

The national manager of human resources for one of the smaller automobile firms thought that his company "does a good job of trying to meet its commitment to affirmative action. We have quite a few women who have moved into senior management positions. We also have a very good minority representation." A black corporate services supervisor with only a high school education was very happy with her electronics firm. "My husband has been very supportive in my career with this firm. They expect a lot, but the rewards are great. Working here pushes my talents to the limit. My overall experience here has been very favorable."

The middle-aged Hispanic accounts receivables supervisor for a large electronics firm also was extremely pleased with her experience:

> With my limited education, I'm very fortunate to have this job; it's the best I've ever had. The Japanese are always very polite and treat me with respect. Some of my friends say the Japanese are chauvinist, but they [the Japanese] remind me of all the Mexican men that I know and I don't have any problem with that [*laughs*].

The electronics firm's manager of procurement and materials believed that:

> the minorities and women do fine, probably better than most American firms.
>
> The Japanese that are here have a high level of acceptance when having to deal with women. I have not seen any indication of prejudice on the part of the Japanese.

The female communications manager has also had positive experiences with her medical technology firm:

> I've made presentations to the Japanese many times and have always been listened to with respect. This may not be the experience that some woman have had and might be due to the specialized expertise we have. [The Japanese have a financial interest in her firm, which deals with medical systems—an area in which the Japanese are still behind.]

A black accounts payable clerk for a large bank with a few years of college education and five years with her firm felt that:

> so far the experience has been favorable. I am trying to reach beyond what I have learned to be promoted. My husband has been

impressed with the firm's attitude toward employees that does not exist at American firms for which he has worked. There is a family atmosphere here, with each person a part of the team.

A Vietnamese-born Yankee Samurai found that his advanced degrees meant little when applying at American, as opposed to Japanese, firms:

> America is supposed to be a melting pot, but there is discrimination everywhere in the job market. It is deep-rooted and difficult, or impossible, to eradicate. But I am accepted by the Japanese. My family knows how hard I searched to find an appropriate place to work in this great land. Here at [bank name] I feel stable, secure, pride, and comfort.

Finally, the auto firm's vice president of marketing said, "The minorities and women here do quite well. We are located in a community that is heavily Hispanic and there are several women managers."

WOMEN AND MINORITIES: A MIXED PERFORMANCE

Almost a third of the Yankee Samurai felt that while women were doing fine, minorities were not, or that the reverse was true. Some felt that while women and minorities were perhaps not excelling, neither were they being discriminated against. And finally, many saw considerable progress over the years.

Here, for example, is the senior credit officer who commented:

> Minorities and women are doing much better than historically. The Japanese are becoming more Americanized and are starting to understand the issues in the United States. They know they have to adapt to local customs and rules.
>
> I am sure that at one time there was discrimination against minorities and women, but that is changing. The Japanese may not like it, but they are adjusting.

The advanced printer project manager, a recent UCLA engineering graduate, felt that:

> Generally, women do fairly well up to a certain level. [The] Japanese still have a difficult time dealing with women; more so than minorities.
>
> Right now there is a strong push to increase the number of women and minorities in management, but we are still dealing with traditional Japanese.

The electronics company's vice president of marketing, on the other hand, felt that minorities were doing quite well, but that women were having problems:

> Women here do terribly. We are recruiting for a program manager who will have a lot of contact with Japan. I have a woman who is a great candidate for that job, but when I discussed her with the Japanese, while they would not say it, she was not acceptable because of gender.
>
> Minorities are doing okay. There is a black guy from Bermuda who holds a pretty high position. And our Asian minorities are of course all overachievers; we have R&D and repair departments full of them.

The bank customer service representative was a black woman with a few years of college. She says: "There is no management future if you are a woman or minority without a master's degree and a working knowledge of the culture. Otherwise, though, you are treated fine."

The Australian-born senior consultant is in his late sixties and highly respected by the Japanese. His thoughts:

> The question of women and minorities is a tough one. Under American rules they are doing pretty good, probably about the same as at an American firm. But the Japanese believe, like the Germans did years ago, that the woman's place is in the home, not the office.
>
> The company lost two cases in court because Japanese was spoken in a meeting, which the women felt was unfair. Over the years I have come to know the Japanese well enough to be sure that in the long run those kinds of suits won't help the women here. They [Japanese] highly value harmony and have contempt for those who resort to the legal system to resolve differences; it is uncivilized to them.

After a long pause for thought, the electronics firm's legal counsel responded:

> There are women managers and I don't see any serious problems, although there are none who are very high up. There are not too many blacks around here, but I am not aware of any problems. There are a large number of Hispanics and non-Japanese Asians. An effort is definitely being made to maintain racial harmony. The policy of the company is very clear in that respect. But, I don't think we are different from any other company.

The general manager of accessory marketing thought that his electronics firm was doing pretty well:

> We are probably about average regarding minorities and women. I hired the first black for the company. I didn't know what I was doing, I just did it. Then I saw all of the Japanese parading through and looking at this person. However, we ended up having some very serious problems with him. I do have good hiring skills, but I sure blew it on that one; it was pretty bad. It really set things back for a while.
>
> However, since then we have done very much better. I think that the problem with the Japanese not promoting minorities and women in this country is long gone. At least it is in this company.

WOMEN AND MINORITIES: NOT DOING AT ALL WELL

About half of the Yankee Samurai believed that women and minorities were not doing at all well with their firms. One such view was held by the outspoken young Japanese-fluent, trading coordinator who said:

> This sounds bad, but Japanese people don't like minorities. The blacks and Mexicans that come through don't last long. They are never fired, they just leave of their own volition. It is a sad thing. The Japanese are not friendly to the minorities.
>
> The Japanese like to refer to "lady staff" and "men staff." I tell them that they have to get out of that habit. A girl working here can just forget about any serious chance of advancement. It will never happen. The Japanese will immediately start to find faults and mistakes with her; she will get no positive reinforcement.

The bank business research clerk is a young black woman with a junior college degree:

> I have a lot of good feelings about working here, but some days the bad outweighs the good. The bad is that women, American or Japanese, are just utility. Only two women have positions where they meet "outside" people. The Japanese are conscious of looks. I am small and blend right in. The larger ladies are in the back room and not seen.
>
> At my bank the Japanese don't like to hire minorities, especially blacks. There are no black men here, and only three other black women. The Japanese view blacks as Michael Jordan, Michael Jackson, Michael Tyson, or as thugs and undesirables.

A young woman in her early twenties who learned Japanese while working in Japan for several years modeling and doing secretarial work had this to say about her current employer:

> I am closely watched and constantly told how to act and what to do. I feel stifled. I've been ordered to perform certain secretarial duties right in front of clients. It was very embarrassing.
>
> The Japanese management style has been a turnoff since I am female and not Japanese. Japanese people are extremely prejudiced, especially against blacks and women over thirty.
>
> There are codes put into the computer indicating age and looks. That is highly illegal. The company has served as a stepping stone in my career, but I do not want to ever work for a Japanese firm again [Update: she now works for another Japanese firm. While still sometimes complaining about "male chauvinism," she likes and respects her current Japanese boss, who is quite "westernized." She is doing well.]

The large auto firm's information manager noted that:

> I have not seen too many women in management here. I can't tell you why, but traditionally cars have been a macho male thing.
>
> There is the long-standing view of the Japanese that women are good to have around but should not make any important decisions. I don't know if that has an effect or whether it is just a lack of qualified women in the automotive field.
>
> I'm not sure if there is any black management here or not. If there are, there must be only a few. There might be some Hispanic managers. It is probably a lack of their education.
>
> The Asian-Americans who work here have been treated pretty much the same as the [Caucasian] Americans. They don't move any faster or slower and special hiring targets are not needed.

The manager of special projects, with his strong interest in Japanese culture and hint of American male chauvinism, observed that: "Japanese have a difficult time with females. In Japan, women will work for five to ten years and then get married, leave the company, and raise a family. The situation here is totally different . . . and I'm not sure better."

The electronics firm's advertising and public relations coordinator is an outspoken woman in her mid-twenties:

> I think that the Japanese have a long way to go when it comes to women. There are no women vice presidents and I really don't

see that happening. There are some women managers, but even they are viewed differently.

I know that women are not terribly happy in American firms, but I think it is a little worse with Japanese firms.

I am tall and aggressive, and I think that scares them. I have met some Japanese men and they are kind of taken aback because I am usually a foot taller than them and am pretty confident. They don't know how to take me.

There are a lot of minorities here, but the majority of them are in clerical positions or in the warehouse.

The Japanese-American loan officer for business development with a major bank commented:

Because of cultural differences the Japanese think of women differently, almost as if they are secondary to men. You can see that in the things they are expected to do. If some of the women allowed it, they could be turned into a personal secretary.

One secretary who recently left was not happy about serving tea every day to the Japanese officers.

I don't see any bias against minorities. There are some blacks and Hispanics, but only at the clerk level. The senior people are all Japanese, Japanese-American, or Caucasian.

Of all the interview questions, it was only this one dealing with minorities and women which seemed to somewhat unsettle people. On several separate occasions those interviewed requested that my tape recorder be turned off, either to make a comment off the record or to gather their thoughts. Here, for example, was the otherwise very articulate credit manager of a powerful trading company, who suddenly turned oblique after the tape recorder was switched back on:

The question of minorities and women is a hot topic, and I don't know how this information will be used. There are basically two groups: rotating and nonrotating employees. And I think that is a good way to look at it and I don't try to look any further than that. I don't think it would do any good.

The Japanese-American associate trader for the same firm was more direct:

If I were a black or Hispanic, I don't think I would get very far in the firm. The Japanese really stick to their kind.

> In Tokyo if you go to an office, there are nothing but men. The Japanese think in stereotypes and will keep women as clerks. If I were a woman, I would not work here.
>
> The Japanese-Americans seem to be doing about as well as the nonminority Americans.

The electronics firm's travel coordinator is a black woman in her mid-thirties who raised a point made by a few others: bias might just be appropriately placed at the doorstep of the American men working for the firm rather than the Japanese. Her comments:

> I don't think that women and minorities do all that well here.
>
> I am pretty limited as to how far I can go unless I really change. We don't have a single black manager; not one. But then maybe no one has applied, or perhaps no one is qualified.
>
> For a woman, it is very hard to climb the corporate ladder in a Japanese company. It is harder than in an American company. When we did get the first female manager, all of the visiting Japanese used to come in and look at her because she was such a novelty. They were like tourists at a zoo; we used to joke about whether they would take pictures.
>
> American men are a little more subtle about their belief that women are not quite as good as they are. The Japanese lack that subtlety.
>
> I think the Japanese feel that women are a little softer or may need more time because they have children . . . or something. But I really don't know; I can't get into their heads [*shrugs*].
>
> I find that American men working for Japanese firms are a little more chauvinistic than they would be in an American company. I do feel that. They take on an even stronger view. They convey a feeling that we are just not all that important.

Sensing the same possibility—that it was the American male managers and not the Japanese who were at fault—an accounting supervisor offered her opinion: "The higher levels of management are typically male; I don't know if that is a Japanese style. It could just as well be an American style of discrimination."

SUMMARY

Over the last few years, various claims have been made that Japanese manufacturing plant sites are purposely located where there are few blacks, and that some firms refuse to hire and promote women, minorities, and people over forty. It has also been alleged that Japanese and Asian-Americans are given hiring preference, and that Japanese expatriates are paid and promoted differently from the Americans.

Recently, several Japanese firms have had charges of race, sex, and age discrimination brought against them. "The men who run these subsidiaries bring their biases from Japan with them. They treat women like office flowers," said Lewis Steel, an attorney who has represented several plaintiffs.

Before this research I might have been skeptical of those bringing allegations against Japanese firms, as well as our sanctimonious Mr. Steel, as perhaps being opportunists. We are, after all, the world's most litigious society, with 800,000 lawyers—Japan has 20,000.

Mr. Steel and some of his potential clients may simply view the Japanese as deep-pocketed and vulnerable targets. Concerned with their image, the Japanese companies are reluctant to battle charges made against them, and out-of-court settlements have been frequent. More recently, however, they have begun to defend themselves, even though there is a strong sense of shame and humiliation in resorting to the legal system.

Still, after listening to our Yankee Samurai, there appears to be something here. The perception is that women and minorities generally have limited opportunities in their Japanese-owned firms. There is nothing unique to the Japanese companies about this. A survey of women and minorities among a range of American firms brings a very similar litany of complaints to those you have heard here. A recent EEOC study dealing with American firms showed that black women held only 2 percent of management jobs and black males 3 percent; blacks are 12 percent of the population. It was also found that throughout American industry black women, behind their backs, were commonly referred to disdainfully as "twofers," meaning that they satisfy de facto hiring quotas for two categories: women and minority. Hispanics are doing even more poorly, with less than 1 percent of management jobs, even though they make up over 10 percent of the general population. Asians are doing only a little better in corporate America; Native American management presence is essentially unknown.

Hundreds of thousands of individual and class-action discrimination lawsuits have been brought against American firms over the last two decades. The settlements for these legal actions total multi-billions of dollars. This is no small cottage industry for the legal profession, whose friends in Congress, to whose campaigns they contribute, continue to generate new legislation and cattle-prod the EEOC to enforce it; it is a beautifully symmetric system, with both plaintiff and defendant corporate attorneys making very nice livings.

Some good has come out of all this. Progress has been made in eliminating blatantly unfair practices applied to women and minorities. American corporations, which for all practical purposes can be equated to a small number of senior management white males, are much more sensitive than they were decades ago. However, Americans are beginning to ask whether a point has now been reached where there are too many 30 percent contingency-fee lawyers—they even brazenly advertise on television. One of the lessons Japan has to teach is the critical importance of group harmony (*wa*) within an organization. Lawsuits, or tacit threats of lawsuits, are anathema to that harmony. Victories in the courtroom are Pyrrhic if they heighten tension within the company—which they invariably do. The alternative is a slow and patient working *within* the corporate culture to achieve equal opportunity. There should be a way to achieve this, and America will be the better for it.

The difficulty the Japanese firms here in the United States have with this issue is two-fold. First, the role of women and minorities in the United States is so very different from that in Japan. Adjustment for the Japanese has not been easy, but considerable progress has been made. You heard that in many of the interview responses, and you see it with many Japanese companies, including Sony and Toyota, which have recently been praised for their efforts in recognizing women and minorities.

Overall, more and more Japanese companies have become aware of the kinds of adverse perceptions reported here and are taking corrective action. That translates into both more training for Japanese expatriates newly arrived in the United States and more aggressive programs in attracting and promoting all qualified people. As the Japanese adjust to the United States, we can look for a hiring and promotion system based upon merit, which is gender- and race-free to an extent at least on a par with American firms. It makes solid business sense to do so, the talent is needed, and it appeals to the Japanese for that reason. The Japanese have largely overcome their initial shock of America's cultural mores and are responding accordingly.

The second difficulty is more intractable; it deals with that same practical business sense. It is beyond the ken of the pragmatic Japanese business mind to hire or promote someone simply because that person's gender or race is not statistically represented in sufficient numbers. These de facto quotas also are beginning to be questioned by a number of American businessmen. The Japanese have arrived in the United

States amidst a growing national debate over quotas, not only in business, but in academia and the political arena; the outcome is uncertain. The Japanese firms will no doubt keep as low a profile as possible in this debate and go along with the American decision, whatever that may prove to be.

Are there opportunities for women and minorities in Japanese firms? With several important exceptions, Japanese companies in general are perhaps five years behind American firms in their hiring and promotion practices. But the Japanese are continuing to learn and adjust. They will ultimately seek talent wherever it can be found.

Today, if a man or woman of any race is educationally qualified and has personality and character traits similar to the ideal Yankee Samurai (discussed in the last chapter), Japanese companies offer wonderful career opportunities. Some of the very positive responses among the interviews that you have read attest to this, as does the 74 percent overall Favorable or Very favorable view the Yankee Samurai have of the Japanese companies. It may well be that by the turn of the decade Japanese companies will be the employers of choice for qualified women and minorities.

The Family/Group ... in Japan

To an extent far beyond most westerners' understanding, the Japanese firm is able to provide an almost family-like environment for its employees. Indeed, the Japanese word for home and company can be used almost interchangeably. It is difficult to imagine an American CEO making comments like the following from Mr. Ishida, the past president of Idemitsu Petroleum:

> The philosophy of Idemitsu is application of the Japanese home life to enterprise. We bring our employees up men of good character because they were left to us by their parents. Even in the very poor years after World War II we put priority on constructing dormitories and company houses for them. Our company is our home; it is our family.

And here is a glimpse inside Matsushita, the giant electronics firm. As one of its senior executives puts it: "At Matsushita at 8:00 A.M. every morning across Japan there are 87,000 people reciting the firm's code of values and singing together. It is like we are all a community."

This strong family orientation is coupled with a corresponding emphasis upon the group rather than the individual—we saw this in consensus decision making, where even if "better" decisions could be made top down, it is believed that the resulting ill-will and disturbance of group harmony far outweigh any benefits. Any individual who dares openly to assert him- or herself is isolated from the group—"The nail that sticks out gets hammered down." The singling out of an individual, for either praise or censure, is barely known.

Fujitsu's president, Taiyu Kobayashi, has said that, "The strength of Fujitsu lies in our group approach. We stress evaluation of group capabilities rather than the individual."

The group is a manifestation of the sense of corporate family. The management system is structured to ensure group cohesiveness; indeed, this is one of the major responsibilities for management. Rewards are based on group, not individual, performance. After hours, the group socializes informally together at restaurants and bars; formally, the company arranges for group trips, sporting events, and other activities.

Confucianism and Buddhism both stress that an individual's goals should become integrated into the larger society. Couple this with a Bushido and Samurai tradition of absolute loyalty to the *Daimyo*, or liege lord—which translates to a modern day loyalty to one's superior and company—and what results is a powerful sense of corporate family.

The companies with a revered founder such as Matsushita, Sony, Kyocera Toyota, Honda, Canon, and Suntory are special cases. They are viewed as one large family with a patriarchal head, and as enterprises of communities where management and employees are bound together by a common fate, interests, and philosophy.

In Japan, the company is largely a social entity operating in an economic environment. Strong paternalistic and familial aspects of the corporation and a sense of camaraderie among the employees prevail. Paternalism is evidenced by the richness and scope of the benefits package discussed earlier. There are in fact characteristics of the old American company town, where the company *was* the town. In Toyota City, for example, Toyota is embarking on a $700 million investment program for company housing, dining halls, and recreational facilities. Matsushita Electric has budgeted $820 million for employee housing; Hitachi Zosen, Sanyo Electric, and Olympus also have major projects under way for the same purpose.

FAMILY/GROUP . . . FOR THE YANKEE SAMURAI

What about the sense of family and group orientation for the Yankee Samurai? Go to the numbers.

Family/Group

Statement		C	P	J
1.	Some organizations are built around just a few superstars. This organization is like that.	2.6*	3.2	1
2.	The firm's internal environment tends to emphasize the importance of the group rather than the individual.	3.7*	2.8	5
3.	Individual initiative is valued more than the harmony of human relations.	2.7*	3.3	1
4.	There is a sense of family here.	3.3	3.0	5
5.	I sometimes feel that the firm is as much my family as is my real family.	2.3	2.4	4
6.	There is widespread trust, goodwill, and loyalty between superiors and subordinates.	3.0	2.9	5
7.	People will not leave the firm, even if higher pay or promotion is offered by another company.	1.8	2.0	4
8.	Employees have a strong sense of identification with the company.	3.4	3.3	5
9.	People stay alert to job opportunities outside the company.	3.5	3.6	2

The first three statements deal with the concept of group as opposed to individual orientation. In each csae, there is statistical significance. To a greater extent than is true in an American firm, it is the group, not the individual, that is emphasized. This is profound and has emerged as one of the important findings here. We have seen that not too many of the Japanese management style traits have been experienced by the Yankee Samurai, but this is one of them. Although still modest by Japanese standards, the Yankee Samurai do operate in a much more group-oriented environment that they have ever been accustomed to before.

At the same time, statements 4 and 5 deal with a sense of family, where it is observed that the results are little different than what might be expected in an American firm; the group orientation does not translate into the closeness of family.

Finally, the last four statements probe the Yankee Samurai loyalty to the firm; this is little different from that at a corresponding American firm, and a far cry from that of the Japanese expatriate who works at his or her side for the same firm.

Let's look at the interview responses.

Roughly 25 percent of the Yankee Samurai felt that their firm did offer a family environment, while another fourth believed that a once-existing family environment was being lost. Finally, about one half experienced little or no family feeling.

A FAMILY ORIENTATION

The legal secretary sensed a family orientation and noted that it played a role in the firm's control system:

> This firm tends to have a family-oriented approach to control. The last firm [American] I worked for was ruled with an iron fist and people were leaving right and left. Things are not real authoritative here.
>
> There is a friendliness around the building and people know your name. We have a company party which enhances that. It is the way they treat you. The Japanese do not insist that you call them by their last names.

You should recall that there is evidence that Japanese management style is practiced far more vigorously in the *manufacturing* subsidiaries of the Japanese firms than in their white-collar operations. For example, there seemed to be much more intense hiring practices and far more training and job rotation in the blue-collar environment. There may also be more sense of family. Listen to the auto firm's public relations manager, who compared the family environment at his manufacturing facility to that at corporate headquarters:

> In our manufacturing facility, I think there is a much stronger sense of family. It is more important that there be that sense where there are thousands of workers who are both hourly and salaried.
>
> Everyone there wears a uniform, there are no reserved parking spaces, and there are not big deluxe walnut offices.
>
> The plant manager probably knows every employee by his, or her, first name, or 80 percent of them. He spends most of his time on the plant floor.
>
> Here at our national headquarters there is less need, but it still

does exist. The company does a lot of things that are appreciated. There is a strong sense of loyalty to the company.

A Family in Transition

The senior consultant for the major electronics firm felt that his company had lost the family feeling that existed earlier:

> At the beginning, we were a family. Now we are more rigid, with many rules within the company. Now that we have become more regimented, much of the strong personal feelings we had, both up and down, are being lost. I think we were a Japanese firm but are not anymore.
>
> We have standing operating procedures now. I fought for this, arguing that things had to be put down on paper. I am rather sorry that I did.
>
> We have grown and things have become rigid, with an American sales manager. We are not as Japanese as we were ten years ago.

The travel department coordinator also believed that the feeling of family was slipping away as her firm became larger:

> When I first came here I felt a real sense of family, but we have become so large that I don't know people anymore. Even though everyone is friendly, I still feel lost sometimes.
>
> The company tries to bring people together with softball and volleyball teams. There is a picnic and Christmas party. These events are well attended. Even those who have left the company are frequently there. The company is doing its part.

The office services supervisor for still another electronics firm saw similar change:

> The company has grown enormously since I came aboard. In the first few years, everyone pretty much knew each other and there was a sense of family. We didn't have a lot of rules and regulations. Everyone just more or less understood what was appropriate behavior.
>
> But now we are putting rules and regulations in place. I don't think the Japanese really want to do that. However, they are being forced to because there is now such a broad spectrum of people.

We don't always have everybody who is honest and hardworking. We have introduced security, behavior, expense account, and dress-code regulations. These now try to do what family used to do.

NO FAMILY ORIENTATION

Finally, about half the Yankee Samurai experienced no feeling of a corporate family environment at all. However, the Hispanic bank cashier felt that the sense of family was strong for the Japanese:

> The feeling of family *is* very strong among the Japanese. They have a different network. They are all from Japan and know each other.
>
> It is hard to get the family orientation across to my American staff . . . it is impossible. We don't really have a network. We don't socialize together.

The electronics firm's director of marketing for the mobile radio division had this to say:

> I don't feel a family approach. Rather, I feel that I am a foreigner in a Japanese company. I really cannot think of many family things that go on. We do have the obligatory summer picnic. But it is not well attended and is very superficial.

The major bank's executive vice president and CFO compared the Americans unfavorably to the Japanese:

> All of the Japanese staff members are working entirely for the benefit of the bank. They don't look at their own interests separately as most Americans do. You don't find a Japanese staff member fudging on his expense account, for instance, but I do see it among Americans.
>
> So, among the Japanese staff there is definitely a sense of family-type feeling. We try to encourage that among the Americans, but it is just not the same.

The manager of procurement and materials added:

> The Japanese tried to foster the family concept. For them the company comes first, the country second, and the family third. That is how they see things. In contrast, for the Americans the

individual comes first, family second, country third, and company last.

These two contrasting mentalities come through all the time. However, the Japanese don't push the family issues on us.

The attitude of the American staff here is far superior to what I have seen elsewhere but still not even close to that of the Japanese. If push comes to shove, the individual is still first.

The customer services rep of another electronics firm thought that "they [the Japanese] are trying to make things like a close-knit, family-oriented-type group. But you are dealing with Americans, whose way is not the Japanese way. They cannot adapt to it; there are too many of them who are out to step on others."

The airline sales manager who has been with his firm for over twenty years responded:

> There is a great sense of family within the company in Japan, but that does not carry over to overseas operations. That's because of the different ethnic people involved. In those operations, the top people have all been Japanese and they had no training in dealing with a foreign staff.
>
> The Japanese here prefer to surround themselves with other Japanese, eat Japanese food, speak Japanese, and mix with Japanese. They are comfortable with that and I can understand it.

Finally, the electronics firm's vice president of marketing thought that "The Japanese do not feel that the *gaijin* [foreigners] are loyal, or that they are capable of being managed by intuition as in a family. They turn all the way over to the other extreme and introduce overly stringent controls."

GROUP ORIENTATION

The Yankee Samurai were generally agreed that the group orientation was much stronger than in their earlier experiences working for American companies. This was true even without the corresponding feeling of a corporate family. The physical office structure may have contributed to that. Here, for example, is the Chinese-American trading coordinator:

> We emphasize the concept of working together and the team approach. The physical set-up of the office contributes to that. It

is like offices in Japan. It is all open, with no partitions. If you walked through the area, you would not be aware that on the floor are different departments handling very different commodities. The most senior people are in the same area, seated by the windows, facing inward. The general manager is the only one with a private office. All of this creates a group orientation.

And here is the auto firm's general manager, who contrasted his earlier experience with an American firm:

Compared to the corporate culture I saw at Ford, where there was a lot of individual initiative, force of personality, and political maneuvering, what I learned there is that all managers are working toward a consensus kind of approach. For the Americans, that means learning the art of compromise. Personal credit that one might get in an American corporation is not so readily obtained here. One's individual contribution tends to get a little blurred. Things get done in the name of a committee or group.

In our company there *is* place for the cowboy. But they are where they belong: in the field, interacting with American clients. But to really be successful here, you have to cycle through national headquarters. They [cowboys] would have a difficult time with that. So our cowboys become field generals, and they pretty much top out there or they might just move on.

The auto firm's public relations manager had previously worked for an American auto maker:

If you have a real strong ego, this probably isn't a good company to work for. We don't have palatial offices. And the kind of thinking around here is not that *I* came up with the idea for something and that it is *my* baby. The Iacocca mentality is completely contrary to [company name]. You will not find anyone in our top management taking full credit for success in an operation or any other activity.

In summary, then, for the Yankee Samurai, compared to their previous experience, the group orientation of the firm was quite strong; the "star" is much less likely to be found in the Japanese firm. But that did not translate into either a sense of corporate family or loyalty to the firm. This, of course, was in sharp contrast to the Japanese expatriates with whom they work, who did feel a sense of family among themselves as well as an intense loyalty to their firm.

THE "WHOLE MAN": SUMMARY

The cornerstone of the Japanese firm is the employee. The company nurtures that resource with an entire body of policies, practices, and traditions, all directed toward making the workplace an environment where the employees can reach his full potential . . . become a "whole man." The Japanese firms, in Japan, largely succeed.

The elements that have been described here combine to form an almost seamless system that treats the individual as an economic, social, and psychological entity. The worker experiences spiritual fulfillment. Socially, and spiritually, the employee is fused to the firm and becomes an integral part of it. It is this approach that is the unique—and arguably the most important—feature of the Japanese management style; it is fundamental to the firm's success.

The value placed upon the employee in Japan is reflected in the policies that have been discussed which are constantly reinforced by senior Japanese managers. There are thousands of examples of this reinforcement, but here are two.

Mr. Shige Yoshida, an executive vice president of Honda who has been instrumental in that firm's American success, told me:

> We believe that the most important asset of the company is people. It is not the production equipment or computers; it is the human resources which makes the organization competitive.
>
> Of fundamental importance is how the company treats people. If people are satisfied with management, they will perform well. The issue is not pay alone but overall management. If people feel that they are treated well, they will stay with the company.

And here are the words of Matsushita's almost mythic founder, Konosuke Matsushita:

> "The company builds people before it builds things. It is a fundamental tenet of Matsushita to develop extraordinary qualities in ordinary men."

Japanese management system proponents believe it is this focus placed upon the "Whole Man" that does indeed develop extraordinary qualities in ordinary people. It is a basic factor of the management style . . . as practiced in Japan. This chapter has reviewed several of its key dimensions and the extent to which each is experienced by the Yankee Samurai in America. The following chart summarizes what we have found:

	IN JAPAN	FOR THE YANKEE SAMURAI
Intense hiring practices	Yes	No; little different from American firms, but with some indication of strengthening.
Job rotation and training	Continual	Little training and essentially no rotation, but with signs of change.
Human resource department	Powerful	Even weaker than in American firms.
Lifetime employment	Yes	No, but much more stable than American firms.
Seniority pay/Promotions	Yes	No; largely mix of merit and seniority.
Women/Minority opportunities	Few	Much more than in Japan, but somewhat less than American firms; situation improving.
Group/Family orientation	Strong	Group orientation strong; sense of family/loyalty little different than in American firms.
Pay/Benefits	Good	Good.

It is evident that the Yankee Samurai experience a working world significantly different from that of the Japanese, but at the same time also different from that at corresponding American firms. How do the Yankee Samurai feel about this "whole man" concept and the way their firm views them? The numbers speak for themselves:

The Whole Man

Statement	C	P	J
1. People truly are our most important asset.	3.7*	3.3	5
2. There is a sincere concern here for the economic, social, psychological well-being of the employee.	3.3*	2.9	5

This is pretty favorable, and I want to share with you a very personal feeling about these numbers. It is a mix of anger and I suppose sadness. The Yankee Samurai are given just a very small measure—by Japanese standards—of recognition, decision-making involvement, group orientation, reasonably secure employment, training, good benefits, and fair compensation. And yet that elicits a surprisingly positive response— significantly more positive than for corresponding American firms. The Yankee Samurai believe that compared to their experience with American companies, their Japanese company is more concerned about their economic, social, and psychological well-being, and that it views them, to a greater extent, as being the firm's most important asset. Through a variety of means the Japanese firms have been able to communicate to their employees that they do care. Certainly the politeness and respect that the Japanese managers show toward the Americans is an important part of that. So, too, is the Japanese egalitarianism in terms of unreserved parking, all-employee eating areas, and Japanese executive salaries that are sometimes less than those earned by the Americans. The Japanese work ethic is also a factor. The Yankee Samurai know that top management is carrying more than its share of the burden. Finally, many of the Americans experienced the reward of a feeling of pride, knowing they are part of a company with an international reputation for quality products or services.

Have you ever had a dog that you did not pay an awful lot of attention to? Remember its response when you took a moment and stooped to pet it? Its tail wagged joyfully, its whole body shook in ecstasy, and it no doubt would have been willing literally to die for you—all for a pat on the head. Now here are American employees, the strength of America, and someone comes along and gives them a little pat, which nevertheless is hungrily welcomed. Recall that 74 percent of the Yankee Samurai felt Favorable, or Very favorable, toward their work experience. It doesn't take a lot. But what if the one pat became two, or three, or a hundred? The Japanese are onto something with their Whole Man, although they have certainly not pursued it among the Yankee Samurai nearly as vigorously as they could. Should the Japanese choose, they have it in their power to build a highly dedicated American work force. It is evident that a basic foundation has already been put into place. But, as you will see in the last chapter, that means using more, not less, Japanese management style.

I said that I felt some sadness and anger. The sadness is for those among the 110 million men and women in America's work force who labor eight to ten hours a day for perhaps thirty or forty years of their one, single, God-given life and yet do not feel "whole," and who miss the joy and satisfaction that derive from fulfillment at work. My anger is for a system that keeps this from happening. The workplace should not have to be that way. Perhaps the Japanese will be the vehicle of change in America.

9

Mission

> If a Samurai fails in his mission, but dies
> a fanatic's death, it is not dishonorable.
> Such a death is in fact the way of the
> Samurai.
> —JOCHO YAMAMOTO (1659–1719),
> Samurai turned priest

Early in the year 1701, Lord Asano became embroiled in a bitter personal dispute with Lord Kira, an adviser to the shogun. Losing his temper, Asano drew his sword and slashed at his antagonist. Kira received only a superficial wound, but even to strike a member of the shogun's court was a shocking breach of conduct. The shogun commanded Asano to commit *hara-kiri* (ritual suicide), confiscated his fief, and ordered his samurai retainers made *ronin*—warriors wandering the land without a master.

Oishi Yoshio was Asano's leading retainer. After their master's suicide, he and forty-six other loyal samurai retired to Kyoto pledged to a singular mission: revenge for the death of their lord. Realizing that Kira would be suspicious of any overt action, they adopted the pose of a drunken and dissolute life, all the while secretly planning vengeance. Their shabby appearance brought disparagement from the town people; their friends and loved ones were shamed by their behavior and abandoned them. The samurai stoically accepted the scorn and contempt heaped upon them, even though these were proud men for whom maintaining face and honor were more important than life itself. Two years passed, with the samurai never losing sight of their mission to kill Kira; it was their reason for living. Every precise detail of their plan and every aspect of their behavior was guided by that mission.

Then, on a snowy evening in December 1702, the forty-seven *ronin* with Oishi in the lead finally struck. Lord Kira's stronghold was attacked, his guards overwhelmed, and Kira himself murdered. Only one of the *ronin* fell in the brilliantly planned and executed assault.

Just before sunrise the next morning, the surviving forty-six *ronin* solemnly gathered before Lord Asano's tomb. The air was freezing and pristine clear as the samurai watched Oishi slowly unwrap a bloody rag that was wound about an object he had reverently placed upon the icy ground. He finally pulled forth the grimacing, severed head of Kira; the sightless eyes stared back at them. As one man the *ronin* bowed deeply. Moments later the first rays of the new day's sun pierced the darkness; the world seemed somehow cleansed. There on that isolated, snow-covered field the *ronin* stood, each lost in his own thoughts; utter silence and the now-avenged spirit of Lord Asano surrounded them. Shortly thereafter the *ronin* committed group *hara-kiri*. The mission was complete. There is pure beauty and poetry as well as magnificence in this true story from Japanese history.

One important postscript: when Oishi first heard that his lord's fief was to be confiscated, he took immediate steps to distribute much of the holdings to creditors, which deprived the shogun of sizable funds; the money-counting abacus was seldom far behind the sword.

Over the centuries the forty-seven *ronin* with their unswerving sense of mission have become Japanese folk heroes. Their deeds have been celebrated in the great Kabuki play, *Chushingura*. Forms of the tale are told and retold in movies, novels, ballets, puppet theaters, and even adult comic books (*manga*)—a respected literary form in Japan. It has become part of the Japanese ethos.

Today, the same sense of mission—the same driving purpose and over-riding vision—permeates successful Japanese business organizations and transcends all else. The mission is far more complex than the singular objective of the forty-seven *ronin*, but just as in their case, it is a powerful motivator and critical factor in integrating and directing the organization. Mission, like consensus decision making and the "Whole Man," is another fundamental concept of the Japanese management style.

MISSION OF THE JAPANESE FIRM

For the Japanese firm, the company's mission is taken simply as "the reason for being." It sets forth the ultimate—and perhaps never attainable—destination, as well as the values adhered to while pursuing that destination. The mission is introduced to the salaryman at the initial training program, and is then daily reinforced through company songs, anthems, management speeches, and printed slogans. It becomes inculcated in the employee. Because it is so deeply believed in and completely understood by organization members, it provides an implicit control mechanism, far more effective than the strongest iron hand, or the most complete set of rules and regulations. The values set forth in the mission become the individual employee's values; everyday actions are guided accordingly.

As discussed in the next chapter, it serves as the framework within which strategic and tactical planning takes place. Any plan of action must pass the acid test: Is it consistent with the larger mission?

Typically, the mission summarizes the firm's belief in itself as eternal, the employee as part of a harmonious corporate family, the desire to contribute to national well-being, the constant advancement of technology, the aim to better the future for humanity, and the code of honor. Passages from the mission statements of two of Japan's finest firms clarify the point:

> We recognize our responsibilities as industrialists, to foster progress, to promote the general welfare of society, and to devote ourselves to the further development of world culture.
>
> Progress and development can be realized through the combined efforts and cooperation of each member of our Company. Each of us, therefore, shall keep this idea constantly in mind as we devote ourselves to the continuous improvement of our Company.
>
> We value national service through industry, fairness, harmony and cooperation, struggle for betterment, courtesy and humility, adjustment and assimilation, and gratitude.
>
> We are dedicated to achieving leadership in consumer electronic technology to enrich the lives of the people of our nation and the world.
>
> There is a primary obligation to employees to assure a harmo-

nious family environment in which they can learn and grow so as to pass the firm on to the next generation.

We will maintain trust and honor in all of our business relations and assume full responsibilities as a citizen of society.

Some of you might have read those passages and shrugged, having expected something stronger. The language appears to be rather vague, hardly the stuff that would galvanize an entire organization and guide it in determining strategy as well as forming the basis of an implicit control system. But it has to be understood that the words are *lived* every day and so take on a life of their own.

Let me put this in a Western context. At a visit to West Point just before his death, the aged and ailing General Douglas MacArthur spoke to the young cadets:

The shadows are lengthening for me. The twilight is here. But my memory always comes back to West Point, and there echoes and reechoes in my ears—Duty, Honor, Country. When I cross the river my last conscious thoughts will be of the Corps, the Corps, and the Corps.

Now, the West Point mission can be captured simply as "Duty, Honor, Country." Those three words in and of themselves are almost without meaning for anyone who is not of the Corps. But for those whose minds and hearts are filled with the traditions of West Point, dating back to 1802, for those who commune with the ghosts of Lee, Jackson, Grant, Pershing, Eisenhower, Patton, and Marshall, and for those officers who daily are surrounded by fellow members of the Corps who share and live the mission, these words and all they imply are enough for a man to die for . . . it is a battle cry. A Japanese firm's mission statement, such as NEC's "Computers and Communication," is like that.

Mission . . . For the Yankee Samurai

Given, then, this fundamental role of mission in a Japanese firm, what is the impact on the Yankee Samurai? Is the mission deeply imbued within each of them, as it is in the Japanese expatriates? Does it serve as a moral compass and an implicit control system? Is it the starting point for strategy setting?

As always, let's begin with some numbers.

Mission

Statement	C	P	J
1. Strategy is guided by the mission statement, which indicates the firm's reason for being and its basic values and beliefs.	3.4[*]	3.1	5
2. While strategies and plans are adjusted to reflect changes in the environment, the mission, or vision, remains unchanged.	3.7[*]	3.3	5
3. There is an absolute commitment to the mission, and the firm is quite willing to endure even fairly long failure and losses to achieve success.	3.4[*]	2.7	5
4. I understand, and have largely memorized, the firm's mission statement, or philosophy.	2.8	2.6	5
5. The firm's mission, or basic philosophy, is extensively discussed at hiring, and is constantly reinforced.	2.6	2.6	5

At first glance, the results appear to be sharply contradictory. The first three statement responses showing statistical significance indicate that, compared to American companies, the Japanese firms do have a mission to which the firm is highly committed and which serves as a guide to strategy. At the same time, the response to statements 4 and 5 show that the mission plays little role in the working lives of the Americans. They have only a vague understanding of it, and the firm has not made a strong effort to share it with them.

The firm itself does have a mission that fulfills its classic role as both a control mechanism and a lodestar for strategy setting—among the Japanese. But while the Americans are generally aware of this fact (statements 1–3), they either have no interest in the specific mission or believe that the Japanese do not share it with them (statements 4–5). Thus, the Yankee Samurai observe that the firm seems to be committed to its mission, and that mission serves as an immutable guide to strategy setting and control; but at the same they themselves are only passive observers.

Not more than a half dozen of the some 250 Yankee Samurai interviewed and questioned believed their firm had a Japanese management style mission *and* were able to articulate it themselves. There were a few more who indicated that their firm was in the process of developing a mission. The great majority of them had no idea what the mission was, even though many among them were nevertheless convinced that the Japanese knew. The following are representative remarks.

MISSION: YES, WE HAVE ONE

Only a relatively small number of the Yankee Samurai believed that their firm had a mission which they themselves shared. The Japanese-American vice president of an auto firm's trading company subsidiary was one of them:

> Our company philosophy was put together by the American staff and is on all the walls. Here we are guided by the belief that every decision we make should either help to sell products or reduce their costs. We seek profits just enough to meet our costs, contingencies, and growth.
>
> If a certain product is exported, we may lose money, but it might have high visibility and would be good for P.R., so we continue. We spend money like heck. We get good people, pay them well, and promote them. When the big push comes, we will be ready.
>
> In Japan, the company mission points out the need to be internationally minded and produce a product that goes beyond the expectations of the customer at a reasonable price. That mission guides the strategy and management decisions. Hopefully our mission does the same.

The forty-year-old public relations manager of a large auto firm had been with General Motors for eleven years. He seemed to think his Japanese company's mission came down largely to quality and service:

> It may sound trite, but our mission is to sell the highest-quality product and provide the best customer satisfaction possible. Everyone in the company deeply understands that. It is not so much a stated philosophy, but everyone just knows [it].
>
> There is more satisfaction around here about winning the Customer Satisfaction Index than breaking the sales records that have been broken.
>
> When we have to do a recall, it hurts . . . it hurts everybody; they feel bad about it. Everyone hates it when we have to do one. We ask, "What will people think and will it inconvenience them?"

Quality and service are the absolute building blocks for our being here.

The corporate marketing manager of a different auto firm also believed that his company had a mission:

The mission for the firm as a whole is to obtain 10 percent of the world market. Our firm in the United States has a percentage of that. Our mission is to build the best-quality products, satisfy people [customers], and provide growth opportunities for employees. I think that is fairly well understood down through levels of the organization, but probably not beyond the management level.

The personnel manager of one of the world's largest electronics firms had an idea of his company's mission:

The firm is trying to promote the "Computers and Communication" concept. They are trying to develop more locations throughout the world. I don't see profit being put forward as the bottom line of things. They seem to be more concerned that the employees are happy, that we fit into the community, and that we are representing ourselves as an American company.

MISSION: JUST NOW BEING PUT INTO PLACE

On the other hand, several of the firms, having recognized their lack of mission, were in the process of putting one into place. Here, for example, is the bank executive vice president, a man in his early sixties:

We have just established a mission statement for the bank and put it out for the staff. Upon until three months ago we did not have a mission or corporate objectives [shrugs shoulders in amazement]!

The mission basically says that we want to be a provider of quality financial services to the markets which we serve, provide professional opportunities for our staff, and be recognized as a positive contributor to the communities within which we operate.

The statement is relatively short; only about half a page. We are also in the process of establishing corporate goals and objectives. This was a first shot . . . that is kind of mind-boggling; we were essentially operating without any direction [shakes his head]!

The manager of corporate computer and data network resources for a major electronics firm also spoke of a mission statement that had just been introduced:

We recently developed a mission statement. Prior to that, we didn't have one. It is a strategy for the next three years. It describes the business we want to be in and sets certain goals; there is a large emphasis on customer service. I haven't got it memorized so I can't quote it back to you. I don't think the mission is deeply ingrained.

MISSION: THERE ISN'T ANY

Large numbers of the Yankee Samurai were either unaware or only vaguely aware of the existence of a mission. Typical was the electronics firm's somewhat cynical accounting supervisor:

I think that we are here to sell a product. There is some stated credo, but I honestly cannot think what it is right now. There is a theme and I am trying to recall the words. We had a contest and everyone was allowed to put in ideas; a trip for the winner was awarded. But it is not something I pay a lot of attention to. They are just trying to sales-pitch me in some way.

The executive vice president noted the lack of his bank's mission:

The question of mission is a very significant deficiency that we have here in the bank. We do not have a well-defined direction from the Japanese. I am responsible for planning and control, but there is no way I can do the job. We largely abrogate the responsibility to the Japanese because we cannot get enough real information from them. We could do a much better job if there was a clearer mission statement and if there was better communication.

The advertising and public relations coordinator of a well-regarded electronics firm was one of the more outspoken of the Yankee Samurai. She commented:

Within the company there is no sense of mission, but I think it is important to have one. We have no corporate mission! If there is one, it is not evident to me. We just kind of show up and do our job, without really understanding why or where it fits into the larger picture.

The auto firm's personnel manager described her company's mission in only the vaguest of terms:

One of the problem areas of this firm relates to communicating our mission. Different people are likely to have different views as to the mission.

> It is my understanding that our mission is to reach a certain market position with a good-quality product.
>
> There is nothing written about this that I am aware of.

Another auto firm's product information manager thought that: "The average [company] person doesn't see much of a mission beyond 'the customer is king.' "

The office services supervisor for a large electronics company had little or no idea of his firm's mission:

> I don't think the everyday employee out there has a sense of mission. He or she is just doing their job and getting a paycheck every week.
>
> We have so many divisions here that each one is sort of doing its own thing without any common direction.
>
> There probably is some mission statement somewhere, but I don't know what it is.

The auto company's vice president of marketing had experience both with Ford and another Japanese automobile firm. He spoke of his current company's lack of mission:

> This company is missing a mission. Neither the people in Japan, nor the top people here, have been able to enunciate what our mission is. There have been demands for corporate mission statements because everyone is hungry for that.

The young Hawaiian-born Japanese-American didn't have much idea about his bank's mission: "I guess the mission is to come to the United States; it is pretty vague. I have not seen anything written down [shrugs]."

MISSION: ONLY THE JAPANESE KNOW

Finally, many of the Yankee Samurai believed that the firm did indeed have a mission, but that only the Japanese knew what it was. The young, highly insightful Hispanic banker held that view: "We have no mission that I know of, although we have often thought about it. We do have basic operational goals but we don't know the big picture. We get the impression that somebody knows the long-term goal but it is not us [Americans]!"

A major bank's assistant manager of administrative planning made the same point:

> The mission is not that clearly communicated, but I believe it is, "To expand and become known as a worldwide international

bank." That has been our goal over the last decade. [*Pause*] At least I think so.

I am sure that the bank does have a basic corporate philosophy that the Japanese are aware of. However, that has not been shared with the American employees here.

The account representative in the textile department of a major trading firm also contrasted American and Japanese knowledge of the mission:

There are several elements of the company's credo that traces back to the founding of the firm in the last century.

That credo is not at all a part of the American thinking. But in Japan every employee has this credo in their mind, all the way down to the telex operators.

The electronics firm's senior buyer was himself unaware of the firm's mission, but again thought the Japanese knew what it was: "There is no mission that has been made clear to anyone other than the Japanese or maybe the American top management. They are very secretive among themselves."

The vice president and head auditor of a major bank, a man in his late thirties, believed that:

A lot of Americans who come here become frustrated because they feel they do not know where the corporation is going or what are the long-term plans. They feel shut out from these things. They don't know where the organization is heading. They don't know the higher strategy or why we are here.

The contrast between American and Japanese sense of mission was reflected in the remarks of the national manager of human resources of a dominant electronics firm: "While we [the Americans] do not have a clear mission here, I think the Japanese do have a mission and are struggling to get there, while doing it through the Americans."

Finally, the manager of special projects of a large electronics firm spoke most clearly to the point: "One of the biggest problems we have is that the Japanese do not tell the Americans where the boat is going."

CONCLUSION

It is not only Japanese firms that recognize the importance of mission. About ten years ago, Johnson & Johnson confronted its Tylenol crisis, in which arsenic-laced tablets were discovered in Chicago retail stores.

J&J was well prepared—with its company mission, or credo. It is captured today, as it was then, in a fairly long statement that includes language making clear the absolute top priority given to customers and the infinite importance of the company's reputation for trust among physicians and the health-care community. J&J people deeply believed then, as now, in the mission. Employees in the field—far removed from corporate headquarters, and unable to obtain direction—automatically knew what right action should be taken when the Tylenol crisis struck; the guiding principles were in the mission statement. Regardless of the cost, the product was immediately removed from the entire distribution system and a candid appraisal of events was given to the media. Senior management's high-pressure decisions were made almost simple by using the mission as a North Star to guide them. The company not only survived the crisis but managed to strengthen its reputation.

Another American company, certainly one of the finest of this century, was founded by Thomas Watson. He has given his views of the importance of mission at IBM:

> The basic philosophy, spirit, and drive of an organization have far more to do with its relative achievements than to technological or economic resources, organizational structure, innovation, and timing. All these things weigh heavily in success. But they are, I think, transcended by how strongly the people in the organization believe in the basic precepts and how faithfully they carry them out.

IBM's mission statement includes references to customers, technology, employees, strategy, stockholders, society, nation, and the world.

There are, unfortunately, not many more examples, although Hewlett-Packard, 3M, DEC, Merck, McDonald's, Wal-Mart, Herman Miller, Mars, and Harley-Davidson might be cited as companies with a well-thought-out mission. It is no coincidence that these are among the most successful American companies.

In the early eighties, the idea of a meaningful corporate mission was all the rage among management theoreticians and consultants. Many companies rushed to put one in place. Top managements went off for week-long retreats in the Bahamas, say, to hammer out a mission statement—in between rounds of golf. Upon their return, a series of meetings were held at which the CEO personally addressed the troops to share the newfound wisdom. Copies of the mission, printed on heavy bond paper, were printed and widely distributed. Time passed and . . . nothing changed. Within months it was business as usual. Management apparently failed to recognize that it takes perhaps decades to establish a credo that is embraced by the totality of stakeholders—employees, customers, suppliers, creditors, stockholders, and community. It must be practiced and lived daily for years. Myths and legends must build. Heroes and heroines must be sanctified. There can be no deviation from the mission, even in times of crisis; indeed, that is when adherence to it comes to the fore.

The mission fad has now largely passed. By the mid- to late eighties, amidst merger and acquisition mania, the de facto mission of many American firms took on a whole new meaning. RJR Nabisco was a classic case in point. The firm's top management, led by the chairman, Ross Johnson, failed in its late 1988 leveraged buy-out putsch. The company was put into play, and ultimately Johnson and nine vice presidents reporting to him were forced to resign. They walked away with a $100 million or so golden parachute to be distributed among them; Johnson himself obtained a windfall $26 million. Had their proposed deal been successful, these ten would have enriched themselves as a group even more—one estimate was $2.6 billion. Given that a firm's actions are a reflection of its mission, its reason for being, it would appear that RJR's defacto mission was primarily to make a modern-day Croesus of Ross Johnson himself and mini-Croesuses of his executive team.

Lincoln's Gettysburg Address ends with reference to government of the people, by the people, and for the people. A forthright statement of many of the *Fortune* 500 company missions, based upon the actual actions of the firm, would include language to the effect that the company is of top management, by top management, and for top management.

Too many American companies are being managed solely for the benefit of senior executives. Peter Drucker refers to "corporate capitalism" as the establishment of management accountable only to itself. The tacit mission of those firms practicing this corporate capitalism is centered on the welfare of senior management, with their multi-million-dollar packages of perquisites and compensation.

It would be difficult, if not impossible, to find a "corporate capitalism" mission among Japanese firms. At the same time, what we have seen in this chapter indicates that while the Japanese subsidiaries do have a mission, it is basic to the working lives largely of the Japanese rather than the Yankee Samurai. Either the Americans were not interested in the mission or the Japanese chose not to share it with them.

This has significant implications for planning. Without a mission, planning—the next chapter's topic—becomes impossible. Lincoln once commented: "If you don't know where you are and whither you are going, you cannot judge what to do and how to do it." The Yankee Samurai, for the most part, do not know where their firm is going. Their lack of a sense of mission precludes meaningful involvement in the critical responsibility of setting strategy.

Contrasting American to Japanese companies, Akio Morita, Sony's chairman, has said, "American companies struggle for a next quarter's vision. Our vision looks forward thirty and more years." That's fine, and it is unquestionably a great strength of the Japanese firm. But the Yankee Samurai of those same firms are largely unaware of the vision.

When Morita was still a young boy, Thomas Watson wrote of the importance of mission and vision for *foreign* affiliates: "You have to attract the best people in the host country and give them the same objectives, values, and vision [mission] as the parent company. Everyone then shares a common view of the company, its products, direction, and purpose."

The Japanese firms operating in the United States might take note of Watson's sage counsel.

10

Destiny

> *We will put a man on the moon before the end of the decade.*
> —John F. Kennedy
>
> *Good tactics can save even the worst strategy. And bad tactics can ruin even the best strategy.*
> —General George Patton
>
> *When you start to take Vienna . . . take Vienna.*
> —Napoleon

Destiny . . . in Japan

Some two decades ago, Alvin Toffler wrote his best-selling *Future Shock,* in which he described the dramatic technology-wrought changes that were buffeting the lives of Americans. In retrospect, those were almost sleepy halcyon days. The pace of change has accelerated; life is now on fast-forward.

How does a firm face the uncertainty of the future in such a way that it has a measure of control over its destiny? Is it possible to hammer, or perhaps cajole, destiny to its will? The performance of many Japanese firms over the last half century cautiously suggests a positive reply. Their rise to dominance in the areas of banking, autos, steel, electronics, robots, computers, industrial equipment, and more cannot be due simply to pure chance and benevolent gods. How does the successful Japanese firm approach the future? With the three elements represented respectively by the epigraphs at the start of this chapter: mission; a flexible strategy, with an emphasis on tactics; and an absolute commitment both to the task at hand and the larger mission.

MISSION

As we saw in the last chapter, a powerfully articulated mission that is imbued in the hearts and minds of those within the firm is fundamental; everything else builds upon that. Without a mission, the firm flounders; it is at the mercy of change, with no compass or direction, and is whipsawed by the swirling events about it. The mission is the firm's ultimate purpose, its reason for being; and it transcends all else.

President Kennedy's tersely stated mission became reality when Neil Armstrong did indeed before the end of the sixties step on the moon and say, "That is one small step for a man and one giant step for mankind." Yet once that was accomplished, no new mission replaced it; America's space program has been largely adrift ever since.

Having stated the mission, a strategy must be designed to fulfill it.

STRATEGY

Strategy is taken here as meaning a *long-term* plan of action to realize the mission. The Japanese think far into the future; government agencies and individual firms periodically develop ten- and twenty-five-year plans. Yet a careful and thoroughly thought-out plan provides only a starting point. Its primary benefit is to serve as the mechanism that forces thinking through as much of what is known as possible. The process, and what is learned from it about the key issues among all those involved, is of far more value than the completed strategy itself.

Even the most brilliantly designed strategy falls prey to the vicissitudes of the battlefield. General Eisenhower once commented, "Every war is going to astonish you. No plan ever survives the first contact with the enemy." One of his subordinates General Patton noted that, "Good tactics can save even the worst strategy and bad tactics can ruin even the best strategy." Generals deal in strategies; privates, sergeants, and lieutenants deal in tactics or short-range plans. It is implementation of the plan at the tactical level that matters.

Military experts generally agree with that. The published works of Count Helmuth von Moltke, the brilliant nineteenth-century Prussian military officer, are still studied at war colleges around the world. He believed that strategy should not be based upon a lengthy and detailed battle plan, but rather should evolve from a central mission through continually changing circumstances. "A plan is valid only until the opponent makes his first move."

Napoleon suggested a similar approach: "One commits oneself and then one sees." If an apparent weakness appears in the enemy lines, it should immediately be tested and if in fact it is an opportunity, exploited. If it is not, there is an immediate withdrawal, and another opportunity is sought.

These military examples easily carry over into the business arena. Business is of course war. Any American who thinks that it isn't should be aware that the Japanese think that it is.

Chaos Theory

A new concept in strategic planning dubbed "Chaos Theory" has been gaining some popularity and is a fair approximation to what so many Japanese firms practice. It is based on the view that the world has become so complex, and situations so mercurial, that no matter how carefully a firm may plan, unanticipated events will occur that raise questions of whether long-term strategy is even possible.

Some MIT researchers have explained the source of these unanticipated events as the "butterfly effect." In theory, a butterfly flapping its delicate wings on a warm day in Tokyo, while hovering over a cherry blossom, may set into motion an extraordinary mix of random circumstances culminating in a New York snowstorm. The theory argues that even infinitely small variations in subsystems, under special circumstances, may lead to large and totally unexpected consequences on the outcome of the system as a whole.

History, as well as your own personal life, is replete with examples that validate the theory; it intuitively seems right. Did you set out to be what you professionally are now? What series of extraordinary, fortuitous events led to your current career position? How big a role did chance play in meeting your spouse or special friend? She may have been born in a desert town in Arizona and you in a balmy California beach city. What is the probability of the infinity of events that occurred for your two lives to have come together at that chance first meeting as

college students in a campus library in San Diego one summer afternoon?

An almost impossibly complex and improbable series of events have
followed one after another, making our current individual lives what
they are. Had even one of them been altered, so would our current
reality; sometimes in a barely perceptible way, and sometimes pro-
foundly. For a firm, this is multiplied a million-fold by variables in the
work situation: employees (a 3M man invents the Post-it), CEOs (RJR's
Ross Johnson decides to make a few hundred million dollars for himself
with an LBO), competitors (Ricoh, Canon, Minolta, and Sharp suddenly appear to challenge Xerox in copiers), green-mailers (T. Boone
Pickens's surprise siege of Unocal), inflation (Brazil freezes prices im-
pacting Caterpillar profits), vagaries of international finance (the dollar
strengthens against the Yen and Boeing's jets are less competitive in
Japan), pirates (a shipful of Merck pharmaceuticals is hijacked in the
Strait of Malacca), litigation (Texaco is sued for $10 billion by Pennzoil
for alleged improper bargaining), unions (Eastern Airlines is forced into
bankruptcy because of union intransigence—Lorenzo didn't help
much), psychopaths (J&J finds its Tylenol capsules laced with arsenic),
revolution (EDS employees are arrested and imprisoned by the Ayatol-
lah Khomeini), Mao's legacy (Reebok is forced to rethink operating in
China after Tiananmen Square), accidents (Union Carbide's Bhopal
plant explosion killed 2,000), not to mention consumer caprice, computer viruses, technological breakthroughs, wars, and earthquakes. All
these random and largely unpredictable events continuously impact a
firm. It is literally chaos.

Yet, what appears as chaos to some, in fact creates opportunities that
randomly present themselves. The ideal approach to exploiting these
opportunities is to design a strategic process that is highly flexible and
adaptive, all the while maintaining absolute commitment to the over-
arching mission, which is the one constant. To achieve that, information becomes the ultimate weapon. These are the two lessons of this
Chaos Theory: information and flexible strategy. The Japanese know
both lessons well.

Information

The Japanese are omnivorous consumers of information. Their educational training, with its emphasis upon rote memorization and the
discipline of concentration, develops the skills to assimilate massive

amounts of it. The seemingly endless meetings with the Japanese that the Yankee Samurai endure, and barely tolerate, are manifestations of a national obsession for information gathering, sharing, and analysis.

The Japanese read twice as many books per capita as Americans; some 93 percent of them read a daily newspaper—per capita newspaper reading in the United States continues to decline—and television news broadcasts are in-depth and thoughtful. Japan's NHK is easily on a par with the BBC and produces outstanding cultural and educational programming.

No government agency or corporation begins a new venture until it has ferreted out all relevant information. And there are mountains of such information. Polls and surveys are constantly taken on domestic and international issues. Within a corporation, detailed quantitative data about all aspects of the firm and its industry are constantly captured and analyzed.

Japanese firms operating around the world make a practice of forwarding relevant information to the Tokyo government. The great trading companies have been doing this for well over a century. Information is shared among the myriad of Japanese business organizations: Keidanren, Nikkeiren, Keizai Doyukai, the Japan Chamber of Commerce, specialized trade associations, and more . . . everyone is communicating with everyone else. With its universal literacy, single language, population homogeneity, and high density—coupled with leading-edge hardware technology—Japan is an information society like no other nation in the world.

Many have pondered just what the post-industrial society will look like. It will look like Japan, and will be called "the information society." More than at any time since history began, information is becoming the singular source of wealth and power. And Japan is cornering the market.

One of the most important and reliable sources of information for the Japanese comes as feedback from actions they have already taken. The Japanese do not believe in theory; they believe in action. Not every action has a positive outcome. A recent *Fortune* article entitled "Great Japanese Mistakes" began with the words:

> In the dazzling glare of Japan's economic success, it's easy to forget that the Japanese make mistakes. So stop worrying about the Japanese challenge, put away the latest best-seller on Japan's plans to conquer the world. Kick back, put your feet up, and enjoy a tour of Japanese bloopers.

There followed a recounting of multi-billion-dollar failures: a nuclear-powered blast furnace (blocked by anti-nuke organizations—

even Japan has a few dissidents); a remote-controlled, undersea drilling rig (not cost-effective); an electric car (no battery technology break-through); Mitsui's $4.8 billion Iranian petrochemical plant (held hostage by the Iran-Iraq War); Sony's Betamax (VHS became standard); Sanyo's 1977 Arkansas plant (serious union conflict); and a state-of-the-art $9 billion bridge connecting Honshu and Shikoku (insufficient traffic).

There were a dozen more examples indicating how poorly the Japanese had apparently thought through their actions. The article closed by quoting some unnamed source saying, "They [the Japanese] have more money than sense."

I pondered this, then wrote the following poison-pen letter to the editor:

Dear Sirs:
Regarding your article . . . you gleefully and smugly chastise the Japanese for their myriad failures. There is a pompous smirk behind your words as you catalogue Japan's mistakes, duds, losses, messes, bloopers, disasters, and failures—your thesaurus must have been well thumbed looking for all those synonyms.

You miss the point entirely. The Japanese have no doubt analyzed and reanalyzed the outcome of these projects; each is a bonanza of information. In each case the state of the art has been advanced and new technology developed. Be assured that lessons learned will be applied to related projects whose financial outcome may be quite different. Try to shift your myopic American mind-set to understand that immediate short-run financial results *do not matter*.

You might have asked what American firms were doing during the 1980s while the Japanese were inventing, innovating, and constructing these "failures." In 1989, the equivalent of 41 percent of all U.S. capital investment went into mergers and acquisitions; it was 4 percent in Japan. A handful of American top executives, lawyers, investment bankers, green-mailers, and lobbyists made buckets of money playing a paper-churning game called Mergers and Acquisitions.

But they built nothing, created nothing, produced nothing, and invented nothing. These paper entrepreneurs have left in their wake towers of debt, billions of dollars in defaulted junk bonds, disillusioned employees, and a vastly weakened economy.

There was a time when Americans looked beyond quarterly earnings and constructed railroads to nowhere (across the des-

olate West), cut a canal across mosquito-plagued central America (which would surely never pay for itself), purchased a giant
iceberg (Seward's $7 million Alaskan folly), built automobiles
(never replace the horse), Rube-Goldberged a thing called an
aeroplane that would fly (you can't be serious), invented tele-
phones (no one will use them), and designed things called
computers (that might sell ten or twenty a year). Railroads,
computers, airplanes, autos . . . none of these came without
countless early failures.

    Failures, as you call them, are the very essence of growth.
We learn from them. They are rich sources of information,
indicators of economic vitality, engines of progress, and a plat-
form for future advancement. Oh, that America had a few of
them today.

I received back a very polite and apologetic response, which made me
feel pretty guilty because my letter was kind of nasty and *Fortune* really
does an excellent job of reporting about Japan. Still, this particular
article was misdirected. The Japanese focus is upon action. The outcome is almost irrelevant; neither cause for celebration or remorse. It
merely provides a knowledge base for further advances.

Information—continually gathered and constantly updated—obtained from a variety of sources, especially first-hand company experiences, and broadly shared is a sine qua non for dealing with chaos. The
information is used continually to revise and adapt the strategy, which
remains highly flexible.

Flexible Strategy

The great British economist, Sir John Maynard Keynes, was an outspoken free trade advocate all of his life—until the depression years of
the 1930s, when he suddenly reversed his position and became protectionist. Called to task on this in a public meeting by one of his many
detractors, Keynes turned to the man and said, "When the facts change,
I change my mind. What do *you* do, sir?"

The Japanese well understand that story. They have never been terribly concerned with theoretical arguments; they are archetypical prag-
matists. When the facts change, the strategy changes—but always within
the guidelines of the immutable mission. Strategy simply evolves.

What is at work here is the concept of *kaizen* with its incremental
approach of gradual, unending improvement, doing little things better,
and achieving ever higher standards. Out of the day-to-day advances on

a myriad of fronts come evolving changes to long-term plans. Hitachi, for example, in computers has had a policy of acquiring knowledge in nearby markets and then moving elsewhere step by step—*ippo ippo*, as the Japanese call it. Formal planning is not a sacred cow; actions tend rather to be unplanned, pragmatic responses to a changing situation. Sony's corporate executive in charge of strategy described his firm's computer business as "kind of a trial and error."

For the Japanese firm, great success seldom results from bold strategic thrusts. Rather, it comes from half good ideas that are incrementally improved upon. At Matsushita, structured planning is not overly burdensome. NEC's move into semiconductors, Honda's entry into automobiles, and more recently several firms' pursuit of high-definition television (HDTV) may have appeared to be dramatically new strategies, but in reality they were built upon existing strengths of the respective firms. These were not strategic leaps; they were tactical steps.

Ichiro Hattori, Epson's chairman, indicates that his company's diversification strategy simply evolved. Heavy investment in the 1970s by the Seiko division in race timers and indicator display systems bore fruit a few years later in the form of digital printers and personal computers. Quartz electronic watches paved the way for electronic components. The firm's precision-machining techniques led to the manufacture and marketing of machine tools, automatic assembly systems, and robots.

Toshiba's chairman has said that "Strategy is the result of a steady and continuous accumulation of effort. Strategy comes almost after the fact." Matsushita Electric's erstwhile president Toshiko Yamashita has commented, "At Matsushita we don't really have a master plan. The system guides the company in a positive way. We have no long-term plans, only a long-term vision [mission]."

In summary, then, once the mission is in place, a strategy is designed to realize it. It comes as a result of the gathering of enormous amounts of information, study, and analysis that is widely disseminated and discussed. Yet once action is taken, the strategy is constantly adjusted to changing realities. Those new realities become known by a continual updating of information and the step-by-step seeking of improvements.

The firm is able to adjust to shifting strategies, at least partly, because the men who staff it have been trained as generalists; they are not locked into a singular approach to a problem based upon specific training. Nor are they concerned about changes of strategy costing them their jobs; lifetime employment guards against that. Consensus decision making assures that all the relevant issues each salaryman may raise will be explored. Strategies can be shifted without setting the firm adrift because a constant eye is kept on the mission: flexible strategies fit perfectly within the larger Japanese management style.

There is one more thing about these salarymen and their companies. They are committed.

Commitment

"The Samurai thinks not of victory or defeat but merely fights insanely to the death." That was the Bushido warrior code of centuries ago. But the samurai of the past has been reincarnated into today's business executive, most of whom have the same sense of commitment.

Commitment—not to strategy but to mission and the immediate task at hand, in the form of patience, determination, and the willingness to allocate sometimes inordinate human and capital resources—is a basic quality of Japanese management style.

Japanese firms rarely abandon a product line; there is shame in doing so. Rather, they tend to pursue *kaizen* (continual enhancement and improvement) until it finally succeeds, albeit in a final form perhaps different from that originally intended.

Nissan lost money in the United States for ten years before turning a profit, and it took Minolta six years to stanch its flow of red ink in the U.S. copier market. Five of the ten largest banks in California are now Japanese; they account for almost 25 percent of all construction loans. Yet the banks have been shaving profit margins and buying market share, and are showing a relatively poor (though slightly improving) return on assets. That does not matter. They are here for the long term; they are committed. Other Japanese financial institutions in the United States are prepared to lose money for years. In electronics, NEC invested heavily in semiconductors for thirteen years before earning its first Yen of profits. Japanese Hollywood movie investors have now backed several stinker films, which has not deterred them from launching new projects. There are a thousand other examples.

These short- to mid-run losses can be tolerated because of a combination of factors. Japan's high savings rate that has kept capital costs relatively low certainly helps. Beyond that, the *keiretsu* structure allows the burden of low, or negative, earnings for a given product or firm to be borne by other more successful products of the firm, or by other members of the *keiretsu*. With large equity holdings by other *keiretsu* members, including the core bank, there is little pressure to show short-run profits. The undertaking of a risky new venture by a consortium of firms, along with a mix of government subsidies, also helps to mitigate poor short-run performance.

The commitment of company resources is complemented by each individual employee's commitment. We talked about this in an earlier chapter, where we saw the inordinate dedication of the salaryman. But for a quick refresher, consider the Nomura men and the Kyocera men.

Kyocera, the world's leading high-tech ceramics maker, during its first years of business thirty years ago required its workers to live in crude dormitories on the company grounds; they were allowed to see their families only on occasional weekends. Even today, the young employees still live in dormitories. At morning formation, supervisors snap the plant foreman a military salute and report the number of workers present. The company's operation in San Diego had some very serious technical start-up problems. Two dozen engineers were flown in from Japan. They spent the next three months working eighteen-hour shifts seven days a week—the problems were solved.

One of the world's finest companies, Nomura Securities, has forged committed salarymen that military generals throughout the ages would have yearned to have in their ranks. After morning exercises and status meetings at Nomura branch offices, the newest recruits begin their day of calling upon customers. As they leave one by one, each man turns back toward his department and bellows at the top of his lungs: "I am off to serve my customers and inform them of the latest trends." He then bows respectfully to his colleagues and sprints—yes, sprints—out the door.

When the tricolor of Napoleon's legions was moving across Europe there were occasions when it was blocked by stubborn resistance; the Austrians in particular proved intractable. After mounting battle losses, Napoleon addressed his disheartened troops, exhorting them, "When you start to take Vienna . . . take Vienna." They did. This commitment to the immediate objectives and to the larger mission is evident in the successful Japanese firms. There may be more than one way to take Vienna (flexible strategy) but it *will* be taken. The personal commitment of the salaryman, complemented by the corporation's culture of commitment, has been fundamental to success.

Culture plays a role in personal and corporate commitment. The popular Western adage, "A rolling stone gathers no moss," is a case in point. To an American, its meaning is clear . . . move on, get some action, if you stay where you are, you'll become rusty; a rolling stone is good. The Japanese interpretation is just the reverse. The rolling stone shows a lack of perseverance, staying power, and commitment. A rolling stone is not good. From its very inception, America has been a nation of immigrants, of rolling stones. Its vast frontiers always beckoned and our forefathers were constantly pulling up stakes and moving on. Yet for Japan for perhaps the last millennia there has been little or no immigration; and the land was so densely populated that there was no alternative but to stay where one was and make the best of the situation.

SUMMARY

James Abegglen, a recognized Japan expert, has said that, "One of the paranoid fantasies Westerners have about Japan is that they can see the future. They can't."

I'm not so sure. The postwar performance of the nation and its top companies is simply too remarkable to be explained by chance. Perhaps the extent to which a firm—or for that matter a nation—may be able to control its future and write its own destiny has been underestimated. We have talked about the three elements that combine to determine how it might be done: a carefully crafted and completely accepted mission; a flexible strategy, with an emphasis on constant improvement and a never-ending flow of information; and finally, an absolute commitment to success.

The Japanese firms that practice the policies described here may not be able to see the future, as Abegglen said, at least not in HDTV sharpness. But that isn't necessary. A rough and vaguely outlined but still discernible picture will do; the details can be filled in when the firm gets there. And when the future arrives, the picture that it has fashioned *will be* the reality. The rest of the world will simply have to accept it as a given.

How do the Yankee Samurai figure in all of this?

DESTINY . . . FOR THE YANKEE SAMURAI

To what extent have the three elements of the Japanese approach to dealing with the future crossed the Pacific to become a part of the thinking of the Yankee Samurai?

Is the mission inculcated in the Yankee Samurai? Do they approach strategy in the same spirit as the Japanese? Do they share the same sense of commitment as their Japanese colleagues?

MISSION . . . FOR THE YANKEE SAMURAI

The last chapter made clear that the Yankee Samurai realized that while strategies and plans were adjusted to reflect changes in the environment, the mission or vision remained unchanged. Strategies were guided by the mission, and there was an absolute commitment to it, regardless of apparent failure or loss. So far so good.

But at the same time most of the Yankee Samurai, while realizing the importance of their firm's mission, did not know specifically what it was. It had not been explained to them at hiring, nor was it discussed in day-to-day operations. While a few firms did have a clearly articulated mission, and a few others were in the process of getting one, most of them did not. Somewhat typical was the major electronics firm whose national manager of human resources commented: "While we [Americans] do *not* have a clear mission here, I think the Japanese *do* have a mission and are struggling to get there, while doing it through the Americans."

So, this fundamental of the successful Japanese firm, the mission, is missing for the Americans who work in most of the subsidiaries operating in the United States.

STRATEGY . . . FOR THE YANKEE SAMURAI

In Japan, management style relating to strategy is characterized by developing a thorough and detailed initial plan that may look ahead a decade or quarter of a century. That is, however, only a starting point. The plan is constantly updated and altered as circumstances change. Is this what the Yankee Samurai see? Look at the numbers. Recall that the asterisk* indicates statistical significance, and that 5 means Definitely true while at the other extreme 1 means Definitely Not True.

Strategy and Tactics

Statement	C	P	J
1. The strategy is guided by the mission statement, which indicates the firm's reason for being and its values and beliefs.	3.4*	3.1	5
2. The firm seems to believe that great results are obtained not from major strategic thrusts but rather from rough ideas that are incrementally improved upon.	3.2*	2.9	5

3. While strategies and plans are adjusted to re-   3.7*   3.2   5
    flect changes in the environment, the mis-
    sion, or vision, remains unchanged.

4. A given product or service is seldom aban-   3.1*   2.9   5
    doned, it simply continues to develop until
    market success has been achieved.

5. Once the mission has been established, the   3.3*   3.0   5
    strategy simply evolves from steady and con-
    tinuous effort.

6. Incremental adjustments to the strategy are   3.7*   3.4   5
    continually being made.

7. The development of strategy occurs from the   2.4   2.3   5
    bottom up in the organization, not from the
    top down.

You have to begin to appreciate the Japanese penchant for quantitative analysis; numbers really can tell a story by themselves. The
responses to the first six statements indicate that for the Yankee Samurai, their current (C) Japanese employer practices the Japanese management style relating to strategy to a statistically greater extent than
did their past (P) American employer. Mission plays a fundamental
role, and strategy simply evolves with it incrementally as events
change. The responses are directionally what might be expected in a
survey of salarymen in Japan.

The response to statement 7 is another matter. While the *firm* has an
approach to strategy similar to that practiced in Japan, with perhaps the
exception of a few senior Americans, the Yankee Samurai are often
rather passive onlookers. The Japanese hold all or nearly all of the top
positions, and it is they who apparently are setting the strategy. We have
already seen that the Yankee Samurai tend to lack familiarity with the
mission. The response here indicates they play no more of a role in
setting strategy than at corresponding American firms, where top management typically is calling most of the plays.

Consider some of the interview responses.

Detailed Planning and Flexibility

The Japanese planning process is characterized by a highly detailed
and well-thought-out strategy consistent with the mission's objectives.
Once this is in place, it continues to evolve as new information and new

facts become known. This indeed is what the Yankee Samurai saw.

The national manager of human resources has been with his second-tier automobile firm for three years and observed:

> Each year a five-year plan is put together. It is a very comprehensive plan that is not taken lightly. The Japanese do a very good job of planning, decision making, and follow-through.
>
> Having said that, things are not so set in concrete that as we go through time there are not adjustments. There may be several changes along the way, dealing with regions, dealers, new products, scheduling, employees, and so on. These changes are not a question of missing the mark, but rather of being flexible.

Another auto firm's corporate marketing manager said something rather similar: "We have a five-year plan that is updated yearly, based upon changes in the environment. We are always planning but we are always changing the plan."

The sales vice president from the same firm agreed, and made note of the vast amount of information the firm deals with:

> We spend a lot of time strategizing. Sometimes I think that we have too many facts to deal with. These facts are woven into short-, mid-, and long-range plans. The plans are very detailed. They also are very dynamic and flexible, in that they include contingencies should the environment change.

The auto firm's human resources manager saw much the same thing:

> The strategies very much shift. That is a unique asset of the company, its phenomenal flexibility. We learned that by having been in the motorcycle business long before the automobile business. That business was highly competitive, with many new models developed every year. It is a constant evolution of change and has become natural for us.

The general manager of accessory marketing described his electronics firm's approach:

> We have strategies both short term and long term. We try like hell to hang on to them, but we are pushed and shoved by our competition and have to keep changing them.
>
> Our goals, and certainly mission, are pretty much stable, but how you get there changes a lot.

The manager of computer and data network resources noted:

> If a decision is made that is seen to be a mistake, I sense no
> hesitation to accept that and turn 180 degrees and go somewhere
> else. They do that with amazing speed.
>
> If I were to pick one thing out from my whole three years here,
> it is the rapid change of strategies. We go full speed down a path
> developing a product or a market or consolidating warehouses. But
> if it is concluded that there was a mistake and a given strategy is not
> working, we stop, shut it down, and close it out.
>
> But we remain definitely committed to the product. We focus
> on the global policy statement [mission]. We are, and will con-
> tinue to be, in the computer business.

Finally, the trading firm's assistant to the general manager added:

> Japanese trading companies are acutely aware of changing fac-
> tors that influence the business and international climate. They
> have a long-range view and plan ten years ahead. That plan is
> modified according to conditions. Timing is all-important and the
> Japanese are very aware of that. They are concerned about whether
> a product is before its time, or perhaps has arrived too late.

Yankee Samurai: Not Included

The planning process seems to follow the basic approach consistent
with Japanese management style. But to what extent are the Yankee
Samurai participants and to what extent are they merely observers in
setting strategy? The evidence would seem to indicate they are largely
watching the game from the bleachers. Notice how frequently the words
"they," "them," "their," and "Japanese" appear below when discussing
the issue. The young trading coordinator, for example, in the short
quote that follows speaks almost entirely in the passive.

> The Japanese are very flexible in the way they look at their job.
> When something goes wrong, they don't ever get hung up on it.
> They just move on to the next thing. When a major financial
> mistake has been made, they will look at the problem, find the
> causes, see if there is a way around it, and then move on; it doesn't
> bother them. They seem to be able to roll with the punches and
> keep things in perspective very well.

You will see the same passive usage in much of what follows. The word "we" is seldom evident. Here is the electronics firm's human resources manager:

> The Japanese do plan things way into the future. But they are pretty flexible if the product turns out not to be adaptable to the American market. They have in their mind a three- to five-year business plan, but within that they have a tendency to be flexible.

Strategy setting, in Japan, is understood to be largely bottom up, yet the electronics firm's customer service rep isn't much involved: "I am kind of down at the bottom of the ladder, so I'm not sure what the strategies are. I just go and do what I am told." Nor is the manager of special projects for a large electronics firm: "In Japan, the top people in the company do not do the key marketing planning; the bottom controls the top. Yet here we [Americans] are not asked what products we want. The boats just keep coming . . . that is what happens."

The travel department coordinator also feels a little left out of things:

> All we hear is that there are a lot of changes. They are working new products very hard. But no one has sat down with me and explained where we are going and how it will be done. I am assuming they have some mission or strategy, but it has not included us.

The manager of procurement and materials has been with his firm since it first set up operations in the United States. Even so, he felt that:

> No one tells us what the strategies are and we don't know what the mission is. The Japanese see that, but the Americans don't. All that we see is that here is a company that has to make a profit. Our visibility stops there, but the Japanese see much farther than that.

The senior vice president described his bank's approach:

> Every six months, strictly dictated criteria are passed on from headquarters to us as to our targets over the next period. There will be no excuses as to why these targets are not met. Therefore this becomes a Tokyo-driven and not necessarily a market-driven environment.

The electronics firm's Louisiana-born project manager was actually angry when he said: "I have yet to see any kind of strategic plan, whether it be five, ten, or twenty years. I have not seen anything tactical, either. I have no idea as to where we are trying to get to. There is no downward

communication about our objectives!" The pattern continues with a
marketing services manager, who says: "The strategies set in Japan are
fixed. I am not privy to a lot of that." Another firm's national account
manager added: "Unfortunately, I don't know what the strategies are."

Finally, the vice president and head auditor of a major bank noted
just how distant his operation was from Tokyo:

> Much of the bank's strategy is dictated from Japan. In the eyes
> of Tokyo, our president here is the equivalent of nothing more
> than a branch manager at a large office in Tokyo. While he might
> have a lot of good ideas, if Japan doesn't agree, then that is the end
> of it. If our Japanese president here is not involved in strategy, I
> can assure you that we [Americans] are not.

All of this is not to say that the Yankee Samurai are playing no role at
all in strategy setting or that changes are not under way to give them a
greater voice. We know that the Japanese do gather a great deal of information from the Yankee Samurai—consultative decision making. But
beyond that, only a few firms were actively involving the Americans.

The auto firm's corporate import distribution manager, for one, indicated that Americans were beginning to play a larger role in strategy
setting: "The strategies are pretty flexible; they have to be. The long-
range plan has historically been determined in Japan, but that is beginning to shift."

The young Hispanic banker talked about flexibility and his involvement in setting strategy:

> We are constantly reanalyzing our efforts to achieve a goal.
> Many times I will give my view about how a strategy should be
> approached. If it is totally wrong, we just go back and try again.
> We are very flexible.
>
> There is a lot of talking, almost too much, about how we are
> doing and whether something else should be tried.

There were a few other examples of this, but the basic trend was
otherwise: strategy setting seems to be largely out of the hands of the
Yankee Samurai.

COMMITMENT: FOR THE YANKEE SAMURAI

The third element of the Japanese management style is an absolute
commitment to the mission and task at hand. That commitment is
manifest both by the firm and by its employees in their individual tasks.

Do the Yankee Samurai see their firm's commitment and are they personally committed? Check out the numbers first.

Commitment

Statement		C	P	J
1.	There is an absolute commitment to the mission, and the firm is quite willing to endure even fairly long-term failure and losses to achieve success.	3.4*	2.7	5
2.	Return on investment is perhaps the most critical factor for consideration in the decision process.	3.0*	3.6	2
3.	I work harder here than I ever have.	3.5*	3.2	5
4.	People stay alert to job opportunities outside of the company.	3.5	3.6	1
5.	My work ethic seems to have improved as a result of my employment here.	3.1	2.9	5

The responses to the first two statements are entirely consistent with the concept of the Japanese firm's commitment compared to corresponding American companies. The responses to the last three statements probe the issue of personal Yankee Samurai commitment. The results are mixed. The Yankee Samurai are essentially no more loyal or committed to their Japanese firms than they previously were to their American employers; however, they do seem to work a little harder.

Listen to the interview responses regarding their firm's commitment; the Yankee Samurai see it as being very real. Here, for example, is the electronics firm's manager of procurement and materials:

> The Japanese seem to be fairly inflexible. I think that is one of their weaknesses. Once they make a decision, they just go for broke . . . to a point. When it becomes obvious they are riding a dead horse, there will be a change. They will make it work. They will shove a square peg into a round hole and do whatever is necessary to make it work. That goes back to their culture and society. They don't like failure or to lose face and are absolutely committed to succeed.

Another electronics firm's director of material controls felt the same way:

> [Company name] has made a commitment to the U.S. market to manufacture on-shore. We are moving in that direction. We are taking long-term planning five to twenty years in the future.
>
> Short term there are many changes and [company name] is flexible. But the firm is here for the long haul; they are making the investment. They are not going away.

The vice president of marketing for a major laptop computer company also underscored the Japanese commitment:

> The Japanese certainly are committed. Suppose a Fourth of July picnic was planned in the strawberry field just to the west of our Los Angeles plant. If the big one [earthquake] came along the day before and instead of the strawberry field there was the Pacific Ocean, then by God, on the Fourth of July, we would all go marching into the water [laughs].

The manager of new product marketing commented that, "The Japanese are very long-term planners. They will set a goal ten years out and will suffer the ten years to get there. They will run in the red for ten years, but Americans won't do that." The auto firm's Japanese-American vice president said tersely, "[Company name] is absolutely committed to this market. We will live or die with America."

Another auto firm's marketing vice president made the same point: "It is not just lip service to say that we are committed to the American market. I have to believe there is commitment when the firm is investing $500 million in a new manufacturing facility."

The distribution manager of another auto firm, a man in his mid-fifties, said that his "company is extremely committed to the market. They came in here with an attitude that they would not fail under any circumstances. We have had some horrible situations develop but we have always had support from Japan."

The bank lending officer, a woman in her mid-thirties, said:

> I sense a very strong commitment. The Japanese are very long-term players and think about the future many more years out than the Americans. They have committed a lot of capital resources here. Losses, even extended losses, don't seem to matter.

Finally, the electronics firm's marketing vice president noted:

> The Japanese cannot understand why Americans give up so easily. It took us thirteen years before we made our first dollar in

the semiconductor business. Three years later, we became number one in the world.

They will begin projects that they will not complete in their lifetime. American management wants to start a project and turn a profit with the first quarter. Certainly no American CEO is interested in any long-term investment that will not bear fruit until after he retires. The short-run investment losses will drive down stock prices and hurt his precious stock options. I know; I've worked for American companies.

The personal commitment and work ethic of the Yankee Samurai was explored in chapter 5, with the conclusion that both seem somewhat stronger than in corresponding American firms. Still, the degree cannot compare to the Japanese. Here are two somewhat contrasting Yankee Samurai views.

The human resources manager for one of the smaller automobile firms felt employee commitment was very good:

> The team spirit has caught on, but I don't know if it can be maintained. You don't find a lot of people here working eight to five. You see many coming in early and staying late. People have an attitude of doing what they have to do to get the job done.

The Yankee Samurai commitment to work may be reasonably strong, but that does not always translate into a commitment to the firm. The major bank's senior consultant has been wrestling with the issue of lacking Yankee Samurai commitment:

> [Japanese] employee commitment to the organization is very deep and therefore there is no question that the commitment to the mission is total. It is not like an American company today that has little regard for its people and the people have little regard for it.
>
> Here at our bank, the Americans feel absolutely no loyalty at all. How we bring our American troops into this thing is another matter. I don't think anyone has the answer to that.

Certainly, no single factor can explain the success of a Japanese firm. At the same time the planning process described here of an articulated and inculcated mission, a detailed but flexible and constantly updated strategy, and commitment to the mission and task at hand, do combine to give the firm some control over its own destiny. Yet from what we have seen here for the Japanese U.S. subsidiaries, it is a destiny largely forged by the Japanese themselves, and not by the Yankee Samurai.

11

The Role of Culture

Two cultures cannot exist on equal footing side by side. That is out of the question. Hellenic culture could not live under Roman influence. Roman culture disappeared. The one in time must destroy the other.
—HOUSTON CHAMBERLAIN

INTRODUCTION

Ultimately this book is about culture and the clash of cultures. To the extent that only a modest amount of Japanese management style was observed among the white-collar Yankee Samurai, the explanation is cultural. And to the extent that Japan's economy is strong, and getting stronger, while America's is at best holding its own, the explanation is again cultural.

National culture matters. And yet American management theorists, when musing endlessly about leadership, motivation, decision making, planning, staffing, and the rest of what is presumably known about the science or art of management, have seldom taken it into account. They simply accept the American culture as a given. American economists also too often disregard the impact that culture has on national well-being. They assume that people all around the world are driven by the same forces that drive Americans. Yet per capita savings in Japan is

$45,000 while it is $6,000 in the United States, and American CEOs take home four times the compensation of their Japanese counterparts. There is nothing in economic theory that explains this; but culture does. As international trade increases and multinational firms expand their operations abroad, and as our knowledge about other lands and other peoples grows, narrow egoistic cultural views are becoming increasingly untenable. Much of what has been written in American management and economic textbooks and what is being taught in America's business schools will have to be amended. The United States is not the world; management is not U.S. management, and economics is not U.S. economics. And American culture is most assuredly not the world's culture.

Ideology, ethics, and culture more generally, all play a very significant role in a people's economic condition, including the management style of their public and private institutions. A society's culture influences societal cooperation, trust, decision making, communication, perceptions, work ethic, and behavior. It determines the society's mission and commitment to that mission, and it defines the control mechanism whereby a nation governs itself. This carries directly over to the economic institutions within the society. These institutions in turn influence the societal culture by the products and services produced, wages paid, merit orientation, hiring and firing practices, autocratic or collegial management approach, sense of social responsibility, competitive practices, and treatment of minorities and women.

In the case of Japan, its unique societal culture is mirrored in the management style of its business institutions, as well as being fundamental to the nation's overall economic success.

THE EXPORT OF MANAGEMENT STYLE

If culture is indeed a decisive factor in determining a nation's economic strength and the structure of its management systems, then the question arises as to just how transferable a management system is from one culture to another. An effective system operating within a given culture may not be similarly effective when practiced within a different cultural environment. The approaches to management that are successful in Japan may prove to be unworkable elsewhere because of differences in national ethos. Another nation may not be able, or want, to emulate Japan's management style because of cultural differences. Adoption, then, of Japanese management style by another nation can-

not come without the rest of the Japanese cultural package . . . a price
that another nation may not be willing or able to pay.

Can the Japanese management system be effective in the United
States, with its strikingly different cultural base? You have seen some
partial answers to this earlier in the book, and perhaps made some
preliminary judgments on your own, but the final answer will have to
wait until the last chapter. For now, let us examine just how distinct
those two cultures are when comparisons between the United States and
Japan are drawn.

CULTURAL CONTRASTS

Culture has been referred to as the set of important assumptions that
members of a community share in common, the way ordinary people
voluntarily behave, or the collective programming of the mind, determined by history and geography. The elements of culture include language, ritual, and social structure. The *World Book Encyclopedia* says
that "Culture is the sum total of the ways of life of a people." Daniel
Webster thinks that, "Culture is the totality of a society's behavior
patterns, beliefs, and institutions."

This could go on for a week since almost everyone who has ever written
about this subject adds his or her own definition. Here is mine, and the
one that will be used here: a society's culture is *the totality of its beliefs,
traditions, values, institutions, myths, language, history, and vision.*

Armed with that, how can we go about measuring and comparing
cultures? One sociologist, Geert Hofstede, suggests four dimensions:
individualism versus collectivism; population inequality; uncertainty
avoidance; and masculine versus feminine. That's not bad, but I'm
going to consider a more inclusive set:

CULTURAL DIMENSIONS

Ultranationalism
Homogeneity
Primacy of Education
Religious Underpinning
Group Precedence
Law and Order
Separate Male/Female Roles
Continuity with the Past

Defining and contrasting each of these for the two countries will not be easy. The dozens of definitions of culture make clear just how slippery the concept is; each of the dimensions themselves has a certain subjectivity about it. Nevertheless, we will begin to see within just a few pages just how very different the cultures of these two nations are from one another—in fact, they are at near-polar extremes.

ULTRANATIONALISM

Ultranationalism is taken to mean a citizenry's united and deep sense of identity with its country, respect for its symbols and traditions, belief in preserving its independence and influence, acceptance that its actions internationally (whatever they might be) are right and just, and a willingness to pay, the ultimate price—to die for it.

Nearly all Americans bristle when challenged about their patriotism. Yet, in America, flag burning goes unpunished, while in Japan the mayor of Nagasaki was the target of an assassination attempt for having done nothing more than remark that perhaps the emperor, the very symbol of Japan, had played an active role in World War II.

During that war, for every one American who died fighting in the Pacific, four surrendered—a ratio of 1:4. For the Japanese, the figures are reversed—10:1 (that is, ten died for every one who surrendered) and they are as high as 120:1 for some campaigns. A Japanese philosopher once wrote: "To believe and not to act is not to believe." These men, who willingly sacrificed their lives, did believe. This is ultranationalism.

After hostilities in the Gulf War had ended, Peter Arnett, the American newsman for CNN who had been stationed in Baghdad during the conflict, was asked if he, as a professional reporter, would have withheld information even though it might have cost the lives of thousands of American troops. With only a moment's hesitation he answered, "Yes." It is impossible to imagine a Japanese newsman responding that way—impossible.

Japanese national holidays are generally respected, with millions attending shrines and temples. On the other hand, holidays for millions of Americans have all but lost their meaning beyond blazing newspaper ads: "July 4 Bargain Day," "Memorial Day 50% Off Sale," "24 Hour Veteran's Day Clearance."

If you have ever had a conversation with a Japanese man or woman, invariably you will hear him or her use the term "we Japanese," indicating just how strong is their feeling of nationalism and how close is their identity with one another. Such terms are rarely used in America.

Nationalism is closely linked to a people's sense of their history. Japan's history, which goes back some 6,000 years, is a very real part of the Japanese conscience. The people know, understand, and are proud of it. Precisely because of that, efforts have recently been made at revising school textbooks written during the MacArthur occupation that refer to Japan's "aggression" in World War II. More benign and euphemistic terms are being proposed, and Japan as the victim of the war rather than the aggressor is being suggested. Whatever non-Japanese may think of this—the Chinese and Koreans certainly don't like it—it is in fact robust nationalism. Particularly because a case can be made that the American, British, Chinese, and Dutch powers gave the Japanese little choice in the 1930s between fighting or accepting a secondary role to their own in the Pacific. History—the links to the past—matters to the Japanese; it is fundamental to a sense of nationalism. Yet three fourths of America's high school seniors cannot determine within fifty years when that nation's Civil War was fought and do not know what the Emancipation Proclamation is; 90 percent of black students do not know.

Japan's actions internationally are nearly unanimously supported by the citizenry, another indicator of nationalism. In America there is literally no government foreign policy action that will not bring dissidents to the streets. Now, the dissidents may assert that it is they who are the true patriots, and they may indeed be right. But that is not the point. America lacks a nationalist uniformity of viewpoint—"Our country right or wrong, but our country." Ultranationalism is directly linked to consensus. It cannot exist without it.

In Japan, company mission statements invariably include references to the nation and the importance of advancing its interests. No such statements are generally found in an American firm's mission—assuming the firm even has one. Japanese workers on assembly lines actually believe that they do a disservice to their nation if they produce a product purchased by a foreigner that is in any way flawed. This is a factor in their work ethic and quest for quality. When was the last time an American worker was seriously motivated out of a concern for letting his or her country down? You would probably have to go back to "Rosie the Riveter" in 1945.

Nationalism affects the Japanese workplace, then, as a motivating work force that has no equal in the United States. But it does something more. For over a century, Japanese firms abroad have served as the eyes and ears of the Tokyo government by communicating relevant information back home. And Japanese companies have built their long-term strategies taking account of national goals. There is no American equivalent to this, although CIA operatives no doubt are in contact with American firms operating in the Middle East, Latin America, and Europe. Certainly, American companies have not coordinated their plans with a well-thought-out national industrial policy because there isn't one.

HOMOGENEITY

Japan is perhaps the most racially and culturally homogeneous nation in the world. There have been virtually no new additions to the gene pool since the eighth century, allowing its culture to develop in virtual isolation. That has been the foundation of Japan's single community, language, way of thinking, acting, rules, and customs. Only about 3 percent of Japan's population are "minorities," and they are almost entirely segregated from the rest of society. It is a tight-knit, almost tribal, nation-state, with a shared sense of purpose that places a high value on the purity of its race and uniqueness. The Japanese call it "Yamamotoism."

Geography has played a role in this homogeneity not only of race but of behavior. Because of Japan's mountainous terrain, the majority of the nation's population lives on the relatively narrow Kanto Plain on the central island of Honshu in and around Tokyo. The resulting extremely high population density has led to an extraordinary cultural uniformity. It is as though the condition of overcrowdedness simply could not tolerate aberrant behavior, which might lead to a loss of harmony.

A homogeneous people can more readily come to a national consensus decision; over the years, a large percentage of the legislation voted upon by Japan's Diet (Parliament) has passed nearly unanimously. A single party, the LDP, has been in power since the 1950s. There are factions within the party, but they are based on personality cults, not ideological differences.

While Japan is arguably the most homogeneous of nations, the United States is the most heterogeneous. The time is nearing when half the population will be of non-European heritage. That will happen in California within this decade, and California has always been a bellwether state. In Los Angeles, 18 percent of the public school population is Caucasian; 17 percent black; 57 percent Hispanic; the remaining 8 percent are a mix of Asian and "other." By the turn of the century, nationwide 85 percent of industry new-hires will be women, or black, Hispanic, and Asian men.

With the exception of what was the USSR, heterogeneity in the

United States is quite unlike that of other nations that are made up of two or three groups at most, such as the English- and French-speaking peoples of Canada. It is not so simple in America. The black population represents 12 percent of the whole. Its roots trace to dozens of African nations and hundreds of tribes within those nations. More recently there has been growing legal and illegal immigration from Nigeria, Sudan, Cameroon, Haiti, Jamaica, and the Dominican Republic, which renders the black population even more diverse. Added to this are almost three centuries of miscegenation between blacks and whites—forced upon the blacks at least until 1865—that have resulted in a whole spectrum of "blackness." Some 10 percent of the country are Hispanics who are of Puerto Rican, Cuban, Mexican, and Central and South American heritage. Except for the Spanish language, cultural differences among them are far greater than similarities. The Asian population is estimated at 5 percent; it contains people from a dozen nations, including Cambodia, Vietnam, South Korea, Thailand, Hong Kong, and Taiwan, who share little common history or culture. In addition, there are Indians, Pakistanis, Lebanese, Iranians, Filipinos, Armenians, Tibetans, Azerbaijanis, Egyptians, Latvians, New Zealanders, Turks, Afghans, Icelanders, Samoans, Palestinians, and more. Dozens of school districts across the country have the responsibility of somehow educating children when one hundred and more different languages are spoken among the students.

The United States is not heterogeneous in the sense of two or three major groups; rather, it is moving toward becoming a "mini-United Nations." This is a relatively new phenomenon. Until only a generation ago, the United States was basically white European, with a small black population, and even smaller Asian and Hispanic ones. But, beginning in the 1960s, when Lyndon Johnson quietly imposed sweeping changes in the immigration laws, America's demographics have shifted dramatically. The rate of legal—and especially illegal—immigration in the 1980s far surpassed that of any other decade in U.S. history. Also unprecedented is the ethnic mix of immigrants. Historically, the "huddled masses" who sailed past the Statue of Liberty and were processed at Ellis Island came predominantly from Eastern and Western Europe. The new wave of immigrants on the other hand are largely Asian and Hispanic; immigration laws favor them.

Arthur Schlesinger, Jr., in a recent book, has commented upon the impact these recent trends have had in America: "A cult of ethnicity has arisen among non-Anglo whites and among non-white minorities to denounce the idea of a melting pot, to challenge the concept of 'one people,' and to protect, promote, and perpetuate separate ethnic and racial communities."

The contrasts between the two nation's cultures will become even more evident in the following pages. But few differences are more striking than this Japanese homogeneity and American heterogeneity. It has profound implications for other cultural factors because culture implies a *commonality* of belief, traditions, language, institutions, values, and so on. But if a body of people is so diverse that they do not share these things, then almost by definition, how can such a people even be said to *have* a culture?

PRIMACY OF EDUCATION

A pronounced cultural disparity between the United States and Japan shows up in their respective educational institutions and attitudes toward learning. The structures of the two institutions are radically different, as are the results. With a literacy rate of 99 percent, the Japanese people are the most highly educated in the world—that translates into an elite work force.

In the United States, the National Assessment of Educational Progress recently completed a survey of college graduates. It was found that 53 percent of them could not restate the main argument of a newspaper article, 48 percent were unable to figure out a bus schedule, and 52 percent were incapable of calculating a 15% tip for a simple meal. Among seventeen-year-olds, only 6 percent of them could answer questions such as, "If Mary borrows $850 for one year and pays 12 percent simple interest, what is the total she repaid?"

New York Telephone had to interview 60,000 entry-level job applicants in order to hire 3,000 reasonably qualified people; Polaroid is teaching basic English and arithmetic to one third of its hourly workers; at the Prudential Life Insurance office in Newark, New Jersey, 44 percent of the applicants for nonmanagement or professional positions could not read at the ninth-grade level.

Illiteracy is not America's only problem; so is innumeracy. The Educational Testing Service reports that half of America's seventeen-year-olds are unable to answer multiple-choice questions such as:

> Which one of the following is true about 85% of 10?
>   a. Greater than 10
>   b. Less than 10
>   c. Equal to 10
>   d. None of the above

The report also indicated that about 35 percent of the nation's eleventh graders—to say nothing of the 25 percent who have already dropped out of high school—write at or below the following level:

> I have been experence at cleaning house Ive also work at a pool be for I love keeping thing neat organised and clean. Im very social Ill get to know peopl really fast.

A recent congressional study concluded that 80 percent of the nation's eleventh graders could not write a note applying for a summer job; two thirds of high school seniors could not distinguish between the Revolutionary and Civil wars, and 25 percent of them could not name the nation on the U.S. southern border; the majority of eighteen- to twenty-four-year-olds cannot locate England or France on a world map; less than 10 percent can find Japan!

Of the country's 4 million eighteen-year-olds, one fourth drop out of high school and another fourth can barely read the words of their diploma. That translates into a future population that is 50 percent functionally illiterate. Today, the functional illiteracy rate has been estimated as high as 30 percent; it is greater still for blacks and Hispanics.

Japanese students' training in math and science is unsurpassed. Recent U.N.-administered tests placed Japan first, while the United States finished fifteenth among nations of the world, not too far ahead of Swaziland. The lowest 25 percent of the Japanese high school student performers did better than the United States' top 25 percent.

With a one-third longer school year, young Japanese spend hundreds of hours more a year in class than their American counterparts. And beyond that, most of the high school students attend after-hours private tutoring schools, called *juku*.

Japanese primary school children study at home for two hours daily. The *Japan Times* reports that fourth through sixth graders average 7.3 hours a day of study; the figure for high school students is 8.1! Fourteen-year-olds still at their desks at 1:00 A.M. are not unusual. In preparing for college entrance examinations, high school students cram late into the night for months on end. There is a saying, "Pass with four and fail with five," which refers to the limited hours of sleep the young scholars are able to get while preparing for *shiken jikoku* ("examination hell"). Two thirds of the test-takers fail and take another full year, or two, to study for a second and third try.

By contrast, over the last decade homework in the United States has declined by 30 percent. Sixty percent of high school seniors study less than one hour a day.

In the United States, elective courses such as cooking and driver's education may count as much as English, history, and science toward a high school degree. The readings of Albert Einstein, Madame Curie, Theodore Roosevelt, Washington Carver, and dozens of other great historical figures have now been replaced in many American schools by study of contemporary athletes, musicians, and actors—it is the only way to get tomorrow's American leaders to read. In high schools around the country, but especially those in the inner cities, young males spend perhaps twenty-five hours a week practicing on a football field, track, baseball diamond, or basketball court. The same young men spend literally no time studying and often skip class, yet they continue to advance from grade to grade. At the college level, 80 percent of black athletes use up their four years of athletic eligibility and do not graduate.

The head of the National Teachers Union believes that only 5 percent of American high school graduates are truly qualified to do college work. The proof of this is evident on almost any college campus, where first-year students are overwhelmingly enrolled in remedial math and English courses that a generation ago were taught in the ninth and tenth grades.

Recent polls contrast high school students' attitudes and lifestyles in the two countries. The Japanese students' greatest interest is in mastering subjects, and friendships are drawn from one's own sex. For their U.S. counterparts, the primary interest is in extracurricular activities and their friendships are mostly with the opposite sex.

Many schools in the United States, particularly in the inner cities, provide an all but impossible learning environment. Buildings are filthy, decrepit, and graffiti-covered; drugs are openly sold and violence is common. Student assaults on teachers in New York City alone are six times greater than for all of Japan; the Los Angeles school system employs two hundred full-time armed security personnel—their responsibilities include frisking students for guns and knives. It is a near miracle for any inner-city youngster to succeed under such circumstances.

There are other characteristics of the Japanese education system that are strikingly different from the United States. One example is the Japanese use of the educational environment as a mechanism to inculcate morality. Students are taught discipline, nationalism, and to apply themselves with a single-minded effort and intense dedication. Group orientation is instilled and encouraged by requiring that the students wear school uniforms and have nearly identical haircuts. Japan's citizens are being sculpted in the classroom. On the other hand, prayer, moral training, and the inculcation of a sense of citizenship and nationalism in U.S. schools have essentially disappeared over the last quarter of a century. So too have uniform dress and haircut codes—as the parent of any of today's teenagers are well aware.

The Japanese system is merit-oriented, with a selection process that begins as early as primary school. Only the outstanding students are accepted into the best junior high schools. The winnowing process continues, with only the strongest junior high students gaining entrance to the most outstanding high schools. And the training from a good high school is critical in helping to overcome the rigors demanded for entrance into the most prestigious universities—at the apex of which is Tokyo University. Its graduates go on to fill top positions at the most powerful government ministries and largest corporations.

Americans, on the other hand, are generally discomfited by this merit orientation in their schools. In Alice's Wonderland, all of the creatures approached the wise Dodo bird and told him they wanted to race. He agreed, and without laying out a course or starting or finish line, he told them they could begin any time they chose. Some began immediately to run in large circles and some in small. Others sprinted madly back and forth. Still others walked or skipped. A few sat under shade trees and idly chatted. After about an hour, tired of this game, the creatures returned to the Dodo and asked who had won. The Dodo pondered long and hard, and finally concluded that, "Everybody has won, and all must have prizes." That is America's education system. For those who are willing to put in their time, all receive a prize—a high school diploma—even though large numbers of our students, our children, our treasures, our future, cannot read the language written upon it.

Fundamental to the academic success of the Japanese youngsters are their mothers, many of whom are referred to as *kyoiku mama*, or "education mother," who dedicate themselves to their children's achievement. These are largely nonworking mothers. There are relatively few "latch-key" Japanese youngsters returning home from school to an empty house with no supervision. In contrast, today only about 12 percent of American children are raised in a two-parent home where the father is working and the mother is a homemaker.

Corporal punishment administered by Japanese teachers—ruler slaps—is an everyday matter, and class sizes range from thirty to fifty students. In America, corporal punishment went out of vogue a generation ago—a teacher even touching a student today runs the risk of immediate dismissal and of course a lawsuit. And for all the grousing we hear from American teachers about the large size of their classes, they in fact are smaller than in Japan.

The Japanese focus on education is evident from polls that continue to show it as the nation's first priority; it ranks fifth or sixth in the United States. Teacher salaries in the United States are still not high enough to attract top people—the lowest university SAT scores invariably are found among students in the School of Education preparing to become teachers. Just how important education is at the university level is reflected in a telling statistic: the average salary of a professor at Ohio State University is $52,000, while the same school's football coach makes $550,000.

There is evidence that the Japanese have the world's highest IQs. Studies at several universities, including Michigan and Belfast, indicate that Asian IQs are measurably higher than Europeans'. James Fallows notes that by most estimates, Japanese IQs average about 10 points higher than American. This may be the cause of Japan's literacy . . . or the effect with heightened literacy improving IQ test scores. While there is debate among scholars as to the validity of IQ tests, the fact remains that the average reported Japanese IQ score is higher than that of three fourths of Americans.

Beyond providing the tools for tomorrow's jobs, the Japanese education system yields a commonly shared body of knowledge of history, language, geography, and the arts, which becomes the bond holding a society together. It is not clear that America's system achieves this; it could get worse. The Nobel Prize–winning economist Milton Friedman has had a lot of good ideas. However, the voucher system, which he has been pushing for over a decade and which now has many proponents, is not one of them. The system would allow parents to use government-provided vouchers for any school to which they choose to send their children. Granted that it will probably bring more competition to our schools, but it will do so at too heavy a segregating cost. Peoples of the same race, ethnicity, religion, and general philosophical belief will inevitably be drawn together as though by some powerful invisible magnet where like attracts like. We have way too much of that already. The schools must serve as an integrating force. They are one of the few institutions we have left that can do so.

Several of the Yankee Samurai commented on the American level of academic achievement. The corporate employment manager for a large Japanese automobile firm was one of them. He was an English major in college who voiced frustration and anger as he said:

As I look at the young people coming into the work force, I'm convinced we are seeing a terrible decline in educational levels. The workers coming in are substandard. I see it daily.

I have seen people with college degrees who cannot fill out an employment application. Perhaps 95 percent of them make mistakes in spelling and half have trouble writing a simple sentence.

People coming into the clerical ranks can't spell and can hardly speak English in many cases. Part of the problem is California. We have the charge of assimilating a lot of these different cultures.

I remember in college reading about the Dark Ages where civilization and learning almost disappeared in Europe. America is moving into its own Dark Ages. In Dante's *Divine Comedy*, he described Hell as some pit deep in the earth. I hope there is a special hell reserved for those who have allowed our education system to become what it has.

Religious Underpinning

As the "Age of Reason" dawned in the early eighteenth century, Voltaire wrote that "Mankind will be free when the last king is strangled with the entrails of the last priest." Men of "reason" have always rebelled against authority (kings) and religion (priests), because these two sources of power constrained them and limited their thinking and behavior. True; but religion, for all of its sometimes narrow-mindedness, meanness, and extremes, does bring order to a society. When Moses came down from the mountain with the Ten Commandments, he found his Hebrews, who had just been freed from Egypt and the Pharoah, stealing from one another, fornicating, lying, killing, and just generally having a good time—sort of like Times Square in New York City. The Ten Commandments, which the Hebrews believed came from God, was adopted by them and brought resulting order and stability to the society. God's appointed priests proceeded to interpret the law and pass judgment, and in the process built an entire religious system of tradition, ceremonies, and dogma—it was this kind of temporal power that Voltaire despised. Yet it served the Hebrews well. A now unified people, under God and the Law, they went on under Moses' successors to build a nation.

Perhaps if we were all men and women of "reason," we could, as Voltaire suggested, ". . . reach conclusions not by recourse to religion, rule, prejudice, or passion, but rather by bringing our minds fully and comprehensively to bear upon all the relevant and available information. Thus should we act." Unfortunately, the Age of Reason has not yet arrived. And like it or not, religion does bring order to society. Granted, this may not be desirable order in the eyes of some, but it is order nevertheless. A society that sets religion aside without replacing it with another set of moral standards does so with the nearly certain danger of disorder, nihilism, anarchy, and ultimately tyranny that will bring its own "new order."

None of this is a problem for the Japanese, where religion plays a critical, although largely subconscious, role in the society.

Confucianism

In the sixth century, Confucianism crossed the sea from China and became Japan's first major religion. Its teachings formed an ethical, as much as religious, system by providing the rules for social convention. Those rules include complementary filial, fraternal, and junior-senior relationships. The teachings also emphasize the importance of work, education, group harmony, and proper etiquette.

Loyalty, or devotion to one's *Daimyo* lord, is a basic principle of the religion. The voice of a samurai warrior, dead for over a thousand years, whispers from the grave of absolute loyalty to his sovereign:

> *At sea be my body water soaked*
> *On land be it with grass overgrown*
> *Let me die by the side of my sovereign*
> *Never will I feel regret*
> *—Yakamochi*

Confucianism has been the dominant moral principle in Japan for well over a thousand years and, although many Japanese people may not even realize it, remains so today. Its elements are manifest in contemporary Japanese management style.

Shintoism

Shintoism, with its worship of the sun goddess Amaterasu, developed from Taoism in about the eighth century, and has been fundamental in creating a strong sense of nationalism. That nationalism is apparent in the mission statement of many firms. Workers assiduously perform their duties to ensure that the quality of the product or service being produced will bring pride not only to their company but to their nation.

Buddhism

Buddhism flourished in Japan from about the seventh to twelfth centuries, and is still a force today. It taught individual salvation, and formed the basis for the arts, including architecture, writing, sculpture, and painting.

It was the religion of choice for the roughly 10 percent of the population who were samurai—the last of whom disappeared in the late nineteenth century. The teaching of the transience of life and the naturalness of death made these warriors fearless in battle. And the concentration learned from meditation was invaluable in the mano a mano combat so typical of Japanese warfare.

The religion underscored the importance and nobility of work. There is a story of a very old and frail Zen Buddhist master who taught his young acolytes at a monastery. Concerned about his health, one morning the followers hid their master's farming tools, which he used daily in the fields where the order grew its own rice. That evening, and for two ensuing evenings, it was noticed that the master declined his dinner. When finally asked why, the old man responded, "No work, no eat." His tools were returned. That work ethic is unchanged today, and is evident in the commitment of the labor force with its six-day work week and stingy welfare system.

Christianity

Christianity came to Japan early in the sixteenth century. It was brought by the Portuguese, whose interests were both religious conversion and lucrative trade opportunities, not necessarily in that order.

By 1543, Japanese Christians numbered nearly half a million, with the majority living in, or around, the port city of Nagasaki on the southernmost island of Kyushu. At least part of the new religion's popularity appealed to the secular side of the Japanese, with their interest in the West's trade and technology. However, beginning with Hidetada, the second Tokugawa, early in the seventeenth century, Christianity was brutally suppressed and all foreigners were banished.

Christianity has had very little impact on Japan. The pragmatic Japanese have never been terribly interested in wrestling with theoretical questions of the Trinity, good and evil, Heaven and Hell, existence of the soul, and original sin. Some of the basic principles, including "love thine enemy" and "turn the other cheek," are all but incomprehensible to most Japanese. The Christian concept of fairness would have a wealthy man give a poor man charity or some opportunity. Fairness in the eyes of the Japanese would mean exploiting or spurning the poor man, who has clearly failed as a person.

Today, although Japan has fewer than 2 million Christians, the entire nation celebrates Christmas—albeit in a highly commercialized version. This is consistent with the eclectic Japanese view of religion. Japan's religions have comfortably commingled, and an individual may well practice elements of several of them.

By contrast, over its brief history, the United States has been heavily influenced by the Judeo-Christian credo. Even though in recent decades growing numbers of non-Christians and secularists have considerably muted that influence, some 70 percent of Americans still call themselves Christian. Further, unlike Japan, there has historically been conflict between the various organized religions.

While religion has influenced the Japanese workplace significantly in terms of work ethic, group harmony, loyalty to firm and nation, and emphasis on training and education, it is difficult to see a corresponding influence in the United States—at least over the last forty years. The Protestant work ethic that equated leisure with sin is a relic of America's past. Americans today work for more pragmatic reasons. And the business world demonstrates little "ethical" behavior based on religious principles. Corporate social responsibility is driven at least as much by external political and market forces as by an internal ethical code of religious origin.

In America over the last generation, religion has been virtually severed from government, schools, and the workplace—its influence on these institutions has been marginal at best. For better or worse, religion, and what it teaches, does not play nearly as strong a conscious or subconscious role in America as it does in Japan.

Group Precedence

A winter visitor to Japan will notice some individuals on the street wearing white cotton masks. The visitor will probably assume that these are to protect the wearers from pollution or catching colds from someone. In fact, the mask is worn by people who already have colds and do not want to infect strangers. This extraordinary sensitivity to the group and responsibility to the larger society is characteristic of the Japanese culture.

The Japanese are probably the most group-oriented people in the world. It is rare for an individual not to belong to some group, whether

it be work or hobby, religious- or sports-oriented. Group outings, group
sightseeing, and group drinking are common, and there is a strong work
group identification.

A fundamental responsibility of the education system is to teach
cultural uniformity and impress upon students the importance of group
obligation. Children are taught to be attentive to other people and
sensitive to their concerns. The group orientation is felt to be critical for
a nation believing itself vulnerable to outside forces. Cooperation and
harmony become a matter of life and death. The Japanese simply accept
that their individuality will be restrained by the collectivity for the
common good.

The business environment is just one more manifestation of the
larger society's group orientation. It is natural to the employee. With
that comes individual loyalty to the firm, a sense of family, and a
facilitating of control and consensus decision making.

The situation in the United States is the exact reverse. Much of
Western culture is based upon views similar to Rousseau's that society
corrupts and debilitates the individual and restricts his self-expression—
directly contrary to the Japanese view. Expanding on Rousseau, Walt
Whitman wrote of the perfect and free individual; Thoreau—while
exiling himself to Walden Pond—rebelled against the intrusion of government; and Emerson championed the view that each man must think
for himself and act on his own instincts. The poet Robert Frost wrote
that "Good fences make good neighbors." All of these philosophical
principles are in sharp contrast to a group orientation, and are a reflection of an American cultural system largely based on a fierce individualism.

America's Revolutionary War patriots championed the belief that an
individual's right to life, liberty, and pursuit of happiness took precedence over even the survival of the state. Reflecting upon that, George
Washington commented that "I do not have a fighting army of 10,000
men, but rather an army of 10,000 generals." From its very inception,
America was a nation of individuals.

As geography has played a role in Japan's culture, so too it has greatly
influenced the American ethos. The vastness and relative emptiness of
the country during much of its history has encouraged individuality and
discouraged commonality. Beginning with the earliest colonial times
and later the opening of the West, a typical family of settlers fought off
freezing winters, scorching summers, disease, hostile Indians, and out-
laws. And with the nearest neighbors often many miles away, they
carried out their noble struggle largely unaided. Of necessity, then,

individualism with its dependency upon self has become almost genetically implanted into the national character.

The rugged "Marlboro Man" has entered into American folklore. On billboards, and in print ads—whether he is shown on horseback riding in a light, clean rain, sitting on a jagged rock at the edge of a precipice staring off into a golden sunset, or roping a recalcitrant steer to the ground—he is always alone. He is isolated from the rest of society. Yet that is his strength. He neither needs nor wants another human being. That is his appeal to the men who seek to emulate him and to the women who find him attractive. There are very few Marlboro men in Japan.

Group decision making is against the Western idea of working for something that will not bring individual distinction or reward. It is unreasonable to expect individualistic Americans to behave like group-oriented Japanese, yet group orientation is fundamental to Japanese management style.

Several of the Yankee Samurai commented upon the Japanese sense of group orientation. One of them was the director of materials control, who is on a fast track with his electronics firm, having just returned from a six-month rotation in Japan:

> When I was a kid, if it said, "Made in Japan," that meant that it would break in a day. Now, if it says, "Made in the U.S.A.," *that* means that it will break in a day.
>
> Quality starts with the individual employee. You have to understand that the Japanese people are a tribe. They work with the concept of what is good for the tribe. They do whatever it takes to make a quality product, and to support their firm and country. That tribalism is Japan's strength.
>
> The Americans are too self-centered and shortsighted. It is, "What is good for me today?" Our people don't seem to have a high enough caring level. That attitude leads to quality product differences.

America's unrestrained individuality and Adam Smith's "invisible hand"—every individual pursuing his or her own self-interest is guided as if by an invisible hand to do that which benefits all of society—has served America well for much of its history. But beginning in the early 1960s, something started to go horribly wrong. The myriad of cultural threads that were holding the country together were being torn. A sense of the "common good" and of national harmony began to slip away. Today, with our quotas for gender, race, and the handicapped, and our never-ending battle over rights, we are constantly pitting one group against another.

The titles alone of Lester Thurow's *The Zero-Sum Society* and Milton Friedman's *Tyranny of the Status Quo* tell of an America that is approaching societal gridlock. The advancement of one group, perhaps to correct a previous injustice, can come only at the expense of another, which of course fights back; the result is the status quo. Hundreds of small special interest groups, across the political spectrum, have gained enormous power to block actions that might benefit the vast majority of Americans but not themselves. We have become an entire nation of such groups, and the country has lost the ability to move forward together as a single people; the Japanese, with their strong racial identity, for better or worse, have not.

Law and Order

No city streets in the world are safer than Japan's. A woman can walk without fear throughout Tokyo at literally any hour of the day or night. Bicycles are left unchained at train stations for hours. Nearly all of Japan is like the small-town U.S.A. of the 1950s. The society largely polices itself.

The contrast to the United States is stark, where per capita murder, assault, robbery, and rape are the highest in the civilized world. The prison population has increased by two thirds since 1980; on a given day there are about 1 million prison or jail inmates; there are another 2 million on parole, two thirds of whom will ultimately be reincarcerated. For every black male in college, there is one that is in prison. All of this translates into the largest and most active criminal class in the world, numbering some 3 million. Compare this to Japan, with its almost negligible figure of 300,000.

Statistics show that a critical contributing factor to America's violent crime is illegal drugs. Cocaine alone accounts for 20 percent of the $100 billion annual drug trade business. In Los Angeles, where rival gangs wage war on one another with Uzis and assault rifles, there were four hundred drug-related murders in 1988, six hundred in 1989, and seven hundred in 1990. And at the other end of the country, there are twice as many murders in New York City as in all of Japan. Washington, D.C., is more than the nation's capital. The city, which is home to the seat of government of the most democratic and freest people in the world, is one of the most violent and dangerous in that same world. With the full power of the federal government behind him, the past drug "czar" William Bennett in 1986 thought that "It will take perhaps six or seven years to come to grips with the Washington, D.C., drug problem." That period has now passed and the problem is worse. Nationwide, the death rate among inner-city black males due to gang-related incidents now approaches the annual black casualty rate of the Vietnam War. Today, a black teenage man living in the inner city of Detroit, New York, Atlanta, Los Angeles, Chicago, and a dozen other large cities, would have been far safer facing 500,000 Iraqis in the 1991 Desert Storm battle than stepping out onto his own streets.

The drug problem in the United States is unique to that nation, and is all but out of control in many low-income minority communities. The National Institute of Drug Abuse estimates that nearly 40 million, or one in every six, Americans consume illicit drugs. Yet, when a group of Japanese are interviewed on the street and asked about Japan's drug problem, a puzzled look crosses their faces. "Do you mean like aspirin?" they ask. Heroin use, for example, is rare, and measures taken against its distribution are merciless. Japan has only the most minor of drug problems, mostly dealing with amphetamines—no great surprise for seventy-hour work week salarymen.

Nonviolent crime in the United States, from Boesky-Milken, to Clark Clifford and the BCCI scandal, to retail shoplifting, to David Keating and the entire S&L debacle, to worker compensation fraud, to welfare cheating, to corrupt televangelists, is part of the American scene. The loss to society, and the expense of administering the criminal justice system, totals hundreds of billions of dollars annually. White-collar crime alone is estimated to cost business $40 billion a year, and the FDIC estimates that one third of all bank failures are due to fraud.

American public law enforcement agencies are unable to cope. The Justice Department reports that America spends more today for private security than public—$52 billion compared to $30 billion. And the number of private "rent-a-cops" is now larger than the nation's combined sheriffs, highway patrolmen, and police—1.5 million compared to .6 million. Some jails are even being built and run privately.

We have been talking largely about order here, but what about the law part of "law and order"? The dissimilarity between the U.S. and Japanese legal systems is almost absolute. With over 800,000 lawyers in the United States—70 percent of the world total—America is by far the most litigious. The U.S. courts are clogged with criminal and civil cases. In 1985, Richard Ramierez was arrested in Los Angeles, accused of being the "Night Stalker" who raped and murdered some two dozen women. Five years later, after over $3 million in court costs, a jury brought in a guilty conviction and imposition of the death penalty. In 1992, seven years after the arrest, the appeals process is just getting under way—the souls of the victims will have to rest uneasy yet longer. These protracted, Kafkalike legal circuses have become the rule in America; they do not occur in Japan.

Americans file 18 million lawsuits a year, or one for about every fourteen of us. Only one generation ago the vast majority of these suits would have been laughed out of the courtroom. Yet today, a man who lost a leg by jumping in front of a Chicago El train in a failed suicide attempt is suing the transit authority because it did not have adequate guard rails to keep him from his self-destructive act. Cases such as this and hundreds of thousands far more frivolous are unknown in Japan, where plaintiffs in civil cases must pay a large nonrefundable fee.

Japan has only 20,000 lawyers, many of whom deal with foreign business interests. That is only one twentieth the per capita lawyers of the United States; there is a like percentage of civil suits. Policemen often work out traffic accident settlements on the scene, and business disagreements are generally resolved without recourse to the law. Medical malpractice suits are rare; if a patient dies under somewhat questionable circumstances, generally an apology by the physician and his attendance at the funeral is considered adequate compensation. In criminal cases, there is no plea bargaining and no trial by jury. The confession rate is 89 percent; defense attorneys are not allowed in interrogation rooms, and suspects can be detained for up to twenty-three days without being charged. In 1986, of 63,204 people receiving a criminal trial, only 87 were acquitted. That was a typical year. Conviction rates generally run over 98 percent and in 1981 hit 99.81 percent. In Japan, legal technicalities are not very relevant and certainly not decisive. It is the spirit, not the letter, of the law that matters.

In America, with overworked law enforcement officers, exclusionary rules that bar "tainted" evidence, overcrowded courts, and jampacked prisons, there is roughly one chance in a hundred that a felon will be caught, convicted, and do hard time. The economist Gary Becker among others has studied the economics of crime objectively and largely concluded that in America, crime pays.

These differences within the larger Japanese culture are reflected in the business arena, where control is not based on explicit legally drawn contracts, rules, regulations, and procedures, or accounting and auditing systems, but rather on a sense of family and mutual trust.

By contrast, the very pervasiveness of the law in the United States is a reflection of the near-complete collapse of any national sense of trust, family, or morality. That comes as little surprise given the population's marked heterogeneity, secularized religion, value-free educational teaching, and the lawlessness on Capitol Hill, in the boardroom, and on the streets. We try to compensate for the lack of these things with infinitely detailed codes of law, but it fails. Ultimately the law can achieve little more than what is in the hearts and minds of the people. And what exists in the broader culture of the United States is of necessity reflected in the management style of American firms, with their generally quite explicit policies, procedures, and control systems.

With mutual trust all but gone, employee-employer conflict grows. On the one hand, employee lawsuits brought against corporations for perceived discrimination (sex, age, race, sexual preference, and even obesity) are common, and organized labor continues to challenge management. On the other hand, senior management often responds to any few quarters of poor financial performance by vast across-the-board employee cutbacks that largely exclude its own ranks. General Motors senior management is not the only one that has recently ordered plant shutdowns and layoffs while at the same time awarding itself generous multi-million-dollar bonuses. The highly popular 1990 film *Roger and Me*, which pilloried G.M. and its chairman Roger Smith, while unfair and inaccurate in many respects, did touch a national nerve on the striking disparity between the treatment of top-level executives and the blue-collar work force.

The corporate environment is not isolated from the society as a whole. The men and women of a corporation bring into the workplace largely the same ethics, beliefs, and traditions they hold outside.

Separate Male/Female Roles

Partly because the Confucian ethic asserts the superiority of men over women, women in Japan face a world quite different from their American counterparts. It is a world where youth is celebrated with a separate Boy's Day and Girl's Day, but only the former is a national holiday. The highlight of Girl's Day is the *Hina Matsuri*, or Doll Festival, which has roots going back to the eighteenth century. Japanese men, by Western standards, are blatant chauvinists, who practice a double sex standard. Although women comprise 40 percent of the work force, their jobs are overwhelmingly in the lower brackets. The fields of higher endeavor are exclusively, or predominantly, the preserves of men. It is a man's world (*otoko no shakai*).

The culture is characterized by male dominance in professional and public life and philandering in private life. Men view women who are not family-oriented as either sex objects or economic cannon fodder. To the Japanese, a "feminist" doesn't have the meaning it has for Americans; instead, it refers to a man who is "kind" to women.

From early age, in preparation for marriage, girls learn the tea ceremony, flower arrangement, and traditional dancing. Career-oriented educational investment for women is generally viewed as unimportant. At the same time, the Japanese home is largely a matriarchy, with women having full responsibility for finances, the children, and aged in-laws. Remember the great strength and wisdom of Ma Joad in holding the family together in Steinbeck's *Grapes of Wrath*? A lot of Japanese women are like that. Polls show that 76 percent of Japanese women believe that life's task is to be a good wife and wise mother. They see little in the life of men that they wish to emulate.

Japanese management style has been built around a system of male dominance that is a reflection of the larger culture. The corporation is a male sanctuary. A myriad of management subtleties, practices, relationships, and communication styles flow from this.

In the United States, the women's movement may not have achieved all of its objectives, but it is still by far the most advanced in the world and light-years beyond what some view as the "Stepford" women of Japan. This raises questions of how effective Japanese management might be when encountering the culture shock of an American environment where the role of women is so very different.

Continuity with the Past

A nation's culture builds slowly over time—decades, centuries, millennia. History with all its myths and legends is crucial to that process. Yet Americans, especially the young people, are abysmally ignorant of their past. And even what is known is being challenged by those who question America's perceived racism, imperialism, and treatment of women and minorities. Our heroes—Christopher Columbus, General George Custer, even Thomas Jefferson with his black mistress—are being taken from us. Yet they and the myths and legends that surround them are part of American culture. Icons from the past are part of the glue that holds society together. Destroy them, and you destroy the culture. That may be good or bad depending upon one's point of view, but it is destruction nevertheless.

Japan, on the other hand, revels in its myths and legends. There are the forty-seven *ronin*; the great warrior-philosopher Miyamoto Musashi;

and the first shogun, Ieyasu Tokugawa, all of whom you met earlier. Ieyasu came to the shogunate following the largest pitched battle between samurai ever fought, on October 21, 1600, at Sekigahara. It was a day of fog, sleet, bitter winds . . . and blood. The heads of 40,000 of Ieyasu's enemies were taken on the field that day. And for wonderful drama and the stuff of legends, there was the "kamikaze." In the twelfth century, Genghis Khan sent a fleet of overwhelming power against the Japanese. But the fleet was destroyed at the last moment by a miraculous "divine wind"—the *kamikaze*. There is a special place in the hearts and minds of the Japanese for all of this. They maintain a continuity with the past that strengthens their contemporary culture; one newspaper carries a feature entitled "This Day in History," where a reader on October 3, 1991, would find that on that day in 1616 the Tokugawa Shogunate banned tobacco production. Only a people who sense their heritage would care about this.

Americans on the other hand seem hell-bent on either revising or forgetting their history. If an individual man or woman does that, they are changed in the process; so too with a nation.

Space does not permit us to examine the other cultural factors that might be compared, including future orientation, language, a strong work ethic, the family unit, and sexual constraints. But the basic conclusion once again is that the two cultures are different . . . very different.

VIEW OF THE YANKEE SAMURAI

It has been the premise of this chapter, and really the entire book, that a nation's culture plays a significant role in determining its economic structure and the management style of its industrial organizations. Can the management style in Japan, which reflects so many cultural elements, be effective in the United States with its diametrically opposed culture? Several of the Yankee Samurai did not think so.

The assistant to the general manager of a powerful trading company has traveled the world many times and worked for several international firms. She commented:

> The Japanese management style really doesn't work in the United States because here there is an emphasis upon the individual in the American culture. His development, and self-expression, are paramount. Whereas in Japan the emphasis is

upon integrating oneself into a group and submerging oneself in deference to one of a higher level.

A similar point was made by the young Claremont economics graduate, a metals specialist with a large Japanese trading firm:

> . . . I realized that it is a cultural thing. For the [Japanese] culture, the Japanese management style works fine. There is a saying in Japanese that "the nail that sticks out gets hammered down." That is very descriptive of the Japanese culture; you want to blend in. Consequently, you have a *ringi-sho* decision-making process. You don't want to be the one making a decision. You want to be part of the clan.
>
> Whereas as an American—and I think I am typical—I *want* to make the decision and take the responsibility. I want the kudos if things go right and am willing to take the consequences if they do not. Culturally, it just doesn't work.
>
> Ouchi [author of *Theory* Z] makes the point of how successful and effective the Japanese management style is and how on the other hand the American management style is not that successful. Something must be wrong with what we are doing and we should transfer to what the Japanese are doing. But it simply does not work. The Japanese management system was developed with the Japanese culture in mind.

Professor Bill Ouchi's Theory Z was mentioned several times by other Yankee Samurai. For example, the Japanese-American assistant manager of administrative planning was quite outspoken in her views of the theory:

> It is very difficult for an individual to change styles and philosophies. I see the difference between the American and Japanese cultures and the problems with the Japanese management style.
>
> But much depends upon the individual. Some of the Japanese managers do change, but others, even at the end of their stays, still strongly believe that the Japanese management style is the best. They are inflexible in trying to understand the American culture.
>
> There is no way that you can bring the management style that works in one culture and transpose it into a totally different culture; you must make adjustments.
>
> Despite all of the publicity that we hear about how great Japanese management is, and what impact it has, it is in Japan that it is so effective. But you cannot bring that here and expect it to work

100 percent. Several of our Americans and permanent Japanese
have discussed this. We all agree that you cannot implement the
Japanese management style here and expect everyone to respond
accordingly.

When I was in school we studied Bill Ouchi's Theory Z, which
argued in favor of American firms practicing Japanese management style. Those of us who worked for Japanese firms disagreed
with the concept. We knew that while it sounded nice as an ideal,
in all practicality it does not work here.

The marketing services manager of a large electronics firm observed:

The Japanese belief that they can bring their management style
to the United States and expect it to work is very naive. The
cultures are too different.

In graduate school we saw a film of Mexican workers in a
Japanese-owned U.S. subsidiary; they could not speak English
or Japanese. They were being led in calisthenics by English-
speaking Japanese; it was hysterical. The Mexicans' cultural identity with America is not very strong, let alone that with still another
nation.

The American culture is so diverse that it makes it more difficult
to mobilize workers, whereas Japan is so homogeneous.

The Iranian-born customer sales assistant for a large trading firm
again recognized the role of culture:

The kinds of problems that you see here are not unusual. American firms would have problems in Japan and an Italian company
would have problems in Libya. It doesn't make any difference.
When there are cultural differences there are managerial problems. It is universal.

The Japanese-American vice president and secretary of a rapidly growing auto company also stressed the impact that culture has on management style:

The United States is a nation of people with tendencies toward
nonconformity, impatience, and confrontational relationships.
Disagreements are solved by a battery of attorneys in an almost
stifling litigious environment.

On the other hand, for centuries the Japanese have been locked
into a Confucian-type social structure, with obedience to authority, conformity, and unswerving loyalty. Disagreements are settled

by time-consuming consensus, and nonverbal implicit and intui-
tive understandings among individuals.

One nation is heterogeneous and the other homogeneous in
racial makeup; one breaks tradition while the other clings to it; one
is uninhibited, the other inhibited; one is upfront and confrontational, the other vague and nonconfrontational; one openly ver-
balizes hurt feelings, the other suppresses it; one publicly greets
each other with a hug or slap on the back whereas the other is
embarrassed by any physical contact in public; one is women-first,
and the other men-first; one prefers a top-down management style,
the other a bottom-up style; for one the squeaking wheel gets the
attention, for the other the protruding nail gets hammered down;
and the list goes on and on and on.

Is it any wonder that we have problems understanding each
other and making Japanese management style work here?

WESTERN INFLUENCES ON JAPAN

There is a measure of hyperbole in the picture of Japan that has been
painted in this chapter. It is a little too idealistic. The Japanese culture
is not a pristine thing untouched by Western ways. Its people are becoming the most well traveled in the world and there are few nations
where the men of the trading companies (soga shosha) do not operate.
Salarymen typically spend three- to five-year rotations abroad and more
often than not their families join them. In the process of all of this, the
Japanese have been touched by Western ways. To what extent do they
bring back to Japan what they have learned?

And what of the impact of Western influences in Japan itself? Japan
is not the isolated citadel that Commodore Perry happened upon in
1853. U.S. stockbrokers are members of the Tokyo Stock Exchange and
there are a growing number of American advertising, consulting, legal,
and accounting firms successfully doing business in Japan. Coca-Cola,
McDonald's, Disney, Texas Instruments, IBM, Xerox, Schick, Merck,
Procter & Gamble, and dozens more with operations in Japan are
making money there. At the same time, their presence in ways both
subtle and unsubtle must have some cultural impact upon the host
country—a Japanese friend told me how during his family's drive from
the airport after having just arrived in the United States, his five-year-old
son sat quietly transfixed looking out the car window until he suddenly
yelled out: "Look, look, they have McDonald's here too!"

Today's leaders of Japan, just as their Tokugawa forebears almost four centuries ago, worry that the presence of Western ways in the Land of the Gods is a Trojan Horse which brings with it the destruction of Japan. Well, the Trojan Horse has in fact slipped inside the gates and its influence is beginning to be felt.

LIFETIME EMPLOYMENT

Lifetime employment is the linchpin of the Japanese management style, yet over the last few years thin cracks in this basic principle are appearing. Japan's baby bust, beginning in the 1970s, has continued with that nation today not even reproducing itself—1.53 children per married woman. Yet at the same time Japan's economy has continued to grow, some years faster and some years slower, but always growing. This has led to Japan's most serious economic problem—a severe labor shortage.

Today, every new college graduate receives at least several job offers and the best receive dozens. Almost half a million jobs will go unfilled in 1992. There is an increasing need for technical experts, who cannot always be trained in-house, and competition for specialized talent is savage. The result has been the new but once condemned phenomenon of job-hopping and the emergence of temporary employment and executive search firms. A recent poll showed that 38.5 percent of Japanese managers aged twenty to thirty-nine had given thought to changing jobs. They are doing more than thinking about it. For the first time in well over half a century, some employees are leaving their firms for better opportunities elsewhere. Konen Suzuki rose to the level of managing director of Toyota, but after twenty-nine years left in late 1991 to head Ford's Japanese operations. Mitsuo Hirose, the fifty-one-year-old CEO of a Tokyo printing company, recently resigned to lead the medical arm of J&J in Tokyo. There are growing numbers of such men. A stint in America appears to be especially dangerous. One in ten of the salarymen who have had an American assignment later jump ship.

At the same time, severe competition has forced several Japanese companies to encourage some older and less productive people—incompetent employees called *madogiwa-zoku* (those who sit along the windows and do not perform meaningful work)—into either early retirement, partial retirement, accepting salary reductions, or transfers to second-tier, lower-paying subsidiary firms. Nomura is one of several companies that began as early as 1987 to use merit to a greater extent than seniority in its promotion process. Companies, then, have also begun to break their part of the lifetime employment and seniority system pact.

Earlier, in chapter 8, we saw the cornerstone role that lifetime employment plays: every other dimension of Japanese management style depends upon it. And yet the cornerstone is weakening—not seriously or irreparably, but weakening nevertheless.

WOMEN AND MINORITIES

Partly as a result of its labor shortage, Japan has begun to rethink the largely industrially unused resource of women. The trend is not yet very strong, but there are stirrings.

The 1986 Japanese Equal Employment Opportunity Act, while having no language for noncompliance, has had at least a modicum of influence on the workplace—the first ever sexual harassment lawsuits have recently been filed. It is viewed by some as a significant first step in altering the role of women in society. As has been the case in the United States, there is little question that women are as capable as men in nearly all business fields and indeed can be superior in many. At the same time, no one can doubt that women's entry into the labor force has a significant cultural impact. It is nearly impossible for a woman to assume serious management responsibility and at the same time play the traditional role of homemaker. Yet, abandoning that role cannot help but to influence mother and child, wife and husband, daughter-in-law and mother-in-law, mother-teacher, and even neighbor-to-neighbor relations, which in turn must alter in some way the society's culture.

More Japanese women seem to be speaking out and demanding—perhaps politely requesting is more accurate—entry into the man's world. And in fact a few changes can be observed. More and more women are delaying marriage; 40 percent of women aged twenty-five to twenty-nine are unmarried, up from 20 percent in 1975. There is even a new term: *kekkon shinai kamoshirenai shokogun* (the "I Might Not Get Married" syndrome) for those women enjoying the comforts of single life. And to attract married women with children back into the labor force a few large firms have been experimenting with on-site day care centers. Change is in the air.

An alternative to women in the labor force is the importation of foreign labor, both legal and illegal. To do that, as both the United States and the Western European nations have found out, can have a major impact on altering the culture. While legal immigration into Japan is all but unknown, the number of documented and illegal workers is growing. They come primarily from various surrounding Asian countries. The men take low and unskilled work, while women for the most part are recruited as bar girls. There has already been a backlash; the *Japan Times* reports that right-wing groups, have called for the immediate expulsion of foreigners, who they say molest women, commit crimes, and have brought AIDS to their country. By American standards, this is not yet a problem for the Japanese. But illegal immigration to the United States was also modest twenty years ago. Today, well over a million people a year enter the country without documentation, bringing with them their own cultures which, for better or worse, alter the American culture.

CORRUPTION

In late 1991, the outlines of a scandal were emblazoned across the pages of Japanese newspapers. The major securities firms—including Nomura, Daiwa, Nikko, and Yamaichi—had secretly reimbursed select customers for their losses during the 1987 stock market crash. Although it has never really been made clear exactly what law was broken, now foreign investors and many smaller Japanese investors have a heightened sense of cynicism about big business practices.

This is not Japan's first financial scandal. Most have involved questionable joint government and business dealings. They seem to occur with some regularity: the Lockheed affair in 1972, and the Recruit scandal in 1987. At this writing a story has just broken about the Tokyo Sagawa Kyubin Company, which allegedly was involved in millions of dollars of fraudulent loans and massive payoffs to politicians; this scandal may surpass in scope anything that Japan has yet seen.

Dealing with business ethics and morals across cultures becomes difficult. What an American might view as corruption, the Japanese may see as both moral and honorable. Let me give you an example. A major American oil company signed a ten-year contract with a Japanese trading company to provide it coal from one of its mines in Australia. Japanese payment would be made at the ongoing world price. Everything was fine until several years into the contract, when world coal prices surged. The oil company, of course, demanded that the higher price be paid. The Japanese were stunned. This was something that needed to be discussed and worked out. The Americans saw nothing to discuss; the contract was clear. Ultimately, the Japanese yielded and the Americans won—in fact, they had lost. Japanese business relationships are built upon decades of mutual trust and loyalty. If either party in a relationship is damaged by unanticipated changes in the environment, then adjustments are made; that is the Japanese way. The American oil firm discussed here may have made a few extra million dollars, but it lost the opportunity to forge a genuine long-term relationship with the Japanese company.

This story is relevant to the financial scandal introduced above. The best customers were hurt by an unexpected untoward event—1987 stock market crash. Of course it was the responsibility of the securities firms to make these customers whole. This is the right, moral, and just action to take. It is the Japanese way, and not seen as corruption at all. American and Japanese perceptions can be totally at odds. What does corruption mean when viewed from quite different cultural perspectives? And just when does business and government working in very close cooperation become corruption?

Japanese business is the primary supporter of political figures in the Liberal Democratic Party. This is money politics to an even greater extent than in America. And unlike America, almost all the money comes from business—by far the most important special interest group. The system is not unlike that which existed in the United States from roughly 1860 to 1925—more or less America's golden age of capitalism. The analogy to modern-day Japan is strong, but with a singular exception. In America during that period the government was little more than a handmaiden to business interests, and did its bidding. In the case of Japan, there is a much closer sharing of power and decision making between business and government. Government is of course understood to include the ministries.

Americans, then, forgetting their own history, look at Japan's working relationship between business and government and see bribery and corruption. The Japanese, on the other hand, look at the adversarial running battles between a watchdog American Congress and American business, and see not moral superiority but stupidity.

Nevertheless, in the days ahead, the foreign investor and foreign media presence in Japan will assuredly cast a sharper spotlight on the nature of business and government dealings previously carried out behind closed doors. Some confidence in the Tokyo stock market has been lost. The Japanese Ministry of Finance has recently imposed some fairly severe penalties on the offenders and proposed some considerably strengthened controls. A crack has appeared in Japan Inc.

PLASTIC AND MORE

There are dozens of other signs that the Trojan Horse has been loosed in Japan and that the malignant forces of the dreaded Western malaise are spreading, including . . . plastic.

Japanese consumers, particularly the young people, have discovered the credit card. Its use has grown in double digits over each of the last several years. Recently, a twenty-three-year-old Tokyo secretary earning $800 a month ran up $56,000 in debt before declaring bankruptcy. A credit company executive observed: "Creditworthiness and honor have become dead words in today's Japan." This, along with other factors, including the graying of Japan, is raising concern about the ability to maintain savings at past levels. Japanese have historically been almost compulsive savers—thrift is a pronounced samurai trait that goes back centuries. Yet hints of change are evident.

Questions are also beginning to be raised about the work ethic of the young people compared to their postwar parents. The word *rekreeayshon* has had to be invented (there had been no word like it in the vocabulary before), and although the people still do not know exactly what it means, they are working very hard at it. Even the government is helping by requiring that its offices, as well as banks and brokerage firms, will now close every other Saturday and employees are being encouraged to actually take allotted vacation time. A recent survey by the Japanese Productivity Center showed that only 26 percent of white-collar workers believe it is appropriate to sacrifice their outside life for the company. Older Japanese shake their heads disapprovingly and have coined a new word for the younger generation, with its heightened consumer patterns and lessened work ethic—*shinjinrui*, or the "new human race," the elders call them. To the extent that significant changes are occurring in the lifestyles of younger Japanese, that nation's economic machine must be affected, as will the larger culture.

Then there is *zaitek*. At the very heart, or perhaps soul, of a Japanese firm is the mission, with its dedication to the consumer, product, employee, nation, society—and investors. The mission for many firms has been in place for more than a century. It has been a guiding principle. Yet in some cases it has been perverted for the glamour and attraction of *zaitek*—a word having the connotation of making money the new-fashioned way, through electronic wheeling and dealing from a desktop. Traditional manufacturing firms are doing this. Toyota has more cash than any other company in the world. It uses a portion of its $14 billion hoard to invest in a variety of purely financial activities, including stocks, bonds, real estate, works of art, and currency transactions. Other firms are following suit, and it has not been unusual for half the profits of some firms listed on the Tokyo Stock Exchange to come from such investments. There has even been a growing interest in mergers, acquisitions, and diversification. This should be troubling to thoughtful Japanese. Granted something has to be done with their vaults of cash, nowhere in the mission does it say, "Let's go long on December pork bellies." An appropriate, and often justified, epithet hurled at Americans is that they have become little more than "paper entrepreneurs"— referring to creativity only in the field of finance, with ever more bizarre financial instruments to trade. Japan's strength has been to leave that to the Americans. *Zaitek* is a change of direction. Sadaharu Oh, Japan's Babe Ruth, would say: "You can't hit the ball if you take your eye off of it." *Zaitek* takes the Japanese corporate eye off of the ball—the mission. As the Nikkei Index reaches five year lows in early 1992, hundreds of firms, especially banks, with large stock portfolios are realizing the truth of this.

Still another western influence is the pressure brought to bear on Japan's farmers. Redistricting and gerrymandering is beginning to lessen the power of the farm lobby; proposals to eliminate all tariffs on rice, beef, and citrus fruits are being discussed on Tokyo's Nagata-cho— Capitol Hill. Good farm land is being plowed under to build needed housing, highways, and factories. The culture of nearly every country is greatly influenced by its farm traditions. Break them, and the national culture changes. Japan's are now being broken.

Finally, there is the Yakuza. Some have compared them to America's Mafia, but the analogy is not perfect. The Yakuza have something of a Robin Hood past and a reputation for being ultranationalist that is extreme even by Japanese standards. They have generally been respectful of private citizens, indeed, known for their chivalry to women, and have served as a kind of second police force keeping street crime at a minimum. There are perhaps 100,000 of them, affiliated with some 2,300 gangs. Individual members are easily identified by their body tattoos and finger stubs—cut off as a ritual. They show a loyalty and obedience to their organizations unknown in the Mafia, or at least the modern Mafia.

Over the postwar years the Yakuza have become increasingly involved in prostitution, pornography, drugs (amphetamines), loan sharking, gambling, extortion, and gun smuggling—citizens do not own guns in Japan. They serve as strong-arm guards or *sokaiya* (corporate bouncer) at annual corporate meetings, suppressing troublesome or antagonistic questions; such meetings seldom run more than twenty minutes. The Yakuza are also firmly established in legitimate construction and entertainment businesses.

The Yakuza represent something of a Stygian side to Japan. Every nation has such a side. Yet the Yakuza, in typical Japanese fashion, seem to have brought order and neatness even here. Nevertheless, there is clearly potential for the Yakuza to go beyond its current bounds—for example, by entering the cocaine business or manipulating the stock market—that could have a far-reaching impact on Japan.

Wakon Yosai

It is too easy for an outsider to view Japan as an almost perfect, albeit perhaps somewhat repressive, nation-state, with a culture only superficially changed from the days of Tokugawa. Yet, from credit card abuse to a more carefree younger generation to organized crime, Japan's newfound enormous wealth and contact with Western ways have begun to influence the country. Shifts in Japan's culture since the 1950s are modest but measurable.

A premise of this chapter is that a nation's economic power ultimately comes down to its people and their culture. The Japanese had literally nothing following the end of World War II—except themselves and their culture. From this they built an economic machine that is poised for world leadership by the turn of the century. But what if the Japanese lose their culture along the way? It is a kind of Catch-22. Japan needs its unique culture to achieve world leadership. But to achieve that leadership results in the loss of culture. Perhaps this is why every great empire has ultimately fallen. Japan may be the exception with its *wakon yosai*.

The term translates roughly as "Western technology and Japanese spirit." In the seventh century, the Japanese brought Chinese Confucian teaching to their land—and changed it. It was altered to fit the "spirit" of Japan, which has a strong element of nationalism about it not found in China, for example. The Japanese adopted their criminal and civil code from France, Germany, and Switzerland; their navy from England; their army from Prussia; and their quality-control methods from America. In each case, appropriate adaptations were made. From Arnold Schwarzenegger TV commercials for Oreo cookies, to baseball, to democracy, to the transistor, to Mickey Mouse, the Japanese have taken it all and reworked it. They have infused Western technology with their own Japanese spirit—*wakon yosai*.

Will that spirit continue to serve Japan? The answer will determine Japan's destiny.

Summary

The Japanese management style is only marginally practiced in the United States. It is not practiced more because it cannot be . . . the cultures are simply too different. What works in Japan, it appears, will not work in the United States. Differences in culture also of course have much broader implications for the economic, social, and political future of the two nations.

So far the cultural differences between the United States and Japan have been discussed subjectively. The following table attempts to summarize and quantify the issues. The assignments below of A for Americans and J for Japanese are admittedly open to much debate. There is no intended precision here. You might try to assign the As and Js yourself. Your choices will depend upon personal experiences, including how and where you were raised, what you know about Japan, and how you are defining each of the terms. While you and I may disagree somewhat, I think that the same basic pattern will emerge. Reading the table should be straightforward. For example, Group precedence over the individual has a Japanese score of 9.5, indicating a strong Yes, while the American 3.0 score is much closer to No, indicating a greater degree of individualism.

The elements of culture are all here: beliefs, traditions, values, institutions, myths, language, history, and vision. What is evident is just how very different the peoples of the United States and Japan really are. It is no wonder that Japanese management style, so much a function of Japan's culture, is not thriving in the white-collar environment of the United States.

At the same time it *does* seem to be functioning pretty well in many of the smaller rural areas of the American Midwest, Southeast, and Northwest, where dozens of Japanese manufacturing facilities have been built. Why the paradox? The answer is very significant for both Japan and America. The cultures of many of those small communities are much more similar to Japan than are those of America as a whole. Indeed, they are very similar to America's culture of the 1950s. The America of today is a strikingly different nation from that of one generation ago. The changes were hardly discernible year by year, but

1992 America-Japan Cultural Differences

	No								Yes	
	1	2	3	4	5	6	7	8	9	10
Ultranationalism					A			J		
Homogeneity				A				J		
Primacy of education			A						J	
Religious underpinning					A		J			
Group precedence			A					J		
Law and order	A							J		
Separate male/female roles				A				J		
Continuity with the past				A				J		
Future orientation			A						J	
Language (common)						A			J	
Strong work ethic						A	J			
Family unit strength			A					J		
Sexual constraints	A						J			

looking back collectively over the whole generation, America today is a substantially different country.

What cultural shifts in fact have occurred since the 1950s? The table below should be compared to that above. As before, it is open to debate, and you will have your own ideas. But once again you should end up with a similar pattern. America, and Japan, have both shifted culturally over the last generation to the left of the scale. Japan's shift has been relatively marginal; America's has been dramatic.

Several points follow. First, the cultures of the United States and Japan today are as night and day. A generation ago they were considerably closer, but major shifts in the American ethos have changed that. Japan, too, has changed, but not nearly to the same degree.

Second, these basic cultural differences are critical to management style. The management style of any nation's institutions is influenced by the larger society's culture. If Japan's culture is so different from America's, that raises some serious obstacles to transferring the Japanese system to the United States (the final chapter is going to suggest a way to deal with those obstacles). One clue as to how that might be done is suggested by the relative success of the Japanese manufacturing facilities operating in small Midwest, Southeast, and Northwest communities.

Finally, as both Japan and the United States move into the next century, the ability of both nations to compete in the world arena will

1952 U.S.-Japan Cultural Differences

	No									Yes
	1	2	3	4	5	6	7	8	9	10
Ultranationalism								A	J	
Homogeneity							A		J	
Primacy of education							A		J	
Religious underpinning							A	J		
Group precedence					A				J	
Law and order								A	J	
Separate male/female roles						A		J		
Continuity with the past							A	J		
Future orientation						A			J	
Language (common)								A	J	
Strong work ethic								A	J	
Family unit strength							A	J		
Sexual constraints								A	J	

ultimately come down to culture. Both nations must look carefully at the international cultural shifts that have occurred over the last generation, as well as trends that are now developing. Some of these trends strengthen the nation and some do not. *Nothing* is more important than for each country to give infinite attention to this issue. Culture is destiny.

12

The Japanese View

> *There never were in the world two opinions alike, no more than two hairs or two grains; the most universal quality is diversity.*
>
> —MONTAIGNE

INTRODUCTION

To this point you have been listening to Yankee Samurai views and opinions. But what about Japanese managers with whom they work? What are their thoughts on the Yankee Samurai, their own personal experiences in the United States, the differences in cultures between the United States and Japan, and future relations between the two countries? What message do they have for their American competitors and for the roughly 40,000 other Japanese executives and managers in the United States?

These men—they are all men—face a great challenge. During much of the work day they are forced to speak a second language, operating in a totally foreign and diverse culture that has a bewildering array of laws, customs, and traditions; and late in the evening they are on the phone with an often unsympathetic or uncomprehending Tokyo. Their wives

and children sometimes do not adjust well to the United States, or to the
contrary they adjust too well and are not terribly anxious to return
home. Frequently, older children are left in Japan to study for critical
upcoming college examinations, and the separation can be painful. If
the Japanese executives have been in the United States for extended
periods, they may be viewed with some suspicion upon their return to
Japan. And not infrequently they find themselves caught up in the
middle of troubled U.S.-Japan relations. Overriding all of this, of
course, is the day-to-day task of working with and managing the Yankee
Samurai.

I separately interviewed almost two dozen senior Japanese who were
chairmen, vice chairmen, CEOs, presidents, senior executive vice
presidents, and general managers of a mix of auto, electronics, banking, and service firms. They ranged in age from the mid-forties to
mid-sixties, and had backgrounds that were quite different. Three of
them had worked for an American firm before joining their current
Japanese company. One of them is married to an American woman
and another has an American son-in-law. Two of them plan on retiring in the United States. Several have children attending American
universities. One of them had slightly longish hair and a stylish
Brooks Brothers wardrobe, another is the archetype salaryman, with
his slim build, short haircut, wire-rim glasses, and an almost palpable
intensity, while still another has the appearance and demeanor of a
wise, kindly grandfather.

For a few this was their first rotation to the United States, while others
had been posted to English-speaking countries for as much as twenty
years. Overall their English was very good; one spoke with a distinct
British accent, while another had the hint of a southern drawl—it would
be impossible to find a like number of senior Americans in Tokyo with
a comparable fluency in Japanese. One of the most senior and successful among them was concerned that somehow through the interview his
wife would find out that he was still smoking; these are not only professional, educated, hardworking, and thoughtful men, they are men
you would like to know and befriend.

Listen to some of their thoughts, with the understanding that it is
generally not in the Japanese nature to be openly critical or speak too
bluntly. The Japanese also tend to be self-effacing in the extreme and
are not known for boasting, no matter how much it might be deserved.
The quotes that follow should be viewed as somewhat muted under-
statements.

AMERICAN AND JAPANESE WORK ETHICS

The Japanese tend not to be openly critical of American workers, although they are troubled by the adversarial character of American unions. The predominant view is that the ultimate responsibility for productivity lies with management. They noted the variations in American work ethic from region to region around the country and made their decisions on plant locations accordingly. They were concerned about the questionable work ethic of young people in their own country. There is a sense that work is almost a way of life for the Japanese as compared to the Americans. Here are their own words.

Regardless of nationality, people have strong points and weak points. I believe that it is management's responsibility—by training, communication, exchange of views, and so forth—to assure that people perform the job correctly. I believe that everyone wants to do a good job—management must make that happen.

I don't think that the manufacturing problem in the United States is the worker—not if he is properly trained and treated well. I think that Americans are good workers. We do not have quality problems in our manufacturing here. We pay a lot of attention to factory layout and product design, and most importantly, provide our employees with a clean environment, good training, and a spirit of pride in their work and the company.

In America, I think the top managers work harder than their Japanese counterparts. The chiefs work harder than the Indians. But the Japanese are certainly always busy . . . very, very busy [laughs]. In America you never have a meeting unless you have a purpose. If there is no purpose, then there is no meeting. For the Japanese, it is a different thing. It is the reverse. If you do not have any special agenda with someone, then you try to meet him. There may be some future benefit. So "busy" does not mean hard work.

I am over fifty years old and people of my generation work very hard. But since Japan has become rich, the younger generation is not so driven. They just want enough money to buy things and enjoy themselves. This is a major attitude change. I worry about it.

The Japanese [in America] do work longer hours because we have to communicate with Japan late in the evening. Also Japanese tend to work harder overseas because there are fewer of us and the responsibility is greater.

I find that Americans work hard and also seem to enjoy life. The Japanese tend to work hard, doing nothing else or going home and doing work. The Americans might be missing a satisfaction that comes from work, but the Japanese too are missing something.

I think that American unions are a problem as they are in the United Kingdom. That has to be changed in some way. I am not saying that unions should not exist, but they should be run a different way. They have to cooperate with management and have the same objective. I think that the Japanese way is better.

I find that how hard Americans work depends upon what part of the country you are in. There really are very different patterns. Smaller communities away from the bigger cities seem to be much better.

For many of the young men we send to the United States, this is their first assignment out of the country. They have to work very, very hard. I tell them that three years goes by very quickly and they must take advantage of every minute of it. The first year should be spent learning what their predecessor has done. In the second they should begin to create new ideas, and in the third start to think about the future for their successors. The important thing is to use every moment of those three years.

Americans work hard just as do the Japanese. But for the Japanese, work is more a way of life. We think about it more and spend much more time at it.

U.S.-Japan Relations

The Japanese executives feel the pressure of strained relationships with the United States, although most of them believe that for better or worse the destiny of the two countries are inextricably linked—"almost like marriage," said one of them. They are concerned about what they feel to be unfair Japan bashing by various American politicians and the media—criticism of Japanese actions in the Gulf War angered the executives, who felt that their country did more than its share. They see the grass-roots ties between American and Japanese businessmen as being important in strengthening relations between the two countries. Several of them called for a more aggressive Japanese stance toward America and the world, including a stronger military. Many of them worried about America's inability to compete.

American criticism of Japanese investment in the United States is very shortsighted. The investment has had very positive economic results. Part of the problem is the American media. If a European company buys a U.S. property, it is not newsworthy, but if Sony buys Columbia, then it is a major story about how Japan is taking over all of the United States. This appeals to American emotions and is very dangerous. Americans believe everything they see on TV, even if it is very superficial.

The Gulf War strained relations between the two countries, but economically they cannot stand alone. We are very strongly interrelated. Political talk between Washington and Tokyo sometimes is not good. But at the grass-roots level between businessmen it is very positive. There are hundreds of joint ventures between American and Japanese firms that are cementing relations.

Politically, Japan will be forced to take a more important role in world politics. Japan has been hiding behind the United States. We are like children always asking for permission and counsel. But when we begin to make decisions on our own, there may be conflict.

The relationship between America and Japan is almost like marriage. Whether we like it or not we have to understand each other. We need to take care of the children, grow larger, and have a nice family.

Sometimes I am not happy with the Japanese government attitude. At the same time American politics can become very emotional. Japan bashing doesn't help. People-to-people relationships are so important in overcoming that. They are the key. I would like to see more informal communication. If we can get together, eat together—maybe sushi and maybe hot dogs—play golf together, or just talk together, more understanding will result. Hawaii is a good place to do that. I hope to build a guest house there and bring people together.

By the year 2000, relations between the two countries will very much depend upon how American industry performs. If you fail to compete with us, that will be very dangerous because people will start to look for excuses and scapegoats. Japan will be blamed; it is already happening.

America needs more confidence. I think that the [Gulf] war has helped to strengthen that confidence. If this feeling translates into industry, that will be very positive.

For myself, this is really a personal feeling, the Japanese lifeline is not rice, it is oil. To protect our lifeline, we should have sent a force to the Middle East during the Gulf crisis. But the Japanese people have a sentiment of no more war. The teaching of General MacArthur was so strong that it was written in the constitution that we do not rely on force to resolve international problems. For myself, I think it is time to review the constitution.

In my opinion, relations between the United States and Japan are getting worse. The Gulf War made matters more difficult. From our standpoint, we made a substantial $9 billion contribution. That was very generous and within the framework of our constitution and culture. But Americans didn't think we did anything and that made Japanese feelings more negative.

I was talking to a *very* senior American CEO recently. He told me that American business and political leaders have to keep bashing the Japanese because it provides an easy excuse for why the country is doing so poorly.

Americans complain about Japanese buying various real estate properties. But if they don't sell, we cannot buy. The Americans come to Japan and push us to buy the properties. They put big ads in the newspapers and send us videos of properties. The majority of Americans don't care about that. Americans have a more difficult time buying property in Japan, although many do, because we don't like to sell, even for a quick profit.

In the United States, Japan bashing comes from the evasion of domestic problems seeking international scapegoats.

A Message to American Companies

Several of the older Japanese executives grew up after the war admiring everything about America. They proceeded to pattern their own businesses on the American model. Today, it is evidently almost painful for them to observe that their idol has slipped badly over the years. The Japanese raised concerns about shortsighted planning, executive greed, autocratic management style, loss of quality consciousness, merger and acquisition money games, lack of concern for the employee, and failure to compete internationally. Far from taking comfort from this, they call on American companies to return to the "shining stars," as one very senior auto executive put it, that they once were. The Japanese message to American companies would seem to be: "You need not copy us. Everything we know we learned from you. Return to what you were only a generation ago."

Unlike most American companies, Japanese companies are long-term-oriented. But that requires being people-oriented. People are not like a disposable component. If the company treats people well, they will work hard and be loyal. Most American companies don't do this.

American companies play the money game too much. They forget the most important point, which is to continue to grow the company. Their thinking has become too shortsighted. The egos of top executives have grown too large and they think that their own short-run projects to run up profits are so important—but they leave nothing for those who follow.

Right after the war, [WWII], American cars were number one. I so respected America's technology and styling. G.M., Ford, and Chrysler were always the shining stars. Everything they did, we did. I was a very strong admirer of those companies. But today, I am sorry they are losing their competitiveness. They are no longer the shining stars we can look up to. I am sorry to see that. Unions are part of the problem but so is management. Management doesn't care about people and is overly concerned with shareholders.

About fifteen years ago, Japan, voluntarily cut back on auto exports. But nothing improved on the American side. How can you blame that on Japan? You have to blame yourself. Five years or so ago when the Yen strengthened, the American companies had a great opportunity to increase market share. But, unfortunately, the U.S. financial system seems to call for short-term profits. The only interest is in making quick money. That holds for both management and the investor. The tax system should be restructured to change this.

If there is one thing that the American companies should do, it is to love their employees. That does not mean just money. It means sincerely caring about their security and fulfillment in the workplace. They are not just something you buy and then sell like a piece of equipment.

I think that American top management gets too much money. They do not realize who really is doing the important work in the company. I think that has to change. Japanese manufacturing is strong because we treat the factory workers the same as white-collar workers.

Before the war, Japanese products were known to be cheap and perishable. But after the war, we learned methods of mass production from the United States. Dr. [W. Edward] Deming came to Japan and taught us about quality-control systems. We followed his advice and gave full participation to the work force. We learned to be more democratic from the MacArthur people after the war. So even our executives eat in the same cafeteria with the workers and communicate with them. Everything we know we learned from the Americans. But the American *sensei* [teacher] got sick.

In Japan for the last 150 years working overseas has been treated as an important promotion. But Americans do not think it is a promotion and are concerned about their jobs when they return. American companies should change their policies so that after an employee is posted abroad for three to five years, he returns and is assigned to a good general manager position. This policy exists in Japanese companies.

The United States has been our teacher or *sensei*. We are still students in so many ways. Everything that the Japanese do in their management style we learned from the American textbook. But Americans themselves have forgotten these things. They have become too shortsighted, and money-chasing. They have forgotten about product quality and the importance of their employees.

If an American company finds itself in financial difficulty, it immediately lays off people. But a Japanese company does think about its employees and their families, and does everything possible to avoid that. The employees understand and appreciate it. It is reflected in their loyalty and work ethic. The Americans don't think through the long-term impact of their actions on their most important asset—their employees.

Many American companies do not realize that their most valu-able asset is people. It is not production equipment or computers; it is the human resources which make the organization competi-tive. How people are treated is of fundamental importance. If they are satisfied with management, they will perform well. The issue is not pay alone, it is overall management.

So many American companies take over another company and then begin selling off pieces with no concern for the employees or the long-term life of the company. Short-term profits and the wealth of a few bankers, lawyers, and top managers is all that matters. That doesn't happen in Japan, where short-run profits and immediate stockholder interests are not important. In some ways, Japan is almost a socialist country. Maybe American companies should start to care more about their people.

American companies care only about profits. But profits take care of themselves if you care about people and work together as a team.

I have looked around the United States for products to export back to Japan and all I see is hamburger. A company comes to me and says, "This is what I have to sell—hamburger." But in Japan you don't sell hamburger; you sell a whole meal, with a nice restaurant, polite waiters, beautiful table setting, salad, service, and so on. The Americans don't understand just how demanding Japanese consumers are. American manufacturers must pay much more attention to the quality of the products they produce.

We try to establish consensus here among our associates. That creates a lot of enthusiasm. It takes a longer time, but the result and execution is always better. That has long been a Japanese tradition. But American top managers like to make all of the decisions. Perhaps they should encourage their lower-level people to participate more.

Maybe American companies define jobs too narrowly. Since we are emphasizing the team concept, everyone is expected to reach out beyond one's assignment whenever it is necessary. This helps people understand the company from a broader perspective and results in total productivity increase.

American companies should be more aware of international competition. After the war [WW II], America was the most productive and technologically advanced. But after fifty years of peace, Japan and Europe grew their own industries. Because the dollar was the currency of the world, all the nations wanted to export to America to obtain the dollar for their own needs. The United States did not have to worry about that. They could spend as they wished. And the U.S. market was so big that there was no need to export. But now the world has changed. Not many American companies recognize that, but they will have to if they are to compete . . . if they are to survive.

Successful Yankee Samurai

The Japanese have come to recognize that not all Americans do well in their companies. The more successful of them seem to be less aggressive, more team- and consensus-oriented, patient, understanding of Japanese culture—knowing the language helps—willing to accept job rotation, and show a heightened attention to detail; and of course they must be willing to work long and hard.

The most successful Americans working for Japanese firms tend naturally to be the ones who like the management style, although they might get a little frustrated sometimes. People who are overly independent and who like to decide things by themselves don't do that well here. The ones with a very aggressive style tend to have more difficulty.

Rotation is a part of the management system. It provides a new stimulation that is lost when you have been in a job for too long. Everything comes naturally and there are no new ideas. However, the American staff have a hard time adjusting to this. If offered the opportunity to be transferred to Japan, they generally refuse. That is very limiting for career advancement. Our more successful Americans, however, have no problem with this.

When I interview Americans for a job, I like to be certain that they have a personality that suits our firm. They have to know our style of operation and be comfortable in that environment.

An American working here at [company name] or at any other Japanese firm is part of a much more exciting global world. I would encourage those Americans to take advantage of the opportunity and learn about Japan and the Japanese language and culture. I think they will be better employees.

I really don't want to suggest that the only way an American—or Yankee Samurai, as you call them—can succeed at [company name] is if they speak Japanese. But knowing the Japanese culture is very important and certainly an understanding of our language can be very helpful.

If we recruit higher-quality people, they tend to be more aggressive and independent and difficult to control. We need intelligent people who can also be good team players.

Productivity here comes down to a problem of communications. Some Japanese managers do understand English very well and the speaking skills of the younger Japanese continue to improve. However, sometimes communications crisscross and don't reach the other side. It is bad with yes, yes, yes spoken, but no, no, no in the belly. This is a problem. I am afraid that my Americans do not speak Japanese except for the few that have been specifically recruited for key positions—and they are doing very well.

A big problem for us is to find top Americans who are familiar with Japanese management style. We do want to Americanize and have Americans in top positions, but the Americans have to be familiar with our management style. The managers should be patient, have a long-term perspective, accept *kaizen* [practice of continuous improvement], and be comfortable with consensus decision making.

Generally speaking, Americans are responsible for a specific area but do not want to do anything in other areas. So, in the United States, one plus one is two. but in Japan, where we rotate our people, one plus one is three or four. We like our Americans here at the bank to accept rotations and broad job responsibilities.

A Message to Japanese Managers

The experienced executives with whom I spoke call upon other, especially younger, Japanese managers in the United States to thoroughly familiarize themselves with the American culture, encourage the rotation of Americans into positions of authority, including postings in Japan, recognize the quite different role of personnel departments in the United States, emphasize the importance of corporate social responsibility, and lead both their Americans and Japanese with enthusiasm. In a later section you will see that they also encourage the assuring of opportunities for women and minorities.

It is vital that Japanese managers understand the culture of other countries. Less than two hundred years ago, the belief throughout Japan was that we would not deal with other countries. Now the consensus is that we will do business throughout the world. But we cannot do that without accepting foreign cultures. My children and the children of other Japanese businessmen who have gone to school abroad have lived through the difficulties and become immersed in new cultures. So often when my daughters were young, they didn't want to go to school because their stomach hurt or they had a headache—of course they were just nervous. But they went anyway and met new people and now love America. They didn't just read about foreign lands, they experienced it. More Japanese managers should be like their children, even though it isn't easy.

I am trying to become involved in various community activities. This is quite different from the Japanese system, where community concern is the work of the bureaucrats. But the Japanese managers must learn that in the United States this is important.

In my second assignment in the United States, I requested to be a field salesman. I was very handicapped because of my poor English, but I worked very hard and accomplished reasonable results. I think that actually working directly with the Americans is very important.

My uncle was a naval officer during the war [WWII]. He told me that when he was being educated at the Japanese Naval Academy, he was taught that while the U.S. Navy was very powerful, it would not fight and would easily give up. So if Japan just fought very hard, we could win. But Japan miscalculated because the information about America was limited. This is why networking among American and Japanese businessmen is so important today. Japanese managers should do much more of it.

We have been implementing a program to dispatch our American associates to the factory or R&D centers in Japan. Some will stay as long as two years with their family. This serves to accelerate the transfer of technical and engineering knowledge to American associates, who will themselves be taking the future initiative. Perhaps more Japanese firms should put this trust in their American associates.

I would tell the Japanese managers who are coming to the United States to first work for an American company in Japan for a few years. I did that while working at [American company]. Without that experience, at the very least, I would say when they come here they should not hire secretaries and assistants who speak Japanese; that helps a lot.

Most of my classmates from college went into major corporations and stayed with the firm. I am one of the few who joined a small start-up company which I left before coming here. Changing jobs is still very unusual in Japan and is very different from the United States, but it does provide a different perspective that can be useful to the new employer.

It is very important that your associates should always be kept enthusiastic. Sometimes one plus one is not always two. Sometimes it is three or zero. Humans can be emotional and should be kept enthusiastic. That might mean one plus one is three. A good manager can make his American and Japanese associates see that, and then go on to make it a reality.

When I was posted in Thailand, I became a Buddhist monk to try to better understand the people of Thailand. The Buddhism they practice is very different from ours. It is important to understand the culture of the countries where we operate, and managers should try very hard to do that.

Japanese managers have to understand that personnel matters are handled very differently in the United States. In Japan, the personnel department is the center of power. It recruits college graduates without referring to the various other departments, and has the main responsibility for rotation, education, and promotion of employees. So even if one manager does not like an employee, he usually does not have the power to fire him; the personnel department will reassign him for another chance. But in this country it is the reverse. The American personnel department has no power at all. This is not well understood by the newly arrived Japanese expatriates. Sometimes Americans fired by other Americans complain to the Japanese, and this causes difficulties. So the Japanese managers have to gain some understanding of human resource issues in the United States.

LESSONS FOR AMERICA

Most of the senior Japanese executives with whom I spoke were young boys during the peak of American power in the post-World War II years. They have watched a year-by-year erosion in that power and believe that America has lost its confidence. They think that in America there is too much freedom, greed, and crime, and not enough attention paid to education or learning how to live together under conditions of high population density. They suggest that America should return to its cultural roots. The Japanese, on the other hand, have mastered most of these things and believe that America might learn from them. They strongly encourage Americans to find out more about Japan.

Americans have lost their confidence. They become too nervous about small matters. That doesn't sound like Americans. They have lost their traditions and values. This is not the America I grew up knowing.

American greed has become too excessive. Over the last ten or twenty years, American top executive salaries have reached amazing levels by Japanese standards.

America has created too many losers who should not be given welfare. Ways should be found to make them more independent and especially to educate them. I was surprised that bus drivers make more than teachers. No Japanese can understand why you tolerate so much crime.

American society enjoys too much freedom, democracy, and so forth. Democratic principles have been pushed too far, and it is now time to step back and consider the need for more control.

I hope that Americans will go to Japan. You can't just read your newspaper or watch CNN. The media cannot be depended upon—it is too emotional. You have to go there and see the country itself and meet the people. The flow of understanding between the countries is almost only one-way. For every one piece of information going to America about Japan, there is a thousand going the other way. I would like Americans to learn more about Japan.

Japan has learned how large numbers of people can live together. Americans have to learn how to be a little more respectful of others. We are very concerned about other people's feelings. We don't want to say no to someone because that might upset them.

After the Vietnam War, the American people seemed to lose their confidence. Today, your politicians and leaders need to provide hope and direction. In the auto industry many Americans have lost confidence. In Japan, the workers at Toyota and Nissan have great pride and are respected by people. This kind of thinking is important. Americans need to recover their confidence in their products and strengthen their work habits and culture. In Japan after World War II we lost our confidence. But we looked back to our roots and who we were as a people and what our true culture was. America should do this also because America too has lost, or is losing, a kind of war.

We Japanese have no natural resources and only a small amount of land area. To survive, we have to work very wisely, very hard, and as a team. We are so crowded as a nation. So we have learned how to live with each other, with our neighbors, and colleagues. In the United States, especially in Southern California, where it is becoming so very crowded, Americans might learn from Japan how to be more personally considerate of others and how to use limited space more wisely.

Democracy is good, but only if it is kept in some framework. There is too much freedom here. People are always fighting with each other and saying rude things that cause hurt feelings. You need some controls.

HOW AMERICAN EMPLOYEES DIFFER

The Japanese see Americans as having certain work characteristics different from their own. The Americans seem less attentive to detail, do not really feel comfortable with numbers, are more impatient, less team-oriented, more narrow and superficial in their thinking, and try to avoid being rotated to other positions, especially those outside of the country.

Japanese tend to be much more generalists than the Americans. We think more broadly and do not like to specialize in one area. Japanese have always thought like this.

In the banking industry, providing clients with good service is important, but we have to constantly check the quality of the Americans—they seem to lack attention to detail or just do not think it is that important. They like to work independently and don't follow our rules, policy, or culture. It causes a big problem.

By and large, Americans don't really feel comfortable working with numbers as the Japanese do. Numbers seem to mean more to Japanese. We communicate with them. They tell stories and capture preciseness that ordinary words cannot. Perhaps it is a lack in the American educational training that explains the reluctance to work with numbers and charts.

Americans want their privacy and do not like an open office environment. But my experience is that such a structure is very important for good communication, especially in a sales organization. You need good information and a high volume of it. Sometimes even informal conversations can be very helpful— perhaps just overhearing a telephone conversation.

In Japan, managers work for the good of the company and help others, which is not necessarily what the Americans do.

Americans are always so impatient. In some ways that is good, but they complain about how slow our promotion system is here. The Japanese accept that but the Americans do not.

Americans like job descriptions that determine a quite specific range of responsibility. Unless you have that for them, they will not know what to do. But this limits the capabilities beyond the job description. In Japan we really do not have job descriptions. It is naturally understood what you should and should not do. It is common sense. It is a vague system. But it works to give each individual participation in the management.

I have been posted to five different locations overseas. It is a great challenge and an accepted part of being with the company.

But Americans do not like to be assigned to other countries or even be transferred to another location in the United States. We Japanese seem more willing to do what the firm asks of us.

Americans have a very difficult time with silences and always want to fill every moment with conversation and talking. The Japanese like to think about what has been said and what they will say next. Silences themselves have meaning to us. Sometimes Americans just talk too much.

WOMEN AND MINORITIES

The Japanese recognize the very different role of women and minorities in the United States compared to their own country, but feel that they themselves are beginning to adjust well to the American environment. They spoke of the strong family role played by Japanese women at home and their personal belief that women should be given an equal opportunity.

It is very difficult for the Japanese to adjust to America's diverse culture. At home we have a completely homogeneous environment. The Japanese who first come here are shocked at how different things are. But we have been learning, and [company name] does have women and minorities at management levels.

Japanese women are very strong. They run the household and have total control over all the finances and the children. But even in Japan, because of an accelerating labor shortage, women are beginning to play a greater role in the workplace. Within a very short number of years, whether we like it or not, the role of women in Japan is definitely going to change.

In Japan, women believe it is important to stay home and raise children. But things are changing and I think that is good. Every woman should have a right to be happy. If that means selecting a career path, then that should be all right. Japan is perhaps twenty years behind the United States with regard to women.

We have made a lot of progress in hiring minorities in our manufacturing plants. Also, we now have hired African-American and Hispanic advertising agencies. We are committed to doing the right thing and I expect will surpass the American companies on this issue.

Japanese men greatly rely upon their wives to raise the children. This is because most of their wives do not work. Just because a Japanese man does not accept a Japanese woman in the workplace does not mean he doesn't respect her. In fact, it means he respects her more.

Usually in Japanese companies today women only do "complementary work," which means they stay in the same office and do not rotate to other jobs. However, gradually companies have developed a system where if a woman wants to do the work that men do, she will be given "general work." She would then be transferred anywhere and would accept that just like a man. This system is working now. In the case of government bureaucrats, quite a few women are advancing. I have always advocated this opportunity for women. Because our bank is international, we need people who major in foreign literature, and many women do that.

America is really not a melting-pot society. You are a salad bowl, with many different races and religions and beliefs about the role of women. This is why you need a lot of lawyers, because there is a lack of understanding. This is not a problem in Japan. Our managers are learning to deal with this in the United States.

CULTURAL DIFFERENCES

In speaking of the cultural differences between the two countries, the Japanese particularly noted America's heterogeneity compared to their own homogeneity. They are clearly troubled by this issue, recognizing strengths and weaknesses in either extreme. They also spoke of America's poor education system, lack of order, strong sense of individualism, and extreme dependency on the legal system.

Japan has always had a concern for keeping order. The strong should not eat up the weak. But the strong have a good appetite. So someone has to check the strong. The system that has been constructed in Japan gives that responsibility to the bureaucrats— the feudal lords did that in the olden days. Their motivation is to protect the people. It is purely good. American society lacks order and everyone fights with one another; there is no harmony.

Originally, we don't know if people came to Japan from the north or south. But for the last 1,000 or 2,000 years we have had no immigration. So, one of our strong characteristics is homogeneity. Because of that it is unnecessary to consult attorneys and lawyers. We can just talk. We do not need specific rules.

Japan is an exception in its homogeneity compared to other parts of the world. So it is America that is the reality. Heterogeneity, I think, is a weakness of the United States. But, on the other hand, we Japanese respect America's generosity and ability to absorb people from all over the world. This is really the only place for those people to come. This is a dilemma. The Japanese people want to stay as they are. They want to keep their way of living forever. But I think it is time to change our way of thinking. It should be done slowly so that it does not upset our society.

In Japan there are only a few people who cannot read or write Japanese. Part of the education problem in the United States are the immigrants who do not speak English. People of lower classes are coming to the United States to start a new life here. That poses a problem.

Americans have no respect or concern for one another. Everywhere here [Los Angeles] there is graffiti. It is even all over the freeway signs so that a stranger cannot even read directions. To write all over another person's property or on public property is something we just cannot understand.

America is a legal society where human rights are respected. That is very good, but these days I see some excessiveness where people sue so many times. Whatever happens, they go to court. There are no conversations between people to solve their problems by themselves. In Japan, it is the other side of the coin. Community discipline is very strong, so that any dispute is somehow solved without the intervention of the government. It is a good system but sometimes goes to excess.

People came to America because of political or religious pressure and sought their own freedom. That freedom is most important to them. But in Japan, after the historic era, we had kings, lords, and rulers. So the Japanese people are much more accustomed to subordination and group pressure. I think freedom is good—but not too much of it.

We Japanese are many people on a few small islands. We have had to learn how to live with limited resources. We know that if we quarrel with one another, we lose. It is better to negotiate and compromise. Here in the United States you always fought for rights and if you were defeated you went elsewhere—to the West. But in Japan that is impossible. There is no place to go. So, "the nail that stands up gets hammered down." This makes the two cultures very different.

A strong point of America comes from its ethnic populations and a weak point is the other side of the coin. I admire the diversity of the United States. But it also creates difficult problems in bringing the country together. Spanish people come here and can live without speaking English. But if they are going to live here, they should be taught English. Language should never be split as it is in Canada. Without a common language there is no nation.

The independence of the American people is a strength, but there is no organization. There is a great deal of illiteracy and a clash of cultures. Japan's homogeneity has been a strength. It is easier to manage an employee. It is much harder in America because there are so many different cultures. But that American weakness could become a strength in the next century. Business is crossing national borders and we will all have to accept people of different cultures. Japan needs to do that, but it will create a lot of conflict—we have no immune system, so to speak, as the Americans do.

I think that U.S. heterogeneity is a strength and that we Japanese should learn from you. A lot of Japanese, Korean, Taiwanese, and Singaporeans are coming to the United States, not only as visitors and expatriates; they want to stay here and become U.S. citizens. So America accepts these so-called "hungry people" that will revitalize the country. That won't happen in Japan.

The group-minded nature of the Japanese and our homogeneity makes it very easy for us to communicate with each other. Also for hundreds of years education has been very important to us. We are a small and poor nation. The only thing that we have is our people. We always try to do better, and competition is intense. We want to win. We are very different from Americans in these ways.

PERSONAL EXPERIENCES AND FEELINGS

Over and over throughout this book and in our everyday thinking we use the term "the Japanese," as though they—there, I have done it again—are a single entity. As in the case of any generalization, or stereotype, there are elements of truth. The Japanese population is in fact very homogeneous, with a strong group orientation. And the Japanese pride themselves on their stoicism. Still, this can be carried too far. The Japanese have a saying that "Every man has three faces. One is shown only to acquaintances, another only to loved ones, and the third only to himself." The following personal experiences and feelings will give you at least a peek at that third, very human face.

In this international situation I am some use in the bridging between the United States and Japan. Because I can speak English so-so, I can communicate. I make friends with people, which is very difficult for newcomers. While Americans and Japanese have different backgrounds, I still see only human beings. My rotation here [in the United States] has been a great experience, although I still have a very hard time fully understanding American culture.

My wife is very lonely here. She does not speak English and does not know how to drive. She spends almost all day watching TV videos that her mother sends her from Japan. She is very lonesome for home and I just don't have time to be with her more—this is a problem.

I really like the freedom here in America and the fact that Americans are basically very kind. When I first came here, I could not speak English very well and was not a very good driver. A policeman wanted to give me a ticket, but I didn't understand what he was saying. Finally, he just shook his head and said, "Please be careful," and drove away. I remember how concerned about my safety he seemed to be; that was very nice . . . I still don't drive very well [laughs].

My wife loves the weather here, we have a very roomy house, and she drives wherever she needs to go. She tells me that she is like an American woman now and does not really want to return to Japan [*shakes his head*].

My earliest recollection of the war as a child was the bombardment by B-29s. So many people died and we were of course destroyed. We have very bitter memories about that. But after the war it was a night-and-day difference. The American GIs were so tall, shiny, bright, enthusiastic, and friendly. I was very impressed. They were so generous, especially with children. We were always hungry while the war was going on, but during the occupation they gave us chocolate, chewing gum, and I remember Lucky Strikes—LSMFT, Lucky Strikes Means Fine Tobacco [*laughs*]. I thought it was so wonderful. So the Japanese have not forgotten the war, but the impression of the generous GIs and the Red Cross is very strong. I will never forget what they did.

Globalization and the information age make it difficult to maintain the old ways. For example, my daughter was born in the United States and was educated here. She tells me that she is already spoiled by American society. With CNN, newspapers, and foreign travel, it is impossible for Japan to remain segregated. I wish every country, not just Japan, could retain its tradition and culture. That would keep the world so much more interesting.

A Japanese man works very hard and is not able to spend much time with his children. But in his heart I think he cares just as deeply about them as the American father.

My first job was with an American company in Japan. My boss was an American. I said to myself that if I ever had a chance to manage another people in another land, I would never do what my boss did, which was to force American management on me. I remember he had me translate a contract into Japanese and told me to take it to a customer to sign. I told him that in Japanese culture the seller has to sign first, which is the reverse of the American way. The Japanese way underscores how important we think the buyer is. But my boss insisted. It was very, very embarrassing to me when I presented it to the customer. I remember how ashamed I felt. So now I like as much as possible to adjust to the local country's culture.

There are so many differences between the two cultures. We drive on different sides of the street. Our saws cut when you pull and yours when you push. We call people with the same hand motion you use to say goodbye. Once I did that to an American I was calling over and he thought I wanted him to go away [*laughs*]. But even with the differences, the one thing I really like here are the people.

When I am in Tokyo, I speak up for the American market. Sometimes I am a little challenging. That is my responsibility and obligation. But some people in Japan prefer a softer approach and the building of consensus. They think I have become too Americanized [*laughs*].

Sometimes I worry about the future of Japan. In our main Tokyo office there are people who do not like to follow company policy. That is a new problem. People come to us just after graduation without really knowing the company. After a while they start complaining about rules, policies, working habits, and everything. Many people quit after only one or two years. This tendency is getting more serious.

Americans seem more concerned with Japanese investment [in the United States] than with purchases by the Italians, British, or Canadians. Perhaps that is because we are a different race. This is a very delicate issue for us.

I have seen articles and books that say the Japanese are now trying to buy people's minds with their investment in the community. That is very discouraging personally to me. [Company name] is trying very hard to be responsible and wants to work and grow with the community.

I learned that giving away money in corporate contributions is not enough and that in fact it can have a negative impact. So I try to spend a lot of time myself meeting with nonprofit organizations. I have met many new American friends this way. But most Japanese managers either have too limited an amount of time or communication problems to do this. They prefer not to do anything that might prove embarrassing. Pride and maintaining face is very important to us.

I am very broad-minded, but when my daughter called me in Italy to say she was going to marry an American boy, I remember the first thought that I had. I saw her in my mind, there in California alone, divorced, feeding the children spaghetti out of a can, and dropping them off at a day-care center [*laughs*]. She wanted me to talk to him on the phone but I thought that was too informal. But then she started to cry, "Papa please, Papa please," so I did. He is a very nice young man. They seem very happy. I hope they have children.

SUMMARY

Several times in the text it has been noted that the Yankee Samurai are caught up in the very midst of historic change. They are players in the drama of world history. So, too, are the some 40,000 Japanese expatriates here in the United States.

A century or two from now, writers may well note how these Japanese—like the Roman proconsuls of 1,500 years ago, the Spanish conquistadors, the nineteenth-century British colonial officers, and Yankee traders of the last century—prodded history in a direction it otherwise would not have chosen, and how the world was the better for it.

13

Lessons

> *Still I am learning.*
> —MICHELANGELO

What does all that has preceded this final chapter mean for today's and future Yankee Samurai, for the Japanese firms employing them, for American firms competing against the Japanese, and beyond that, for the peoples of two great world powers? What lessons are to be learned?

THE LESSONS FOR JAPAN

There is a long shopping list of concerns that Americans have about Japan's domestic and international policies. Earlier you heard many of the Yankee Samurai and Japanese expatriates touch upon several of the most delicate of them. What can the people of Japan learn from these concerns and what action should they take? Let's begin with a basic Japanese staple: rice.

RICE

The Japanese diet has included rice for over one thousand years. During World War II it was referred to as "grains of silver." It fed the 70 million people of Japan for four years. But for the Japanese, rice goes beyond mere sustenance. It has been to Japan what cotton was to the antebellum South—an inseparable part of the culture itself. In centuries gone by, rice even served as an important currency—one koku was the amount of rice required to feed one man for one year. The very nature of rice growing required the close cooperation of villagers, which strengthened the communal instincts of the Japanese. Wars fought in pre-Tokugawa times were waged basically over rice. The Kanto Plain where much of it was grown was soaked with the blood of samurai warriors who fell in battles for its control. Today, as the Japanese salaryman races across the countryside in a 170 mph bullet train, he looks up from his newspaper and gazes outside to a blurred sea of lush emerald green rice paddies—they are a link to his past, and at least one of his older relatives is probably still lovingly nursing rice plants on a small one- or two-acre plot of land.

At issue is the fact that U. S.-produced rice is largely shut out from the Japan market, even though it sells for one eighth the price of that raised domestically. American rice growers are complaining, as are a growing number of Japanese consumers. The Japanese farm lobby—a major supporter of the LDP—has been vigilant in opposing actions that might alter the status quo. Yet, like their peers throughout much of the First World the farmers are fighting an ultimately losing battle against industrialization. Since 1982, farm subsidies in Japan have fallen 16 percent, and recent redistricting will give Tokyo and other urban areas increased political power. The Minister of Agriculture recently announced his support for eliminating all obstructions to the importation of rice, with the exception of a 600 percent tariff that would be phased out over several years. The driving force behind this "tarification" was the effort to break the impasse in GATT talks whose successful outcome is very important to the Japanese. Thus, the proper steps are already being taken. This matter will simply fade away over time. Given the situation, the pace of change is reasonable, and the Japanese need do no more. At the same time, there is a lesson for American trade negotiators: cease the preoccupation with this peripheral issue, when the Japanese are sprinting ahead on a dozen other fronts.

DISTRIBUTION SYSTEM

Another common complaint made by the Americans is that the Japanese distribution system is so antiquated, inefficient, and tight-knit that it deprives American products from gaining access to the market. For every 1 worker in the U.S. distribution system between the manufacturer and the customer, there are about 2.3 in Japan—hence the "inefficiency." In the recent round of Structural Impediments Initiative, or SII, talks, Japan agreed to do something about this.

There are several points to be made here. First, even if the Japanese altered their system, it is not immediately evident how that will greatly help American exporters. The Japanese have for example begun to import foreign cars in fairly substantial numbers, but it is the BMW, Mercedes-Benz, Audi, and Volkswagen that are seen on the streets of Tokyo, not the products of Detroit. Michael Basserman, president of Mercedes-Benz, has said flatly that "the Japanese market is not closed." American quality is not up to Japanese standards; pitifully, the Big Three have not even been willing to make the investment to move the steering column to the right-hand side of the automobile, which is conventional in Japan. Nor has Detroit been willing to invest the huge sums required to build showrooms in high-rent Tokyo. BMW recently spent $0.5 billion for its facilities.

A second issue is that what Americans call "inefficient," the Japanese might simply call "exemplary service." Remember the last time you were in an American retail outlet and were looking for someone to help you and there was literally no one in sight? When a salesperson was finally located, it turned out to be a recently hired teenager who knew little more than you. On the other hand, there is a premium on customer service throughout the Japanese distribution system, with its "greeters" at the door, gift wrappers, and myriad small mom-and-pop wholesale and retail operations, that is often missing from much of the American scene.

Beyond this, there are unintended cultural benefits from the Japanese system. Many of the small retail operations provide a source of income for people, some of whom are well into their sixties, who might otherwise be on welfare. Further, the proprietors know the local community and the people in it, thus becoming "eyes and ears" that add to neighborhood stability; so unlike the massive and anonymous American shopping mall.

Whatever the arguments regarding Japan's "inefficient" distribution

system, this, like rice, is another nonissue. The system is already changing as the demands of a quicker-paced and labor-starved society make
themselves felt. The government has streamlined its licensing procedures for opening large stores. The recently completed LaLaport Fun-
abashi 360 store mall east of Tokyo is now Japan's largest. More like it
are on the drawing board. Even so, look for the system to maintain
much of its almost fanatical solicitude for the customer. This is going to
find its way to the United States as Japanese retailers begin to cross the
Pacific in the years ahead. If the U.S. retailers think they have problems
now . . .

The Japanese can no doubt learn some things from America's product
distribution system. But it would be a terrible mistake simply to abandon
their own—a mistake that likely will not be made. Efficiency is not the
operative word for the Japanese; effectiveness is.

REARMAMENT

The American Congress, ever on the alert to cut spending (military
spending, that is, and so long as it is not in one's own district), has been
admonishing Japan to share a larger burden of defense in the Pacific.
Japan's military spending, limited by its constitution—imposed by the
American occupation forces—to defensive purposes and not to exceed 1
percent of GNP, is felt to be inadequate by the majority in America's
Senate and House. Many of our Yankee Samurai, taking a cue from
their representatives, seemed to agree.

Yet this is another example of American shortsightedness. Try for
once, we should beg our leaders, to think a decade ahead. Do we really
want to *encourage* an already mighty economic power, which today has
a standing military ranked variously from fifth to eighth in the world, to
embark upon a vigorous armaments-spending program?

With technology playing an ever more important role in military weaponry, and with Japan rapidly becoming recognized as the world electronics leader, the Japanese need little encouragement. Join together Japanese twenty-first-century *Star Trek* weapons with a seventeenth-century
samurai warrior code, and you would have a military machine the like of
which the world has never before seen—ever.

Often over the last few decades the Japanese leaders have used Western pressures as a pretext to do what they wanted to do anyway; the
Japanese even have a word for this—*gaiatsu*. Streamlining the distribution system against the will of small shopowners is an example of that.
Rearmament may be another. Polls indicate a general opposition to an

expanded military; memories of World War II are still sharp and painful. Yet there are stirrings. One of the greatest Japanese writers of this century, Yukio Mishima, wrote the script for his own death and played it perfectly. Calling upon Japan to turn away from Western ways and return to its proud and honorable past, on November 25, 1970, dressed in a military uniform, he committed public ritual suicide. Mishima, who had been born into a samurai family, was a still vital forty-five-year-old at the height of his professional career. It was a magnificent gesture. Just before his death he had written:

> Purging away the evils of the West,
> Let us be faithful to our land.
> Stalwart, giving no ear to traitor's pleas,
> We shall hand down our great cause
> Without the least fear of death.

The Japanese people did not then respond, but they have remembered. More recently, Japanese prime ministers have begun to visit war shrines, including the almost sacred Yasukuni Shrine, honoring those who have died in battle. These are important symbols.

Nearly every Japanese friend I have ever spoken with has disagreed when I shared my belief that Japan's rearmament is inevitable. The arguments that I make with them are two-fold.

The first is a matter of reality. No individual, family, or nation has *ever* been able to hold its wealth over an extended period of time without the physical or armed means to do so. That is simply the way it is—and the Japanese are wealthy and getting wealthier every day. It must use, or have the ability to threaten to use, physical force in order to protect its wealth.

The second reason is admittedly open for argument. In one of Aesop's fables, a scorpion asks a frog for a ride across a lake. Very reluctantly the frog agrees, only after the scorpion vows not to sting him. Halfway across, however, the scorpion plunges his stinger into the frog. "Why, why," cried the frog, "now we will both drown?" "I couldn't help it," the scorpion replied. "It's in my nature."

Nature (culture) matters. The Japanese are a strong, proud, and sometimes arrogant people, with an almost mythic warrior past. Japan's closed borders over the last many centuries ensured that the same blood that flowed through the veins of samurai forefathers flows through contemporary Japanese. Can a millennia and more of samurai blood be simply shrugged off because of a new world of frivolous electronic gadgetry, foreign travel, BMWs, and all the rest that newfound wealth will buy? My Japanese friends think so and I believe that they believe what they tell me. But that may be wishful thinking on their part.

A 1967 survey taken among Japanese high school students showed that nearly 80 percent supported the "peace clause" of the constitution. A similar 1987 survey found the figure falling to barely half; the nation's youth with no direct memory of the war are returning to their samurai heritage.

What is the lesson here for Japan, with the Yankee Samurai and other Americans calling for increased military expenditures? The Japanese should proceed on this issue without paying an awful lot of attention to the Americans, or at least to the U.S. Congress. The Japanese can be absolutely certain that the same myopic congressional leaders who today call for increased Japan armament, a decade from now will be badgering Japan to *dis*arm.

Does a military buildup in today's relatively peaceful world make sense? History should provide the answer. War has been a near constant throughout the ages; even now, there are a dozen and more rogue states and an equal number of potential hot spots around the world that could threaten Japan's interests. The oil-rich Middle East is a tinder box of high-tech weaponry. A government that fails to take that into account is irresponsible. This is not warmongering. To the contrary, a well-armed nation can as much deter as incite war; the comparative military weakness of Hitler's neighbors, coupled with their lack of martial courage, was an open invitation to Nazi aggression. Conversely, the 1947 George Kennan "containment" policy aimed at the USSR, with the aid of nuclear and conventional forces, averted a direct conflict for almost half a century and led ultimately to that empire's dissolution.

Irrespective of military aspects of rearmament, the fact is that weapon sales internationally can be not only good business but an excellent way to align smaller foreign nations to Japan's sphere of influence. Commercial spinoff from military weaponry is still another benefit of defense expenditures; America's commercial aircraft and electronics industry have clearly benefited from weapons development. At the same time, Japan must realize just how nervous even the hint of rearming makes its neighbors throughout the Pacific region—their memories of World War II are still vivid.

This is another issue to be decided ultimately by the Japanese themselves, although close working relations with the Defense Department and Pentagon are certainly a good idea; this will build a continuity of high-level American and Japanese officer relations that could become important in the future if politicians of the two governments have a falling out with one another. Exchange of military officers to serve in one another's armed forces is a good idea.

A bill calling for Japan to participate militarily in future U.N. peace-keeping efforts was recently killed in the Diet. Sooner or later, a similar bill will pass. It is inevitable. It is also inevitable that Japan—and Germany—will take a permanent seat on the U.N. Security Council. The United States, Germany, and Japan will almost certainly emerge by the turn of the century as the world's uncontested three great powers. Great powers are militarily strong. The Japanese will have to learn how to deal with that without terrifying their neighbors—and without repeating the history of the 1930s by yielding their own government to the militarists.

KEIRETSU

The *keiretsu*, or family of companies, are integral to Japan's industrial structure. Yet they have become targets of American detractors who believe them to be anti-competitive and impediments to American firms attempting to gain access to the Japanese markets. The matter has now hurdled the Pacific as the *keiretsu* begin to clone themselves in the United States. This runs headlong into U.S. anti-trust laws. What should Japan do about this concern? Absolutely nothing beyond the continued evolution that is now unfolding.

We have already seen that the *keiretsu* compete savagely with one another and assuredly are not anti-competitive. And even if they were, the *keiretsu* structure itself is beginning to weaken somewhat as a growing number of family members are breaking ranks and doing business outside the group—in early 1992, Toyota began buying auto parts from Hitachi, a member of the Fuyo Group that includes Nissan. In fact, American companies can become de facto *keiretsu* members by forming a joint venture with one of the family's firms; hundreds have already done so.

There is a related critical issue to consider here. The United States is beginning to rethink its own anti-trust laws. A growing number of American firms are pursuing a variety of joint research and other ventures with one another. The government has voiced no concern and in the case of Sematech has actively encouraged it. Lester Thurow, the dean of Sloan's School of Management, even calls for a return of the bank holding company of J. P. Morgan days. So America itself may be moving toward an industrial structure similar to Japan's.

For all of these reasons, the *keiretsu* issue is not one the Japanese should concern themselves with, beyond politely listening to the Americans and trying to explain the facts.

INCREASE CONSUMER DEMAND

What many Americans really mean when calling for the Japanese to increase consumer demand is that they should not work quite so hard and save so much. They should spend not for new plant and equipment investment (which is greater than that in the United States, even though our economy is nearly twice as large) but rather for more consumer goods, even going into debt if necessary. What Americans are in essence asking the Japanese to do is slow down some, enjoy life, live beyond their means; to become more like us.

In fact, the Japanese government has proposed a new five-year plan aimed at reducing the work week, increasing the availability of housing, improving the environment, and decentralizing to reduce the overcrowdedness of greater Tokyo. Some steps then are being taken, but not at a rapid pace, and not at the behest of the Americans. This is a natural and sensible evolvement. First, the industrial machine is put in place; only then do the needs of the people begin to be met.

What of American calls for the Japanese to provide women with full rights and opportunities and to open their borders to foreign immigrants and workers? Once again, there are hints of change in Japan, but not because of any urging by the Americans. This is after all the internal concern of a sovereign state—and a very powerful one at that.

For all of these and other internal societal changes, the great lesson for Japan is to look carefully at the experiences of the United States. To the extent that social engineering by fiat and tax code has strengthened the American culture, the action can be emulated by the Japanese. And to the extent that it has weakened the culture, it should be eschewed.

WORLD MORAL POSTURE

One of the most often-voiced American criticisms of Japan is that it is too nationalistic and concerned only with its self-interest. The Japanese, for example, are major trading partners with South Africa, have generally supported the Arab boycott against Israel, refused to take up arms against Iraq, and maintained close relations with China in spite of the Tiananmen Square massacre. Many Americans condemn these actions, and accuse the Japanese of being amoral and concerned only with their own nation's interest.

Yet, America's foreign policy hardly bears close scrutiny. Lord Palmerston, Britain's Foreign Secretary in the last century, wrote, "We have no eternal allies and no perpetual enemies; our interests are eternal." The British were blunt in their days of glory. In fact every nation, including the United States, has exactly the same belief.

One might say that, well, America is different; we are concerned about the immorality of apartheid, Israel's legitimate right to exist, and the freedom of the people of Kuwait. Set aside emotions and personal feelings; look at cold, hard *realpolitik*. Suppose that an accident of history had brought 5 million Palestinians and only a few hundred thousand Jewish people to the United States, instead of the reverse. And suppose that the evil of slavery never happened and that America's black population was less than 1 percent instead of its present actual 12 percent. Would that influence American foreign policy in the Middle East and South Africa? And quite irrespective of right and wrong, Israel has served as a Western outpost challenging several of the region's Communist surrogate states. America needed Israel in its Cold War battle against the USSR—it has been in our geopolitical interest to support that courageous and beleaguered country. Certainly no one seriously believes that we would really have deployed some 30 percent of our total military might to return the people of Kuwait to its repressive monarchy were it not for oil. How, then, can Americans argue on the basis of morality that Japan should have sent troops against Iraq, particularly when it was our own General Douglas MacArthur who forced the addition of Article IX in the Japanese constitution that forever barred the use of offensive military force?

In fact, Lord Palmerston's quote also holds perfectly for the United States. Morality ultimately comes down to self-interest. The difference between America and Japan is that the latter makes no pretense that it is anything else, and the former is so divided internally that it often cannot figure out where its self-interest lies—Vietnam, Iran-Contra, and so on. Morality, right and wrong, is another nonissue in the *realpolitik* of the modern world. Moral arguments, no matter how rationalized, come down to self-interest.

Japan now has surpassed the United States in terms of foreign aid: roughly $13 billion compared to $10 billion. Much of the Japanese money is targeted for neighboring Asian countries. Is there self-interest involved? Of course. The majority of it will result in critical friendships for the Japanese, and the grants often come in the form of loans earmarked for the purchase of products or services of Japanese firms. Americans complain about these "strings-attached" loans. Yet, are we so

naive as to believe the Japanese will simply make cash grants to Third
World nations, who will use the money to repay loans that U.S. bankers
fecklessly made to them over the last decade which they are now unable
to repay? American diplomats have actually asked the Japanese to do just
that.

The Japanese need not worry about American charges of amorality.
America has no corner on "righteousness"—no nation does. The only
concern the Japanese should have, and the Americans as well, is that
every effort be made to assure that their individual self-interest is reasonably congruent with that of others; ideally, self-interest becomes
mutual self-interest.

From Pebble Beach to the Level Playing Field

None of the issues raised thus far suggests a need for immediate and
aggressive actions by the Japanese. But there are four areas of concern
voiced by the Yankee Samurai, and generally supported by the American people, that might be of value to the Japanese in terms of lessons
worth acting upon.

First, in spite of the fact that it takes an American seller as well as a
Japanese buyer to consummate a real estate transaction, the downside in
terms of American animosity is an inordinately heavy price for the
Japanese to pay for the ownership of an American "trophy" like the
Rockefeller Plaza or the Pebble Beach Golf Course. A more circum-
spect policy would likely have greater long-term benefits. In fact, economics may determine the future policy. The Dunes Hotel purchased
by Japanese interests in 1987 is losing $500,000 a month and is now
valued at only two thirds of its $158 million purchase price. The Pebble
Beach operation, purchased in 1988 by a Japanese real estate tycoon for
over $800 million, has recently been resold to a Japanese syndicate for
$500 million. Heavy Japanese investment in the late eighties came just
as the market peaked; since then, declines of 30 percent in commercial
properties are common. Japanese real estate investment in 1991 was a
meager $5 billion, with much of that targeted for the residential sector.
Still, this remains a sensitive matter for Americans.

The second issue relates to American knowledge of Japan, or lack of
it. The Yankee Samurai were in near-unanimous opinion that Americans know very little of Japan. The Japanese government and various
private organizations are doing a great deal today to change this, with a
variety of television programming and exchange of students, scholars,
and influence makers. But much more needs to be done. American

ignorance about Japan is vast. Overcoming the lack of understanding does not mean acceptance, but it is a critical prerequisite.

Third, every effort by the Japanese should be made so that American firms have the same opportunities in Japan that their firms have in the United States. That means parity in the rules for investment and trade. This does not mean guaranteeing American companies a percentage of the Japanese market—a terrible idea. Quotas such as the target 20 percent of Japanese semiconductor sales, or 20,000 American automobiles, only reinforce Japanese belief in the poor quality of American products. The same argument holds in reverse in the United States, where Congress (or at least the Michigan delegation) is attempting to limit the number of automobiles the Japanese can produce in their American factories—an even worse idea. Apparently, American industry needs its government to protect it from Japanese competition both internationally and domestically.

Yet Japan has already largely dismantled its formal barriers to American goods. Informal obstacles—including bureaucratic red tape, public bias in favor of Japanese goods, and close working relationships among Japanese businessmen—can and have been overcome by hundreds of American firms that show the necessary commitment. The Japanese government has helped by sponsoring trade fairs, making information available about how to do business in Japanese, and encouraging the business community to be open-minded in seeking American suppliers. It has gone further by providing start-up funds to several American firms, including Ford, to locate research centers in lesser-developed regions outside of Tokyo. Even the Japanese private sector is easing the American path. Canon Trading U.S.A. was formed in 1992 with the dedicated mission of exporting American products to Japan. A dozen other Japanese companies have been formed for the same purpose. The "playing field" is a lot more level than some Americans might be willing to admit. Nevertheless, these affirmative actions by Japan should continue. They contribute to harmony between the two nations.

Finally, many of the Yankee Samurai were concerned about the strong influence the Japanese seem to have on the U.S. government; influence purchased by the services of high-priced Washington lobbyists—the best that money can buy. Recent best-selling books have pilloried the Japanese for this. In fact, the Japanese neither broke nor even bent any law. If there is a moral or ethical question here, it should deal with Americans who by design first serve their own country in trade matters, either writing, negotiating, or enforcing the law, and then (having mastered the issues and made the necessary contacts) leave government and go to work for the very same people they have earlier been opposing—and do so at generous six-figure salaries. You don't see much of the reverse in Japan.

Thus far the lobbying efforts have proven largely successful, but there is an amorphous and very dangerous anger in America. An ominous backlash is building. At all costs the Japanese must avoid a possible future *Washington Post* headline: U.S. GOVERNMENT RIDDLED WITH JAP-ANESE AGENTS. It is suggested that the Japanese cut back high-level politicking and began to advance their interests bottom up at the grass-roots level, using the Yankee Samurai—a natural constituency. There are about 25 million Americans who directly or indirectly are positively affected by the Japanese presence in the United States; their views and political support should be sought. (More on this below.)

In sum, then, with the exception of circumspection in buying U.S. high-visibility real estate, increased efforts to improve America's under-standing of Japan, the assurance that U.S. firms can compete in Japan pretty much by the same rules under which Japanese firms compete in America, and a rethinking of the use of high-powered Washington lobbyists, Japan should do no more.

The best service Japan can do for America—and for that matter for the world—is to continue as an economic and social model demon-strating the success that hard work, sacrifice, commitment, and internal harmony can bring. Nations throughout the Pacific Rim are looking to emulate the Japanese. In essence, Japan should keep on being Japan, while at the same time heightening attention to foreign sensibilities and preparing for world (or at least Pacific Rim) economic, political, and military leadership. Whether the Japanese want it or not doesn't matter. The crown will fall to them.

The Lessons for Japanese Companies

It is not often that managers have an opportunity to find exactly what the people who work for them feel—in fact, most really don't want to know. With this book, the Japanese have had such an opportunity. What are some lessons from this for the Japanese companies in the United States? How can they better manage their Americans and how can they more effectively operate in American communities?

Early in the book we posited similarities between the Hessians, mer-cenaries hired by the British in the Revolutionary War, and our Yankee

Samurai. While there are significant differences among the firms, from what you have already read, it is clear that some general patterns do emerge.

	HESSIANS WITH BRITISH	YANKEE SAMURAI WITH JAPANESE	JAPANESE WITH JAPANESE
Communication problems	Severe	Moderate and improving	None
Acceptance management/fighting style	Limited	Moderate and improving	Total
Leadership opportunities	None	Modest but growing	Unlimited
Mission acceptance	None	Modest	Total
Consensus decision making	None	Moderate	Total
Loyalty	None	Modest	Strong
Commitment	Limited	Modest	Total
Strategic planning participation	None	Marginal	Total
Pleased to serve	No	Yes	Yes

The table suggests that the Yankee Samurai assuredly are not Hessians, mere hired mercenaries. They are too much an integral part of their firms to be called that. But neither are they fully accepted and equal contributors to their firm as are the salarymen (third column).

As the Japanese companies continue to expand their overseas empires, they are confronted with a basic choice: continue to control the far-flung enterprises from Tokyo, using Japanese managers, or begin to localize operations that take advantage of foreign manpower.

Some companies are already beginning to do the latter. Honda is even talking about making its headquarters in the United States, and has made a point of trying to localize its products, profits, production, and management. Several Japanese companies have moved their European headquarters out of Tokyo to Europe, and Sony has appointed an American and a European to its board of directors. At the same time, don't discount the possibility of a centrally run operation. Though Japanese manpower is spread very thin, modern communications and travel technology may make it possible to do so. But even with a strong Tokyo hand it will still be necessary to draw loyal Americans, and other nationals, into the ranks. How can this be done?

JAPANESE MANAGEMENT STYLE: MORE, NOT LESS

A key finding of the book has been that only a modest amount of Japanese management style is practiced among the white-collar Yankee Samurai—more of it seems to be evident in factory environments. It is not that the Japanese have not tried; but many Americans lack the patience and team orientation required for consensus decision making, reject the seniority system, feel uncomfortable in an open office environment, dislike being rotated out of their current jobs (particularly if it means relocation), and do not want to be committed to a firm for life. Many feel uncomfortable with the ambiguity of job responsibility in a Japanese firm, which encourages a broad perspective, while others simply do not adjust to the *kaizen*, or continuous improvement, philosophy.

What has resulted, then, is neither Japanese management style nor American—whatever that might be. It is a new management style struggling to find itself. What is evident are patterns that show considerable dilution of management methods as practiced in Japan. The primary lesson for the Japanese firms operating in the United States is to change course *away* from accommodation to American customs and pursue *more*, not less, of Japanese management style.

Everyone in the company, for example, should know the firm's mission, which may or may not be identical to the parent's mission. It should be inculcated in every Yankee Samurai just as it is in the Japanese. With this and the other elements of the management style, the Yankee Samurai will almost naturally begin to play an increasing role in setting strategy and making key decisions while moving up the organizational ranks. Over time those who feel comfortable with the system will stay and those who do not will leave—a kind of samurai Darwinism. Word will spread of the Japanese management style of the firm, and those who are drawn to it will come for that reason.

Of course, necessary adjustments should be made to the local customs when operating abroad, but the envelope should be pushed to the very edge by the Japanese. Japanese management style has much to offer, and for those Yankee Samurai whose personal belief system is consistent with it—either because of the way and place they were raised, or because they have been trained that way—it is a perfect fit. If the Japanese firms simply yield to American management style—as many seem to be doing—they are likely to end up not with the best of both worlds but rather the worst.

The Japanese should have more confidence in their ability to promote elements of their management style among the white-collar Yankee Samurai. They have been reasonably successful in doing this on the factory floors of their U.S. installations. Recall one of our Yankee Samurai describing the differences in hiring, training, and a sense of family in his firm's manufacturing facility compared to white-collar headquarters. In fact, the Japanese practice something of a double standard: using their management system in the blue-collar environment, and then abandoning much of it in the white. Granted there are greater difficulties in the latter environment, with a work force that is more highly educated and specialty-trained, more urban, more diverse, and generally more "sophisticated." The white-collar work itself is also fundamentally different, tending to be more abstract, dealing with ideas rather than things. Still, the Japanese should push for more, not less, of their management style among all their Yankee Samurai.

But there is the dilemma pointed out in an earlier chapter. Any institution's management style is a function of the larger society's culture, and the culture of the U.S. and Japan remain at polar extremes. How, then, is it possible to deploy the Japanese management style in this country?

The answer is to build so strong a *corporate* culture that it serves as a shield from the larger society. That is done by first crafting a mission that becomes part of every employee's thinking. This is coupled with a scrupulously careful selection of employees to ensure they have the right personal qualities, followed by an intensive training and orientation program, and then the daily practicing of policies and procedures that serve to reinforce the corporate culture. This is difficult to do in America, but it is possible; the U.S. military achieves it. Young men and women who have been acculturated in the broad society are essentially reeducated into the military way. Certainly several American companies have been reasonably successful at building a strong corporate culture—McDonald's, Federal Express, Hewlett-Packard, Johnson & Johnson, and 3M, to name a few.

The physical location of the facility is also important in building corporate culture. American culture is by no means uniform across the country. The Japanese know this, which is why they have built so many manufacturing operations in relatively rural areas of the Northwest, Southeast, and Midwest; the cultures of these communities, markedly different from major urban centers, lend themselves to Japanese man-

agement style. Site location is no less important for white-collar operations in building a corporate culture. A recent survey shows that the
best places for a business to locate are the smaller cities like Phoenix,
Nashville, Albuquerque, Tucson, Salt Lake, Charlotte, and Orlando.
Suburbs, some fifteen to twenty miles from major cities, are also becoming much more attractive locations, and for the same reason: the
community culture.

Another critical key to achieving this strong Japanese corporate culture is the recruiting of a special cadre of Americans—the *hatamoto*.

THE HATAMOTO

Realistically, it may not be possible for a Japanese company to recruit
and train an entire work force of totally dedicated Yankee Samurai,
every one of whom is imbued with the company culture. But it certainly
should be able to obtain a special select few. That should be all that is
needed.

Centuries ago, samurai were generally known for intense loyalty to
their masters, but there was a special group, the *hatamoto*, who were in
a class by themselves. Each *Daimyo* surrounded himself with these
dedicated warriors, a kind of Praetorian guard, who were completely
faithful and could always be depended upon. These were the *hatamoto*.
The word literally means "under the standard." During battle, it was
they who stood unyielding unto death under their *Daimyo* lord's battle
flag. The Japanese subsidiary firm can build its small cadre of Yankee
Samurai *hatamoto*.

Their role would be two-fold: to serve as a direct link between the
America and Japanese staffs, and to advance Japanese management style
within the firm among the Yankee Samurai to every extent possible.
They would act as a bridge between the Japanese and Yankee Samurai:
as loyal to their company as any salaryman, yet still sensitive to the
needs of their American co-workers and fully accepted by them. This is
a task of enormous complexity and requires subtlety, judgment, and
careful training. Having said that, where will these *hatamoto* come
from?

No university offers a curriculum to train such people, but a two- to
four-year program could certainly be put into place. It would be a mix
of Japanese language and culture training, along with a broad survey of
business fundamentals that would include an emphasis on managing
global firms. After graduation and recruitment by a Japanese company,
another intense in-house training program both in the United States

and Japan would follow, along the lines of Nomura's program described earlier (see p. 151). The dropout rate, at least initially, might be high; that is a price the firm should be willing to pay. But for those who survive, these *hatamoto* would be perfectly positioned for a fine career and an opportunity to be of great service.

JOB ROTATION AND TRAINING

Many American management consultants have argued that Japanese companies should rethink the policy of rotating top Japanese managers every three to five years and lengthen their stay. Earlier, we saw that the policy did often create discontinuities. Still, the degree of disruption should lessen over time. More and more Japanese are rotating through America, creating a critical mass of knowledge and sensitivity at the home office. Better decisions are likely to flow from this.

The argument for lengthened stays might be overstated. But that is only true if the Japanese managers in the United States really "live" the experience. For example, in the last chapter we heard the electronics firm's chairman suggest that it is desirable for a senior Japanese to hire an American secretary, as well as American direct reports, to ensure against isolation from the American staff and becoming too comfortable surrounded by other Japanese. Further, when evaluating the Japanese expatriates, how well they have managed the Yankee Samurai should be a factor.

Opportunity, indeed, strong encouragement, should also be afforded to more Americans—the *hatamoto* and other Yankee Samurai who have demonstrated their loyalty—to be rotated, especially back to Japan, as well as to different American plants and facilities. Sumitomo is beginning to do some of this.

Cross-cultural project and work teams could also be effective. Mitsubishi International Corporation has a program whereby twice a year it brings together thirty of its top people, half Americans and half Japanese, in an isolated setting to review manager relations as well as operational efficiency; special effort is made to break down cultural differences.

The Japanese should be integrated throughout the organization to every extent possible, so that both Americans and Japanese can benefit from the interchange. This is far preferable to separate or parallel operations, and again is consistent with the principle of more, not less, Japanese management style.

While many Japanese companies have launched language training for their Yankee Samurai, it has seldom been taken very seriously. The effort should be advanced again with emphasis on Japanese culture, thinking, and practices. This can be achieved with in-house programs that include both lectures and videos—some excellent ones have recently been produced. Mirror-image courses should be designed for the Japanese so that they can better understand America and the Yankee Samurai. The idea of appointing American mentors to the Japanese, suggested by one of our Yankee Samurai, is a good one.

AMERICANIZATION—AND THE SPINOFF

Many Japanese companies operating in the United States are wrestling with an identity problem: there is often a rush to "Americanize." One simple way to help achieve that is to add the word "America" or "U.S.A." to a company title: American Isuzu Motors, Seiko Instruments U.S.A., Epson America, Toyota Motor Sales U.S.A., and so on. It should even be possible over time to spin these operations off as wholly owned separate companies, with an entirely American staff reporting to a board that would be comprised largely of Japanese parent company managers. This would certainly make many of the Yankee Samurai feel a little more independent and salve the egos of the most senior among them. It ostensibly puts a more American face on the firm.

This is fine, but carried too far it might not be such a good idea. If the purpose of the spinoff is public relations, it is an easily seen-through facade—the operation is still largely controlled by a Japanese-dominated board. The Japanese companies should not fear being what they are. So long as they maintain harmonious community relations, allow participation by American labor, capital, and management, make every effort to use American parts/vendors (even providing technical or capital help if necessary), reinvest in the local economy, and cooperate with other American business enterprises, they are doing all they should do. Americanize, yes, but *not* to the point where the Japanese roots are lost, for that is where the strength lies. America needs to learn the lessons that Japan can teach.

COMMUNITY ACCEPTANCE, SPEAKERS' BUREAUS, AND PACs

The whole arena of corporate social responsibility as part of doing business in America is new to the Japanese, yet it is crucial that they come to understand its importance and act accordingly. Their ability to do so must be greater than for American firms, because fairly or unfairly they are being judged by a higher standard. When one of the Japanese automobile firms decided in the early 1980s to build a major manufacturing facility in the United States, a key man assigned to the task, one of the Yankee Samurai you have heard from, was sent to Japan and spoke personally with the chairman. He told him: "Remember one thing. We cannot consider this project a success unless we are accepted by the community."

By every measurable standard, the project has indeed been a success. But not all Japanese firms have done so well. A late 1991 survey by the Keidanren showed that philanthropic practices are not common for overseas operations of Japanese firms. While the longer-established and larger Japanese companies in the United States have developed fairly sophisticated corporate social programs, including corporate contributions, others have floundered. They are easy targets for a myriad of nonprofit causes, not all of which have much merit. This is an area where the Japanese have little expertise and need some help. American "advisers" have provided some direction, but it is not evident that the direction has always been the best.

For one example, the Japanese like the United Way mode of corporate giving because it is nicely structured and easy to participate in. Little more than writing a check is all that is required. One of the Japanese executives in a given city is appointed to head the "Japanese sector" of the annual campaign; he proceeds to solicit funds from the other local Japanese companies, who generally do their fair share. But there are problems with this. First, the Japanese money is lost in the United Way bureaucracy. Not all of it finds its way to the community—the national president in 1991 made $467,000—and that which does no longer has its source identity. To the ultimate recipient, it is United Way money—not Nomura, Toshiba, or NEC money. The Japanese firm will gain far more recognition if it can get directly to the community organization. United Way is a convenient vehicle for a corporation, and the organization certainly does some fine work; Japanese firms should continue to support it. But such giving should be augmented by direct company-to-community programs.

Further, it is suggested that direct giving be done through a foundation funded by the company itself: 0.5 to 1 percent of before-tax income is about right. Giving should take place primarily in those communities where the firm operates, and a matching grant program should be introduced so that every dollar contributed by an employee to a local cause can be matched by the foundation. That gets the Yankee Samurai themselves involved in the community, which is critical. The foundation should be staffed by a few professionals who review grant requests and make recommendations. Its board makes the final grant decisions and should include members of the corporation, as well as an outside adviser or two.

The Japanese should understand that corporate giving is a science, which should be handled by specialized professionals. A well-intentioned effort that inadvertently funnels money into a politically noncorrect or activist cause can have a serious backlash; AT&T recently found itself picketed because it unknowingly supported an organization that had strong ties to "right to life" groups.

The Japanese should also consider being a little less elitist in their giving. One Japanese company a few years ago made a $1 million grant to a major university. But the university was already heavily endowed, and far more might have been bought by spreading that $1 million over a dozen smaller universities, or perhaps an inner-city school system. It was easy to understand the choice of a major university. The Japanese have always been hierarchy-oriented, and the university is certainly a fine one—so you give to the best and strongest. It is far more difficult and time-consuming to reach out to the local community and address its true needs. But the firm that made that university contribution has learned rapidly and has now gained a deserved reputation for being one of the most sophisticated in its philanthropy. Among other things, it has discovered that corporate social responsibility means more than just giving away money; it also means personal executive involvement. You heard some of the Japanese talk of that in the last chapter.

In the final analysis, money is not nearly as important as personal involvement by the executives themselves. Critical to the success of a firm's sense of corporate social responsibility is putting a human face on the corporation. That means having the executive sit on the boards of nonprofit organizations, visit the sites of the nonprofit facilities, and perhaps participate directly in various programs. One Japanese executive spending an afternoon on an athletic field working with the Special Olympics for handicapped children is easily worth the equivalent of a $5,000 contribution.

In early February 1992, Benjamin Hooks, the president of the NAACP, called for a boycott of Japanese automobiles, claiming that the Japanese had too few black dealerships. The charge may or may not have been true, but in any case this is potentially very serious and must be dealt with aggressively, positively, and with complete integrity. Many of the Japanese firms have a fine record in the minority community, but much more needs to be done. Simply giving money to nonprofit minority organizations won't do it. Programs should be designed that lead ultimately to increasing minority hiring, outside suppliers, and higher educational performance; these are the bread-and-butter issues. Every effort should be made for the Japanese executives to interface directly with the people of the minority—black and Hispanic—community; both will have something to learn.

In an earlier chapter we saw that the Yankee Samurai tend to be far more objective in dealing with U.S.-Japan trade and policy matters than the average American. They are far more supportive of the Japanese presence in the United States than their fellow Americans. This is a great potential resource for the company. Every firm of reasonable size should establish a speakers' bureau, comprised of volunteer Yankee Samurai men and women, including a good representation of minorities. They would be carefully trained in the fundamentals of public speaking, and then familiarized with a series of sample speeches dealing with their company, industry, and perhaps key U.S.-Japan issues; supporting video material could also be prepared. There are thousands of local Kiwanas, Lions, and Chamber of Commerce groups always looking for speakers. Only the part-time effort of a manager and a secretary should be required to run the bureau. The speakers themselves are out of the office perhaps two hours a week, giving breakfast, lunch, or dinner speeches. The speakers' bureaus should have a disproportionately favorable impact on the community because once again they put a human American face on the company. They also by the way serve to improve the speaking skills of the Yankee Samurai. The company president should make a high-level issue of this and host an annual awards banquet for the speakers.

It is not only the Yankee Samurai who must develop speaking skills. The American media, both print and electronic, are doing an increasing number of stories on Japanese firms in the United States, as well as on U.S.-Japan relations. The U.S.-based Japanese executive is being called upon for his views by the media—he has become a de facto spokesman for his country. But few of these men are trained in the give and take of American journalism. The Japanese firms should immediately begin special training for their top executives, including simulated hostile press interviews, as well as making sure that executives posted in the United States have the skills to deal with this. Every Japanese firm should have at least one articulate high-ranking spokesman. Many, but not all, already do.

Sooner or later, one or another Japanese firm will encounter some highly embarrassing situation. If there is one lesson in damage control that has been learned from the stonewalling of Exxon following the *Valdez* oil spill and Dow Chemical following revelations about problems with silicon breast implants, it is that full and quick disclosure must be the rule. The Japanese media does not have much of a reputation for investigative reporting, but the American does. Less than complete candidness will badly exacerbate an already difficult situation.

Earlier we discussed the bitter attack upon the Japanese for their buying of Washington lobbying power. The detractors make a point. To the extent that political influence can be gained locally by the Yankee Samurai themselves, that is far more preferable. A company-oriented political action committee (PAC), in which employees have volunteered both their time and money to advance political interests of their firms, can be very effective. Company retirees should also be included in the PAC and letter-writing campaigns orchestrated on those occasions when that is required. Quarterly newsletters should be distributed that deal with the key political issues confronting the firm and the larger society.

There is nothing Machiavellian about all of this. So long as the intent of the Japanese firm is to help build a better America through its presence in the United States, then philanthropic giving, speakers' bureaus, and PACs are ways to achieve that end. But they must be approached professionally and ideally, without any sense of cynicism.

Corporate social responsibility is part of doing business in the United States and should be built into strategy, side by side with other major disciplines. When American Express, for example, announces that 10 cents will be donated to the Olympics Fund every time its card is used, that is good social responsibility and good marketing. When Ford nurtures and develops a minority parts supplier, that is good social responsibility and good manufacturing. And finally, when Mercedes-Benz makes a $1 million grant to the Chicago Symphony in return for its cars being displayed in the theater lobby during performances, that is good social responsibility and brilliant target advertising. Properly done, both the firm and the society benefit. This dimension of business is new for the Japanese, but they are learning fast.

THE LESSONS FOR THE YANKEE SAMURAI

Slowly and very tentatively, the Japanese have begun to yield power to the Yankee Samurai in whom they have confidence; there are not yet that many of them. Confidence is of course based upon competence and ability. But the Japanese demand something much more. Hiring practices in Japan are based largely upon the candidate's personality, character, and fit with the organization. Mutual trust is essential. So, too, with the Yankee Samurai. What are some of the personality traits that seem to be manifest by the more successful among them? How would you characterize the American men and women who are likely to step into leading positions in their Japanese subsidiaries over the next several years?

Granting the inability of anyone to fit this profile with perfection, certain traits stand out among the more successful of the Yankee Samurai.

The Perfect Yankee Samurai: A Profile

Patience
Self-control
Team orientation
Puritan work ethic
Hunger for information
Tolerance for ambiguity
Respect for age and rank
Long-term planning horizon
Enthusiasm for *kaizen* approach
Sensitivity to Japanese culture
Lifetime commitment to the firm
Identity with the company mission
Willing job rotation/relocation

If you now are a Yankee Samurai, review the profile and match it against yourself and the culture of your own company. For many factors where there is a personal lack, in-house training programs can be helpful—for example, a sense of company mission, long-term planning, *kaizen*, Japanese culture, and team orientation can all be taught. But other characteristics are integral to your personality and probably can not—indeed, should not—be changed. Adjust what you can and what you think is appropriate for the organization. Don't try to do more than that. Ultimately you must be true to yourself, and not everyone is a candidate for work at a Japanese firm. But for those who are a reasonable fit to this profile, a superb future awaits them. And this is more than just a career; it is an opportunity to participate in a historic sea-change as the great international firms accelerate their globalization.

A special note for Yankee Samurai human resources managers: recall that your organizations are not held in especially high esteem by the American staff. Treat that as a Japanese would: as neither good nor bad, just information. Act on it, and take a much more aggressive stance by beginning to build a department along the lines of that which exists in Japan. That means pushing for more intensive hiring practices, thorough training, ongoing job rotation, building a company sense of family, lifetime employment, instilling the importance of company mission, and so on. You could be the driving force for change in your firm.

A very positive sign that this is occurring is the recent appointment at Toyota of an outstanding man to head the human resources department. He has been with his company for over twenty years, and has rotated through a number of ever more responsible positions, none of them in human resources—he was one of the Yankee Samurai we have heard from, although he was not in his new position at the time of the interview. This is the first occasion that a very strong nonhuman resources manager has been assigned to such a post in any major Japanese company in the United States. It signals a growing recognition by the Japanese of the importance of their Yankee Samurai.

Today, there are roughly 400,000 Yankee Samurai; the number could well rise to 1 million by the turn of the century. Readers of this book may be among those who will be joining the growing ranks. How best to prepare? Assuming that you fit or roughly fit the profile, a solid business or technical grounding coupled with a knowledge of Japanese culture is an ideal mix. You should also be aware that there are vast differences between companies. Some practice almost traditional Japanese management style; some are so American in appearance that few but the American senior managers seldom even see a Japanese; others fall somewhere in between.

Women and minorities should not be deterred in their thinking about working for a Japanese firm. The Japanese are rapidly adjusting to the American workplace and assuring equal opportunity. A senior executive at Honda has said that he expects his firm to outperform the American companies in this regard. And in a major breakthrough, Sumitomo recently announced the appointment of a woman as president of Sumitomo Bank Securities.

In the 1850s, Horace Greeley, the St. Louis newspaper editor, counseled those seeking a challenging career to, "Go west young man." Our forebears, a century ago, listened to him, cracked their whips over teams of oxen that hauled Conestoga wagons filled with all their earthly belongings, and headed west. They made a new life for themselves, built a nation, and fashioned history. Greeley's advice is still fitting today, but now it includes women, and going west means standing on the shores of the Pacific and looking to the setting sun in the west—to Japan. Today, the only belongings of value one need have are a solid education and proper training; the Conestoga wagon has become a JAL Boeing 747 headed for Japan. "Go west young man and woman."

THE LESSONS FOR AMERICAN COMPANIES

The great irony of the paeans being sung to the wonders of Japanese management style is that much of it is American in origin. The interviewed Japanese executives themselves said this in the last chapter. The vaunted Japanese obsession with quality is the gospel of Deming. And the principles of participative decision making, empowering the worker, and providing an environment where the employee can reach his or her full potential were being proposed half a century ago by the American behavioralists: McGregor, Maslow, Barnard, Simon, and Mayo. In 1930, Mayo was saying, "You increase productivity when you pay attention to employees!" That may have been a revelation then, but should not be today—yet all too often it is.

A basic theme of this book is the importance of national culture in influencing the management style of its economic institutions. America's culture is marked by individualism and heterogeneity, which militates against consensus decision making; by poor education, which makes bottom-up strategy setting and worker empowerment problematic; by an adversarial larger society, which makes the achievement of a cooperative worker-management relationship difficult; the loyal "Organization Man" that William F. Whyte wrote about in the fifties is gone, replaced by nomadic workers for whom a company investment in training and job rotation may make little sense. The American culture, broadly speaking, produces a work force that does not readily lend itself to the kind of management style described above. The Japanese subsidiaries in the United States have encountered this culture.

But the counsel that holds for the Japanese firms also holds for the American. The larger culture can be overridden or at least blunted by building a powerful corporate culture, which essentially buffers the employee from outside forces.

CORPORATE CULTURE

That culture is built the same way the Japanese would build it, with a powerful sense of mission, leadership by example, intensive hiring and training, and the slow evolvement of myths and legends. This is no short-term undertaking. And it must be so thorough and complete that it remains largely intact as one CEO retires and is replaced by another. Each of the issues discussed below will contribute to strengthening the corporate culture.

BONUSES

The Yankee Samurai fully endorsed the principle of year end company bonuses, amounting to as much as 30 percent of total compensation, for those firms that made them available. With payment a function of the firm's performance, the employee's destiny is directly linked to the firm's—this is an ideal motivator, and crucial in building a sense of company family. This should translate well into the American workplace. The transition can be done either cold turkey or phased in over a five- or ten-year period (the latter approach is probably preferable). The employees themselves should have an important voice in designing the system. Properly done, it should lead to greater profitability even though total compensation costs might rise. All of the benefits discussed earlier to the employee, firm, and even nation are possible. This is one lesson for American companies—taken from the Japanese—whose time has come.

IN-HOUSE TRAINING

The campuslike facility at Crontonville, in Ossining, New York, has all the appearance of a small and exclusive ivy-covered college. In fact, it is G.E.'s training center, which offers hundreds of courses, ranging from manufacturing to marketing to personnel relations, that are being taught by an elite nontenured faculty. Every course is highly relevant to the working life and environment of the company. Both General Electric and more recently Westinghouse and Motorola have discovered what Japanese firms have known for some time: the employees and the company can benefit much more from a tailor-made in-house training program than from an outside MBA.

Almost all of America's larger companies provide education reimbursement to their employees. Many of the plans cover 80 to 100 percent of all costs. For a $30,000–60,000 MBA program at some elite school, that is a lot of money, especially if what is learned is not directly relevant to the firm's concerns and if the employee cashes in the MBA and moves on. An employee's career with a firm should directly benefit from a specialized in-house program, paid for by money that otherwise would have been spent for outside educational reimbursement.

Most American firms need not build their own "universities" as General Electric has done. An alternative that is growing in popularity is to custom-tailor programs in cooperation with local universities; instructors travel to the companies. There is resistance among many business school "scholars" who feel this to be somehow debasing and a distraction from "research." Perhaps, but look for more of these programs in the future. The Japanese have taught us that a great economic machine, perhaps the most powerful in the world, can be built without one single MBA! That is worth pondering.

In addition to this, the American firm can certainly copy the Japanese intensive one-year socialization and training program, as well as the practice of job rotation. Many of America's better companies now do something similar. Most, however, show a half-hour video to new employees telling him or her about the firm and then send them off to work in an area where they will likely spend much of their career. Consensus decision making, work teams, and cross-functional communication— all common to many Japanese firms—serve as mechanisms for sharing knowledge and learning. An American firm willing to tear down walls can emulate this. The model described here can lead to a targeted and pragmatic education that no MBA can offer.

THE ROLE OF THE SENIOR EXECUTIVE

The Yankee Samurai experience with Japanese senior executives offers some thoughts about leadership. One of Genghis Khan's young generals had just successfully fought a major campaign and rushed to the great Khan looking for his reward. "Ah, your reward . . . it is not a bigger tent as you apparently so desire, but rather more responsibility." Leadership certainly has its bigger tents, but overwhelmingly leadership is about more responsibility.

Within one year the entire ethos of any major American company can begin to change from one of executive privilege and employee grumbling (keep them restless but not mutinous) to one of a company family dedicated to company success. How is this done? For starters, without making a single public announcement, all reserved parking spaces are painted over, the executive dining room is shut down and the full-time private chefs fired, executive chauffeurs are let go, and construction begins to reconfigure the palatial executive offices (which often include fireplaces and built-in golden-fauceted basins) into one large open space for the entire team of senior executives. When not working in that environment, the executives will be seen meeting with people in the organization no matter how far flung domestically or internationally it might be. They are building harmony, listening, sharing their knowledge, articulating the mission, and encouraging top performance. They begin to yield their autocratic decision-making approach to bottom-up consensus. Well before the year is over, existing employee cynicism will begin to fade, replaced by a sense of team spirit and a surge of enthusiasm and heightened motivation.

Small things matter. In many Japanese companies, managers (or white-collar people generally) are not allowed to have coffee at their desks because assembly-line workers cannot have it on the factory floor. And no office will ever be air-conditioned before a factory is. Executive speeches about how important workers are to a company fall on deaf ears, but actions and symbols such as these mean a great deal.

A second most critical step is for the senior executives to address their own compensation. It is largely a myth that "an independent subcommittee of the board" determines these salaries. Everyone knows that. It is likely that members of that subcommittee were appointed by the CEO. It is also likely that some of those board members are CEOs themselves of other companies, and that our CEO sits on their board; the whole set-up is lasciviously incestuous.

American executive salaries have been an issue of discussion now for the last decade, when they began to accelerate well beyond that of the average employee, and in no correlation whatsoever with profitability. Stock options to be triggered at, say, $50 have simply been lowered to $25 when the firm encountered financial difficulty. They have become guaranteed 30–40 percent additions to income which conveniently the SEC does not require to be included when reporting executive compensation. Although a good deal of effort is made to bury executive salaries deep in the back pages of annual reports relying on the most cryptic of terms, an even greater effort is made to maintain a shroud of silence regarding munificent benefits. While the average worker waits his or her turn in the crowded office of an HMO to be treated, the executive is receiving private care from renowned physicians. There are company boxes at sporting and entertainment events, secretaries handling largely personal matters, access to company-owned vacation condos, golden parachutes, million-dollar life insurance policies, and multi-million-dollar retirement packages for him. We do mean *him*; roughly 95 percent of senior executives are male. Rank has its privileges. No one is arguing with that. But no CEO should expect loyalty from the work force when those privileges are pushed too far.

Many of the Japanese managers in the last chapter noted and disapproved of American compensation practices. The Japanese salaries are roughly 25 to 50 percent of their American counterparts, and they believe it would be inappropriate for themselves to be making more. The *Wall Street Journal* reported that in 1990, Lee Iacocca's direct compensation was $4.6 million; in 1987, it was $18.7 million. In addition, he receives 62,500 free shares of Chrysler stock every quarter he stays on the job—an apparent incentive so that, God forbid, he won't leave. Over the last five years, his counterparts at far more successful Japanese companies have taken home barely a tenth of his compensation.

The argument that CEOs, like professional athletes, are worth their million-dollar salaries does not hold up. Athletes can leave one team and be paid the same or even a higher salary with another. There is a market for them. But suppose there was a "free agent" system for *Fortune* 500 CEOs. How many of them would be drafted by another firm at the same, let alone higher, salary? Five of them, ten; twenty at the most? The marketplace does not set their salaries—they themselves do.

The first CEO of a major company who breaks ranks to rein back his firm's executive payroll may not be applauded by his peers at the Business Roundtable, but he will do a great service to his firm and perhaps his nation. Other large companies will follow, union and worker intransigence will lessen, and a sense of corporate family will grow. With that will come increased performance and productivity—worker and executive salaries will grow together.

There can be no grandstanding here. A few well-known executives have taken $1-a-year salaries and widely announced their selfless act. But not announced were buckets of future stock options and other contractual tiny print yielding benefits worth millions of dollars even if the firm failed. This won't do. In fact, little or nothing need be publicly said about executive compensation reductions. Soon enough the employees will learn the facts. Their view of the executives and the company itself will be significantly changed for the better; it will be manifest in their performance. De Tocqueville observed that, "the more equal social conditions become, the more men display a reciprocal disposition to oblige each other." The Japanese understand this. Our CEOs might paste that line above their shaving mirrors. It could turn their companies around.

The initiative for this must come from the executives themselves. It would be the ultimate in hypocrisy to have the Congress enforce more austere corporate practices. In the still of the night, with no one but Ralph Nader looking, the members of Congress increased their own salary 23 percent in 1991; they would have lost a national referendum on the issue 90–10. Even if it were not for this, government lacks the ability to control executive compensation. Congress has attempted to take action, for example, by taxing executive perquisites such as life insurance and limousines as "imputed income." But this kind of thing invariably fails because executives are simply "made whole"—their salaries are increased to the point where the taxes are covered. No, executive compensation is not the business of the government.

Stockholders, pension fund managers, and boards have an oversight role to play here in controlling executive salaries. Over the last year they have become more aggressive; G.M.'s board recently forced some changes and the United Shareholder Association (USA) has coerced several companies including ITT into reining in outrageous executive compensation plans. Realistically, however, the current corporate structure and the limited SEC reporting requirements largely preclude that. "The only limits are the gall of the CEO," writes Ralph Whitworth, president of the USA. Watch for a maverick CEO to step forward and say, "We are building a company here, not my personal wealth. I am taking a 50 percent pay cut." It will happen.

Several of the top Yankee Samurai executives felt very strongly about this issue. Here is an electronics firm's chief operating officer:

> [American] managers also need to rethink salary structures where they make so much more than the workers, which is quite different from Japan. If I were a Chrysler worker and saw Iacocca getting a $6 million bonus, I would say, "*#$[]@ 'em," and do everything I can to get mine. The high salary and unbelievably generous retirement package for G.M.'s Roger Smith [$1.2 million a year for life] has to be very demoralizing for the worker on the line. And Scully from Apple Computer in that company's heyday was just throwing huge bonuses at people. He is not doing it anymore and I don't think he had to do it then.

It is the leader's singular role to carry the torch of the firm's mission, and to keep it burning among not only those inside the company but outside as well. He or she must help initially to shape that mission and then later to reinforce it. The mission must be articulated, evangelized, and *lived as an example* by the leader. This is the most critical responsibility.

Beyond that, the leader must assure internal harmony and speak for the firm to the outside world. Inside the company, he or she should be fully accessible to people. Indeed, the leader should be reaching out to those in the organization by visiting plant sites and seriously soliciting concerns and ideas. These should be more than mere visits. Perhaps five days a year should be set aside serving in five different capacities. First-year schedule: retail clerk, environmental coordinator, customer sales rep, lab assistant, and planning analyst. There was a time when a business leader worked his way up through an organization and knew these kinds of jobs firsthand. No longer; and in the process, leaders too often have become isolated.

Fairly or unfairly, the leader must take full responsibility for any failing of the firm. In late 1991 when G.M. Chairman Robert Stempel announced a $6 billion loss, the closing of 21 plants, and the firing of 74,000 workers, Peter Drucker commented: "In Japan someone like Mr. Stempel would have announced his resignation by now."

Finally, the leader must assure that strategy is properly directed, that conflict within the organization is resolved, that people are motivated, and that training and management succession is effective.

These are the leadership characteristics found inside a good Japanese company. There are lessons here for senior Americans who choose to listen. Future leaders will have no choice. The imperatives of international competition will force changes.

Go Global

The American firms must learn, as have the Japanese, to think global and to act global. For too long American companies have had ready access to the world's largest and richest market in the United States itself. That is changing as foreign competition has come to America, and as new opportunities are opening up in Canada, Mexico, Europe, and throughout the Pacific Rim. American firms must go global if for no other reason than to protect their own domestic market. Dozens of them have already done so very successfully, but *every* company must now think in global terms.

One of the most effective ways of entering or expanding global interests is with the joint venture. Ties should begin to be built, perhaps informal joint research projects at first, with compatible foreign firms.

Cooperative efforts, which can take a bewildering array of forms and multiple arrangements, are the wave of the future. One firm might have dozens of them. American companies should not limit these to foreign firms, however. The American equivalent of the *keiretsu* is a coming new reality. American partners should be sought.

Entering the global arena creates special challenges in terms of financial and marketing strategies, offshore manufacturing, organization structure, and compensation and career choices for employees. None of this is easy; it multiplies by at least a factor of two the difficulty of operating a domestic operation. But the Japanese experiences can be of help.

One lesson to be learned from the Japanese is the effectiveness of the trading company. There is no American equivalent to the giant Mitsui, Sumitomo, Marubeni, or Mitsubishi; each of these firms does billions of dollars a year in export-import business. A good way to start might be with American firms that are already selling their products abroad. It should be possible for such firms to gather together their in-house expertise and spin off a fully owned trading company—Boeing Trading Inc., say. The firm would buy and sell a range of products in the international marketplace. Honda International was built in exactly this way. Beginning about ten years ago as a means to fill empty cargo ships returning to Japan, the operation is now doing half a billion dollars a year of business importing and exporting.

DESTINY

American top management often claims that it would like to plan long term but the constraints of the capital market make that impossible. With almost half of corporate equity held by retirement funds, there is great pressure for quarter-to-quarter performance by fund managers who churn their portfolios looking for even small percentage gains; they are personally judged by those gains. Short-term performance matters. There is some validity then to this management complaint, but it is vastly overstated. Too many American firms don't think long term either out of habit or simply because it is very hard work to do so.

Wall Street would likely welcome a firm that came forward with a plan that would take it into the next century, albeit perhaps with poor early returns. So long as that plan took the general form (discussed earlier) of a compelling mission, infinitely detailed but flexible strategy, and absolute commitment to the task at hand, investors would likely embrace it. There is of course a role for government here in terms of complementary tax incentives.

This long-term perspective is of critical importance in building corporate culture. That culture must have about it a sense of the eternal. Employees, customers, investors, suppliers, and other stakeholders cannot view the company as a transient entity. That does not build loyalty. One wants to link his or her fortune to an eternally burning star, not a comet.

In the last chapter we heard many of the Japanese executives criticize American firms for their shortsightedness. It is generally a legitimate criticism. American firms need only develop a new mind-set. Boeing, Hewlett-Packard, Merck, Disney, Johnson & Johnson, and 3M are some of the many fine companies that do plan years ahead. But they are too few in number. This is not a choice that American firms have. The Japanese think well into the future, and it is they who will be setting the business agenda, with shortsighted American firms always playing catch-up—that is a loser's game.

THE LESSONS FOR AMERICA

An underlying theme of this book has been the clash of cultures. If history is a guide—and it has been consistent on this point—as the economic and military power of a nation grows, so too does its culture begin to lap onto shores outside its domain. To an extent that many Americans may not yet realize, the Japanese have begun to influence our thinking and, by extension, our culture. Here are a few dimensions which the Yankee Samurai at one point or another commented upon. There are several lessons here for America to learn or at least consider; each deals with our culture.

KEIRETSU AND INDUSTRIAL POLICY

A Japanese card game popular around the turn of the century when the *zaibatsu* were most powerful was called *daiheimin*. In each hand the loser of the previous hand had to turn his best cards over to the winner of the previous hand. This is profound. The strong get ever stronger and the weak ever weaker, until they die. The Japanese have no problem with this principle. It is right, natural, and the way life in fact is—it is Herbert Spencer's theory of social Darwinism, and is manifest in their economy. Big and strong is good. The powerful *keiretsu* are witness to this.

At about the same time in history that this game was being played in

Japan, "trust busters" were at work in America breaking up the large industrial combines, including the vast steel holdings of Andrew Carnegie, the oil kingdom of John D. Rockefeller, and the financial empire of John Pierpont Morgan. Big and strong is bad. A card game that might have been played at that time in America would have had the *loser* of each hand receive the best cards from the winner.

Americans have always distrusted pockets of power, especially economic power, and have felt the need for government to serve as something of a restraining force. Unfortunately, they are discovering, as the people of what was the Soviet Union have already discovered, that big government can be just as repressive as big industry; in fact, far more so.

Japanese success with government-industry cooperation and de facto cartels is causing America to rethink its banking, anti-trust, and industrial policy views. This is a healthy dialogue, and there may be aspects of the Japanese paradigm from which America can learn. On the other hand, there must be a good deal of caution. "Big" works in Japan partly because of a Confucian principle that with strength and power comes a corresponding communal responsibility; that may or may not hold here in the United States. And industrial policy works in Japan at least in part because of the elite cadre of the men who forge it in the major ministries, and in part because of the underlying cooperation between business and government. Americans have to ask whether our bureaucrats have the same level of competence and unselfish commitment to the national well-being, and whether it is possible for business and government to cooperate; cultural factors may preclude this.

LONG-TERM PERSPECTIVE

As this book is being finalized, America has just begun one of its favorite quadrennial pastimes: presidential elections. If this one turns out to be like so many of its predecessors, it will be a largely empty and vapid exercise; we love the excitement nevertheless. Yet there is a genuine opportunity here for leadership—quite a different concept from caretakership.

We have heard much discussion of the fundamental importance of a firm's mission. But a mission is of even greater importance for a nation; it is the basis of a long-term perspective and gets to the very core of who a people are. What is America's mission, its reason for being? No one in the country knows! There are 250 million of us, and we are simply drifting into the future with no agreed-upon national reason for being. It has been said that the most corrupt man is one without a purpose.

What, then, of an entire nation without a purpose, without a mission? If leadership means anything at all at the national level, it means the ability to articulate national mission.

Few of our leaders seem anxious to do this. The reason is obvious. We have become so heterogeneous as a people that no matter what is said, someone will be alienated. There is virtually no mission of any substance that can be universally accepted. But that is what leadership is about. Not everyone need agree. It is the leader's responsibility to maintain the integrity of his or her vision and to evangelize its message to all who would follow. But that is not enough. The leader must also *fight* those who stand in opposition. American politics has not seen real fighting over principles for a long time—the politics of confrontation. This brand of leadership may mean not being elected, at least this time around. Churchill tenaciously held to his views, ever warning of the Nazi threat while out of office for nearly a decade—the "days of the locusts," he called them. No one listened until his moment came and he was called.

Vision is the starting point for long-term thinking and planning. The Japanese as a people excel at this and Americans can learn from them. The well-known Japanese architect and urban planner, Kisho Kurokawa, has made public his latest project, "The New Structure of Japan in the Year 2025." He has brought together the best minds in Japan to address the demands of that distant future. There is nothing unusual about this . . . for the Japanese. They naturally think in these terms; so should we. The President should order a series of State of the Union 2017 papers, in which every effort is made to foresee the impact twenty-five years hence of current trends in energy, demographics, the environment, crime, education, drugs, technology, immigration, trade, and so on. A presidential commission, comprised of a broad spectrum of interests, would analyze each of these areas, and based on current trends project where America will stand, along with recommendations as to what might be done. This would force Americans to begin to think in terms of the future and just exactly what legacy is being left to our children. It would also be a step toward getting us to think and act cooperatively.

We used to think long term. The writings of the country's founders are replete with references to posterity; the policies of Washington, Jackson, and Lincoln clearly had an eye on the future. Teddy Roosevelt was another forward-thinking President. At the turn of the century he launched the "Eighth Wonder of the World" Panama Canal project, knowing that he would have long since left office by the time of its completion. All that his administration would see would be costs—no glory. It didn't matter. He knew it would serve America for a hundred years. Roosevelt was thinking of empire and spreading the "American Way" around the world. He, and the nation, had a sense of mission, of manifest destiny. When was the last time America as a people launched *any* undertaking whose rich fruits would only begin to be reaped decades into the future? You have to go all the way back to John F. Kennedy, and Camelot, with America's space program—a program that is now in semi-limbo.

When a man or woman loses a sense of personal mission, of purpose, or of reason for living, they take a first step toward death. So, too, with a nation. Mission is the starting point for a long-term perspective and is integral to a society's culture; everything else follows from it. Every great forward-thinking nation has one; America once did. We yearn for a strong leader who will give us another.

HETEROGENEITY

The speeches are majestic and poetic; they ring from the rafters: "America is a beautiful, variegated mosaic of men and women who have come from around the world. Each enriches this great land with his or her own culture. We learn from one another and grow together, sharing the bounty of our mountains, valleys, fields, and streams. This great country with its wonderful diversity of people is our heritage, strength, and destiny. . . ." Yet we are deceiving ourselves. The reality is often very ugly.

Over the last two decades as America's heterogeneity has reached new limits, ethnic and racial strife have become commonplace viewing almost every night on the evening TV news. Martin Luther King Hospital in Los Angeles is now virtually a battle ground between blacks and Hispanics over control. The city of Monterey Park, California, was all white fifteen years ago and is now 90 percent Chinese. Clashes have been bitter, with the once-majority whites demanding English as the official language and Chinese merchants refusing even to use English on their business establishment signs. The University of California at Berkeley, where whites now account for only 25 percent of the student body, has put in place quota systems to assure equal access to all groups, but in the process has satisfied no one. "English only" referendums which are thinly disguised anti-Asian and anti-Hispanic laws have been passed by twenty states. In Los Angeles, which has seen twenty Korean merchants murdered by black assailants over the last two years, a Korean grocer shot and killed a young black woman she thought was threatening her, and the local community has been in an uproar for months. White middle- and upper-class voters in Holyoke, Massachusetts, recently passed bond issues for police and fire protection as well as trash collection, but refused to spend more money for overcrowded schools largely filled with Puerto Ricans. Racist voices of white students raised against blacks and other minorities on many of the nation's college campuses are becoming more strident. Hate crimes against Asian-Americans have increased four-fold over the last five years. And across America today rages the whole question of the very legitimacy of Western culture, history, and tradition being taught in our schools. When we were largely a Western culture only a generation ago, this of course was not an issue; now it is. Never in our history have we been so diverse as a people. The Soviet Union before its collapse was the most heterogeneous nation in the world. The United States today has inherited that diadem.

As the Asian and Hispanic population has grown to some 20 percent nationwide and essentially 100 percent in hundreds of communities, those Americans can legitimately ask why they should be studying Eurocentric history, tradition, and culture. Of course, one response is that they are now in America and that's the way it is. That may have been acceptable when the minority population was still small. No longer. Henry Cisneros, the erstwhile Mexican-American mayor of San Antonio, has said that the greatest challenge America faces is to assimilate its vastly disparate population. This will be America's most daunting task.

America must now begin to ask why our land is somehow different and free from what is a worldwide phenomenon of racial, ethnic, and religious hatred between groups. Why do we think (hope?) that America is somehow exempt? Over the last twenty years we have seen the advent of new kinds of Americans: Mexican-American, Japanese-American, Arab-American, Haitian-American, African-American, Chinese-American, Filipino-American, Armenian-American, Cuban-American . . . Is it possible to have a whole nation of hyphenated Americans each holding dear his own culture, heritage, and language, and still even *have* a nation? If the United States has already made the intellectual leap from "American" to "X-Americans," is it really so implausible that at some point in the future we will take one more small step to simply "Xs"? In fact, this is already happening. Big-city newspapers commonly refer to the "Vietnamese," "Arab," "Cuban," or "Chinese community" when reporting a local story.

The Pulitzer Prize–winning historian Kenneth Jackson has said: "The people of the United States will soon recognize that every nation has to have a common culture to survive."

What is America's common culture? If there is any one characteristic that defines a culture it is a common language. Yet over one hundred languages are spoken in dozens of school systems around the country. And in hundreds of good-sized communities across America hardly a word of English is heard.

A recent Roper Poll indicated that 77 percent of Americans believe that immigration should be halted. Responding to that, the Simpson-Kennedy Bill (passed in 1991) will supposedly shift immigration to those who have adequate financial and educational requirements, that is, to those of European descent, and away from the poor of Asian and Hispanic descent. The latter are now given first choice because they have relatives in the United States. Canada and Australia have long had such financial and educational "means" requirements for immigration.

The Japanese with their nearly total homogeneity, and full intent to stay that way, are forcing us to begin to address the issue. It is a healthy dialogue and better discussed now than later. Racism, ethnicism, and all the rest of the ugly isms are pervasive in the United States. The pernicious virus is already loose; the issue now before all Americans is how we deal with it before it destroys us. We do not seek the good of autonomous individuals, or the balancing of one group against another. We seek the common good. What is that good, and what common banner can we rally behind? The survival of America depends upon the answer.

This is not exaggerated rhetoric. Images from the May 1992 Los Angeles riots included Korean, Indian, and Iranian store owners trading gunfire with marauding gangs of blacks and Latinos. The Justice Department has estimated one-third of the looters to be illegal aliens largely from Mexico and Central America. A predominantly white police force was caught in the middle. Only two decades ago Beirut, the jewel of the Mediterranean, was a thriving and beautiful city; the financial center of the Middle East. A dozen warring ethnic and religious factions have destroyed it. It is now ungovernable. The seeds of hatred sown in Los Angeles, with its bewildering babel of one hundred twenty spoken languages, and insular ethnic enclaves, may well bear the same fruit of anarchy over the next decade. How many more American cities will follow?

EDUCATION

Japan's work force is the best trained and educated in the world. That nation's education system is unmatched. At the same time, America's ranks overall anywhere from fifteenth to twentieth internationally. There are large pockets of it that are Third World at best. What are some lessons America can learn from the Japanese?

We have seen that the Japanese education system is characterized by a powerful centralized authority, merit orientation, universal testing, a moral and national dimension to instruction, an emphasis on memorization, long school hours, parental support, deemphasis of dating and athletics, strong student discipline, and study of foreign languages. But these things are not terribly dissimilar from what existed in America just a generation ago. They are not new, and they worked reasonably well.

"See Dick run. See funny, funny Spot. See Jane and Spot. Watch Puff jump." "$9 \times 7 = 63$, $11 \times 11 = 121$, $8 \times 7 = 56$, $12 \times 12 = 144$, $6 \times 9 = 54$." "Argentina's capital is Buenos Aires and its gauchos are like our cowboys but they wear funny baggy pants." "The first shots of the Civil War were fired at Fort Sumter on April 12, 1861." "Custer and all of his men were lost at the Little Big Horn." "I pledge allegiance to the flag of the United States of America . . . ." "NaCl is the chemical formula for salt and this is what a crystal looks like under a microscope." These things have been locked up in my mind since grammar school. Readers over forty or so have similar random memories. Out of it all somehow we became more or less reasonably well educated. Why, then, did the education system that worked pretty well for over a century suddenly begin to fail in the sixties? The answer was provided earlier. The culture changed—dramatically. The educational institution that served one culture so well became dysfunctional in another.

A return to yesterday's education system, which looks very much like today's Japanese system, runs headlong into a brick wall of cultural obstacles. The growing diversity of America makes agreement on a universal curriculum impossible. Merit orientation is deemed to be unfair by many. Teaching of morality and ethics becomes bogged down in the quagmire of whose morality and whose ethics. How can a woman be expected to play the role of a traditional mother when she is working either by choice or because of economic necessity? And indeed how can the mother play this role when she herself is a barely literate teenager? How can the teacher perform her job of teaching when *armed* guards patrol the hallways as if in a federal penitentiary? How can you deemphasize dating and athletics when sex and sports pervade television, movies, and the media? How can you instill the joy of learning in impressionable young people when scholars are pejoratively referred to as "nerds" or "dweebs"?

Institutions, including educational institutions, are part of a society's culture. They are influenced greatly by that culture. The problems of America's educational system have little or nothing to do with education. They have to do with culture. Until the culture changes, all the commissions, blue-ribbon panels, million-dollar studies, and the myriad of pilot programs will fail. None of these gets to the root of the problem. It is the culture that is dysfunctional, not the educational system. Do we then throw up our hands, saying that culture is what it is and beyond our control? Not necessarily, because institutions are not only influenced by culture; they, in turn, influence it. To the extent that changes consistent with the Japanese educational system can and should be introduced to America, they will ultimately influence the larger culture. In fact, if America is prepared to rethink its culture, the schoolroom is one of the places it must start.

SUMMARY

In thinking through the differences between America and Japan, the Yankee Samurai made frequent mention of four dimensions of Japan's culture: *keiretsu*, long-term perspective, homogeneity, and the educational system. We have talked a little about each of these and asked whether there might be lessons here for America.

But these are only a part of the Japanese culture which was compared to ours. The larger lesson and the larger question for America deals with culture. Can our culture, with its totality of beliefs, values, traditions, language, institutions, myths, history, and vision, carry us successfully into the next century?

America's continued influence, power, and wealth is by no means assured. Nations decline. Some have gone from great heights to abject poverty in little more than a hundred years. America's rise to real world power began in 1898 with the Spanish-American War, when we grabbed the Philippines, establishing ourselves as a Pacific power; the two world wars then gave us European and Asian hegemony. This century has been ours. But what of the next? The answer is not hidden: it will depend upon who we are as a people. Nothing else matters. *This is the most important lesson that Japan has to teach America.*

If we close our minds, history will look back and say, "What a shame. They were blessed with the richest and most fertile land any people have ever had. They had a concept of freedom and democracy, unbridled patriotism, and a strong value and religious system. They fought and bled to protect their interests and those of their friends. They were industrious and filled with a sense of manifest destiny. They seemed fated to change the world and make it a better place—in fact, for several decades they did just that. And then, all too soon in one generation, the light began to dim, and sputtered out."

The Japanese firms in the United States and the Yankee Samurai that work for them are only part of a much larger drama featuring America and Japan. Much more quickly than most people think, Japan's military strength might well match its economic power. By the turn of the century, it is not unlikely that Japan will have the world's strongest economy and second or third most powerful military, while the United States will have the world's second-strongest economy and first most powerful military. Are these two nations then on a collision course? Is the Pacific big enough for the two of them? There is cause for optimism.

Long ago two loyal samurai retainers competed for the domains of their childless *Daimyo*. The Great Lord proclaimed that he would make his choice as to which would receive the inheritance of his vast holdings after ten years had passed. The determination would be based upon which of the two became the most complete warrior-philosopher, consistent with the teachings of the celebrated samurai-philosopher Miyamoto Musashi, who recognized that the military leader must have far more than expertise in battle: he needed to be a complete man.

Each of the two then set about assiduously applying himself to sharpening his skills with the lance and short and long swords, as well as developing a thoughtful and deep appreciation for the arts, sciences, and indeed life itself. Each studied how to govern justly so that under his leadership the people of the land could live protected, rich, and fulfilled lives. These things the two samurai did tirelessly and relentlessly. The competition between them was intense and disputes were common—sometimes bitterly so. But as each watched the other's dedication and commitment, mutual respect was strengthened and a grudging friendship began to build.

Ten years passed, and both men were now powerfully built and masters in their use of weapons. Both had accumulated great wisdom and developed an almost delicate aesthetic sense. Both had mastered the art of governing. The decade-long competition brought each of them to their full potential.

The two now stood before the *Daimyo* awaiting his decision. The old man spoke very slowly: "There is poverty, injustice, and fighting in the kingdom. I have grown too old and too weary to deal with it. He who follows me must build a new kingdom where these things are no more. I have watched the two of you very carefully over the years and now must choose, but one . . . I cannot. Each of you has shown yourself by your commitment to be more than worthy of my inheritance. It is yours to share. Make it a better kingdom."

There is good reason to believe this may be the future of the United States and Japan in the Pacific. Both nations have a good deal to offer the peoples of the region and one another. While the two governments have been only modestly successful in maintaining positive relationships, in another entirely different venue, more lasting and meaningful bonds are being forged. These are at the personal and business levels. There are now literally thousands of joint ventures between American and Japanese companies. The building of relationships and the bonding between the American and Japanese business people goes far beyond the reach of the two formal governments. And inside the Japanese subsidiaries here in the United States another phenomenon is evolving. American men and women, Yankee Samurai, are bridging the culture gap between the two countries. It is they and the hundreds of thousands of others who deal directly or indirectly with the Japanese personally or professionally that may well determine the joint destiny of the United States and Japan.

We have seen the structure of the *keiretsu* family of companies in Japan, and in chapter 6 I posited the hypothetical Alpha Group of all-American companies here in the United States. Such a group would compete head-on against the Japanese groups. That may indeed happen. But it is also possible that we are thinking much too narrowly. There is another likelihood that may well unfold—the signs are already evident. Could it be that the "Pac Rim Group" below and others similar to it will take form in the next ten to twenty years?

THE PAC RIM GROUP

Citicorp
Coca-Cola
Nomura Securities

Arco
Honda
Texas Instruments
Apple Computer
R. J. Reynolds
Nippon Steel
Fuji Photo Film
Sony
Westinghouse
Canon
Seiko
Mitsui Manufacturers Bank
Caterpillar
Merck
Bridgestone
Wal-Mart
Prudential
Kirin Brewery
Weyerhaeuser
Nippon Mining

Now, should such an international business colossus and others like it—comprised of both major American and Japanese firms—come to pass, we will indeed have a new world order, with a decisive power shift from the governments of the world to the boardrooms of the monthly *sankin-kai* or presidents' council meeting. Perhaps the entire premise of the United States in competition with Japan—two great nation-states vying with one another for supremacy—is a false one. A new, "border-less world" may be on the horizon, in which industry assumes no national allegiance. This would give enormous power to the corporate world's business leaders. With that power hopefully would come a Confucian sense of responsibility to the larger society.

This is Utopia in the eyes of some, a Stephen King horror story in the eyes of others, and clearly the subject of another book. But one way or another the Yankee Samurai will play a direct role in these most extraordinary of times. They are at the cusp of history . . . so are you.

Glossary
of Japanese Words

amakudari Post-retirement industry employment of bureaucrats

burakumin Former outcasts or "untouchables"

Bushido Warrior's code including duty, loyalty, and self-sacrifice

Daimyo Feudal provincial lord

gaiatsu Foreign government pressure that serves as an excuse for the government leaders to do what they wanted to do anyway

gaijin Foreigner, or sometimes barbarian

giri Duty

hatamoto Particularly dedicated and loyal samurai

Hina Matsuri Doll Festival, celebrated on Girl's Day

Issei First-generation Japanese-American arriving in America at the turn of the century

juku Private tutoring schools

Kabuki Popular theater

kaisha Japanese corporation

kaizen Philosophy of continuous improvement

kamikaze Divide wind that drove back Ghenghis Khan's invading fleet in the thirteenth century

kanban Toyota's just-in-time inventory system

karaoke Singing bars

karoshi "Death from fatigue," i.e., overwork

Keidanren Federation of several hundred of the largest firms, somewhat akin to the Business Roundtable in the United States

keiretsu Group of corporations tied together by interlocking directorates and mutual shareholding

kyoiku mama "Education mother" who pampers, cajoles, threatens, and infinitely loves her child (or children), with the goal of advancing their education

madogiwa-zoku Window watcher—employee who is kept on even though not productive

manga Cartoons, narrative strips, and animated films

Meiji era Period of the reign of Emperor Meiji, 1867–1912—the beginning of Japan's modern era

michi "The way," which refers to work as being the vehicle to personal enlightenment

Nagata-cho Japan's Capitol Hill in Tokyo

Nemawashi Literally "growing the roots" referring to informal discussions to build consensus

Nisei Second-generation Japanese-Americans

otoko no shakai A man's world

oyabun-kobun "Father-child role"; senior-junior mentor relationship

rekreeayshon Recreation

ringi-sho Consensus decision process

ronin Masterless samurai

Samurai Warrior in feudal Japan

sankin-kai President's council of a *keiretsu* that typically meets monthly

Sansei Third-generation Japanese-American

sararimen Salarymen—the elite of the white-collar work force

sensei Teacher

seppuku Suicide by piercing the abdomen; also **harakiri**

shiken jikoku Examination hell

shinjinrui The "new human race"; a term elder Japanse use for the younger generation

soga shosa Trading company

sokaiya Yakuza corporate bouncer

tanshin funin Salaryman's relocation without his family

uchi Home or company

wa Group harmony

wakon yosai "Western technology and Japanese spirit"

wan setto shugi One-set principle in which every *keiretsu* seeks to have an entry in every business line

Yakusa Japan's organized crime families somewhat similar to the Mafia

Yamamotoism Uniqueness of the Japanese race and culture

zaibatsu Family of industrial businesses formed in the late nineteenth century and disbanded after World War II; replaced by the *keiretsu*

zaitek Making money through electronic movement of financial securities; practiced by a growing number of manufacturing firms

Pronunciation Guide:

a as in *art*

i as in *police*

ai as in *aisle*

e as in *get*

o as in *pole*

ei as in *veil*

u as in *rude*

g as in *go*

Bibliography

ABEGGLEN, J. C., "Commentary," *Japan Economic Survey*, November 1988.
————, *Kaisha*. New York: Basic Books, 1985.
ALLEN, C., "Alohas Fading to Sayonaras," *Insight*, October 29, 1990.
ALLETZHAUSER, A., *The House of Nomura*. New York: Arcade, 1990.
ALSTON, J., *The American Samurai*. Berlin: de Gruyter, 1986.
ASSOCIATED PRESS, "Firms Split Americans, Japanese," *Daily Breeze* (Long Beach, CA), May 23, 1990.
BAILE, A., "Education the Foundation of the Japanese Productive System," in S. Lee, ed., *Japanese Management*. New York: Praeger, 1982.
BARRETT, T., "Mastering Being in America," *Newsweek*, February 5, 1990.
BEHR, E., *Hirohito*. New York: Vintage Books, 1989.
BENEDICT, R., *The Chrysanthemum and the Sword*. New York: Signet Books, 1946.
BERNSTEIN, A., "Where the Jobs Are Is Where the Skills Aren't," *Business-Week*, September 19, 1988.
BLUMENSON, M., *The Patton Papers*, Boston: Houghton Mifflin, 1972.

BORRUS, A., "How Real Estate Pumps Up Japanese Stocks," *BusinessWeek*, February 12, 1990.

BRADLEY, B., "Japanese Stand Alone Among Foreign Players in U.S. Real Estate," *Christian Science Monitor*, October 29, 1986.

BURJESS, J., "Japanese Executives Flock to U.S. to Gain Expertise in Service Industry," *Washington Post*, November 21, 1988.

BURNSTEIN, D., *Yen*. New York: Simon and Schuster, 1988.

BYLINSKY, G., "The Hottest High Tech Company in Japan," *Fortune*, January 1, 1990.

CHANDLER, C., "Shifting Gears," *Wall Street Journal*, April 11, 1991.

CHANG, C., "Individualism in the Japanese Management System," in Lee, ed., *Japanese Management*.

CHIPELLO, C., "Easy Riders," *Wall Street Journal*, March 14, 1991.

CHOATE, P., *Agents of Influence*. New York: Knopf, 1990.

CHRISTOPHER, R., *Second to None*, New York: Crown, 1986.

———, *The Japanese Mind*. New York: Fawcett Columbine, 1983.

CLAVELL, J., *Shōgun*. New York: Delacorte Press, 1975.

COHEN, S., *Uneasy Partnership*. Cambridge, Mass.: Ballinger Books, 1985.

CURRAN, J., "Tokyo Stock Market Stronger Than You Think," *Fortune*, April 11, 1988.

DARLIN, D., "Trade Switch," *Wall Street Journal*, July 20, 1988.

DEUTSCH, C., "Business People," *New York Times*, October 3, 1991.

DEUTSCHMAN, A., "The Trouble with MBAs," *Fortune*, July 29, 1991.

DREYFUSS, J., "How Japan Picks America's Brains," *Fortune*, December 21, 1987.

DRUCKER, P., *The Frontiers of Management*. New York: Dutton, 1989.

———, *Managing in Turbulent Times*. New York: Harper & Row, 1980.

———, *People and Performance*. New York: Harper & Row, 1977.

DUMAINE, B., "Beating Bolder Corporate Crooks," *Fortune*, April 25, 1988.

EMMOTT, B., *The Sun Also Sets*. New York: Random House, 1989.

ENDO, S., *The Samurai*. New York: Harper & Row, 1980.

ERLICH, E., "America's Schools Aren't Making the Grade," *BusinessWeek*, September 19, 1988.

FALLOWS, J., *More Like Us*. New York: Houghton Mifflin, 1989.

FERGUSON, C., "Computers and the Coming of the U.S. Keiretsu," *Harvard Business Review*, July–August 1990.

FIERMAN, J., "The Selling Off of America," *Fortune*, May 23, 1988.

FINN, C., "U.S. Campuses Are Bursting at the Quads," *Wall Street Journal*, January 27, 1988.

FISHER, A., "Morale Crisis," *Fortune*, November 18, 1991.

FLANIGAN, J., "Japan Has to Get Used to the American Way," *Los Angeles Times*, July 10, 1988.

FRANTZ, D., "In California Japan Banks Fare Poorly," March 6, 1988.

———, *Selling Out*. Chicago: Contemporary Books, 1989.

FRIEDMAN, G., *The Coming War with Japan*. New York: St. Martin's Press, 1991.

FRIEDMAN, M., *Tyranny of the Status Quo*. New York: Harcourt Brace Jovanovich, 1984.

FUCHSBERG, G., "Education," *Wall Street Journal*, October 17, 1991.

GALBRAITH, J., *The Age of Uncertainty*. Boston: Houghton Mifflin, 1977.

GATES, D., "Say Goodnight, Socrates," *Newsweek*, February 1, 1988.

GIBSON, D., "Organizational Culture, Sub-System Variation and Environmental Context," *Administrative Science Quarterly*, March 1987.

GOODMAN, D., "Reciprovocation in Recent U.S.-Japan Relations," *The JAMA Forum*, March 1991.

GRAHAM, E., "Education," *Wall Street Journal*, March 31, 1989.

GRAHAM, J., and Y. Sano, *Smart Bargaining*. New York: Harper & Row, 1989.

GUENTHER, R., "Japanese Firms Head to U.S. Real Estate Markets," *Wall Street Journal*, October 20, 1986.

GUZZARDI, W., "Looking Ahead," *Fortune*, July 3, 1989.

HALBERSTAM, D., *The Reckoning*. New York: Morrow, 1986.

HARRINGTON, J., *Yankee Samurai*. Detroit: PEI, 1979.

HASEGAWA, K., *Japanese Style Management*. Tokyo: Kodansha, 1986.

HINTERHUBER, H., "Are You a Strategist or Just a Manager?" *Harvard Business Review*, January–February 1992.

HOLSTEIN, W., *Japanese Power Game*. New York: Scribners, 1990.

HUCKSHORN, K., "Hiring Bias by Japanese Firms Alleged," *Orange County Register*, July 24, 1991.

IIGP, "Continuing Frictions: Creating a Common Economic Foundation," Policy Paper 55E, June 1991.

IMAI, M., *Kaizen*. New York: Random House, 1986.

ISHINAMORI, S., *Japan Inc.* London: University of California Press, 1988.

ITOI, K., "Desperately Seeking Akio," *Newsweek*, September 16, 1991.

JACOBSON, G., *Xerox American Samurai*. New York: Macmillan, 1986.

JAMESON, S., "Japanese Government to Its People: Work Less, Be Happy," *Los Angeles Times*, 1989.

KAGANO, T., *Strategic vs. Evolutionary Management*. New York: North Holland, 1985.

KAGASAKI, M., "Karoshi," *U.S.-Japan Business News*, April 1, 1991.

KANABAYASHI, M., "Labor Letter," *Wall Street Journal*, March 14, 1989.

KANTROWITZ, B., "Why School Reform Fails," *Newsweek*, May 27, 1991.

KAPLAN, D., *Yakuza*. New York: Colliers, 1987.

KEYS, J., "The Japanese Management Theory Jungle," *Academy of Management Review*, 1984, vol. 9, no. 2, 342–53.

KIECHAL, W., "Unfuzzing Ethics for Managers," *Fortune*, November 23, 1987.

KOTKIN, J., *The Third Century*. New York: Crown, 1988.

KRAAR, L., "The Drug Trade," *Fortune*, June 20, 1988.

LANGE, R., "Participative Management," in Lee, ed., *Japanese Management*.

LANGGUTH, A., *Patriots*. New York: Simon and Schuster, 1988.

LAURIE, D., "A Study of the Management Style of Japanese Owned U.S. Subsidiaries," Michigan: 1990.

LEE, S., ed., *Japanese Management*. New York: Praeger, 1982.

LUBLIN, J., "Highly Paid Chiefs Hear Criticism from Below Too," *Wall Street Journal*, June 4, 1991.

————, "They Are Making It Big in Human Resources," *Wall Street Journal*, December, 20, 1991.

MAGNET, M., "How to Smarten Up the Schools," *Fortune*, February 1, 1988.

MAIN, J., "How 21 Men Got Global in 35 Days," *Fortune*, November 6, 1989.

McCLELLAND, D., *The Achieving Society*. Princeton, N.J.: Van Nostrand, 1961.

McCRAW, T., ed., *America vs. Japan*. Boston: Harvard Business Press, 1986.

McGREGOR, D., "The Human Side of Enterprise," *Management Review*, November 1957.

MEYER, M., "The Crash of 88 Scenario," *Newsweek*, November 23, 1987.

MISHIMA, Y., *The Decay of the Angel*. New York: Washington Square Press, 1971.

————, *The Way of the Samurai*. New York: Basic Books, 1977.

MORISHIMA, M., *Why Has Japan Succeeded?* Cambridge, Mass.: Cambridge Press, 1982.

MORITA, A., *Made in Japan*. New York: Dutton, 1986.

MURAYAMA, M., "Kazaokushigi and Shudanshugi Management Approaches," in Lee, ed., *Japanese Management*.

MURAYAMA, M., "The Japanese Business Value System," in Lee, ed., *Japanese Management*.

MUSASHI, M., *The Book of the Five Rings*, New York: Bantam Books, 1982.

NATHANS, L., "A Matter of Control," *Business Month*, September 1988.

NUSSBAUM, B., "Needed Human Capital," *BusinessWeek*, September 19, 1988.

OHMAE, K., *Borderless World*. New York: HarperBusiness, 1990.

OUCHI, W., *M Form Society*. New York: Avon, 1984.

————, *Theory* Z. Reading, Mass.: Addison-Wesley, 1981.

PARE, T., "The Big Threat to Big Steel's Future," *Fortune*, July 15, 1991.

————, "The Uncommitted Class of 1989," *Fortune*, June 5, 1989.

PASCALE, R., *The Art of Japanese Management*. New York: Warner, 1981.

PERRY, N., "Saving the Schools," *Fortune*, November 7, 1988.

PETERS, T. J., AND R. H. WATERMAN, JR., *In Search of Excellence*. New York: Harper & Row, 1982.

PICKENS, T. BOONE, *Boone*. Boston: Houghton Mifflin, 1987.

POWELL, B., "Can Japan Work the Street?" *Newsweek*, October 19, 1987.

————, "What Japan Will Buy Next," *Newsweek*, November 11, 1991.

PRANGE, G., *At Dawn We Slept*. New York: McGraw-Hill, 1981.

PRINDLE, T., *Made in Japan*. Armonk, N.Y.: Eastgate, 1989.

PUCIK, V., "Management Culture and the Effectiveness of Local Executives in Japanese-Owned U.S. Corporations." (Privately funded study) University of Michigan, 1990.

RAND, A., *Atlas Shrugged*. New York: Random House, 1957.

RAPPAPORT, C., "How Japan Will Spend Its Cash," *Fortune*, November 21, 1988.

————, "Japan's Big Knack for Coming Back," *Fortune*, November 6, 1989.

————, "Japan's Capital Spending Spree," *Fortune*, April 9, 1990.

————, "Japan's Growing Global Reach," *Fortune*, May 22, 1989.

————, "Now Japan Is Plunging into Oil," *Fortune*, March 13, 1989.

————, "Why Japan Keeps on Winning," *Fortune*, July 15, 1991.

————, "You Can Make Money in Japan," *Fortune*, February 12, 1990.

REICH, R., "Who Is Them?" *Harvard Business Review*, March–April 1991.

————, "Joint Ventures with Japan Give Away Our Fortress," *Harvard Business Review*, March–April 1986.

REISCHAUER, E., *The Japanese*. Cambridge, Mass.: Harvard University Press, 1977.

ROMBERG, A., *The United States and Japan*. New York: Council on Foreign Relations, 1987.

RYAN, J., "Japanese Real Estate Survey," *U.S.-Japan Business Review*, April 1, 1991.

SADLER, A., *The Code of the Samurai*. Rutland, Mass.: Tuttle, 1988.

SAMUELSON, R., "The Boss as Welfare Cheat," *Newsweek*, November 11, 1991.

SANSON, G., *Japan: A Short Culture History*. Stanford, Calif.: Stanford University Press, 1952.

SASAKI, N., *Management and Industrial Structure in Japan*. Oxford: Pergamon Press, 1981.

SATHE, V., *Culture and Related Corporate Realities*. Homewood, Ill.: Irwin, 1985.

SCARDINO, A., "Japanese Pushing Up Prices of U.S. Commercial Property," *New York Times*, December 17, 1986.

SCHLESINGER, J., "Fleeing Factories," *Wall Street Journal*, April 12, 1988.

SELIGMAN, D., "Keeping Up," *Fortune*, July 18, 1988.

SHOOK, R., *Honda*. Englewood Cliffs, N.J.: Prentice-Hall, 1988.

SIGIURA, H., "How Honda Localizes Its Global Strategy," *Sloan Management Review*, Fall 1990.

SOLO, S., "Japan Discovers Woman Power," *Fortune*, June 19, 1989.

————, "Japan Opens More U.S. Plants," *Fortune*, April 22, 1991.

SOURS, M., "The Influence of Japanese Culture on the Japanese Management System," in Lee, ed., *Japanese Management*.

STEINER, G., *Strategic Planning*. New York: Free Press, 1979.

STEWART, T., "GE Keeps Those Ideas Coming," *Fortune*, August 12, 1991.

TAKENAKA, Y., "Challenge Is to Build on Strength," *Los Angeles Times*, October 12, 1986.

TATSUNO, S., *The Technology Strategy*. Englewood Cliffs, N.J.: Prentice-Hall, 1986.

TAYLOR, A., "Who's Ahead in the World Auto War?" *Fortune*, November 9, 1987.

——, "Can Iacocca Fix Chrysler—Again?" *Fortune*, April 8, 1991.

TAYLOR, J., *Shadows of the Rising Sun*. New York: Quill, 1983.

THOMAS, R., "The Pay Police," *Newsweek*, June 17, 1991.

THUROW, L., "Let's Learn from the Japanese," *Fortune*, November 18, 1991.

——, *The Management Challenge*. Cambridge, Mass.: MIT Press, 1985.

——, *Zero Sum Society*. New York: Basic Books 1980.

TOLAND, J., *The Rising Sun*. New York: Random House, 1971.

TULLY, S., "The Hunt for the Global Manager," *Fortune*, May 21, 1990.

——, "Where People Live Best," *Fortune*, March 11, 1991.

TURNBULL, S., *Samurai*. London: Magna, 1986.

WARNER, R., "Major Changes in Japan Belie an Aura of Tranquility," *Orange County Register*, April 2, 1989.

WATERMAN, R., "Strategy in a More Volatile World," *Fortune*, December 21, 1987.

WEICK, K., *The Social Psychology of Organizing*. New York: Random House, 1979.

WEISS, A., "Simple Truths of Japanese Manufacturing," *Harvard Business Review*, July–August 1984.

WHITE, M., *The Japanese Education Challenge*. New York: Free Press, 1987.

WILEY, P., *Yankees in the Land of the Gods*. New York: Viking/Penguin, 1990.

WOLFERAN, F., *The Enigma of Japanese Power*. New York: Knopf, 1989.

WOODWARD, K., "Ideas," *Newsweek*, September 30, 1991.

YAMADA, E., "Globalization of Japanese Management," in R. Bukics, ed., *International Financial Management*. Chicago: Probus, 1988.

YODER, S.,, "Did Loyalty Lead Takeshita Aide to Ritual Suicide?" *Wall Street Journal*, April 17, 1989.

Index

•

ABOUT THE AUTHOR

Dennis Laurie is a Research Fellow at the Drucker Graduate Management Center in the Claremont Graduate School where he earned his Ph.D. in management. He has taught global management at University California Irvine. He recently retired after twenty years as an executive with Arco.